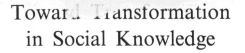
Toward Transformation
in Social Knowledge

To my father and mother

Toward Transformation
in Social Knowledge

Second Edition

Kenneth J. Gergen

SAGE Publications
London • Thousand Oaks • New Delhi

Second edition © Kenneth J. Gergen 1994

First edition 1982

Second edition 1994

The first edition was published by Springer-Verlag New York Inc.

 SAGE Publications Ltd
6 Bonhill Street
London EC2A 4PU

SAGE Publications Inc
2455 Teller Road
Thousand Oaks, California 91320

SAGE Publications India Pvt Ltd
32, M-Block Market
Greater Kailash – I
New Delhi 110 048

British Library Cataloguing in Publication Data
A catalogue record for this book is available from the British
Library.

ISBN 0 8039 8971 7
ISBN 0 8039 8972 5 (pbk)

Printed in Great Britain by Redwood Books, Trowbridge, Wiltshire

Contents

Preface to the Second Edition

Just over ten years have passed since the original publication of *Toward Transformation in Social Knowledge*. It has been a decade of enormous agitation in the social sciences. Many dislocating developments have occurred, fresh sensibilities have emerged, novel lines of thought have been articulated, and new and challenging practices have appeared. Simultaneously, much remains the same. Major traditions have continued to thrive, insulated from the storms of change, and satisfied by the contribution made to both scientific knowledge and society. Two distinguishable cultures are emerging rapidly within the social sciences, removed from each other in vocabularies, values, and visions. Where in this turbulence is the present volume to be placed? What is there to warrant the appearance of a second edition? What, outside historical interest, should motivate the reader to embark on the arduous journey demanded by the present text? In the Preface to the First Edition, I lamented over the inability of scholars periodically to expunge the record of their previous writings, thus removing the burden of temporal coherence and freeing themselves for new endeavors. Why, after more than a decade of creative ferment, should I not wish to see the present volume perish in peace?

In the Context of a Rooted Tradition

These questions must be addressed from two standpoints, the first in terms of the sedimented traditions, and the second with respect to the more recent forces of centrifugal flight. In the former instance, it is simply the case that the empiricist tradition continues to remain stalwart within the social sciences, maintaining a steady grip over the future of the disciplines, shaping decisions regarding educational curricula, journal policy, hiring and firing criteria, the allocation of research funds, and the representation of the science to the society. Given the major aspirations of *Toward Transformation in Social Knowledge* (hereafter *TT*), to challenge this tradition and to open possibilities for alternative futures, the need for this collection of arguments is no less vital today that at its first publication. Judging from the reactions of the readers who exhausted the supply of the first edition, the volume was reasonably effective in achieving its goals. It is hopeful to think that it may do the same now for a new generation of readers.

Yet, I am scarcely sanguine about the effects of this volume alone. In the initial writing I was thankfully naive about the profound force of the empiricist tradition, both in terms of its self-sustaining practices and in terms of its place within the culture more generally. My investment in scholarship was unduly colored by an idealistic vision of intellectual exchange. I believed that once a body of challenging and carefully developed ideas reached publication, they would be responsibly read, duly discussed, and depending on the conclusions of such dialogues, various practices would be altered. With this Panglossian vision paramount, I was wholly unprepared for personal and political micro-processes of resistance. As I came to learn, social scientists have a strong tendency first to categorize a theoretical position, and, depending on its placement, to either appropriate it or disregard it. Required for "getting on" in the profession is a cluster of the "like-minded". Thus, arguments such as my own are scarcely ever confronted by those within the tradition. For, once these arguments are identified–even superficially–as anti-empiricist endeavors, they are seldom given serious regard. To grapple with such an adversary is to risk a loss–even if in nothing more than time and effort. Far more cost-effective is to keep one's gaze firmly fixed on the reliable reward structure of the discipline and render the problematic invisible.

In addition to this efficiency heuristic, there are also matters of professional and personal identity at stake. After devoting the better part of a lifetime to a given tradition, how should the established scientist regard challenges to the validity of such commitments? The existential threat is enormous, and little else can be anticipated than defensiveness, disdain, and disregard. A similar process underlies the relationship between the established professional and his/her graduate students. As several colleagues have admitted, they are disinclined to assign my work to their students because of the disruptions created in faculty–student relationships. They begin to feel ill winds of student skepticism, and are moved to defensiveness. There is finally the insecurity of freedom. If one steps away from the route well-travelled, the sense of direction rapidly erodes. In the empiricist tradition the rationale seemed firmly fixed, procedural prescriptions were in place, and the professional reward system clear and apparent. To thrust all into doubt, to proceed without foundations, leaves open the question of Monday morning: "What am I to do now, why, and with what skills?" I despair to think, with Thomas Kuhn in *The Structure of Scientific Revolution*, that paradigms are seldom changed by those within them. Practitioners may have to retire before the next evolutionary stage is attained.

My initial writing also suffered from a certain cultural myopia. That is, I failed to appreciate the extent to which the social science traditions were undergirded by, and intertextual with, a vast range of cultural practices. I treated the sciences largely as autonomous, free to deliberate their future. It is now clear to me that to argue for transformation in the conception of social knowledge is to tilt against the major institutions of the culture, fortified as they are by centuries of custom and justification. Thus, in the academy alone, when the arguments of the volume are extended, they raise significant questions regarding the division of knowledge by distinct departments, the reliance on lectures and texts as pedagogical practices, the use of examinations to test student knowledge, and the existence of highly select colleges and universities. To extend the theses to the culture more generally, we find the broad array of assumptions–derived from the Enlightenment and informing virtually all our public institutions–thrown into question. Assumptions of *objectivity, rationality, truth, individual freedom,* and *progress* are all placed in jeopardy. No, the changes of the past decade have scarcely rendered my arguments less cogent, or removed the critical and exploratory functions of the volume. But, it is with considerable pleasure that I also see the dialogue of which this volume is a part, expanding exponentially both within and outside the academy.

Tradition in Transition

Unfortunately, the ossification of intellectual traditions is frequently accompanied by a growing incapacity for self-reflection. As various ontological and valuational assumptions are linked, and as they are progressively employed to justify and index a variety of practices, it is increasingly difficult to generate a compelling form of self-critique. The assumptive network and related actions provide precious few resources for assessing their own credibility. And, when appraised from alien standpoints, there is little comprehension of the antagonist; the antagonist's arguments range from the irrelevant to the inane. Once residing within a box there is little means of appraising the box itself. At the same time, however, assumptive languages carry with them myriad historical traces, associations with other uses at other times. The propositions welded together to form a foundation at any given time are inevitably drawn from a variety of hybrid traditions. And each proposition contains within it, by implication, myriad ambiguities and possible negations. Thus, within any tradition one may discover hidden tensions, potential schisms, and subtle invitations to reflexivity.

It is thus that the initial chapter of *TT* depends for its major arguments on many of the assumptions shared within the empiricist tradition. In effect, it raises questions about empirical research from an empirical standpoint. Its starting point is a simple one: how can we reconcile the empiricist impulse toward general principles (or more ambitiously, "universal laws") on the one hand, with the use of historically perishable findings on the other? The data used to support the general principle are inevitably dependent on a host of local conditions—a potentially enormous array of determinants in unique combination—while the conclusions drawn from such inquiry are blind to the local configuration, suppress the circumstantial, and speak only in terms of the timeless. To complicate matters, it is argued, the very articulation of the general may operate to change the patterns of action and their antecedents. In effect, the "generation of understanding" within the sciences serves to undermine (or mystify) the very basis of the general formulation. Of course, empiricists have always staked their claims to legitimacy on arguments favoring the universal and the transhistorical. In this way a rationalization is provided for a national investment in the accumulation of knowledge through continuing research, along with educational curricula to train scientists for the challenge. The promise is nothing less than that of an empirically-grounded knowledge base from which systematic deductions can be made to broad arenas of application. It is a promise of progress for the public good. However, as the chapter asks, if we seriously consider arguments on behalf of the local and historical, can any justification be located for drawing conclusions of a general character? After considering a variety of arguments and rebuttals, a negative conclusion is drawn.

Have there been significant developments since the penning of these pages, arguments that might unsettle or sustain these views? Social psychologists, the audience for whom this thesis (Gergen, 1973) had helped to create what was commonly termed "the crisis in social psychology," rapidly tired of the discontent, castigated me for nihilism, and returned to business as usual. Rather than continuing to grapple with the issues, and possibly suspicious of the conclusions that might be drawn, debate was terminated (even suppressed) in the major journals of the field. Further, alternative means have been found to relieve the irritation. For example, in his historical account of "the crisis" literature in the *Handbook of Social Psychology*, Edward E. Jones attempts to show how the "lavish attention" paid to the thesis stems from such factors as "a widespread need for self-flagellation, perhaps unique to social psychologists" (1985: 99), "rhetorical simplicity," and the creation of "straw men." The content of the arguments is never addressed. This is not to say that the issues have been fully marginalized by the empiricist tradition. There are domains such as social cognition, close-relations research, cross-cultural research, ecological psychology, and developmental psychology, in which the arguments are occasionally made focal. However, the attempt in these instances is more frequently to evoke the historical thesis (*TT*: Chapter 1) to explain research findings than to challenge the warrant of empirical findings themselves.

There has been one substantive attempt to unseat the argument for the historical character of social research. Over the past decade social psychologists have been active in developing the technique of _meta analysis,_ a statistical means of pooling data across studies for a broad assessment of research effects. In this case, the statement of general principles or laws is not derived from a single case but a range of cases. The generality of the conclusion begins to converge with the number of instances on which it is based. In this way, the investigator can lay claim to cross-time validity, or demonstrate historical trends–depending on the configuration of the data. As suggested by Alice Eagly (1983) meta-analytic methods enable the problem of historical perishability to be solved empirically.

Yet, in the end this "solution by method" proves unconvincing. There is first the problem of sampling. Meta-analysis relies primarily on published studies, and because of the problematic logic of hypothesis testing, research publications select for positive results. Thus, as research fails to achieve statistically reliable results, it is usually terminated or never put into print. The problems of biased sampling at the level of the individual experiment are compounded with sample biases at the level of research findings. Second, research studies typically suffer from biases of execution. Once committed to a hypothesis, and a given method of testing, an investigator can scarcely proceed without sensitivity to the research context: who is being placed under study and under what conditions? If attempting to test the effects of sexual arousal on aggression, for example, an investigator will not select just any form of sexual stimulant, but just the kind (for example, sufficient quantities, in a sufficient range of taste, etc.) that will allow the subject to attend to and define the subsequent measure in just those ways that will vindicate the hypothesis. In this sense, positive research findings are the product of culturally sensitive researchers who, through skillful staging, verbal craft, and the like, can bring about a given finding. If a sufficient number of researchers are drawn to a given hypothesis, the results will be a significant meta-analysis. Finally, there is the problem of determining whether all studies purporting to measure the same behavior, or the effects of the same variables, are indeed doing so. Is aggression by one standard, not "assertiveness" by another, or "righteous indignation" by a third criterion, and so on? And if there are competing definitions or interpretations of either independent or dependent variables, whose account is to be judged superior and on what grounds? (See also Chapter 2 of TT.) Thus, if a large group of studies on, for example, the effects of sexual arousal on aggression are pooled, how should we determine that they were all treating the same phenomenon? In short, meta-analysis proves to be a technological diversion from the more substantial conceptual issues at stake.

Rather than seeking solutions to the challenge of historicity, other investigators have been moved to explore the positive consequences of the historical emphasis. If we recognize the historically contingent character of human action, are new forms of inquiry invited? As it is reasoned, the traditional conception of mechanical cause (in the Aristotelian sense) and the companionate method of experimentation have unduly truncated the scientist's understanding of human action. The romance with the psychological experiment, as the exemplary case, reduces our understanding of social life to a succession of fragmentary and disjointed cause–effect sequences. As a counter to such time-freezing investments, innovative investigators have set out to explore cross-time sequences in human interchange–from the unfolding patterns of the face-to-face interaction and shifts in relationships over time, to broad patterns of historical change. Much of this work, as developed in social psychology, is featured in *Historical Social Psychology*, edited by Mary Gergen and myself. More recent study has been less concerned with the actual cross-time patterns of human action than the historical changes in our accounts of human action. The shift is from behavior in historical context to transformations in discourse about behavior. As it is proposed in this case, our conceptions of human functioning–of the sources of human behavior–have changed significantly across the centuries, and continue their metamorphosis in the present century. The nature of these changes, the ways in which they may be understood, and their reflexive implications for the human sciences are all issues of intense interest. A range of significant contributions to this endeavor in psychology can be found in *Historical Dimensions of Psychological Discourse*, edited by Carl Graumann and myself.

While the differences separating these historical investigations–the one concerned with historical change in social behavior and the other with discourse about behavior–may seem unremarkable, the difference in underlying assumptions is enormous. It is essentially a difference that separates the first chapter of *TT* from the remainder of the volume–moving the reader from a discussion taking place within the assumptive grounds of the empiricist paradigm to a discursive territory remote from and unfamiliar to the empiricist. As seen in retrospect, the shift from the first to the second chapter of *TT* is a dramatic one–a single manifestation of what may now be understood as the shift from an empiricist to a post-empiricist philosophy of science, from a structuralist to a post-structuralist view of language, and from a modernist to a postmodernist worldview.

Within *TT* the shift begins subtly. Late in the first chapter (p. 48), the question is raised as to whether the attention I give to historical variations in observable behavior is not myopic. Rather, the traditionalist proposes, the scientific investigator is more specifically concerned with the processes that *underlie* or cause behavior, processes that might themselves be permanently installed and responsible for an enormous range of highly variegated activities. For example: the hunger drive may be universal but variations in food preferences infinitely changing; there may be a universal grammar but an ever-shifting array of well formed sentences. Among the various rejoinders offered to this line of reasoning, I argue (pp. 50–1, and again on pp. 54–5) that a conception of a universal and internal, causal source (for example, drive, knowledge structure, mechanism, instinct), does not itself carry obvious or transparent linkages to observable behavior. Thus, whether a given action is treated as an examplar or instantiation of a universal process at the internal level, is subject to continuous negotiation. In a further variation of this argument (p. 55), I propose that whether a given finding is treated as a validation of a hypothesis depends on a set of correspondence rules enabling one to know whether a given observation counts as support for the hypothesis in question. Again, it is proposed, such rules are continuously open to negotiation. In subtle ways, these arguments begin to set the stage for the transformation that slowly emerges in the second chapter. For if there is no transparent or necessary linkage between the languages of science (scientific description and explanation), on the one hand, and scientific observation on the other, then it is difficult to sustain the traditional empiricist argument that the facts of the world drive or determine the propositions that come to stand as "scientific knowledge."

It is this view, beginning with Chapter 2, that sets the stage for the remainder of the volume. Once the link between language and the world is rendered contentious and contingent, the analysis shifts importantly from what is the case about social life, invariably stated in language, to the languages of description and explanation themselves–from the world to text, from the signified to the signifier. The reader is thus prepared for the major intellectual developments that have taken place since the volume's publication.

The Developing Dialogue

As mentioned earlier, a second academic culture has emerged during the past decade, highly varied in its disciplinary origins, but united in its skepticism of the empiricist project for the human sciences. As many see it, an avant-garde from across the social sciences has begun to share in a sense of common pursuit, and in their common consciousness their marginality is slowly giving way to a new sense of center. In the ensuing discussions they have also found their interests allied with major movements in the humanities–especially literary theory and philosophy. Such discussions have also leaped across national borders; they provoke debate no less intense in Buenos Aires, Brisbane, Bhopal or Barcelona than in Berlin or Boston. To what extent do traditional presumptions of empirical knowledge remain viable, if the modernist tradition of which they are a manifestation is problematic, and if the institutions rationalized by this tradition are thrown into question? And if we cannot sustain the traditional views and their associated customs, how is the future to be shaped? How are we to conceive of research, scientific writing, and the relationship of scientific accounts to politics, ethics, and professional practices? For many scholars, there are no more important issues confronting the academy and the social implications are enormous. Debate has been vital, vigorous, and sometimes vociferous.

It is an introduction to may of these "postmodern" developments that the present publication of *TT* also serves. In particular, it is useful to single out three domains in which recent colloquy has been most intense, and to demonstrate how various explorations in *TT* provide an entry into them. Specific attention is given, then, to developments in ideological, literary–rhetorical, and social critiques of science.

Ideological critique

In the initial chapter of *TT*, there is an extended discussion of the scientist as moral agent (pp. 27–34). In particular, I propose that in spite of their guise of neutrality, all social scientific accounts harbor prescriptive implications. In specifying *what is the case*, other accounts are suppressed. Otherwise significant distinctions for certain persons in certain walks of life are obliterated. Scientific terminologies also carry with them evaluative connotations, subtly coloring the picture painted of those whom they portray. In their modes of explanation, blame and credit are also distributed; and in their methodologies, ideals for social interaction are subtly suggested. In effect, the languages and practices of the social sciences necessarily affect the society–for good or ill according to someone's ethical or political standpoint. These arguments will prepare the reader for what has since become one of the most active lines of inquiry within the academy.

As various minority groups have developed a common consciousness, they have become increasingly articulate in their critiques of the otherwise taken-for-granted presumptions prevalent within the sciences and/or the culture at large. Most prominent within this movement are feminist scholars, who locate patriarchal or androcentric biases in virtually every facet of both the social and natural sciences. The interested reader will wish to explore, for example, the works of Hubbard (1988), Unger (1983), Morawski (1985), and Haraway (1988). In each case, accepted scientific practices are shown to be detrimental to women's interests and to social equality more generally. Further, feminist scholars now press on to inquire into possible alternatives to traditional sciences, especially alternatives that might represent women's interests and sensitivities more fully (see for example, Harding 1986; Fine, 1992). Feminists are joined in these critical and exploratory endeavors by many others, such as those who decry the ways in which the sciences and their allied institutions contribute to colonialism (Said, 1979), greed (Schwartz, 1986), cultural narcissism (Wallach and Wallach, 1983), and the obliteration of nature and community (Berman, 1982). Such concerns have also informed segments of my own work since the publication of *TT*. The critical posture has played a special role in discussions of feminist psychology (Gergen, 1988a), empiricism as a form of colonialism (Gergen, 1990b), and the devastating effects on the culture of mental-illness terminology (Gergen, 1990c).

Literary–Rhetorical Critique

Beginning with the second chapter, a chief concern of *TT* revolves around knowledge as a linguistic construction. As the "dilemma of identification" reveals, any description of a given action essentially relies on other descriptions to achieve its justification. Each "interpretation rests on a potentially immense array of interdependent interpretations" (p. 63). It follows that any scientific account will derive its sense of validity from an array of ancillary and often suppressed assumptions. Further, because the language of description is thus porous and polysemous–undergoing continuous change as meanings are recreated in new and varied contexts– multiple interpretations of any action are the rule. As the argument is pressed on (pp. 70–4), we find that the traditional presumptions of "empirically grounded" propositions are problematic. For, as it is reasoned, all the data used in support of a scientific proposition require just the sort of interpretive process for which there is no point of objective decidability. As it is proposed, there is no principled reason that the data used in support of any given theory cannot be used as support for any number of alternative theories. The limits over such relations are not furnished by the data themselves, but by the interpretive practices (and skills) of the scientific community.

This strong emphasis on the linguistic practices of the sciences is extended further in the volume on pp. 78–93. Here I try to demonstrate the "principled" impossibility of linking behavioral description to observation, thus reinforcing the preceding emphasis on the languages–as opposed to the observations of the science. If we bracket consideration of data and center attention on language, we are free to consider the linguistic (as opposed to empirical) grounds for given theories or accounts of the person. Thus Chapter 3 centers on the intertextual relations among the languages of metatheory, theory, method, and observational description. As I try to show, commitments in any of these domains places reverberating constraints over what can be said in any other. To illustrate, I argue that empiricist metatheory has radically constrained the range of theoretical understanding and methodological techniques employed within the field.

When I first developed these arguments I was but dimly aware of major movements taking place in the domain of semiotic theory. Saussure and Pierce had drawn early attention to language as a system of inter-related signs. But, where structuralists such as Lévi-Strauss and Chomsky launched inquiry into the *underlying* (and typically psychological) basis for such system, what we now view as the "post-structural" movement was to radically alter our conceptions of language. The early signals of post-structural possibilities may be located in various writings of Roland Barthes, Georges Bataille, and Antonio Gramsci. The American writings of the "new criticism" school of literary criticism–emphasizing the internal relations among textual properties–contributed further to the ethos. However, in each case, similar to the narrative developed in *TT*, the movement is away from languages as representation (mimesis), and toward a concern with language as a relatively self-contained system.

Such work prepares the way for an appreciation of contemporary post-structuralist writings. Of foremost significance are the works of Jacques Derrida (especially 1976), and others (for example, Paul De Man, and Geoffrey Hartman), contributing to what is called the deconstructionist movement. The work is of enormous significance, not only in demonstrating the materially ungrounded character of linguistic description and explanation in general, but also in showing the delicately constructed character of acceptable meaning, the internal contradictions necessarily inhering in or implied by our accounts of the world, and the removal of meaning from the psyche of individual authors (actors). With deconstruction theory as background, the curious reader might also profitably explore some of the more recent writings of Baudrillard (1983, 1988). In many respects, Baudrillard's word-plays–concerned with the endless circulation of images in a technologically saturated society–recapitulate deconstruction theory's "crisis in meaning" at the level of pop culture.

Simultaneous to these efforts–and in many ways stimulated by them–there has been a rebirth in rhetorical analytics. If descriptions and explanations are principally exercises in language, attention is then drawn to those specific techniques by which persuasive arguments are achieved, and which form both the forestructure and boundaries within which the sciences can proceed. In the social sciences, Hayden White's (1978) analysis of the literary tropes essential to historical scholarship is of pivotal significance. Novick's *That Noble Dream* (1988), reviews and synthesizes much of the pertinent literature on the rhetoric of history. Similarly catalytic has been Donald McCloskey's (1985) discussion of the rhetorical essentials of economics. A host of additional writers have turned a critical eye on writings from across the spectrum of the social and natural sciences. See important works, for example, by Bazerman (1988) and Spence (1982); and edited anthologies by Nelson, Megill and McCloskey (1987) and Simons (1989).

Certain of my own explanations since *TT*, have also participated in this conversation. Of particular interest have been ways in which psychological theory is guided by and dependent on metaphor (Gergen, 1990a) and narrative structure (Gergen and Gergen, 1986), the ways in which language constraints are reflected in characterizations of the person (Gergen, 1990d), the literary basis for the rendering of objectivity (Gergen, 1992b), and the implications of literary and hermeneutic theories for psychological theories of human understanding (Gergen, 1988b).

Social Critique

A third line of critical work has burgeoned since the publication of *TT*, and the present volume again provides a means of appreciating its drama. Although *TT* is ostensibly concerned with how the sciences can comprehend social life, in the end it offers a social account of science. The focal concern with knowledge as discourse, beginning in the second chapter, is equivalent to transforming the question of scientific foundations from the philosophic sphere to the social. For as it is reasoned, discourse is inherently a by-product of social interchange. In this sense, a focus on discourse alone (too often the case in post-structuralist writings) is insufficient. One must attend not only to the social processes at stake in generating knowledge within (and between) disciplines, but consider carefully the function of the sciences within the broader set of patterns constituting cultural life.

Although laced throughout the work, such concerns become most fully elaborated in the final chapter, especially the discussion of a metatheoretical basis for a unified alternative to empiricist science (p. 200). This discussion is premised on the assumption of knowledge as socially constituted. In certain respects this line of argument owes an important debt to a long tradition of scholarship–from Karl Mannheim, Ludwig Fleck, Peter Berger and Thomas Luckmann, to the more recent and broadly compelling works of Thoman Kuhn and Paul Feyerabend–concerned with science as a social process. Their work, along with others important to the tradition, is appropriately credited.

At the same time, writing within this tradition has continued to expand in enormous proportion since the publication of *TT*. Not only have the sociology of knowledge and the history of science gained substantial status within the academy, but they have been joined by related programs in the social study of science, technology and society, and social epistemology. The works of Latour (1987), Knorr-Cetina (1981), Fuller (1988), and Mulkay (1985) are only a few of the most visible beacons in this active and energizing colloquy.

To this form of critical assessment must be added a final entry, chiefly an ever expanding literature stimulated by Michel Foucault's (1977, 1980) discussions of the relationship between power and knowledge. While the vast share of interest had centered on the manner in which the sciences construct the world, Foucault saw such activities as but a small sector of a broad cultural process. As the languages emanating from the various regimes of knowledge–including religion and state institutions, as well as the sciences–circulate, throughout the culture, so do they become constitutive of social pattern. As actions are codified, and reactions justified, so do people come to understand certain patterns of cultural life as necessary and desirable. In effect, as sanctioned languages are absorbed into society, so do they enable relations of power to develop. To question the authority of the sciences, is thus to challenge the forms of power relations in the culture.

The Rise of Social Constructionism

In my view, the vast share of significant writing to which *TT* is a congenial companion is critical in character. Ideological analysis has been preponderantly devoted to a critical dismantling of various intellectual, scientific, and cultural practices. Literary and rhetorical analyses have raised the critical effort to new dimensions–leading to what many see as a despairing nihilism. And the vast bulk of inquiry into the social analysis of science operates in a critical but parasitic relationship with traditional science–requiring the continued pursuit of these practices as the grounds for continued demystification. Far less attention has been devoted to possible successor projects, of developing viable alternatives to existing procedures.

There are exceptions to this generalized characterization. Feminist scholars are devoting increasing energies to developing forms of human science more congenial to a feminist standpoint (see for example, Lather, 1990; Flax, 1990; M. Gergen, 1988, 1990). A broad array of scholars–phenomenologists, hermeneuticists, symbolic interactionists, and humanists–are also carving out a significant space for qualitative research practices as potential supplements or replacements to experimental research tactics. At the same time, I see *TT* as playing at least some significant role in moving the human science dialogue in the direction of what has come broadly to be known as the social constructionist movement. Social constructionist ideas and practices–while sharing much with the aforementioned movements–differ in their primary emphasis on the social–relational constitution of knowledge. Constructionism attempts to synthesize the various forms of critique outlined above, and to move beyond critique to a more positive account of scientific potentials.

It is largely to developing a constructionist alternative that most of my own work has been dedicated since the publication of *TT*. Following rapidly on the heels of this volume, for example, was the publication of *The Social Construction of the Person* (edited with Keith Davis, 1985), and a programmatic statement in the *American Psychologist* (Gergen, 1985). Further works ensued on such topics as narratives (Gergen and Gergen, 1988), therapy as construction (McNamee and Gergen, 1992), the construction of meaning in organizations (Gergen, 1992a), and constructionism in the postmodern context (Gergen, 1991). Under the editorship of John Shotter and myself a book series was also launched in 1986 with Sage Publications Ltd, entitled *Inquiries in Social Construction*. The series has featured writings from across the social sciences–psychology, sociology, anthropology, communication, women's studies, therapy, organizational management, and rhetoric among them–and scholars from twelve different nations have thus far made contributions. These works, too, must be seen against a far broader background of metatheory, theory, research, and human science practices congenial with and contributing to the constructionist dialogue. The interested reader might wish to explore, for example, ongoing work in discourse analysis (Potter and Wetherell, 1987; Billig, 1987), postmodern feminist theory (Weedon, 1987; Butler, 1990), language and power relations (Rose, 1985), the social construction of emotion (Harré, 1986), historical analysis (Danziger, 1990), and narratology (Sarbin, 1986). For further review and elaboration of these and other topics within the constructionist domain, my volume *Realities and Relationships* (1994) may be consulted.

While I believe *TT* can serve as a useful entry into this array of current and inter-related endeavors, it is not to say that its arguments remain free of difficulties. As I see it now, the volume is insufficiently self-reflexive. It does not robustly challenge its conclusions. Insufficient attention is also given to issues of realism, moral and ontological relativism, practical application, and to the positive potentials of traditional social science. I also feel that the rhetorical form of the volume–formal, defensive, elitist, aggressive–is unfortunate in several respects. I have attempted to rectify certain of these infelicities in writings since this period. However, my hope is that even with the shortcomings of the present volume, the generous reader may be taken on an invigorating journey.

References

Baudrillard, J. *Simulations*, New York: Semiotext(e), 1983.

Baudrillard, J. *The ecstasy of communication*. New York: Semiotext(e), 1988.

Bazerman, C. *Shaping written knowledge*. Madison: University of Wisconsin Press, 1988.

Berman, M. *All that's solid melts into air: Experience of modernity*. New York: Simon and Schuster, 1982.

Billig, M. *Arguing and thinking*. London: Cambridge University Press, 1987.

Butler, J. *Gender trouble. Feminism and the subversion of identity*. London: Routledge, 1990.

Danziger, K. *Constructing the subject. Historical origins of psychological research*. Cambridge: Cambridge University Press, 1990.

Derrida, J. *Of grammatology*. Baltimore: Johns Hopkins University Press, 1976.

Eagly, A. Sex differences in influenceability. *Psychological Bulletin*, 1985, *85*: 86–116.

Eagly, A. Gender and social influence, a social psychological analysis. *American Psychologist*, 1983: 971–981.

Fine, M. *Disruptive voices. The possibilities of feminist research*. Ann Arbor: University of Michigan Press, 1992.

Flax, J. *Thinking fragments, psychoanalysis, feminism and postmodernism in the contemporary west.* Berkeley: University of California Press, 1990.

Foucault, M. *Discipline and Punish.* London: Allen Lane, 1977.

Foucault, M. *History of sexuality, vol. 1: An introduction.* New York: Random House, 1978.

Foucault, M. *Power and knowledge.* C. Gordon (Ed.) Brighton: The Harvester Press, 1980.

Fuller, S. *Social epistemology.* Bloomington: University of Indiana Press, 1988.

Gergen, K. J. Social psychology as history. *Journal of Personality and Social Psychology,* 1973, *26*: 309–320.

Gergen, K. J. The social constructionist movement in modern psychology. *American Psychologist,* 1985, *40*: 266–275.

Gergen, K. J. Feminist critique of science and the challenge of social epistemology. In M. Gergen (Ed.), *Feminist thought and the structure of knowledge.* New York: New York University Press, 1988.(a)

Gergen, K. J. If persons are texts. In S. B. Messer, L. A. Sass, and R. L. Woolfolk (Eds.), *Hermeneutics and psychological theory.* New Brunswick: Rutgers University Press, 1988.(b)

Gergen, K. J. Metaphors of the social world. In D. Leary (Ed.), *Metaphors in the history of psychology.* Cambridge: Cambridge University Press, 1990.(a)

Gergen, K. J. Social understanding and the inscription of self. In J. Stigler, R. Shweder, and G. Herdt (Eds.), *Cultural psychology: Essays on comparative human development.* Cambridge: Cambridge University Press, 1990.(b)

Gergen, K. J. Therapeutic professions and the diffusion of deficit. *Journal of Mind and Behavior,* 1990(c), *11*: 353–368.

Gergen, K. J. Textual considerations in the scientific construction of human character. *Style,* 1990(d), *24*: 365–379.

Gergen, K. J. *The saturated self: Dilemmas of identity in contemporary life.* New York: Basic Books, 1991.

Gergen, K. J. Organization theory in the postmodern era. In M. Reed and M. Hughes (Eds.), *Rethinking organization.* London: Sage, 1992.(a)

Gergen, K. J. The mechanical self and the rhetoric of reality. *Annals of Scholarship,* 1992(b), *9*: 87–100.

Gergen, K. J. *Realities and relationships.* Cambridge: Harvard University Press, 1994.

Gergen, K. J. and Davis, K. E. (Eds.), *The social construction of the person.* New York: Springer-Verlag, 1985.

Gergen, K. J. and Gergen, M. M. (Eds.) *Historical social psychology.* Hillsdale: Erlbaum, 1984.

Gergen, K. J. and Gergen, M. M. Narrative form and the construction of psychological science. In T. Sarbin (Ed.), *Narrative psychology: The storied nature of human conduct.* New York: Praeger, 1986.

Gergen, K. J. and Gergen, M. M. Narrative and the self as relationship. In L. Berkowitz (Ed.), *Advances in experimental social psychology, vol. 21.* New York: Academic Press, 1988.

Gergen, M. M. (Ed.) *Feminist thought and the structure of knowledge.* New York: New York University Press, 1988.

Gergen, M. M. From mod masculinity to post-mod macho: A feminist re-play. *The Humanistic Psychologist*, 1990, *18*: 95–104.

Graumann, C. F. and Gergen, K. J. (Eds.) *Historical dimensions of psychological discourse.* New York: Cambridge University Press, in press.

Haraway, D. Situated knowledges: The science question in feminism and the privilege of partial perspective. *Feminist Studies*, 1988, *14*: 575–599.

Harding, S. *The science question in feminism.* Ithaca: Cornell University Press, 1986.

Harré, R. The social constructionist viewpoint. In R. Harré (Ed.), *The social construction of emotion.* Oxford: Blackwell, 1986.

Hubbard, R. Some thoughts about the masculinity of the natural sciences. In M. Gergen (Ed.), *Feminist thought and the structure of knowledge.* New York: New York University Press, 1988.

Jones, E. E. Major developments in social psychology during the past five decades. In G. Lindzey and E. Aronson (Eds), *The handbook of social psychology.* New York: Random House, 1985.

Knorr-Cetina, K. *Manufacture of knowledge: An essay on the constructivist and contextual nature of science.* Oxford: Pergamon Press, 1981.

Kuhn, T. S. *The structure of scientific revolution* (2nd revised edition). Chicago: University of Chicago Press, 1970. (Originally published in 1962.)

Lather, P. Postmodernism and the human sciences. *The Humanistic Psychologist*, 1990, *18*: 64–84.

Latour, B. *Science in action.* Cambridge: Harvard University Press, 1987.

McCloskey, D. N. *The rhetoric of economics.* Madison: University of Wisconsin Press, 1985.

McNamee, S. and Gergen, K. J. (Eds.) *Therapy as social construction.* London: Sage, 1992.

Morawski, J. G. The measurement of masculinity and femininity: Engendering categorical realities. *Journal of Personality*, 1985, *53*: 196–223.

Mulkay, M. *The word and the world.* London: George Allen and Unwin, 1985.

Nelson, J. S., Megill, A., and McCloskey, D. *The rhetoric of the human sciences.* Madison: University of Wisconsin press, 1987.

Novick, P. *That noble dream. The "objectivity question" and the American historical profession.* Cambridge: Cambridge University Press, 1988.

Potter, J. and Wetherell, M. *Discourse and social psychology. Beyond attitudes and behaviour.* London: Sage, 1987.

Rose, N. *The psychological complex.* London: Routledge & Kegan Paul, 1985.

Said, E. *Orientalism*. New York: Random House, 1979.

Sarbin, T. R. (Ed.) *Narrative psychology: The storied nature of human conduct*. New York: Praeger, 1986.

Schwartz, B. *The battle for human nature*. New York: Norton, 1986.

Shotter, J. and Gergen, K. J. (Eds.) *Texts of identity*. London: Sage, 1989.

Simons, H. W. (Ed.) *Rhetoric in the human sciences*. London: Sage, 1989.

Simons, H. W. *The rhetorical turn*. Chicago: University of Chicago Press, 1990.

Spence, D. *Narrative truth and historical truth: Meaning and interpretation in psychoanalysis*. New York: Norton, 1982.

Unger, R. K. Through the looking glass: No Wonderland yet! (The reciprocal relationship between methodology and models of reality). *Psychology of Women Quarterly*, 1983, *8*: 9–32.

Wallach, M. A. and Wallach, L. *Psychology's sanction for selfishness*. San Francisco: W. H. Freeman, 1983.

Weedon, C. *Feminist practice and poststructuralist theory*. Oxford: Blackwell, 1987.

White, H. *Tropics of discourse*. Baltimore: Johns Hopkins University Press, 1978.

Preface to the First Edition

This century has been characterized by a strong and pervasive belief in "certainty through science." It is a belief that has been nurtured by philosophers, scientists, and governing bodies alike. And, where vocal reassurance has failed to convince, modern technology has more than compensated. It has, in effect, been a century in which humankind seemed at last to be making significant headway toward objective and enduring truth. Yet, as the century winds toward its conclusion, this optimistic belief has begun to confront a challenging array of attacks. Widespread signals of concern are increasingly evident, and in the philosophy of science little but remnants remain of the bold rationale that once promised truth through method. One now senses a profound alteration taking place in both the concept of knowledge and of science — an alteration that may prove to be as significant as the Copernican revolution, the emergence of Darwinism, or the development of Freudian theory. As a result of the latter transformations, humans are no longer seen as the center of the universe, as essentially different from animals, or as fully conscious of the wellsprings of their activity. In the present case, however, we confront the loss of the human capacity for objective knowledge. Such challenge is particularly acute within the sociobehavioral sciences, in part because they have never occupied a secure niche within the science establishment, and in part because they have been more keenly sensitive to the dependency of scientific activity on social and personal processes. Thus, as Richard Bernstein observes in his volume, *The Restructuring of Social and Political Theory*, there is at present within the sociobehavioral sciences an "emerging new sensibility" to alternative means and ends for scientific conduct.

This emergent sensibility confronts an array of questions no less profound than complex. On what grounds should the sciences proceed? Are the weaknesses in the logical empiricist conception of science truly lethal? What is to be salvaged from the tradition? What form might a new science take? What are to be the outcomes of such a science? How are such outcomes to be appraised? These and other questions provoke continuous deliberation.

My own odyssey through these issues began in earnest with the 1973 publication of "Social psychology as history" a paper that evoked considerable controversy both within the discipline and without. Since then a number of additional queries have been exposed to public scrutiny and the results have been equally varied. As a result, many bonds of friendship and intellectual exchange were forged and others unilaterally severed by colleagues of long standing. Through these various exchanges, I became increasingly sensitive to the strengths and weaknesses of the various theses, related concerns of colleagues near and far, and the extent of the "revolution" in adjoining disciplines. The result has been a steady intensification of the effort toward understanding.

Upon scanning the results of such efforts, it seemed to me that beneath the clamorous content there was a certain coherence of argument. Speaking about the matter with the editorial staff of Springer-Verlag and Robert Kidd, Advisory Editor to the Springer Series in Social Psychology, I was encouraged to prepare a set of integrated essays that would give expression to the developing ideas. Initially this task seemed propitious enough — a mere matter of honing edges and tightening bolts. However, as the task commenced, it became painfully apparent that this was hardly a matter of fine tuning. The many critical exchanges over the years had left more than scars, and the inadequacy of certain earlier treatments now seemed pronounced. How difficult it is to abandon traditional assumptions once they have entered one's compendium of common sense. It is unfortunate that one is not permitted periodically to expunge portions of the written record. In some instances I have seen colleagues whose public avowals in a single era succeeded in enchaining them for a career. My attitude toward the past is more forgiving; I continue to hope that yesterday's sin may be the forerunner of tomorrow's redemption.

In many respects the present volume is also an outgrowth of recurring controversies in the history of psychology, philosophy and related disciplines. In many instances the present arguments have been vitally informed by these controversies. At the same time, many such battles were isolated from each other and took place over subject matter no longer focal. The present work attempts to revivify and clarify major lines of thinking, but to do so in a way that demonstrates critical relations among the controversies. It further attempts to demonstrate the relevance of this earlier work to contemporary research pursuits. One will glimpse in these pages a reawakening of concerns central to the turn of the century arguments for a *Geisteswissenschaft* as counterposed to a *Naturwissenschaft* However, while this debate is frequently viewed as a neo-rationalist attacks on empiricist doctrines, the stance taken in the present volume is more neo-Wittgensteinian in character. In carrying out this analysis rather extensive use has been made of references and footnotes. It is hoped that such vehicles may be useful in reducing what many take to be an arrogant and debilitating insularity within certain branches of empirical psychology.

The initial chapter of the present volume attempts to elaborate in greater detail the major theses contained in the earlier treatment of social psychology as historical inquiry, and to deal more fully with the various criticisms that have surfaced since its appearance. Although the chapter draws from a 1975 defense in the *Personality and Social Psychology Bulletin*, an invited address to Division 8 of the American Psychological Association in 1975, and a paper entitled "Experimentation in social psychology: A reappraisal," published in the *European Journal of Social Psychology* in 1978, the substance of the present chapter is considerably more extensive than any or all of the previous offerings. In effect the hope is to substantiate, defend, and extend the original thesis of the historical contingency of human conduct and its implications for a science of behavior.

For those who have been immersed in the colloquy over historical change, the initial chapter will hold no dramatic surprises. However, with Chapter 2 the reader will find a radical extension of certain assumptions contained in the initial chapter. While the initial chapter argues that the substance of the sociobehavioral sciences undergoes continuous change, the second chapter proposes that the knowledge engendered by the sciences is not fundamentally objective. Behavioral description, it is argued, does not primarily refer to observables; knowledge of human action cannot in principle be corrected or corroborated through observation. In this light a variety of proposals are made for the function of theory and research in the sciences. As it is argued, such contributions possess far greater potential than are envisioned within the traditional framework. This thesis, drawing in small part from a paper. "Toward theoretical audacity in social psychology," appearing in Gilmour and Duck's (1980) volume, *The Development of Social Psychology*, thus links certain aspects of contextualist, hermeneutic — interpretive, and ordinary language inquiry with the thesis of historical change.

Concern with the function and evaluation of knowledge becomes paramount in Chapter 3. Here the traditional yardstick for theoretical appraisal. namely that of "objectivity" (or truth value), is replaced by the criterion of "generativity" — or the degree to which a theory furnishes alternatives for action. An analysis is also made of major constraints over theorizing in the logical empiricist tradition. This thesis draws in part from a chapter, "The positivist image in social psychological theory." in Alan Buss' (1979c) volume, *Psychology in social context*. and from a 1978 article in the *Journal of Personality and Social Psychology* entitled "Toward generative theory in social psychology." However, both the synthesis and elaboration in the present chapter are far more substantial than the earlier treatments. Chapter 4 is essentially an exercise in extension. The major arguments of the volume grew out of a lengthy period of research in social psychology. And, although most of the illustrative material for the book is drawn from this context, it is argued from the outset that these theses are relevant to a broad range of psychological research as well as inquiry in adjoining social sciences. This chapter attempts to demonstrate this broad-scale applicability by extending the major arguments into the arena of life-span psychology. The choice is perhaps overly fortuitous, for as it is demonstrated, recent arguments in this domain are highly congenial to the present pursuits. This chapter draws from two previous papers, "Stability, change and chance in understanding human development," which appeared in the Datan and Reese (1977) volume, *Life-Span Developmental Psychology: Dialectic Perspectives*, and "The emerging crisis in life-span development theory," published by Baltes and Brim in their 1980 volume, *Life-Span Development and Behavior*, Volume 3.

The final chapter attempts to trace the historical roots of the present-day dissolution of the logical empiricist framework in psychology and to examine several contemporary attempts at developing alternative forms of science. As this chapter demonstrates, implicit in these dissident groups are several key assumptions that form the basis of an alternative metatheory. This metatheory, termed sociorationalist, is found congenial to and sustained by the theses put forward in the earlier chapters of the present volume. This chapter makes use of materials developed for an invited address to the Centennial Symposium at the 1979 meetings of the American Psychological Association, as well as a chapter entitled "An alternative metatheory for social psychology," appearing in Wheeler's 1980 volume, *Review of Personality and Social Psychology*, Volume 1. This latter chapter was coauthored with Jill Morawski at Weslyan University, and she must be credited with a significant contribution to the present rendition.

Whatever strengths are to be found in this work are due in important measure to those friends and colleagues who have given their critical and creative faculties to the endeavor. My indebtedness to Mary Gergen, my most ardent supporter and critic, cannot be overestimated; her insights and vitality are to be found throughout the volume. Among those who have been especially generous in evaluating materials entering into the present confluence are: Irwin Altman, Erika Apfelbaum, Curt Banks, Michael Basseches, Donald Campbell, Peter Dachler, Nancy Datan, Shel Feldman, Edna Foa, Uriel Foa, Gerald Ginsburg, Carol Gould, Alan Gross, Horst Gundlach, Kenneth Hammond, Rom Harré, Robert Helmreich, Clyde Hendricks, Marianne Jaeger, Robert Kidd, Louise Kidder, Sigmund Koch, Hugh Lacey, George Levinger, Ian Lubek, Jacob Meskin, Alexandre Metraux, Jill Morawski, Serge Moscovici, Andrew Okwell, Barnett Pearce, Paul Rosenblatt, Ralph Rosnow, Joseph Rychlak, Franz Samelson, Edward Sampson, Barry Schwartz, Paul Secord, Phil Shaver, Ann Shepardson, John Shotter, Ellen Skinner, M. Brewster Smith, Siegfried Streufert, Lloyd Strickland, Margaret Stroebe, Wolfgang Stroebe, Karl Weick, Diana Whitney, Lawrence Wrightsman, and Ricardo Zuñiga.

Inspiration has been furnished as well by early mentors, Kurt Back, Ned Jones, Sigmund Koch, and Karl Zener. The work of each has embodied ideals to which the present volume aspires.

Work on the present volume was facilitated by a grant from the National Science Foundation (#7809393), a William Fulbright Research Fellowship, and stipends from the Deutsche Forschungs Gemeinschaft. Supporting facilities and a congenial atmosphere for interchange have also been generously furnished at various critical periods by Michael Argyle, Department of Experimental Psychology, Oxford University; Carl Graumann, Psychologisches Institut, Universität Heidelberg; Robert Pages, Laboratoire de Psychologie Sociale, Université de Paris VII; and Wolfgang Stroebe, then at the Psychologisches Institut, Universität Marburg. Finally, the burden of typing countless drafts, along with letters, grant proposals, and reports; the responsibility for arranging all the nettlesome particulars of my professional life; and the struggle of mastering a daily chaos have all been valiantly undertaken by my secretary and friend, Didi Beebe. To all, and for all, I am deeply indebted.

Kenneth J. Gergen
Swarthmore, Pennsylvania

Chapter 1

Traditional Science in a World of Change

The contrasting experiences of permanence and change, of stability and flux, have furnished continuing challenges to human understanding since the origins of intellectual life. For over two thousand years, philosophers, theologians, poets, and scientists have struggled with the implications of this dichotomy. For the most part, treatises devoted to this topic have been characterized by a strong and consistent evaluative stance. The fluctuating and the ephemeral have typically emerged as problematic aspects of human experience, to be overcome by intellectual ingenuity or spiritual transcendence. In contrast, the search for permanence has often been invested with sanctity, whether it be in philosophy, science, religion, or the arts. In John Dewey's words, "The conceptions that had reigned in the philosophy of nature and knowledge for two thousand years . . . rested on the assumption of the superiority of the fixed and the final; they rested upon treating change and origin as signs of defect and unreality. (They laid) hands upon the sacred arc of absolute permanency" (1910, p. 46).

There are many good reasons for valuing the permanent over the ephemeral. As early Greek philosophers were painfully aware, an acceptance of the Heraclitean dictum that "all things flow" was tantamount to nihilism. If the world is in constant flux, then cumulative learning is negated and the concept of knowledge rendered problematic. What is learned or "known" at any given instant may be irrelevant to the next. Indeed, the significance of both Platonic and Aristotelian philosophy lies importantly in their solutions to the problem of how knowledge is possible in a Heraclitean world of continuous fluctuation. For Plato permanence was to be found in the realm of the "pure idea" or ideational form. Aristotle responded to the puzzle by distinguishing between a philosophy of "being" and of "becoming." Other aspects of the human condition also favor the equation of the good with the permanent. Permanent "goods" or enduring ideals lend themselves to solving difficult problems of social control and mobilization. Controlling institutions at all levels of society may deal with the particularized problems of their constituents by invoking, elucidating, and reinforcing various idealizations of permanence. Punishment and coercion are justified in the service of "the law," "democracy," "communism," or "natural rights," and entire societies may be mobilized in defense of such transcendent ideals as "God," "liberty," and "justice." Impermanence also has strong associations with death; indeed, the powerful influence of Christianity in the Western world may well be attributed to its replacement of the finite with the everlasting. The concept of the infinite life of the spirit in Christian theology serves the same function on an emotional level that the "pure idea" does on the intellectual. Too, change is often suffused with feelings of threat or peril. People can accommodate themselves to recurrent regularities; when events are stable, one may adapt through trial and error. However, novelty and irregularity pose continuing threats to ongoing patterns of adaptation, and at any point may thrust existence into jeopardy.

It is this same romance with permanence that has served as the primary impetus behind the development of modern science. As it is often said, it is the purpose of science to discover the constants in the otherwise uncharted flux. As Carnap (1966) puts it, "The more systematic observations of science reveal certain repetitions or regularities in the world. . . . The laws of science are nothing more than statements expressing these regularities as precisely as possible" (p. 3). And the by-products of such discovery can be of untold benefit to humankind. If science can identify systematic and recurring patterns, the society may alter its path or harness the predictable to its advantage. Establishing principles of physics, chemistry, biology, or of human conduct—all enhance the human capacity for controlling destiny. The simplicity of the argument is optimistic and compelling, and the result is a formidable scientific establishment largely (although not exclusively) devoted to the tasks of locating, documenting, and explaining permanence amid the flux of passing experience.

Yet, although behavioral science writings continue to pay homage to the underlying stability of human behavior, one is frequently if not painfully aware of the multitude of disordered and discontinuous events taking place outside the scientific sanctum. Research in the sociobehavioral sciences largely relies on a highly delimited set of systematically constrained experiences. In contrast, outside this arena, wars, revolutions, international allegiances, economic spurts, national and domestic policies, religious institutions, cultural heroes, aesthetic movements, intellectual insights, value commitments, marriages, loving relationships, family ties, personal beliefs, and so on all wend their rapid and disordered way through consciousness, and slip into the quagmire of memory. Is it just a matter of "more hard work" before the sciences will begin to discern the constancies, the enduring principles beneath the vicissitudes of common experience? Will more time, more funding, more research, and greater theoretical effort finally allow the behavioral scientist to master the rudiments of human conduct, and to return manifold to society its investments to date?[1] There is room for suspicion.

One is struck as well by the curious insensitivity to the historical context of most behavioral science. Such investigation typically contributes to what the scientist views as transhistorically valid principles. Yet the research itself is inevitably conducted within the contemporary historical context, one that forces upon the scientist certain observations while precluding others. History itself confronts us with a morass of ever-moving complexity. As Feyerabend (employing Herbert Butterfield's words) has characterized it, "History is full of accidents and conjectures, and curious juxtapositions of events, and it demonstrates to us the complexity of human change and the unpredictable character of the ultimate consequences of any given act or decision of men" (1976, p. 1). Research activity is itself situated within the unfolding and ever-changing web of accidental relations. Yet in general, it remains insensitive to that which has preceded or will follow. Is it legitimate to expect that the discipline can rest transhistorically valid theory on an observation base composed of historically situated patterns?

A third discrepancy adds weight to one's suspicion. In contrast to the mighty oaks of the natural sciences, one might describe the social sciences as a sprawling thicket.[2] The oaks often bring forth widespread smiles of approval; they seem sturdy, powerful, and reliable. In contrast, the sociobehavioral sciences seem to have no clear and dependable product. One becomes perennially entangled in ambiguity. Yet the roots of the latter sciences are buried deep in an estimable intellectual tradition; they have basked in the sum of enthusiastic interest, and they have been fertilized with large sums from public coffers. To what then can one attribute these dramatic differences? The typical answer is that the sciences of human conduct are immature. They are a new breed, it is said, and they will require many years before reaching full fruition. Yet, as careful students of the history of science have often noted, there is little merit in this defense. The history of systematic thinking about human activity is more ancient in origin than natural science (cf. Durkheim, 1895). Observational study has been no less extensive, and it can be argued that curiosity in the former domain has exceeded that in the latter by wide margin. Finally, the number of research publications in the sociobehavioral sciences has multiplied exponentially over the past three decades. Yet, one is hard pressed

---

[1] In Manis' (1976a) words, it is the "researcher's vision . . . that through inspiration, hard work, and continued financial support, [he or she] may discern some relatively stable regularities that appear and reappear" (p. 371).

[2] As Ernest Nagel (1961) has commented in this regard, within the natural sciences "almost complete unanimity (is) commonly found among competent workers . . . as to what are matters of established fact, what are the reasonably satisfactory explanations (if any) for the assumed facts, and what are some of the valid procedures in sound inquiry" (p. 448). In contrast, Nagel points out, the social sciences are a "battleground for interminably warring schools of thought . . . even subject matter which has been under intensive and prolonged study remains at the unsettled periphery of research" (p. 448).

to locate substantial gains in knowledge.[3] Why is it, then, that the natural sciences have experienced such overwhelming success in locating principles with high empirical content, while scientists of human conduct are considerably taxed to demonstrate convincing advances in predictive capacity?[4]

A consideration of phenomenal change, so long disregarded by the field, may furnish insight into the dismaying discrepancy between the productivity of the natural and sociobehavioral sciences. At the same time, if the traditional aim of the sciences, that of establishing a fundamental repository of objective knowledge, can be replaced with objectives that take account of impermanence in pattern, the

---

[3] As Kemeny (1959) has formulated the discrepancy: "A typical law in the physical sciences is stated precisely, usually in mathematical terms, and is quite free of ambiguity. It has been tested repeatedly and has withstood the tests. The usual law in the social sciences, on the other hand, is ordinarily couched in Big Words and a great deal of ambiguity. The law is usually presented with many qualifications and excuses. . . . The law in the physical sciences has enabled us to deduce precisely certain predictions which have been verified. While predictions have been attributed to the social law, the chances are that they simply reflect prejudices or commonsense knowledge of the authors of the law, and that these predictions have not been deduced from the law itself" (pp. 244–245). Farrell (1975) has also commented on the "notorious fact that psychologists have *not* unearthed many satisfactory or invulnerable lawlike generalizations" (p. 253).

[4] Dismay over the accumulation of knowledge in psychology is hardly difficult to locate. For example, as the editor of a seven-volume study of the state of psychological knowledge, Sigmund Koch has summarized, "Consider the hundreds of theoretical formulations, rational equations and mathematical models of the learning process that have accrued; the thousands of research studies. And *now* consider that there is still no wide agreement, even at the crassest descriptive level, on the empirical conditions under which learning takes place" (Koch, 1959, p. 731). In the field of personality psychology, Lee Sechrest (1976) has compared the major issues of study over a ten-year period and asked: "Now why have the themes changed? If it were because issues have been resolved, because important phenomena are now so well understood that they no longer merit attention, it would be cause for encouragement—rejoicing perhaps. Alas, one cannot escape the conclusion that investigators ran out of steam, that issues were abandoned, and that problems were never resolved" (p. 26). Similarly, in reviewing the nearly three hundred studies on individual versus group risk taking, Dorwin Cartwright (1973) concludes: "After 10 years of research (the) original problem remains unsolved. We still do not know how the risk-taking behavior of 'real-life' groups compares with that of individuals" (p. 3). In cognitive psychology, Allen Newell (1973) has commented on the "ever increasing pile of issues in cognitive psychology which we weary of or become diverted from but never really settle" (p. 289). As Brewster Smith (1972) has commented, "After three decades of industrious and intelligent effort, the case for cumulative advance in experimental social psychology remains open to reasonable doubt" (p. 88). And Clara Mayo (1977) has said of contemporary social psychology, "Few theoretical formulations of any power have emerged and few of the empirical findings have proved replicable or generalizable beyond the college sophomore for whom they were developed."

efficacy of the endeavor may be vastly improved. One may hope to fashion a science of vital significance to the society. The present volume will argue that a serious confrontation with impermanence in human action demands a reformulation of the nature of sociobehavioral science and a reconsideration of its potential. In the first chapter several traditionally honored assumptions will be examined in light of what appear to be central characteristics of the subject matter. For those who have been immersed in the various debates over social psychology as history (cf. Cronbach, 1975; Gergen, 1973, 1976; Hendrick, 1976; Scheibe, 1978; Schlenker, 1974, 1976) this chapter will not pose radical departures. Rather, it will attempt a more thorough recasting of the central thesis and a systematic treatment of various lines of criticism. However, as attention is turned to the character of theory within the sociobehavioral sciences (Chapter 2), the form of argument will undergo a substantial shift. Here it will be proposed that the problem of phenomenal change obviates the possibility for a behavioral language linked to observables. In effect, it will be proposed that behavioral science theory is fundamentally nonobjective, and that traditional conceptions of scientific theory are both unwarranted on the one hand, and unduly conservative in their estimates of its potential on the other. As will be shown, when properly understood, scientific inquiry can be of enormous consequence to society.

Chapter 3 will develop the grounds for a generative criterion for theoretical construction and appraisal, a criterion suggested by the characterization of theory as an interpretive implement. Here it will be contended that the commitment to logical empiricist metatheory, along with the favored methodology of experimentation, has significantly impaired the potential of the discipline to foster catalytic theory of broad consequence. As will be argued, one cannot easily commit oneself within either the theoretical, methodological, or metatheoretical domain, without broad repercussions for activity in each of the other domains. Chapter 4 represents an application and expansion of a number of the central ideas developed in the first three chapters. Social psychological research plays a focal role within the initial chapters. However, in Chapter 4 an analysis of life-span developmental inquiry will demonstrate more fully the broad applicability of the central theses.

Finally, Chapter 5 will shift the focus to the historical context in which the present concerns have been nurtured. In particular, attention will be given to the historical developments giving rise to what many view as a crisis within the sociobehavioral sciences in general and social psychology in particular, and to the conception of science currently emerging within a variety of dissident camps. As this chapter will demonstrate, the transformations favored by the present account are congenially related to arguments emerging in several other domains. It appears that the sociobehavioral sciences are engaged in full metatheoretical revolution. The logical empiricist base is gradually giving way to a sociorationalism.

Throughout the volume concern will center most directly on experimental social psychology. There is much to be gained in this emphasis, for this branch of the sociobehavioral sciences has been most zealous in its attempts to emulate the natural sciences. In its endeavor to develop reliable repositories of data, to examine systematically the independent and interactive effects of isolated variables, and to test the objective validity of formal hypotheses, experimental social psychology has been perhaps the most dedicated of the social science disciplines. Its successes and failures may operate as beacons to like-minded colleagues throughout the socio-behavioral sciences. In addition, experimental social psychologists have been uniquely situated within the academic structure. Colleagues pursuing physiological and chemical bases of behavior furnish a continuing impetus toward adopting the natural science orientation. On the other side, social psychologists are frequently sensitized to the more variegated pursuits of sociologists, anthropologists, political scientists, historians, and economists. Social psychologists thus retain a critical vantage point, poised, as they are, at the intersection between the natural and social sciences. Yet, the arguments that shall be developed in the present analysis are intended to cut across the spectrum of sciences dealing with human conduct. That is, they speak not only to all branches of the social sciences but to many sub-disciplines within psychology itself. The fields of learning, cognitive, developmental, and clinical psychology are particularly implicated. Chapter 4, with its special focus on life-span development, should amplify such implications. The immediate focus is thus on social psychology, but the attempt is to elucidate problems and prospects of broadest concern.

Assumptive Bases in the Sociobehavioral Sciences

As we have seen, philosophers have been long concerned with the problem of impermanence and its challenge to the supposition that knowledge can be accumulated. During the past century a new form of solution took shape, one of immense promise and compelling optimism. Philosophers were energetically engaged in what J. L. Austin (1962) has termed "the pursuit of the incorrigible," that is, a means of achieving worldly knowledge, no longer subject to correction. This pursuit, more generally, has come to be identified with logical empiricist philosophy and the associated movement toward a unified science. As maintained by participants in the movement, it should be possible to discover within the variegated activities of the natural sciences a common set of rules for advancing knowledge. If such rules will yield to proper distillation, the resulting elixir might transform the character of human life. Natural scientists might employ such rules to determine what forms of inquiry were productive and thus accelerate manifold the impressive advances of the centuries preceding. And within other spheres of inquiry including the socio-behavioral sciences, the adoption of such rules would ensure progress no less significant than the harnessing of electrical energy, the discovery of genetic transmission, or the smashing of the atom. In Bertrand Russell's (1956) terms, it was hoped that one day there would be a "mathematics of human behavior as precise as the mathematics of machines" (p. 142).

Of course, the conception of proper scientific conduct developed by logical empiricist philosophers of the 1930s has undergone considerable modification over the years, and very few of the assumptions once viewed as fundamental within the positivist framework have remained intact. Such modification has been sufficiently extensive that current philosophy of science is said to be "postempiricist" (Thomas, 1979). We shall touch on several of the major revisions as the volume unfolds. However, it is useful at this juncture to underscore a cluster of assumptions that constitute the "received view," a view that continues to the present to furnish the rationale for psychological research, hope for its future, and existential sustenance to scientists wishing to leave their imprint on the future. A simplified sketch of three central assumptions within the received view will prove useful:[5]

1. *The major function of science is to construct general laws or principles governing the relationship among classes of observable phenomena.* As commonly envisioned, the ultimate product of scientific inquiry should be a set of general statements that describes the systematic relationships among specified observables. Typically, it is argued, such statements should also furnish a "sense of understanding" or an answer to the question of "why" events occur as they do. Further, such statements should enable one to predict the future occurrence of various events. Although alterations in emphasis have taken place over the years, this basic view of the function of science has remained robust in many circles. Braithwaite's (1953) prefatory statement to his classic, *Scientific Explanation*, is virtually conclusive: "The function of science . . . is to establish general laws covering the behavior of the empirical events or objects with which the science in question is concerned, and thereby enable us to connect together our knowledge of the separate known events, and to make reliable predictions of events as yet unknown (p. 1).

2. *The general laws or principles comprising scientific knowledge should be consistent with empirical fact. Scientific investigation is properly concerned with establishing an objective grounding for systematic theory.* This proposition forms a virtual corollary to its predecessor. The laws, principles, or theoretic generalizations forming the product of science are ideally based on systematic observation. In Carnap's (1966) terms, "All empirical knowledge rests finally on observations" (p. 40). Such facts may be used as the basis for initial theoretical formulations, or

---

[5] Just beneath what is here characterized as "the received view" lie a host of distinctions typically made by philosophers but disregarded by most practicing psychologists. Although many of the arguments appearing here are termed neo-positivist, the commonly preferred term for this confluence of suppositions is logical empiricist. When such suppositions are refined (and some abandoned) they are sometimes termed post-empiricist. In Germany conflict over these and related suppositions is viewed as the "positivist dispute." One may also distinguish these positions from those often taken by philosophers of the realist school. The latter typically, though not exclusively, argue for some form of correspondence theory of truth, while recent empiricist philosophy generally takes a functionalist view of the relation between theory and observation (i.e., theories are to be evaluated according to their capacities for prediction, and not against a standard of "what is the case"). This latter view is consistent as well with certain pragmatist arguments, the latter of which played a strong role in legitimizing the hypothetico-deductive method. Popper's refinements of this view are termed critical rationalism. Although such distinctions can be useful for many purposes, they will generally be excluded from the present treatment except where essential for the arguments under consideration.

they may be derivatively sought. In this sense philosophers have traditionally distinguished between the inductive and deductive phases of scientific activity. In the former case the scientist is said to utilize his or her observations to construct the more general theoretic superstructure, and in the latter, the superstructure may be used to deduct hypotheses about as yet unobserved phenomena. The case for the inductive strategy of theory construction has generally failed to be sustained. As is commonly recognized, there is no logical justification for drawing general conclusions on the basis of particular observations (cf. Popper, 1968; Shimony, 1953-54). It is in this context that Popper (1934) developed the challenging thesis that it is not the verification of a theory that furnishes its justification but its resistance to falsification. Universal statements, such as all swans are white, cannot in principle be derived from the continuous observation of white swans. However, the universal statement can be falsified upon the discovery of a single black swan. Further, as argued by Hanson (1958) and others, the identification of particulars from which general theoretical statements are to be drawn already presupposes a theoretical orientation. In this sense, "observation" (entity identification) is theory impregnated from the outset.[6]

Further arguments have been lodged against the assumption that single theoretical statements can be falsified through observation. Quine (1953), along with Duhem (1906) long before, has elucidated the extent to which the outcome of any hypothesis test depends not only on the truth value of the hypothesis, but also on the validity of innumerable auxiliary hypotheses (largely unstated). Thus, negative results do not necessarily fault the articulated hypothesis, but may be attributed to the failure of any number of auxiliary hypotheses. As it is said, most widely accepted scientific theories are "undetermined" with respect to their reliance on observation. However, such controversy has not succeeded in unseating the more fundamental assumption that scientific research should serve to limit or correct theoretical statements. Even for the postempiricist, "the testing of (theoretical) statements against the world is at least one strong criterion for the acceptance or rejection of those statements" (Thomas, 1979, p. 2).

3. *Through continued empirical assessment of theoretical propositions and their deductions, scientific understanding can progress. Scientific knowledge is cumulative.* Scientific research, properly conducted, should enhance the goals of understanding, prediction, and control. This proposition is, of course, fundamental to

---

[6]Some have argued on this basis that no claims to theoretical objectivity can be made in the sciences. If there are no observations outside of those which a theory affords, then all theories are inherently true and data can never rule between them. However, this form of radical extension is a shaky one at best. On this account one should be able to conclude, for example, that there is no sensory discrimination without theory. Infants would fail to recognize their mothers or react to the prick of an errant diaper pin without having arrived at birth with a theory enabling them to single out such events from the swirling confusion. Further, to accept the position would be to forego the possibility of either justifying or dislodging it by recourse to observation itself. If this move is made, one is left with a position that is true by definition—and thus, false by any opposing definition.

the *hypothetical-deductive* conception of science, a conception articulated within early positivist circles and functioning at present as a major source of scientific optimism (Koch, 1959). Essentially it is held that on the basis of an initial postulate set, specific hypotheses should be formulated concerning the state of nature as yet unexamined. Subsequent examination of the state of nature may support or fail to support one's theoretical premises. If the premises receive empirical verification, confidence in their validity may be increased. In the Bayesian sense, the antecedent probability of the proposition's truth value is enhanced. If the empirical test fails to verify the premises, the theory must be called into question. Modification or elaboration of the premise may occur, or, if sufficient negative evidence accumulates, the theory may be discarded. In any case, through this procedure, theories that make valid predictions are retained or conceptually enriched and those at odds with the facts may be discarded. Science may thus undergo continuous improvement.

Of the three orienting assumptions it is primarily this one that has undergone the most intensive philosophic questioning within recent years. Most significant for present purposes is the controversy stimulated by Kuhn's (1970) influential volume, *The Structure of Scientific Revolutions.* As Kuhn argues, the abandonment of a given theoretical paradigm does not primarily depend on the continued accumulation of negative evidence. Scientists are seldom dissuaded from their theoretical commitments by the existence of disconfirming evidence. Rather, states Kuhn, anomalies emerge that do not so much contradict the prevailing paradigm as they raise questions that the initial paradigm is unprepared to answer. As study of the anomalies gains interest, a new paradigm may be generated to replace the old. The paradigm ushered in by the revolution does not represent a negation of its predecessor, but alters the scientist's view of the entities comprising the relevant universe, the relationship among these entities, and the questions that may legitimately be asked. In effect, movement from one theoretical paradigm to another is akin to Gestalt shift in perception: The world is seen anew, but not necessarily more accurately. Kuhn's thesis has, of course, been widely debated, and many remain unconvinced. At the same time, others have attempted in various ways to salvage the fundamental belief in cumulative research. As Lakatos (1970) has argued, it is not isolated theories that are in competition, but extended research programs that may vary in their capacity to derive new predictions. In contrast, Laudan (1977) argues that scientific process is achieved through increments in problem-solving effectiveness. In effect, strong remnants do remain of the belief in progress through empirical research.

To what extent are these foundations of the positivist-empiricist program evidenced within contemporary sociobehavioral science? In his general review philosopher Richard Rudner (1966) points out that the natural and social sciences are similar in that they share "a common logic of justification"; both engage in systematic observation bearing on the "acceptance or rejection of theories." With respect to the theories within the social sciences more generally, sociologist Gordon DiRenzo (1966) points out that a full and proper explanation "is one that has assumed the invariable status as Law . . . whose validity and precision may be established through empirical verification" (p. 251). Within the field of psychology commitment to the traditional program for scientific conduct is perhaps more profound that in any of the related sciences. The preamble to most textbooks in psychology echo the familiar themes. For example, as Morgan, King, and Robinson (1979) state, "Psychology is the science of human and animal behavior. . . . [Psychological knowledge] is gathered by carefully observing and measuring events— sometimes, but not necessarily, in experiments. . . . The observations of events are systematized in various ways, but mainly by classifying them into categories and establishing general laws and principles to describe and predict new events as accurately as possible" (p. 4). Or, as Glenn, Grant, Whaley, and Malott (1976) put it, "Science is a way of finding out. . . . the power of science is in its method. . . . Psychology [is] the science of human behavior. . . . By using the experimental method we achieve three main goals of science: 'explanation,' 'prediction' and 'control'" (pgs. 1-2). Similarly, Houston, Bee, Hatfield, and Rimm (1981) state, "Psychology . . . may be defined as the science that studies behavior. . . . The goals of psychology are to understand, predict, and change behavior. . . . The experiment is one of the most powerful data-gathering methods in psychology" (pgs. 32-33).

As indicated, social psychologists (within psychology, but to a lesser degree in sociology) have been particularly committed to the tenets of the received view. The familiar themes are found throughout its major texts. For example, in their classic text Krech, Crutchfield, and Ballachey (1962) write, "whether we are interested in social psychology as a basic science or as an applied science a set of scientific principles is essential" (p. 3). Jones and Gerard (1967) echo this view in their major text: "Science seeks to understand the factors responsible for stable relationships between events" (p. 42). As Judson Mills (1969) has put it, "social psychologists want to discover causal relationships so that they can establish basic principles that will explain the phenomena of social psychology" (p. 412). These basic principles are to be grounded in systematic empirical examination. Or, in Wrightsman and Deaux's (1981) terms, social psychological theory "provides a source of hypotheses to test predictions about the world. Theory may . . . anticipate kinds of events that we can expect to occur, even if the particular conditions have not yet been encountered" (p. 8).[7] The assumption is further made that understanding may be cumulative. As Dyal, Corning, and Willows (1975) phrase the case:

> We opt for the scientific approach because it has been shown to be a powerful technique of discovery. Although errors of fact and interpretation are sometimes made, the scientific approach tends to be self-correcting in the long run. As a consequence of its self-correcting character and its ability to provide reliable facts, the scientific approach offers the advantage of advancing our understanding because its facts and theories tend to be cumulative, they build on what has been discovered previously. (p. 4)

---

[7]For a recent restatement of these various goals in psychology see McClintock (in press). This particular restatement is of special note as the author makes a serious attempt to reconcile the traditional rationale with more recent lines of critical appraisal.

To be sure, support for these various views is hardly univocal within psychology or related disciplines. The major point is that logical empiricist assumptions are highly pervasive and continue to furnish the general rationale for theory and research in the sociobehavioral sciences.

The Threat of Instability

At this point we must pause to consider a tacit but unquestioned assumption within the traditional perspective, one that appears fundamental to its viability. The core assumption is that the phenomena of nature are enduring, that in the case of human behavior, the essential contours are not ephemeral but are subject to transtemporal stability. Although seldom questioned, it would appear that the strength of the traditional view of science is *fundamentally dependent on the stability of the relationship among events in nature.* The greater the degree of stability in such patterns, the more promising are the traditional assumptions (or some variant thereof) in yielding a body of knowledge, principles, or laws that may enhance the human capacity for prediction and control. Let us examine this position more closely. First, if events in the world of nature were in a state of irregular flux, one would be ill equipped to develop objectively grounded principles relating classes of events. In a major sense the aim of scientific laws is to convert "noise" to information, to reduce chaos by singling out classes of events that bear systematic relationships with one another. However, if events in the state of nature were capriciously related with each other, such conversion would be obviated. Not only would the concept of "class" be irrelevant, but the most veridical statement that could emerge would be that of random variation—in the sciences a principle tantamount to annihilation.

Once it is agreed that general laws are obviated by chaotic change, the empirical test of theoretical propositions and their derivations become superfluous as well. If flux prevails, one could scarcely mount an empirical test of any kind. The empirical test would soon be discarded if the results capriciously confirmed the null hypothesis. And if one is unable to evaluate propositions empirically, the assumption that theories can become increasingly predictive over time capitulates as well. In Popper's (1968) terms, "Only when certain events recur in accordance with rules or regularities, as is the case with repeatable experiments, can our observations be tested in principle" (p. 45).

It would be extravagant, of course, to assert that either the natural or the social sciences are faced with a world of inchoate flux. Human existence would be terminated in short order should events in nature be fully capricious. Yet, it is equally misleading to assume full stability. Who can deny Heraclitus' contention that man never places his foot in the same stream twice? Rather, it seems more fruitful to consider events and their relationships along a *stability continuum*. While some phenomena are sufficiently stable, enduring, reliable, or replicable that they readily lend themselves to encapsulation in lawful principles, others may remain intransigent to such undertakings. For those phenomena toward the stable end of the continuum, science in the traditional mold may prove a valuable tool for prediction and control. For more transient phenomena science of the traditional variety may hold far less promise.[8]

It is the contention of this initial chapter that a fundamental difference exists between the bulk of the phenomena of concern to the natural as opposed to the sociobehavioral scientist. There is ample reason to believe that the phenomena of focal concern to the latter are far less stable (enduring, reliable, or replicable) than those of interest in the former. [9] If this contention is sustained, it may be argued further that the traditional assumptions of scientific inquiry may provide an inadequate basis for inquiry in the sociobehavioral sciences. Further, the unquestioned application of these assumptions, so prominent in core sectors of the sociobehavioral sciences, may be resulting in an immense squandering of time and resources. To place the matter squarely, it may be ventured that with all its attempts to emulate natural science inquiry, the past century of sociobehavioral research and theory has failed to yield one principle as reliable as Archimedes' principle of hydrostatics or Galileo's law of uniformly accelerated motion. As the following analysis will attempt to demonstrate, an additional hundred and forty years, even a thousand and forty years, of the same activity is likely to fare no better.

Of course, few delineations, such as that posed between the various sciences, are without exception. Various natural science phenomena appear to fluctuate in near random fashion. The development of quantum physics was largely in response to this problem, and solution required shifting levels of abstraction. By relinquishing concern with the movement of single particles and focusing on fields, physicists were able to locate reliable patterns. It is just such a solution that has enabled economic theorists to develop principles that successfully predict restricted indicators (e.g., market pricing, rates of exchange) over delimited historical periods.[10]

---

[8] As process-oriented thinkers since the time of Heraclitus often maintain, all nature is in flux (cf. Browning, 1965). That which we take to be stability or endurance is solely conceptual; that is, it depends on abstracting from ongoing experience certain particulars. Critics of this position argue that it is equally defensible to maintain that ongoing experience is made up of a succession of stable states—much as a motion picture is composed of a series of still pictures. There would appear to be no simple way of resolving this antinomy. The present position rests on the assumption that, for all practical purposes, people can come to virtually univocal agreement through a process of observation and referential pointing that certain features, objects, or properties are more enduring or stable than others.

[9] Arguing for essential differences between the natural and social sciences must of necessity be an oversimplification. For example, the natural sciences have undergone many alterations in perspective over the centuries, and there are vast differences among them, even today. Further, we can anticipate changes in the future, some of which will certainly vitiate certain of the present theses.

[10] Anyone believing that the only safe road to a predictive science is that of population (as opposed to individual) study will be sobered by surveying the widespread attempts at economic forecasting. To cite but one instance, Bernholz (1981) has reviewed the relative merits of a variety of econometric models of exchange rate fluctuations. As he shows, such "models tried to explain exchange rate fluctuations

In addition, certain forms of human activity may recur with a high degree of reliability. Processes of breathing, digesting, ovulating, and so on may possess certain
pragmatically invariant properties. However, such activities contribute in only
minor degree to the understanding of the complex range of daily activities in which
humans participate. We shall return to the problem of biological constraints later
in the chapter.

It is also possible that natural and social scientists have been differentially selec-
tive in their choice of phenomena. The success of the natural sciences may be
largely attributed to their restricting attention to highly stable events. If natural
scientists had set out to predict the movement of single grains of sand during the
shifting of tides, or the trajectory of specific maple leaves in a hurricane, their
success would have been far less impressive. As Michael Scriven (1956) has argued,
the good fortune of classic physics and the misfortune of psychology lies to a large
extent in the differential complexity of the prediction problems they confront.
Yet, in the sociobehavioral sciences it is difficult to imagine how the selection of
subject matter could be radically different. Such scientists have been deeply concerned with the behavior of humans as they think, feel, learn, develop, sense the
environment and interact with others. Would it be possible to justify a science of
human conduct that failed to consider such matters?

Over and above these various issues, there is substantial reason to believe that the
comparative success of the two realms may be linked to fundamental differences
in the nature of the subject matter. In particular, it may be argued that the very
nature of the human condition obfuscates the attempt to encapsulate ongoing
activity in a series of abstract principles. In the broadest sense the human being may
be viewed as inveterately law breaking, that is, while constructing order simultaneously generating the grounds for its dissolution. At the moment of its inception,
any principle or law of social conduct may sow the seeds of its own demise. Let us
explore such assertions in greater detail.

Decomposing Patterned Behavior

In what sense can it be argued that human conduct is more "disorderly" than the
events typically studied in the natural sciences? The case cannot be made without
caution. As most natural scientists are quick to admit, stable patterns are discovered
only through "gradual approximation." The social scientist is thus advised to proceed in similar fashion. Yet, after more than a century of apparent failure to gener-

---

as a consequence of such factors as lagged values of relative money supplies, price
levels, industrial products or their changes and interest rate differentials. The expost
results estimates seemed to be quite convincing from an econometric point of view,
but led to very disappointing ex ante predictions when used about two years later
for the developments after the time for which they had been estimated" (Bernholz,
1981, p. 2). As Bernholz goes on to describe, the new predictive models, which are
widely corroborated, are based on the assumption that because "new information
can only arrive randomly and unpredictably, exchange rates will only fluctuate
randomly and independently; they will follow a random walk" (p. 2).

ate such approximations within the sociobehavioral sciences, it is appropriate to reconsider the phenomena under study. In the present case, we may explore four fundamental differences in the focal phenomena within these contrasting domains of inquiry. Three of these differences concern constitutive features of the subject matter of the sociobehavioral sciences. The fourth, which concerns the particular relationship of science to its subject matter, will be given separate consideration. Each of these differences raises serious questions concerning the justification for a logical empiricist rationale for sociobehavioral inquiry.

Stereotypy versus Flexibility: The Biological Stratum

We may first consider the extent to which human biological makeup facilitates or impedes the scientific attempt to locate transhistorical pattern. On a constitutional basis, are we dealing with the sort of creature whose activities are reliably patterned? Let us frame an answer to this question in the language of the neobehaviorist orientation so central to inquiry in psychology. Within this perspective the investigator is centrally concerned with establishing the relationships between stimulus conditions (S) and psychological mechanisms or processes of the organism (O), and between the psychological sphere and external responses (R). The resulting S-O-R principles would thus take the form of reliable stimulus–response connections explained by hypothetical psychological mechanisms. Yet from this perspective certain requirements would have to be fulfilled before one could hope to establish a cumulative science of the traditional sort. Principally, to the extent that the same stimulus conditions precede the same behavioral event for all organisms within a given class, and to the extent that these relationships are reliable across time, one may make a legitimate claim for transhistorical generality of behavioral principles. Such conditions would foster an ideal climate for traditional science, for in this case the investigator might develop a conceptual template capturing observed patterns at t_1, test the adequacy of this template or theory at t_2, revise the template as necessary for further assessment at t_3, and so on. In contrast, to the extent that standardized stimulus conditions precede differing responses within the population and/or across time, one's attempt to construct empirically valid theoretical principles is likely to be abortive. Not only may the investigator experience difficulty in locating highly general patterns at t_1, but templates developed as a result of cursory observation at this point may largely be irrelevant at t_2; theoretical revisions at t_2 may be inadequate or misleading at t_3.

In the case of the behavior of living organisms the chief source of reliable pattern within a given species across time would appear to be furnished by constitutional structure (Greenwald, 1976). Should constitution fail to ensure reliable patterning of activity under standard stimulus conditions, not only are reliable principles obviated, but it becomes unclear how one may properly speak of a "given stimulus." The obvious question, of course, is whether the human constitution favors traditional scientific pursuits. In this case it is instructive to compare those living organisms of rudimentary neurological structure with those of greater physiological complexity. As evolutionary study demonstrates, in the simpler organisms, the protozoans, coelenterates, echinoderms, and so on, behavior is primarily a matter of a single stimulus (or stimulus pattern) triggering a response such as a single movement (taxes). In such organisms activity is highly stereotyped, and the organism is typically said to be *stimulus bound.* Such patterns are essentially innate and, within limits, permanently fixed. However, as organisms become neurologically more complex, further patterns of behavior begin to emerge. The *reflex response,* a more complex set of movements, becomes primary, for example, in the behavior of the metazoans and the flatworm. *Instinctive behavior* involving extended sequences of behavior that may or may not depend on the immediate presence of a given stimulus, and do not appear to depend on learning experiences, gain importance in the life of more advanced invertebrates. As more complex modes of behavior become available to the organism, it is also found that simpler modes recede in prominence (Ford & Beach, 1951; Dethier & Stellar, 1970). Thus, both taxes and reflex behaviors become less prominent in dictating behavior patterns as the instincts gain in potency.

For the vertebrates the dependence of behavior on learning becomes rapidly accelerated. As learning gains increasing importance, behavior gains freedom from the presence of particular stimuli. Modes of conduct are acquired and stored and may be utilized in circumstances far removed from those in which they were acquired. Thus, at any moment, a wide range of capacities may be readied for action. At any moment the individual may "regress" to virtually any earlier period in his or her history and engage in behavior representative of this period. Or, with prompting, one may be moved to act out patterns never practiced but only witnessed in others. In any case, at the human level, the bond between stimulus conditions and subsequent response appears indeterminant. Virtually any stimulus condition may furnish the occasion for virtually any behavioral event. Thus, with the exception of a handful of reflex actions (e.g., the Babinsky reflex, sucking reflex, the eye blink) the human being is from a biological view virtually *stimulus free.* [11] An analog to this capacity of the human organism to acquire multiple patterns of activity that may or may not recur within its life span would be difficult to locate in the physical sciences.

The relatively stimulus-free character of the vast range of human activity has importantly shaped the history of psychological study. Principally, it has thrust the subdisciplines of learning and cognition into a pivotal role. To the extent that human activity is not inherently reliable, then, it is essential from the scientific perspective to illuminate the processes that account for its changing character. Thus, principles of learning are developed, on the one hand, to explain why responses to a given stimulus change over time (e.g., classical conditioning theory) and principles of cognition are elaborated, on the other, to account for the apparent capacity of the organism to repattern stimuli that are otherwise unchanging. The fields of learning and cognition have thus acquired their status as "core disciplines" because of the capacity of the human organism for protean change. How-

---

[11] In effect, this is to agree with those who view the human as an open system. See Hendrick (1976) and Thorngate (1975) for amplification.

ever, such disciplines have not been prepared for the possibility that processes of learning and cognizing may not *themselves* be inherently reliable. The belief that unchanging processes of learning or cognizing best account for the plasticity of human action can hardly be warranted on empirical grounds. If individual patterns of talking, eating, playing, working, and so on are not automaton-like in nature, on what grounds can it be argued that the manner of learning or thinking are inevitable? And what might lead one to suppose, for example, that there are only two basic forms of learning (classical and instrumental), the character of which are sealed by genetics? Similarly, why should one suspect that there are basic principles of information storage, memory, or logic? Is not the range of cognitive heuristics that may be employed in solving problems of adaptation limited only by the human imagination?[12]

One must finally consider the possibility that human biology not only presents to the scientist an organism whose actions may vary in an infinity of ways, but it may ensure as well that novel patterns are continuously emerging. A variety of sources contribute to the plausibility of such an assertion. Early industrial research confirmed very quickly the common observation that the performance of continuous tasks often results in a noxious affective state (typically called boredom). Under laboratory conditions individuals given repetitive mechanical tasks to perform have displayed increasing dissatisfaction, anger, and the desire to escape. Research on sensory deprivation leads to a similar conclusion. With a reduction and leveling of sensory input people are often found to become irritable, to hallucinate, and to experience a deterioration in cognitive skills (Bexton, Heron, & Scott, 1954). A variety of similar tendencies have been studied under other rubrics. For example, Berlyne (1960), Wohlwill (1981), Fowler (1965), and others have carried out extensive inquiry into the existence of an "exploratory drive." As they believe, animals often seek out new and novel stimuli. Similarly, on the basis of their research, Harlow and Harlow (1965) conclude that primates possess a "manipulation motive." Chimps will expend energy to manipulate objects for the seemingly inherent pleasure of the actions themselves. And, as Hebb (1949) long maintained, within a certain range, deviations from any steady state are highly pleasurable for the human.

Alternative interpretations may be located for the various findings in these domains, and whether they are tapping a single generic source for the restructuring of activity remains unclear. However, to the extent that the organism is constitutionally inclined to avoid stasis, to seek novel experience, to search for alternatives, or to inquire beyond the given, the traditional science of human conduct is jeopardized. Behavioral patterning may be in a state of constant regeneration.

---

[12] As Charles Sanders Pierce (1982) wrote at the turn of the century, ". . . no mental action seems to be necessary or invariable in its character. In whatever manner the mind has reacted under a given sensation, in that manner is it the more likely to react again; were this, however, an absolute necessity, habits would become wooden and ineradicable, and no room being left for the formation of new habits, intellectual life would come to a speedy close. Thus, the uncertainty of the mental law is no mere defect of it, but is on the contrary its essence" (p. 100).

The Restructuring of Reality

As we see, human biology largely serves to establish the grounds and limits of human action. Certain functions must be fulfilled to sustain life, and there are biological limits over performance. However, between the poles of grounding essentials and physical limitations there is virtually unlimited potential for variation. Let us now consider in greater detail one widely shared means for understanding variations within the limits of human potential, along with its implications for the science.

As both psychologists and sociologists often maintain, variations in human activity may importantly be traced to the capacities of the organism for symbolic restructuring. As it is commonly said, one's actions appear to be vitally linked to the manner in which one understands or construes the world of experience. The stimulus world does not elicit behavior in an automatic, reflex-like fashion. Rather, the symbolic translation of one's experiences vitally transforms their implications and thereby alters the range of one's potential reactions. Interestingly, while formulations of this variety are widely shared within the scientific community, very little attention has been paid to their ramifications for the theory of science. As these implications are extended, the problematic basis of traditional scientific assumptions becomes increasingly apparent. Treatment of one such implication will be postponed for a later consideration of the hypothesis test. At this juncture, however, it is appropriate to reconsider the earlier contention that a science of human activity depends importantly on regularized or systematically recurring relationships between stimulus conditions and behavior. As is clear, without such regularities the prediction of behavior is largely obviated. Yet, as is equally clear, to the extent that the individual is capable of transforming the meaning of stimulus conditions in an indeterminant number of ways, existing regularities must be considered historically contingent-dependent on the prevailing meaning systems or conceptual structures of the times. In effect, from this perspective the scientist's capacity to locate predictable patterns of interaction depends importantly on the extent to which the population is both homogeneous and stable in its conceptual constructions. The validity of traditional science is, in this sense, at the mercy of its subject matter. The scientist's capacity to predict is precipitously dependent on the conceptual proclivities of the population under study.[13]

It is the capacity for rapid conceptual alteration that much of my earlier work on self-conception attempted to illustrate. Such work suggested, for example, that mere differences in the physical appearance of a bystander were often sufficient to trigger changes in the person's self-conceptions (Morse & Gergen, 1970). People were also frequently responsive to others' reactions, altering their conceptions of self as others communicated their positive or negative reactions to them (Gergen, 1965). When asked to act out a positive role, people often changed their self-conceptions to match the public guise (Gergen, 1965; Gergen & Taylor, 1966). When dealing with others who were senior to them in status, people would fre-

---

[13] See also Toulmin (1972) on the character of conceptual change across history.

quently develop self-conceptions that differed from those adopted when others were inferior in status (Gergen & Taylor, 1969); and, when interacting with an egotist, they would often begin to think of themselves in a way that differed from that occurring when the other was self-effacing (Gergen & Wishnov, 1965). Similar capacities for conceptual alteration would appear to form the basis for the massive research in attitude change. Experimenters have found that with relative ease they may influence people's conceptions of the common cold, racial integration, their personal future, economics, politics, eating grasshoppers, and so on. Such changes may sometimes be influenced by such seemingly trivial factors as the facial appearance of the influencing agent, the spatial distance separating the agent from his or her target, or the number of persons present during exposure to the influencing agent (cf. reviews by McGuire, 1968; Oskamp, 1977; Petty & Cacioppo, 1981).

From the present standpoint none of these findings should be viewed as transhistorically reliable. Each depended in a major sense upon the investigator's knowledge of what conceptual shifts were subject to alteration within a given historical context. However, each of these studies suggests in its own way that people are capable of rapid conceptual alterations, and such alterations may markedly expand the range of available activities.

To this account must also be added consideration of what many believe to be two fundamental characteristics of human conceptual activity. The first is that of *reflexivity*.[14] In Alfred Schutz's words, ". . . I may either live in the ongoing process of my acting, directed toward its object, . . . or I may, so to speak, step out of the ongoing flux and look by a reflective glance at the acts performed in previous processes of acting in the Past Tense . . ." (1968, p. 64). This capacity to consider one's past reflexively has two interdependent moments: In the first instance the past may reassert itself in the present, and in the second the present may transform what is taken to be the past. Thus, in centering one's attention reflexively on the past, any segment of the past may insert itself at any time into the conceptual mix upon which current activity is based. Essentially, "life as the ongoing process of my acting" may thus be vitally dependent on "acts performed in previous processes of acting." One's momentary capacities for conceptualization thus rest on a potentially immense repository, any aspect of which may be rendered salient through reflexive review. Yet, we also see that whatever is given in terms of reflexive review stands itself as subject to reconceptualization. In the same manner that contempo-

---

[14] For a sensitive examination of the grounds for human reflexivity see Rychlak (1980). The present analysis could also be reformulated in a number of ways (including the language of operant theory). In the present case, the thrust of the argument does not fully depend on adopting the voluntarist assumption of self-reflexiveness and creativity. One could also employ, here, a mechanistic model of human conceptual activity with the same outcome. For example, if one argues that the conceptual system is in a continuous state of consistency striving, and to achieve such consistency combines concepts in novel patterns (through principles of randomization, frequency of association, antonym selection, and so on), it can also be concluded that the individual is a semiautonomous originator of novel conceptual schemas.

rary historians are continuously in the process of reshaping what is commonly taken to be the culture's history, so do individuals have the capacity to review their personal pasts in ways that alter their meaning. In this sense, the biography does not dictate social destiny; rather, it stands as a malleable substance subject to contemporary predilection. These two processes, reflexive review and reconceptualization, may continuously interact over the individual's life. Review may yield concepts once abandoned, such concepts may then enter into the process of review itself, and the result may be modification of that which subsequent review can offer. Effectively the individual is furnished a high degree of freedom from the determinative effects of immediate stimuli. The dynamics of internal manipulation and alteration of symbols render the individual essentially autonomous.[15]

In addition to reflexive capacities theorists frequently endow the human with capacities for the *autonomous envisioning of alternatives*. A long line of research on problem solving—presaged by Köhler's (1925) work with apes—strongly suggests that higher organisms possess the capacity for autonomous creation of alternatives to that which is the case. At any moment one may construct alternatives to the prevailing patterns of conduct. One need not accept the given as immutable, but may autonomously develop (1) alternative means for achieving a given end, (2) alternative ends that may be reached through any given means, and (3) entirely novel means-ends composites. With each alternative new patterns of action may ensue and previous patterns be rendered obsolete. So too is the fate of the scientist's predictive formulations.[16] We shall return to the negative relationship between the cognitive orientation and logical empiricism later in the chapter.

The Erosion Potential of Common Values

Thus far we have discussed several constitutional features of the human organism that may militate against stable and enduring patterns of activity. At this point we may turn our attention to the capacity for acquired potentials to operate as well against reliable forms of conduct. Over time one may develop certain capacities, persisting for varying periods of time, that may have destructive effects on existing patterns. In effect, certain dispositions appear to be set at odds with recurring patterns of action; they may interfere or conflict with existing tendencies and ultimately lead to their dissolution. Firm predictions cannot be made with respect to the strength, prevalence, and effects of such disruptive dispositions over time. But judging from the apparent frequency with which they occur in Western culture, and the apparent ramifications of such presence, they broaden considerably the hiatus separating the sociobehavioral scientist from the goal of cumulative knowledge.

Many would argue that the most significant of these recurring dispositions is the quest for *freedom against restraint*. External forces that seem to reduce or diminish one's freedom of action often yield negative reactions. As Fromm (1941) and

---

[15] For an earlier statement of the problem of reflexive awareness on developing laws of human conduct see Gerwirth (1954).

[16] Also see Hendrick's (1976) discussion of autoregulation.

Erikson (1963) have argued, normal development should include the flowering of strong motives for autonomous action. Weinstein and Platt (1969) have discussed the same sentiment in terms of "man's wish to be free," and have linked the disposition to developments within the social structure. Brehm and his colleagues (Brehm, 1966; Wicklund, 1974) have used this disposition as the cornerstone for a theory of psychological reactance. To be sure, the importance placed on freedom in society and its subcultures may vary considerably over time (Müller, 1963). However, to the extent that it prevails, this existing order of conduct is imperiled. This is so because existing patterns themselves can serve as threats to freedom. Whenever it becomes customary, expected, appropriate, proper, or essential to follow the common pattern, the door is closed on an infinity of potentials. Thus, as patterns of conduct ossify within a culture, such ossification may be accompanied by less obvious motives for destruction in the service of freedom.

A similar case can be made regarding the quest for *uniqueness.* Uniformity in society is often condemned (cf. Moscovici, 1972; Riesman, 1950) and praise reserved for those displaying distinctive characteristics. In his studies of French culture, Lemaine (1974) has argued that a heightened awareness of others poses a threat to self-differentiation. In an attempt to reestablish their special identity, ventures Lemaine, the French place a special emphasis on heterogeneity. Fishman (1972) has also argued that nationalistic movements and the attempts to adopt distinct languages often represent a collective search for differentiation. In the same vein, the special linguistic argots developed by subcultures within a nation (e.g., "jive," "hip," "Brooklynese," etc.) are often used as signals of differentiated group identity (cf. Pitts, 1969). And, as studies by Snyder and Fromkin (1979) and their colleagues indicate, when people learn they are highly similar to others, they often experience unpleasant emotional effects, a decrement in self-esteem, and a decreased attraction for those to whom they are said to be similar. In addition, when they are made to feel similar to others, they will often conform less, and change their attitudes in order to decrease their similarity. Such valuing of uniqueness is not without consequences for science. To the extent that people search for means of being unique, there will be a continual erosion of uniform and reliable patterns.

Finally we may consider what appears to be a frequent investment in maintaining *unpredictability.* During any historical period, a certain degree of predictability in behavior must be maintained.[17] If others' actions were in a constant state of capricious change, one could scarcely survive; a society dominated by chaotic dislocations in patterns of conduct could scarcely remain viable. However, coupled with social pressures toward predictability are often individual predilections toward

---

[17]This is to agree with Stryker (1977) that because humans live in interdependent networks there are limits governing the range of activity in which they engage, and thus a certain degree of reliability in behavior is guaranteed at any given point in history. However, there is little to warrant Stryker's contention that by moving from the laboratory to the broader social context the resulting generalizations will gain transhistorical predictive capacities. Laboratory behavior may be more stable for certain periods than common behavior in the social network.

remaining unpredictable. If one's actions are altogether reliable, the outcomes are also problematic. To the extent that one's behavior is predictable, one becomes vulnerable. Others can alter conditions in such a way as to obtain maximal rewards at minimal costs to themselves. In the same way military strategists lay themselves open to defeat when their actions become predictable, organizational officials can be exploited by their underlings and parents manipulated by their progeny when their actions become fully reliable. Knowledge thus becomes power in the hands of others. It is largely on these grounds that Scheibe (1979, p. 106) has argued the sociobehavioral sciences can never gain ultimate predictive advantage over the population under study: "Mirrors, masks, lies and secrets are tools available to anyone" in the attempt to avoid the predictive advantage that others, including scientists, may take of them.

Science and the Shaping of Human Conduct

Thus far we have attended to both constitutive and acquired capacities of the human, each of which would appear to endow the individual with the capacity for infinite variation (within biological limits) and with a certain degree of antagonism toward repetitive patterning of activity. Analogous features among the phenomena of interest to most natural scientists would appear to be rare. A fourth contribution to the historical dependency of human conduct must now be treated—one that has its source not in the phenomena under study but in the study of the phenomena. In this case, there would appear to be little convincing analog within the natural sciences.

From the traditional standpoint, ideal scientific conduct entails a significant separation between the scientist and the phenomenon under scrutiny. As typically advanced, the scientist should ideally function as an impartial bystander whose conduct should not influence the events that he or she hopes to understand. To the extent that such influences exist, the scientist is said to be studying contaminated or artificially altered forms of nature. Such assumptions have proved reasonably serviceable in most natural science domains. Scientists thus observe and record the movement of the planets, the migration of birds, or the reproduction of cells, for example, without altering the character of such phenomena in significant degree.[18] It is out of this same interest in separating scientist and phenomenon that wideranging inquiry in the sociobehavioral sciences has been made into means of reducing the effects of experimenter characteristics on research results (cf. Rosenthal, 1966; Rosenthal & Rosnow, 1969; Webb, Campbell, Schwartz, & Sechrest, 1966). In the case of research on experimenter and subject selection effects, researchers

---

[18] Quantum physics may appear to be an exception. However, as London and Poltoratsky (1958) point out, in quantum physics, "The experiment is recognized as an essential interference in the order or disorder of things, so that resulting theory is a theory of interferences, as it were, rather than one of a so-called objective world whose composition, after interference effects have been 'cancelled out' or 'adjusted for' can be pieced together mosaic-like from the data of experiments" (p. 272).

have thus employed empirical techniques to enhance or ensure proper deployment of empirical techniques within the science more generally.

However, it is shortsighted to limit concern with scientific interference solely to the point of initial observation. Although both natural and social scientist can typically document their observations without unduly disturbing the phenomena under study, the scientific process is not itself terminated at this point. Theories are formulated, explanations are developed, and predictions generated. Most importantly, all such efforts may be communicated to others—including those generating the "phenomena under study." Such communication can, in turn, operate as an input into the population and serve to alter its subsequent character. The socio-behavioral scientist and the society thus constitute a feedback loop, and this fact does pose a radical difference between most sociobehavioral and natural science study.[19] Astronomic theory does not alter the movement of the planets, for example, nor theories of migration the seasonal flight of birds. Let us detail two essential ways in which the sciences of human conduct shape the activity they hope to elucidate.

The Scientific Construction of Reality

As argued above, one may usefully understand alterations in conduct in terms of the human capacity for symbolic activity. As symbols or conceptual systems are altered, so may related patterns of conduct be modified. At the same time, we see that the chief products of the sciences themselves are symbol systems. Thus, the institution of science furnishes to the culture inputs into the existing arrangements of understanding. Science may establish, transform, or sustain common symbol systems of the culture and the resulting patterns of activity. We may refer to the effects of scientific constructions on common modes of thinking and acting as *enlightenment effects.*[20] Let us explore in greater detail.

---

[19] Although Popper's work is frequently used as support by those who defend the positivist-empiricist position in the sociobehavioral sciences, certain of his arguments are uncongenial to this viewpoint. Similar to the position put forth here, for example, Popper (1957) has argued that human history is influenced by the growth of new knowledge. However, the growth of new knowledge itself cannot be predicted. As a result, one cannot predict the future course of society. No comparable restriction need be placed over physical science predictions. Growth of knowledge concerning the solar system will not affect its structure.

[20] In much the same vein Giddens (1976) has proposed, "The concepts and theories produced in the natural sciences quite regularly filter into lay discourse and become appropriated as elements of everyday frames of reference. But this is of no relevance, of course, to the world of nature itself; whereas the appropriation of technical concepts and theories invented by social scientists can turn them into constituting elements of that very subject matter they were coined to characterize, and by that token alter the context of their application. This relation of reciprocity between commonsense and technical theory is a peculiar, but eminently interesting feature of sociology" (p. 79). As the present analysis will attempt to demonstrate

Establishing the ontological inventory. As indicated, philosophers of science are now in broad agreement that the scientist's ideas about nature cannot be derived from observation of nature itself. On the basis of senses alone unlimited distinctions could be made among phenomena. In scanning the present page, for example, should one distinguish among groups of lines, individual lines, word groupings, individual words, letter groupings, individual letters—or should all these possible distinctions be abandoned and attention be devoted to variations in glossiness, or paper texture? All distinctions are possible; innumerable others could be made. Which particular distinctions are made does not seem dictated by or dependent on mere exposure to the stimulus of the page itself.

Such is the case in daily life. The units of understanding human action do not appear to be furnished by observation, but rather through participation in the cultural system of understanding. There is nothing in the mere movement of physical bodies through space that informs us as to when we have a proper unit.[21] In order to know what counts as a unit, we must be informed by the particular culture. That which is a meaningful unit in one culture at a particular time may be "invisible" in another culture or in the same culture at a different time. As a constituent part of a culture, sociobehavioral scientists also furnish an ontological education. In the act of description scientists establish an essential inventory of "what there is." In this sense, such terms as "repression," "socioeconomic class," "schizophrenia," "learned helplessness," "midlife crisis," "dissonance reduction," and so on are not the results of keen observation. Rather they operate as lenses supplied by the theorist to colleagues and society alike. The world is not so constituted until the lens is employed. With each new distinction the groundwork is laid for alterations in existing patterns of conduct.

(Chpts. 2 & 3), reciprocity is far more than "interesting." It may play an integral role in the construction of a new scientific paradigm.

[21] In a series of challenging studies Newtson and his colleagues (Newtson, 1973; Newtson, Enquist, & Boris, 1977) have advanced the position that behavioral units are naturally segmented. Specifically, they argue that separate units of action are perceived when there is a distinctive change in the movement of the body. These "natural units" of perception, it is ventured, might form the basis for an objectively based system of classifying behavior. Such speculation would appear misleading. Although distinctive changes in movement may serve as cues for distinguishing certain actions from others, it would be a mistake to argue that such bodily alterations constitute the basis of the behavioral vocabulary of the culture. First, such an account is at a loss to explain such descriptive terms as honesty, hope, help, hindrance, happiness, and so on. There are simply no bodily movements clearly designated by such terms. We shall explore this point in greater detail in the next chapter. Second, there are many person descriptors that seem to be used upon the occasion of *multiple* changes in bodily movements (viz. serving a tennis ball, peddling a bicycle, doing the tango, laughing). Such terms do not seem to represent composites constructed from simpler, more discrete units, as there are no generally available names for all the separable movements constituting the molar activity.

Theory and the logic of action. Although distinctions prepare the way for altered action, descriptive terms acquire their directive power primarily through their function within the theoretical network in which they are embedded. Thus, the term "chair" in part gains its significance through all the common ways in which people speak about chairs within the culture. People speak of "sitting on," "resting in," and "covering" chairs, for example, and in doing so one is informed of the uses to which chairs are to be put. In Ossorio and Davis' (1968) terms, "Saying something . . . is important because what we say makes a difference in what *else* we do" (p. 356). Thus, to label a phenomenon "a chair" is to place it within a larger system of meaning that specifies the actions appropriate to it. In this sense, the selection of a descriptive term implies a "logic of action."

From this vantage point we see that the scientist's terms, in combination with their theoretical context, may have a powerful directive function. The history of the professional stance toward publicly aberrant behavior is enlightening in this respect. Early in the century psychologists often spoke of "mental illness," a term suggesting that individuals in question might be treated in roughly analogous fashion to the physically ill. Isolation and medical attention were thus appropriate for the afflicted. Over time, however, "illness" theory gave way to "maladjustment," formulations that implied an inability on the person's part to cope with normal life circumstances. The relevance of medical care and hospitalization receded, and attention was directed instead to therapeutic means of facilitating readjustment. However, more recently such formulations have been challenged by forms of "victimization" theory. In this case, society is viewed as culprit and the individual as scapegoat. The previously "ill" or "maladjusted" individual is now the "designated patient," implying, as the term does, that in reality "the problem" lies elsewhere— and most typically within the social system. The latter is thus singled out for the culprit's role, and the individual may even be considered a martyred hero. In Atkinson's (1972) terms, "Insofar as they imply their use as a logic for action, all [behavioral] definitions are at the same time active interventions into social life. This holds true whether the particular [scientist] is aware of it or not, whether he intends this or not" (p. 89).[22]

Sequence specification and the problem of prediction. Over and above the delineation and labeling of social phenomena, normal science typically requires a specification of behavioral sequence. The question for the scientist is not simply "What is there?" but "What leads to what?" Does negative reinforcement lead to a diminution in activity? Do children develop in fixed stages? Does increased contact reduce prejudice? And so on. Yet, in the specification of sequence the scientist does far more than describe; at the same time he or she may alter public expectation. And, with the alteration of expectation, the stage is set for the modification of action. In one respect such alterations in behavior offer no challenge to traditional science. If parents who wish to raise happy and productive offspring alter their child-rearing practices according to the directives embodied in a given theory, they do not

---

[22] Also see Freedman, Cohen, and Hennessy (1974).

thereby alter the validity of the theory. If people alter their behavior in such a way as to produce the end points specified by the theory, their behavior in no way degrades the theory's "truth value." However, the chief problem in this case rests on those instances in which the resulting actions invalidate the specified sequences or lend to them support that would not have been forthcoming in the absence of their specification. As demonstrated in Merton's (1957) discussion of the "self-fulfilling prophecy," predictions may, by virtue of their dissemination, hasten the results which they predict. Merton cites in this case the demise of a private bank in New York City in 1928 that was in no serious financial difficulty. However, because depositors came to believe the bank would collapse, they withdrew their funds and the bank thereby became insolvent. Such instances may be contrasted with "suicidal predictions" in which, for reasons of the prediction, actions are taken that subsequently cause its invalidation. For example, in 1947, available indicators moved economists to predict a recession. However, because of the prediction many businesses lowered the market price of their goods, thus increasing the demand for the goods and averting the predicted recession. In a similar vein, politicans and public opinion researchers have demonstrated concern over the effects of voting predictions on the outcome of elections (cf. Simon, 1957). Predictions of a win may discourage those otherwise voting for the designated loser, thus ensuring his or her defeat.

Extending this line of reasoning, Schwartz, Lacey, and Schuldenfrei (1978) have argued that the implementation of Skinnerian theory serves to engender behavior consistent with its premises. As they maintain, a society that employs a theory of environmental reinforcement, whether it be in terms of broad programs of social change or on the interpersonal level, may undermine the system of intrinsic motives that previously existed. In implementing a theory of extrinsic reinforcement one may essentially create an artificial and arbitrary dependence on a system of extrinsic rewards. The theory becomes increasingly predictive because of its application. As Lacey (1977) has put it, "Applications change the world. If the applications of one theory predominate then the world will increasingly exemplify the principles of this theory."

Direction in explanation. In addition to specifying sequence, normal science typically entails an elaboration of the underlying mechanisms or processes. The scientist not only attempts to describe "what leads to what," but "why" sequences occur as they do. To specify the causal source for a given phenomenon is also to furnish a logic for reaction. Such reactions, in turn, may subsequently change the character of the phenomenon itself. To illustrate, American society has long been concerned with outbreaks of violence in predominantly black sectors of its major cities. The scientist concerned with the problem could set out to study the personality characteristics, moral and political dispositions, and police records of those arrested for these disturbances. Such research would be fully legitimate by common standards of objective inquiry. At the same time this form of exploration also favors a psychological explanation for the activity. The underlying implication of such research is that ghetto unrest is primarily a product of problematic individuals, and

ting policy implication is that stronger police action or stiffer penalties are
The explanation essentially furnishes grounds for *person blame,* and the
results might well be an exacerbation of the very activities that the re-
sea... was designed to diminish. In contrast, should the investigator attempt to
trace the violence to such factors as political and economic oppression, the responsibility for the same actions would be implicitly lodged within the broad social
system (*system blame*), and not the actors. Alteration of the system would thus be
favored and punitive measures deemphasized. The choice in explanatory locus thus
affects social policy, which, in turn, alters the subsequent life forms within the
relevant communities.

The scientific paradigm and social life. It must finally be recognized that the manner in which the scientist goes about the task of generating knowledge may also
affect the patterns of conduct under study. That is, in conducting science a definition of knowledge and how it may be acquired is simultaneously established. In
their commitment to this model, and the claims made for its superiority, scientists
encourage particular modes of conduct. At times such encouragement is more than
indirect. For example, in George Kelly's (1955) theory of human personality, ideal
scientific conduct and optimal human functioning are held to be virtually equivalent. Psychotherapy within Kelly's framework thus makes an active and forthright
attempt to transform the individual into a miniature scientist. Similar implications
underlie Harold Kelley's (1972) theory of causal attribution and the Nisbett and
Ross (1980) investigations of human inference. In both cases people are said to
function like scientists—only less systematically and thus less adequately. More
assiduous modeling of scientific conduct is prescribed. As can be seen, widespread
commitment to a "way of science" thus acts to shape the folkways of the culture.

In this vein, it is important to consider the traditional commitment of the
science to a deterministic form of explanation or one in which behavioral events are
viewed as lawful consequences of specified antecedents. The concept of intention
or voluntary action is thereby rendered both misleading (in its obscuring the "true
cause" of behavior) and obsolete. Yet, as is also clear, many cultural systems of
blame and punishment are importantly based on the assumption that people are
largely in voluntary control over their actions. It is primarily when people are believed to possess self-directing capacities that they can be punished for undesirable
actions and rewarded for positive conduct. Both prison sentences and wage increases are often dependent on the perception that people are not involuntarily
compelled to act as they do. As Skinner (1971) correctly argues, if the scientific
form of explanation is adopted, contemporary systems of blame and praise become
questionable. For example, the punishment of crime is obviated because all crime
may be understood as a function of circumstances beyond the individual's control.
Informal patterns of conduct based on the concept of moral responsibility are
thrown into question. Yet as Shotter (1975) and others have argued, to abandon
the concept of personal responsibility may be to undermine the basis for organized
society. If people cannot be punished for their maleficence and rewarded for their
virtues, and if guilt and self-reward cease to play a role in human affairs, then the

basis for social order may be severely weakened. The essential question is not whether the deterministic view of science is a valid one; its validity is fundamentally indeterminant (Gergen & Gergen, 1982). The important point is that the traditional scientific view of understanding has far different behavioral implications than its alternatives. In accepting a scientific form of understanding the culture may be modified in substantial degree.

We see, then, that in a variety of important ways the conduct of science itself furnishes inputs into the common meaning systems of the culture and thereby establishes grounds for the alteration of common patterns of conduct. In the delineation of "what there is," in furnishing meaning, in specifying sequence, in explicating causal mechanisms, and in adopting a form of scientific conduct, the scientist is engaging in a symbolic interaction with the culture more generally, and as a cultural participant of substantial status, his or her symbols may have potent effects. In many instances such effects include the extinguishing of the data base on which the initial scientific formulations were based; in other instances the formulations may seem to be vindicated because of their broad dissemination. In any case, science insinuates itself into common patterns of conduct.

The Scientist as Moral Agent

Our discussion thus far has centered on the way in which scientific activity may enter the common understandings of the culture. Yet, this concern with enlightenment effects must be expanded in an important direction. In particular, we must consider the valuational character of scientific knowledge, and its capacity to alter society through an inherent and inescapable moral advocacy. In the nineteenth century it was widely believed that science, when properly conducted, could not only generate fundamental knowledge concerning human affairs, but that it would additionally solve long-standing problems of ethics. Questions of what constitutes the good society, what human rights are necessary, what ethical norms are desirable, and so on might all be answered through the application of science. As many hoped, ethical relativism could be replaced by objectively grounded principle. However, it became increasingly apparent that such optimistic goals could not be realized. As Henri Poincaré (1952) put the matter, the principles of science can only be in the indicative mode, and there is no logical means of deriving an imperative (a should or should not) from statements concerning what is the case. With rare exception (cf. Kohlberg, 1971), this position has continued to prevail through the present.

Additional arguments have been added over the years to this fundamental division between "fact" and "value." For example, it is typically maintained that proper scientific posture should essentially be dispassionate. To the extent that the scientific process is guided by ethics, morals, or personal desires, sound observation and logic are denigrated. One might choose to study a given phenomenon for valuational purposes, but the act of study itself should not be contaminated by such purposes. It is further maintained that the fruits of scientific study should be made available to all. How scientific results are used and for what ends are not essentially the concerns of the scientist *qua* scientist. Valuational goals may be admirable but are to be pursued on the scientist's "own time."

Yet, in spite of the understandable desire to transcend the clamorous bickering in the marketplace of competing values, it has become increasingly apparent that scientific conduct is thoroughly suffused with value choices. The claim of value neutrality is but a thin veil obscuring all manner of passionate commitments. Philosophers have generally been successful in showing how such value suffusion does not necessarily threaten the scientist's attempt to establish predictive formulations (cf. Kaplan, 1964; Nagel, 1961; Rudner, 1966).[23] However, for present purposes the important issue is not whether the scientist's values interfere with observation or prediction, but with the *subsequent* impact of such values on the recipients of that knowledge. To the extent that scientific activity is "interest relevant" (Putnam, 1978) it functions as an active agent in social life. Its subtle prescriptions favor certain patterns of conduct and subvert others; they may catalyze resistance, create conflict, generate solidarity, and so on. Let us consider several major sources of valuational communication inherent in scientific activity.

Evaluation in the ontological inventory. At the outset, one's values may influence the way in which reality is segmented. The essential differentiations one makes among entities are almost inevitably influenced by one's "motives for looking." This point was made as early as 1914 when Max Weber (1949) argued that "the very recognition of the existence of a scientific problem coincides, personally, with the possession of specifically oriented motives and values" (p. 21).[24] In the same manner that hunger may give rise to differentiating the environment into "edibles" versus "nonedibles," the scientist's particular values may have a directive effect in establishing his or her inventory of "what there is." Effectively, the primary conceptual distinctions within the sociobehavioral sciences say as much about the valuational goals of the scientist as they do about the phenomena themselves. The fact that the science distinguishes among socioeconomic classes, political ideologies, profit and loss, deviants and normals, racial groups, rational and emotional process, and personality types provides an indication of what ends or goals are valued by the relevant disciplines. Socioeconomic classes, ideologies, profit, loss, deviance, and so on do not exist "out there," waiting for discovery like some sequestered planet. Rather, they are made distinguishable by scientists motivated by specific tastes, values, needs, or motives. Few distinctions are made among people's manner of seating themselves, tying their shoes, combing their hair, and so on. This is so

---

[23] As Scriven (1974), Snow (1962) and others have pointed out, all science is inherently valuational. And, such values may have a substantial effect on the outcomes of research (Mitroff, 1974; Phillips, 1973). The major problem faced by the sociobehavioral sciences, however, is that such values can affect the patterns they seek to understand.

[24] As E. A. Burtt (1957) has written in another context, "what sort of order is discovered depends primarily on the sort that scientists aggressively look for, and what they look for depends in turn on the further ends which, consciously or unconsciously, they want their explanations to serve" (p. 103).

primarily because the value climate of the time is not favorable to distinctions within these domains. To absorb scientific description is at the same time to incorporate its valuational emphases.[25]

It is from this standpoint that Apfelbaum and Lubek (1976) have argued that social psychological knowledge often acts as an oppressive force within the culture. In particular, they have been concerned with the kinds of people or issues that seem systematically excluded from consideration because of the prevailing values and their connected theoretical structures. Special concern has been expressed over the way in which theories of social conflict have been influenced by the scientist's general fear of impending nuclear warfare. Because of this fear, they argue, scientists have typically viewed conflict as a negative state, a problem to be solved. Parties of the conflict are traditionally seen as interchangeable, powerful, potentially treacherous, and so on. As a result of the guiding concern with nuclear disaster, conflict theory takes little account of conflicts of the oppressed in society, the legitimacy of their revolutionary quest, and the possibility that conflicts may play a positive function in producing social change. Essentially, because theories of conflict reflect a restricted range of values, theoretical "blind spots" have developed with respect to other sectors of social life. For Apfelbaum and Lubek, many of society's oppressed peoples have been cast into a state of "invisibility."[26]

Evaluative connotation in descriptive terminology. Not only are the essential distinctions among phenomena typically expressive of the scientists' valuational investments, but so as well are the terms applied to such distinctions. For example, social psychological treatises on conformity typically treat the conformer as a second-class citizen, a social sheep who foregoes personal conviction to agree with the erroneous opinion of others. Theories of aggression typically condemn the aggressor, models of bargaining and decision-making are disparaging of exploitation, and models of moral development demean those at less than the "optimal level." Roger Brown (1965) once pointed to the interesting fact that the authoritarian personality, so roundly scourged in the American literature, was quite similar to the "J-type personality" viewed by German scientists in a highly positive light.

---

[25] It should be clear that behavioral research cannot in itself act as a corrective in this case; rather, such research can only proceed once these ontological agreements have been established. Research cannot verify the concept of "reinforcement," for example; the term is a conceptual tool for interpreting the world and one's actions (including behavioral research) in it.

[26] On similar grounds, Ingleby (1974) has criticized much theory and research on child development. In such inquiry, the child is abstracted from particular social and economic processes and thus such processes are ignored—which is to render unspoken support to the current conditions. In an analysis of psychology in the People's Republic of China, Ching (1980) has also demonstrated how such arguments have played an active role in determining the character of the profession over the past twenty years. For example, traditional psychological study largely collapsed under the political accusation that to abstract psychological processes from economic class considerations was politically harmful pseudoscience.

That which the American literature terms "rigidity" was viewed as "stability" in the German; "flexibility" and "individualism" in the former media were seen as "flaccidity" and "eccentricity" in the latter. By the same token, reversals in valuation can also be envisioned for most of the descriptive terms within the sociobehavioral sciences. For example, high self-esteem could be termed egotism, need for social approval could be viewed as a quest for social harmony, cognitive differentiation as hair-splitting, creativity as antisocial behavior, and so on. If the scientist's values were otherwise, risk taking could be viewed as courage, alienation as lassitude, profit making as exploitative gain, and so on. In effect, with the incorporation of scientific description, the society also absorbs a value structure with widespread behavioral implications.[27]

In this light one can appreciate the importance of Eagly's (1978) survey of sex differences in social influenceability. There is a long-standing agreement in the social psychological literature that women are more easily influenced than men. As Freedman, Carlsmith, and Sears (1970) write, "There is a considerable amount of evidence that women are generally more persuasible than men" and that with respect to conformity, "The strongest and most consistent factor that has differentiated people in the amount they conform is their sex. Women have been found to conform more than men . . ." (p. 236). Similarly, as McGuire's 1968 contribution to the *Handbook of Social Psychology* concludes, "There seems to be a clear main order effect of sex on influenceability such that females are more susceptible than males" (p. 251). However, such statements appear to reflect the major research results prior to 1970, a period when the women's liberation movement was beginning to have telling effects on the consciousness of women. Results such as those summarized above came to be used by feminist writers to exemplify the degree to which women docilely accepted their oppressed condition. The liberated woman, as they argued, should not be a conformist. In this context Eagly (1978) returned to examine all research results published before and after 1970. As her analysis indicates, among studies on persuasion, 32% of the research published prior to 1970 showed statistically greater influenceability among females, while only 8% of the later research did so. In the case of conformity to group pressure, 39% of the pre-1970 studies showed women to be reliably more conforming. However, after 1970 the figure dropped to 14%. It appears, then, that in describing females as persuasible and conforming, social psychologists have contributed to a social movement that may have undermined the empirical basis for the initial description.

Evaluation in explanation. In the same way that selection of descriptive terms typically favors certain valuational ends, so too does the manner in which the scientist explains the relationship among entities. At times such valuational premises are fully evident. To explain one's task performance in terms of "mental capacities" (the superior and the deficient), moral decision making in terms of levels of "moral

---

[27]Also see Bramel and Friend's (1981) critique of the classic Hawthorne research for its implicit message: Workers are irrational and confused, while managers are intelligent and nonexploitative.

maturity," or altruistic activity in terms of "hedonic calculus," has clear implications for the degree of approbation to be accorded the actor. In other cases, the
valuational implications of a given explanation may be more obscure. For example,
in one elucidating analysis Alvin Gouldner (1970) has demonstrated the manner
in which Parsons' structural-functional theory of society provides intellectual sanc-
tioning for the status quo. If, as Parsons maintains, all existing institutions stand in
a functionally interdependent relationship with each other, such that the collapse
of one may threaten the viability of all, then one is disinclined to tamper with the
existing structure. From the structural-functional vantage point, existing institutions are vital to each other; to change one threatens the whole. As Gouldner (1970)
concludes more generally, "Every social theory facilitates the pursuit of some,
but not all, courses of action and thus, encourages us to change or accept the world
as it is, to say yea or nay to it. In a way, every theory is a discreet obituary or
celebration of some social system" (p. 86).

Most relevant for social psychology are Sampson's (1977, 1978) trenchant
analyses of the extent to which American ideals pervade contemporary theories.
As Sampson (1977) contends, many theoretical constructs sustain the cultural
value placed on self-contained individualism or individual self-sufficiency (see also
Caplan & Nelson, 1973; Hogan, 1975).[28],[29] Although a variety of specific cases are
singled out by Sampson (viz. research on androgyny, equity, self-actualization), the
critical argument is that any theory explaining human action on the basis of individual, psychological structures or processes suggests that people should be viewed
as fundamentally independent; narcissistic concern with one's personal systems is
thereby favored. By the same token, concern with interdependency and group
welfare are diminished. Certain social practices, such as the institutionalization of
competition, would be favoreu by the traditional view; in contrast, cooperative
interaction might be favored by a dialectic theory of human activity.

The valuational implications of the scientific process. A final form of prescriptive
bias is contained within models of scientific conduct. The manner in which scientists conceptualize their activity and realize such beliefs in practice contain important messages for the culture more generally. For example, traditional psychology
generally adopts a Humean conception of causality along with a positivist orientation toward observation. The function of science, within this framework, is to
locate reliable patterns of contingency among observable events. Consistent with
this framework is the traditional stimulus-response paradigm. In effect the science

---

[28] Elsewhere, Sampson (1981) has extended this view to argue that the emphasis
on cognitive theory in contemporary psychology places paramount importance on
individual psychological functioning, thereby reducing the significance of collective
social practices. It is these practices, argues Sampson, that serve as the basis for
whatever cognitive processes the individual employs.

[29] See also Wexler's (1982) critique of the individualistic–economic bias of social
pyschological theories of social attraction, and their insensitivity to the broader
social and historical circumstances.

has set for itself the goal of tracing contingent relations between observable stimuli and responses. (Neobehaviorism simply expands the causal continuum by inserting psychological constructs for added explanatory power.) Although such a view of science is ostensibly divorced from issues of value, many critics have discerned within this paradigm a variety of uncongenial valuational implications. For one, if behavior is fundamentally dependent on "stimulus events," then successful functioning in relationships requires that one gain control over the stimuli that control others' actions. To achieve benefit in life, the paradigm suggests, one must adopt a manipulative posture toward others. It is in this vein that Chris Argyris (1975) has shown how the S–O–R orientation had led to a form of knowledge that encourages governmental manipulation of the public. If the form of knowledge specifies a range of stimulus variables necessary to induce a given type of behavior, then achieving a given behavioral end (e.g., reduced crime, reduced racial violence, increased energy conservation) requires that the policy maker manipulate these variables. Implied in the form of knowledge itself is a logic for the way in which people should be treated—one that Argyris and many others view as ultimately inimical to social well-being.[30]

Research methodology congenial to the stimulus–response paradigm serves to sustain the image of the human as manipulable automaton. Experimentation, in particular, is typically viewed as a process whereby the investigator attempts to achieve control over the responses of the subject. The subject is thereby characterized on the implicit level as a "dope," "guinea pig," or "robot." As Hampden-Turner (1970) has described: "It is not that the investigators themselves have a savage eye, but rather that their predicting and controlling tools demand the predictable and controllable man in order to consummate the Good Experiment. And what a misery the man turns out to be. The highly respected Dr. Jekyll discovers Mr. Hyde, the beast in man uncovered by inhuman instruments" (p. 4).[31]

With respect to valuational implications one must also call into question the traditional premium placed on separating the observer from the "object" of study. In effect, criteria for rigorous research demand personal distance between the

---

[30] Of interest to social psychologists in this context is Argyris' (1980) critique of attribution theory. Such theory typically portrays the individual as a "silent-perceiver," proposes Argyris, who goes about the cognitive task of synthesizing information and emerges with a deductive understanding of another's motives, dispositions, etc. As Argyris points out, such a model operates as a desideratum for the public and with poor consequence. Says Argyris of this account of interpersonal understanding, "There is little openness, little sharing of motives, little expression of feeling, little consideration of others as resources for gaining knowledge about interpersonal relationships, etc." (p. 64).

[31] Many have argued that one of the most critical aspects of the behavioral sciences is their masking of the ideological interests of the research by laying claim to objectivity. Claims of objective truth are thus used to rationalize an enhanced position of authority or power (cf. Weimer's 1979 discussion of "justificationism"). To claim objectivity in the behavioral sciences is thus a tactic for social or public control.

observer and the observed. A deep and intimate acquaintance between the two would threaten the ostensible validity of the research findings. Yet the implicit message contained within methods designed by this criterion is that superior knowledge in the social sphere is gained through alienated relations. Intimate relations are implicitly blind and unrealistic. This perspective may be contrasted, for example, with that adopted by existentially oriented psychotherapists. As often argued in this domain, a full understanding of a client requires that the therapist suspend his or her theoretical presuppositions and attempt a full, empathetic incorporation of the other's subjective experience. To treat the patient as an object for scrutiny is to destroy the therapeutic relationship and any hope of full understanding.[32]

Such issues are scarcely academic. As a number of commentators have noted, members of racial minorities have become increasingly resentful over their role as objects for study and actively resist the researcher. As one critic has put it,

> Research and services in psychology have enforced compliant behavior patterns among large numbers of black people.... The distinction between learning how to live better in a pig pen and learning how to escape from a pig pen has not yet been mastered by most psychologists. . . . Paternalistic exhortation has become characteristic of white social scientists working with nonwhites. What these scientists select for attention are the isolated, trivial or marketable elements of the nonwhite experience. (C. W. Thomas, 1973, pp. 58-59)

As another has added, "Black clientele are treated as commodities—useful for a time, but ultimately undeserving of genuine consideration except as may be required to ensure the attainment of investigatory goals" (Gordon, 1973, p. 89). Finally, as Dumont (1969) has ventured, "There has been a vampirish quality to the manner in which researchers sucked the data from their subjects. . . . Moreover, they did so with a sense of righteousness, as if every monograph partook of Galileo's divinity" (pp. 19-20).

We shall have more to say about these valuational expressions in later chapters. However, as we now see, in the designation of "what there is," the terms of description, the explanation for activity, and the process of gaining knowledge itself, scientists generate statements of the good, the proper, or the desirable in social life.

---

[32] As Scheibe (1979) has argued, "The concept of a universalized human science cannot allow a true peerage or equality between the subject and object of study" (p. 151). To adopt the metaphor of the natural scientist in dealing with human beings is thus inherently to place a distance between subject and object. It is largely on those grounds that investigators (cf. Sommer, 1980) have attempted to develop dialogic methods—methods of study that reintroduce peerage in the research domain. The attempt is to ensure that all participants in the research process stand to gain equally in the dialogue. Similarly, Knight (1978) has called for the development of "good faith" research programs. Good faith inquiry would attempt to make the observer–participant relationship explicit, thereby making the context of conclusions and interpretations apparent to research participants.

They serve as moral advocates, and thus act as potential change agents of the persons they attempt to understand.[33] In effect, one may properly replace the traditional belief in the separation of fact and value with the apothegm: no description without prescription.

Fundamental Assumptions Revisited: The Hypothesis Test

As the above arguments indicate, there appears little justification for the immense effort devoted to the empirical substantiation of fundamental laws of human conduct. There would seem to be few patterns of human action, regardless of their durability to date, that are not subject to significant alteration. Should unalterable patterns be located, their proper study is most likely to fall within the natural science realms of physiology, biochemistry, and genetics. In admitting the temporal transience of the data base, we must further be prepared for the possibility that there are few if any predictive principles of learning, cognitive, or moral development, cognitive processing, attitude change, social perception, attraction and hostility, aggression, group productivity, political socialization, personality development, family interaction, educational efficacy, suicide, psychotherapy, social mobility, revolution, social change, economic motivation, wage stability, economic growth, and modernization.[34] And in any realm, the dissemination of "the law" itself may be virtually sufficient to architect its insubstantiation.

---

[33] It is in this context that Parisi, Castilfranchi, and Benigni (1976) have called for a full, explicit analysis of the ideological and political implications of social psychological inquiry.

[34] In this context, Cronbach's (1975) lament over the transhistorical reliability of research findings in psychology is worth quoting at length: "Ghiselli (1974) suggested that even such a reliable finding as the superiority of distributed practice over massed practice may not remain valid from one generation to another. Similarly, J. W. Atkinson (1974) pointed out that when a substantial relation is found between personality variables, it describes only the model personality of a particular society at a particular time in history (p. 408). He went on to say: 'I believe that the early success of Lewin et al. (1944) in the study of level of aspiration can be attributed largely to the fact that their subject samples, drawn from in the decades prior to World War II, were homogeneously high in achievement and low in anxiety.' (p. 409). Of a piece with this observation is the recognition that the California F Scale is obsolescent (Ghiselli, 1974; Lake, Miles, & Earle, 1973). The 25-year old research supporting its construct validity gives us little warrant for interpreting scores today because with new times the items carry new implications. Perhaps the best example of all is Bronfenbrenner's (1958) backward look at research comparing middle-class and lower-class parenting. Class differences observed in the 1950s were sometimes just the reverse of what had been observed in 1930. Generalizations decay. At one time a conclusion describes the existing situation well, at a later time it accounts for rather little variance, and ultimately it is only valid as history." (pp. 122–123)

With the status of fundamental laws thus impugned, traditional research pursuits are also thrown into jeopardy. What function is to be served, it may be asked, in the attempt to verify or discredit basic theories of human conduct? What remains of the guiding assumption that the truth value of a general theory may be influenced, either positively or negatively, by deductive hypothesis testing? And, without answers to these questions, we confront the collapse of the common assumption that with continued research on a given problem, scientific knowledge may accumulate over time. The self-corrective promise of the hypothetico-deductive method does not appear to deliver when applied to understanding human conduct. Because human action is in a state of variable change, the fruits of cross-time programs of deductive research are likely to be marginal. One cannot hope to mount a program of research that will provide "the last word," "solve the problem once and for all," "determine the 'real' answer to the problem," "finally get to the bottom of things," or demonstrate that a theory may be discarded once and for all because of its poor predictive value.[35,36]

With such critical assumptions at stake, it proves useful at this juncture to furnish a more detailed illustration from an existing line of research. In particular, we may examine the traditional attempt to carry out empirical assessments of specific hypotheses. For it is the "hypothesis test," as it is inappropriately termed, that furnishes the putative building blocks in the process of accumulating knowledge. Let us consider, then, a single, widely accepted principle in contemporary social psychology, one for which there is immense experimental support and for which the claims of transhistorical validity could most convincingly be made. This proposition, described in virtually all major texts of the field, is that a person's attraction toward another is a positive function of the other's similarity to the person. At least 50 separate studies now support this general proposition (cf. discussions by

---

[35] In Cronbach's (1975) words, "The trouble, as I see it, is that we cannot store up generalizations and constructs for ultimate assembly into a network. It is as if we needed a gross of dry cells to power an engine and could only make one a month. The energy would leak out of the first cells before we had half the battery completed" (p. 123).

[36] The extent to which the present analysis may be termed "historicist" depends on one's definition of the term. The present analysis is *not* historicist in Popper's sense of the term, emphasizing as it does historical predictability. Nor is it historicist within Fichte's view (with its emphasis on singular ideas in multiple manifestations across time), the view of late 19th century economics (with its emphasis on purely descriptive analysis of economic systems in varying historical periods), nor within the framework of those desiring to understand all phenomena historically. However, the present analysis does share in the historicist arguments of Feurbach against sciences that accept uncritically the universality of existing patterns; and it is in accord with Troeltsch's historicist contention that human ideas and ideals are subject to continuous alteration; with Herder's emphasis on the historical embeddedness of religion, science and philosophy; and with Weber's arguments against the value neutrality of historical analysis. The roots of the present thesis in what is often termed "process philosophy" (cf. Browning, 1965) should also be noted.

Berscheid & Walster, 1978; Byrne, 1971; Newcomb, 1961).[37] To be sure, there are conditions under which the similarity–attraction principle is not supported or in which hostility rather than attraction may result (cf. Mettee & Wilkins, 1972; Novak & Lerner, 1968; Senn, 1971; Taylor & Mettee, 1971). However, as it is said, these exceptions are generally limited by specific conditions. In general, it is argued, over wide-ranging social and behavioral conditions, similarity does engender attraction.

However, for present purposes it will prove useful to break the similarity–attraction hypothesis down into the traditional independent, intervening, and dependent variable format and consider each of the variable spectra in more detail. In the case of the independent variable, interpersonal similarity, one may specify a broad array of dimensions along which people may vary with respect to similarity. After all, not all types of similarity may have the same relationship with attraction. At a minimum, for example, one might wish to distinguish between similarity in opinions and in personality. Most of the data supporting the general proposition have indeed been generated in the former area, and doubts have been cast about the generality of the proposition in the latter case (cf. Lipetz, Cohen, Dworin, & Rogers, 1970). However, for purposes of inquiry, further distinctions might be useful between political opinions, those concerning values and morality, those dealing with family, and so on. There are also a broad number of personality dimensions that may be considered. However, over and above differences in opinion and personality, people also differ with respect to their similarity in physical appearance, educational background, family composition, ethnic affiliation, and so on. Each of these dimensions may also be broken down into a wide variety of subdimensions. For convenience several of these distinctions are featured in Fig. 1.1.

Let us further expand the model to consider a range of intervening variables or processes that might link one or more types of similarity with resulting attraction. For one, another's similarity provides confirmation of one's own perceptions or beliefs; it may also suggest that the other will provide positive payoffs on further occasions; another's similarity can also relieve feelings of isolation or loneliness; or it may ease the course of interaction and thus make one feel more comfortable. Another's similarity may also guarantee one's safety (criticisms are unlikely), or one may be attracted to a similar other as a by-product of attraction to self (the similar other being closer to self on a generalization gradient). All of these intervening mechanisms have been added to Fig. 1.1. (With additional thought, the list might be considerably lengthened.)

However, such an analysis would be altogether biased without considering as well a number of processes that might engender a *negative* relationship between

---

[37]Byrne and his colleagues (Byrne, 1971) have been bold enough to term the similarity–attraction hypothesis an "empirical law." Specifically it is proposed that "the attraction response (Y) of any subject toward a stranger can be predicted by multiplying 5.44 times the proportion of attitudes (X) expressed by the stranger that are similar to those of the subject, and then adding a constant of 6.62" (Byrne & Kelley, 1981, p. 314).

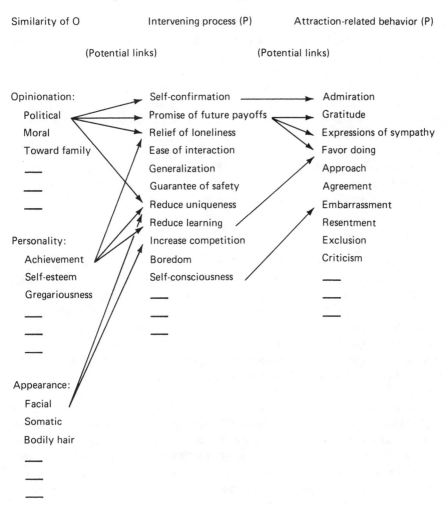

Fig. 1-1. Elaboration of the similarity–attraction proposition.

similarity and attraction. For example, as Snyder and Fromkin (1979) maintain, there is a prevalent desire for uniqueness such that the presence of someone who is similar could evoke a negative reaction. Another's similarity might further imply a constricted set of learning experiences; if the other is similar to self, then one can learn little that is new. The presence of a similar other might also suggest stronger competition for scarce resources, or engender self-consciousness, a state that Duval and Wicklund (1972) contend is negative in character. Finally, a similar other may simply be more boring. Each of these various processes or tendencies should also be taken into account (see Fig. 1.1). Again, with a little imagination it should be possible to extend this list of mechanisms substantially.

In turning to the dependent variable, social attraction, further differentiation is also useful. In particular it is important to consider a variety of forms that attraction may assume on a behavioral level. One may, for example, express attraction through words of admiration, sympathy, or gratitude. Doing favors, appreciating the other, giving agreement, and so on might also be considered signs of attraction. Because we have indicated a variety of ways in which similarity might elicit negative sentiments, we must also add a variety of actions that might reasonably result. Expressions of embarrassment, resentment, and confusion might be included, along with such actions as exclusion or criticism. The formulation in Fig. 1.1 reflects these minimal distinctions. Others could be added.

Having glimpsed a variety of distinctions that may all bear on the validity of the general similarity-attraction proposition, let us consider the types of alteration one might anticipate as a function of changes in the social, physical, or conceptual context over time. Three types of alteration are of particular significance.

Alterations in Entity Frequency

Each entity in each sector of our model is subject to variations in its frequency of occurrence in society. For example, whether strong political opinionation is present in a culture depends on the historical period. Where democracy prevails and differing parties compete for scarce positions, political opinionation may play a very modest role in social life. In the same way it could be argued that whether strong needs for self-esteem or uniqueness exist is also primarily a matter of existing cultural support. For example, in traditional Japanese culture it has been said that strong needs for uniqueness did not prevail among the general population (Benedict, 1946). People generally placed a high value on homogeneity in conduct. Similarly, desires for uniqueness may change as patterns of family life are altered and the society becomes more or less uniform. Likewise, feelings of empathy, admiration, boredom, and so on may also fluctuate in their relevance over time. And the cultural meaning of doing favors, agreeing, or criticizing may shift in such a way that their incidence is increased or decreased. As a result of such alterations in entity frequency, principles of behavior developed at one point in time may be irrelevant at later periods in history. There may simply be no particulars for which the general principle holds true.[38,39]

---

[38] Relevant is the report of British investigators, Perrin and Spencer (1980), who attempted to replicate perfectly Asch's (1951) classic research on conformity. Subjects were drawn from disciplines such as engineering, mathematics and chemistry, and none had heard of Asch's work. The result of the study was that *on only one* of 396 trials did a subject conform to the opinions of the erroneous majority. Although such results are open to myriad interpretations, the investigators conclude that the Asch effect may be a child of its time.

[39] Particulars in this case must be understood as conceptual, that is, as depending on the ontological constructions of human conduct discussed above. To the extent that such constructions also differ from one period to another, the accumulation of knowledge across time is rendered the more problematic. The patterns of human conduct in one period of history would simply be incommensurate with those in other periods as the constituent features would be different. Essentially the com-

Alterations in Independent-Intervening Variable Bonds

More critical to our concerns, we also find that the articulation between the independent variables and intervening processes is subject to alteration over time. Whether a given type of similarity elicits feelings of self-esteem, whether it promises rewards for the future, whether it bodes ill for one's desire for stimulation or information, all seem highly dependent on the prevailing context of experience. Certainly there is little reason to suspect genetically preferred connections between varying types of similarity and varying types of internal processes. Thus, in principle, virtually any type of similarity has the potential capacity to elicit, influence, stimulate, or precede any type of intervening process. As indicated by the arrows in Fig. 1.1, depending on the historical context, political similarity could have strong consequences for self-esteem, or none at all. It could also indicate the likelihood of further rewards, or it could play into one's needs for uniqueness. All such bonds are reasonable, and variations in the type and strength of the various bonds can well be expected within any given culture. As a result, we may anticipate continuous fluctuations in the support rendered to any hypothesis relating external stimuli to internal process or structure.

Alternations in Intervening-Dependent Variable Bonds

In the same way that temporal variation may be anticipated between independent and intervening variables, the relationships between intervening and dependent variables also seem vulnerable to the vicissitudes of history. For example, a positive linkage between anticipation of positive payoffs and expressions of gratitude would hardly appear to be "human nature." Gratitude is not always expressed when one expects to be showered with positive outcomes; indeed, gifts, aid, or help can often evoke hostility (Gergen & Gergen, 1971). In cultures such as Japan, for example, reactions to gifts may include burdensome feelings of indebtedness, the experience of engagement in cultural traditions, hopes for continued contact, and resentment over expectation (cf. Befu, 1966; Benedict, 1946). Similarly, in Western culture, one may express no gratitude toward another who has boosted his or her esteem; many people view esteem enhancement as synonymous with pride or egotism. The feelings attached to the experience of being unique may also vary; there may be important historical periods (e.g., during World War II in the United States) in which finding oneself in a unique political position could be extremely threatening. Whether another's similarity triggers a positive or a negative experience of uniqueness may also have important implications for resulting behavior. In sum, myriad relationships between internal process and resulting effect are both reasonable and

---

parison would be equivalent to testing laws about motor cars with laws about grapefruit growth. In Nagel's (1961) terms, "If social laws or theories are to formulate relations of dependence that are invariant throughout the wide range of cultural differences manifested in human action, the concepts entering into those laws cannot denote characteristics occurring in just one special group of societies" (p. 465). We shall return to this problem in the following chapter.

probable. Which relationships exist and to what degree are primarily historical matters. In effect, we may anticipate continuous fluctuation in the support furnished to any hypothesis relating internal process or structure and subsequent behavior.

Before elaborating further on the implication of these various types of change, it is important to note that almost all contemporary research and theory in social psychology and related domains is subject to such analysis. Not only may the prevalence of tendencies to reduce inconsistency, achieve balance, achieve equity, increase performance in the presence of others, or attribute causality wax and wane over time, but so may the prevalence of opposing tendencies to create inconsistency, negate balance, seek inequity, relax in others' presence, and view behavior as environmentally rather than willfully determined. Likewise, the relationship between demands for obedience and obedient behavior, aggressive attack and aggressive response, feeling good and giving help, a leader's task capabilities and willingness to follow, and so on are subject to alteration in strength and prevalence within society. And for each of these relationships there are several good reasons to suspect a function form opposite in direction from that now accepted as lawful. Over time, as the bonds among the variables are molded anew, these alternative tendencies could increase in strength and/or prevalence.

It is additionally important to consider the possibility that various alterations in intervening mechanisms, processes, or concepts may occur over very brief periods of time. Thus far we have viewed relations among variables much as one would a personality trait: as relatively enduring but subject to slow transitions or modifications over the years. However, it is also quite possible that such relations are subject to momentary fluctuations and thus approximate situationally induced states. For example, in examining one's own experience it should be possible to verify the existence of virtually all the bonds relating independent variables with intervening processes in the illustration above. Many can identify instances in which they have felt self-confirmed when another agreed with their political opinion, and can also imagine being bored by the same agreement; many can anticipate (or remember) praising someone who has given them self-confirmation but also imagine (or remember) reacting in an embarrassed or in a distanced manner. Shifts from one possibility to another could occur within seconds. In this regard, one confronts the possibility that research subjects often shift rapidly from one intervening process to another during the course of any given experiment. For example, the subject exposed to another's opinion agreement may first feel confirmed; he may then begin to consider that he will not be seen as unique by the experimenter ("just another face"), but momentarily subdue this thought by envisioning the ease of interaction with his partner; then, however, he begins to think on the possibility of enhanced competition with his partner, but disregards this possibility upon considering the future rewards he will receive. Other subjects may shuttle through alternative patterns. The "dependent variable" assessment may occur at virtually any point during this multiple array of continuously altering psychological states. At the point of measurement, each subject may be in a different psychological state, preceded by a unique sequence of other states. To the extent that such rapid alterations may occur in intervening process, the psychological significance of experimental results is rendered obscure. They may be viewed as little more than the expression of a frozen cross section of a potentially vast array of processes in motion.

Having specified the major types of alterations within and between the various components of our model, the prospects and limitations of hypothesis testing become apparent. The following conclusions are especially cogent:

1. *That which stands as empirical confirmation (or falsification) may be generated for any reasonable theoretical proposition.* Given widespread and possibly rapid fluctuations in patterns of human conduct, there is no reasonable hypothesis about human activity for which support (or disconfirmation) cannot be generated. Placing hypotheses under experimental test is thus primarily a challenge to the experimenter's skill in discerning the proper time, location, and population in which the most convincing support (or disconfirmation) for the hypothesis may be generated. Given normal familiarity with the culture, the results of such tests seldom inform one of anything not already considered possible. Not only does this argument question the utility of the process of "hypothesis testing"; it further implies that for every hypothesis occupying the literature of the field the contradiction is also supportable. It is possible that all information passing from the discipline to the public is no more valid in a fundamental sense than its negation.

2. *The "critical experiment" is expendable.* Traditionally the experiment has played a key role in ruling between competing hypotheses. It is commonly assumed that the experiment can be used as the crucible against which the validity of alternative or competing explanations may be determined. Such thinking continues to guide research strategy over a broad spectrum. Models of learning, information processing, mental development, schizophrenia, and so on are proposed; research is employed for validation, and the stage is thereby set for a host of experimental challenges. These challenges, designed either to demonstrate limitations in the initial model or to invalidate and replace it, may then be countered by empirical attempts to reestablish the validity of the initial proposal. Further exchange is thus invited, and the resulting dialogue may absorb years of dedicated effort.[40] The history of research on cognitive dissonance nicely illustrates the pattern. For over two decades, social psychologists witnessed an exhausting number of studies attempting to displace the dissonance formulation with alternative explanations or to defend the theory against such attack (cf. Bem, 1967; Chapanis & Chapanis, 1964; Janis & Gilmore, 1965; Silverman, 1964). With respect to the accumulation of general knowledge, the outcomes of such effort have been minimal. The initial formulation remains relatively intact and the challenges remain suspended. From the present standpoint there is little to be gained from such efforts. To the extent that a given stimulus may precede an indeterminant variety of different processes or internal

---

[40] As noted earlier, the assumption of the *experimentum crucis* has long been abandoned in the philosophy of science in favor of a holistic orientation in which entire programs of research are evaluated empirically as opposed to individual cases (see also Forsyth, 1976). The present arguments (and those of Chapter 2) indicate that even this option is closed in the case of behavioral study.

reactions, and the strength and prevalence of such bonds are subject to historical fluctuation, critical tests contain little information value. When perfectly executed, they tell us only that some other process *could* account for observed patterns of behavior at the present time. Given the above premise that all reasonable hypotheses can be supported at some time or place, attempts to employ the *experimentum crucis* may be viewed as unproductive.

These conclusions are reached by adopting the traditional stimulus–response language of "the acquired disposition." However, much the same set of conclusions results if one adopts the view of the human as a conceptualizing agent. This argument is worthy of particular attention inasmuch as it forms the second moment of the preceding contention that the acceptance of the cognitive orientation at the theoretical level flies in the face of the logical empiricist conception of science. As initially ventured, the capacity of the individual to respond to the meaning or conceptualization of a stimulus rather than the stimulus in itself, essentially frees the individual from stimulus control. In the present case we find that this same capacity renders the experimenter impotent to effect systematic variations in stimulus conditions. To the extent that an investigator's account of human action agrees with or is congenial to the conceptual conventions pervasive within a culture, it follows that the results of properly conducted research must be supportive of his or her aims. If the investigator premises research on minority conceptions, the results of the research will appear to contradict the theory, not because the theory is incorrect, but because of the improper generalization. This is equivalent to saying that *any theory is true of those who happen to be employing it at the time as a basis for action.* And by the same token, any theory may be true or false, depending on whether people chose at that time to act upon its premises. Thus, such common propositions as "people like those who they perceive to be similar to self," "people are motivated to avoid inconsistent information," "people do not make use of base-rate information in reaching decisions," "when their options are curtailed, people try to reestablish their freedom," "people who are made aware of themselves begin to feel apprehension over evaluation," or "people faced with inequitable payments will attempt to reestablish equity" are not fundamentally falsifiable.[41,42]

To illustrate further, consider as a social stimulus the question, "What is the circumference of a circle with a radius of four meters?" Appropriate responses to such a query will depend largely on one's conceptual training. Thus, for many people it would be appropriate to respond with some negation of the question (e.g., "I don't have the foggiest. What do you mean by asking me a question like that?"). For others, who may dimly remember that they faced such questions in their earlier years, it might be appropriate to respond with an apology. And for others who are fortunate enough to recall earlier lessons, the only sensible response will be to double the radius and multiply by π. Thus, if placed in an experiment and given the stimulus of a problem in which they were to derive the circumference,

---

[41] See Ossorio and Davis (1968), Smedslund (1978), and Shotter (in press) for related arguments.

it might be predicted, their behavior should reflect the operation of the heuristic for which they had training. (A control group not faced with the same stimulus trigger should not so respond.) Clearly, there are only trivial lessons to be learned from testing the hypothesis that people possess a mental mechanism $2\pi r$. The results would simply demonstrate that all those who possess the mechanism as posited by the investigator would respond as the investigator believed; those who did not would fail to confirm the hypothesis. If the investigator was successful in carrying out the study in an educated sample, the results might be confirmed. In a general population the results would probably confirm the null hypothesis. In effect, to conduct experimental tests to determine whether people reduce dissonance, achieve cognitive balance, respond with reactance, and so on is similar to testing whether people have mastered the mental mechanism $2\pi r$. All such accounts of people's psychological processes may be considered true out of hand of those about whom they are true. Perhaps the only significant empirical question concerns the proportion of the population employing a given theoretical conception during a particular period.

The Retrenchment of Traditional Science

Few readers will probably experience significant reservations concerning the independent components of the analysis thus far. Although minority sentiments may exist in every case, most would probably agree that the vast share of human activity is not genetically programmed, that human conceptual capacities enable people to generate many new and different understandings of the world, and that prevailing investments in such values as freedom, unpredictability, and uniqueness may function as sources for counternormative behavior. Further, most readers would

---

[42] An illustration of this problem in contemporary research is manifest in debate over Seligman's (1975) theory of learned helplessness. In Seligman's initial formulation real world variations in the controllability of events were said to affect subsequent problem solving ability and activity level in both animal and human populations. However, Abramson, Seligman and Teasdale (1978) revised the initial formulation by adding a variety of cognitive mechanisms intervening between the real-world contingency and the resulting responses. Specifically, it was argued, persons must *perceive* noncontingency, make certain attributions regarding it, and anticipate its continuation. Yet, this shift from real-world variations to perceived variations raises severe problems for the testability of the theory. People are fundamentally free to perceive contingencies or noncontingencies in any environment. Thus, variations in real-world contingencies (1) may have little to do with the behavior of the organisms and (2) may be viewed as idiosyncratic constructions of the investigator (i.e., reflective only of his view of contingency) and thus only "real-world" by the investigator's convention. As Wortman and Dintzer (1978) properly point out, the revised theory is not clearly subject to test. Schwartz (1981) has demonstrated similar difficulties with the attempt to extend Seligman's revised theory to the domain of depression.

probably be prepared to admit that scientific theory and its inherent valuational premises are capable of altering the confluence of ideas and values in the society more generally. However, though most of the constituent elements of the present thesis may seem reasonable enough, strong objections do emerge when the implications for hypothesis testing and the accumulation of knowledge are derived. The present arguments suggest that the goals traditionally sought within the sociobehavioral sciences are chimerical, and a new conception of scientific activity is necessitated. These implications have met with strong resistance indeed, and it is to this resistance that we must now turn. Three particular lines of rebuttal will concern us—the pragmatic, the theoretic, and the reductionist.

The Pragmatics of Permanence

An initial line of defense is erected by those who generally accept the fundamental state of behavioral change but who believe that ancillary activity within the sciences may reduce its troublesome implications. As it is argued, there are pragmatic means of reducing the magnitude of the peculiar problems besetting the science. Several such attempts may be considered.

The Reduction of Reaction

Two initial palliatives need be of momentary concern. First, it may be agreed that the task of the scientist is complicated by the transhistorical variation in human behavior. However, it is argued, the primary difference between the natural and social sciences stems from the reactive character of behavioral research: Human beings may respond to scientific formulations in such a way as to invalidate or confirm them. If such enlightenment effects can be prevented or reduced, the problems of the scientist may be considerably reduced. Within this domain many believe that such enlightenment effects are already at a minimum. The sociobehavioral sciences dwell in relative isolation, it is claimed, and the population more generally is either unaware or cares little for their formulations. Yet, it may be replied, to the extent that this condition does prevail, scientists may have serious reason for concern. Public indifference to such formulations may itself stand as a criticism against the banality of much contemporary investigation—a topic to which we shall turn in Chapter 3. There is little reason, in principle, why behavioral inquiry could not command broad attention. Further, to argue that society is inherently oblivious and unaffected by sociobehavioral science would also be to discount the profound social effects of social Darwinism, Freudian theory, Marxism, and Keynesian economic theory, to cite but a few.[43]

---

[43] As Kenneth Boulding (1965) has commented in this respect, "the social sciences are creating a world in which national loyalty and the national state can no longer be taken for granted as sacred institutions, in which religion has to change profoundly its views on the nature of man and sin, in which family and affection become a much more self-conscious and less simple-minded affair, and in which

Others have argued that enlightenment effects may be reduced by developing a value neutral scientific language. As Harris (1976) has suggested, a more formalized or technical scientific language might reduce such effects. The discipline should strive conscienciously for a value-free mathematical language. As we have already seen, however, the specific manner in which scientific language segments the world, the form of its labels (even if ostensibly cleansed of praise and blame), and the manner of explanation are inherently value impregnated. To employ a technical language merely serves to mystify the underlying commitments. Further, in order to "make sense," technical terms must inevitably be tied to terms in the common vernacular. To learn that alpha behavior stands in a curvilinear relationship to gamma conduct is, in itself, a form of cultural nonsense. Such a formulation is neither intelligible nor interesting until its terms are linked to the common categories of the culture. To learn that alpha is emotional arousal, for example, and gamma is task performance reinstates the formulation as meaningful within the culture. Yet, once the technical terms are linked to "sensible talk," the cracks begin to appear in the patina of dispassion. Finally, technical language remains value neutral only as long as its action implications remain unrealized. A term such as "intelligence quotient," for example, may retain its neutrality only as long as segments of the population remain unaware that its deployment thwarts their mobility in society (Kamin, 1974).

A second means of stemming reactive effects is equally impracticable. To preserve the transhistorical validity of scientific knowledge, such knowledge could be removed from the public domain and reserved for a selected elite. This elite might typically be coopted by the state, as no government could risk the existence of a private establishment with means of broad social control. In some degree this situation is approximated in most Western cultures. Economic, political, and social forecasting are all carried out within governing institutions and the results of such work only selectively published. Yet it must also be made clear that scientists in this case continue to remain dependent on the public. Even though the veiling of knowledge reduces one input into social change, such change is not thereby terminated. Through conceptual reconstruction people remain fundamentally free to abnegate long-standing patterns of conduct. The capacity for autonomous creation of alternative understanding leaves the scientist's predictive success in public hands. Let us consider a second and more formidable line of pragmatic retrenchment.

A Science of Enlightenment

As we have seen, the espousal of any behavioral formulation may occasion a variety of differing reactions. For example, one may act so as to violate its implications, conform to them, or ignore them altogether. Given a specified range of reactions, it becomes appealing from a pragmatic standpoint to construct covering laws (cf. Nagel, 1961). Based on the careful documentation of enlightenment effects,

---

indeed, all ethical systems are profoundly desacralized" (p. 886). Also see Cronbach and Suppes (1969).

and with the contribution of research on social influence, of psychological reactance, self-fulfilling prophecy, social expectancy, and so on, one might be able to forge a series of objectively grounded principles systematically accounting for such reactions. Essentially, one might develop a science of enlightenment effects that would allow the prediction and control of the effects of scientific knowledge.

Perhaps the most significant attempt to deal with this problem has taken place in the field of economics. A severe threat to early aspirations for a predictive science was posed by such economists as Vining (1950) and Kemp (1962). As they pointed out, a predictive science of economics is rendered problematic by the fact that once an economic forecast is made known, this information can itself influence behavior, often in such a way that the forecast is falsified. If people alter their behavior so as to take advantage of the prediction, a new factor enters the arena such that the original prediction will frequently be erroneous. For example, if the price of automobiles was predicted to rise 10%, manufacturers wishing to profit from the situation would ensure that automobiles were abundantly available for purchase. However, this increased supply would have the concomitant effect of lowering the price, thus falsifying the original prediction of a price increase.

In reaction to this line of argument Grünberg and Modigliani (1954) asserted that publicly disclosed predictions are not *in principle* obviated by the fact that behavior is altered in light of such a disclosure. Conditions may be specified under which public predictions will not be self-invalidating. As they demonstrate, an accurate public prediction can be made at time t, of the price of a given commodity at $t + 1$ by altering the predictive equation to take into account the reaction to the prediction. Thus, if one knows that suppliers will increase their supply in order to take advantage of the increased price, one's prediction can be altered to take this into account.[44]

Yet, this solution to the problem of enlightenment effects would appear inadequate as more than a temporary palliative. In particular, it fails to take account of reactions to enlightenment theory. If the supplier learns that the public prediction already takes account of his or her past reactions, and realizes that by altering this behavior pattern, he or she may now succeed in driving the price over the announced figure, past observation is no longer predictive. Once established, principles of enlightenment themselves become inputs into the culture. Of course, one could subsequently set out to develop theories of reactions to theories of enlightenment effects. However, it is quickly seen that this exchange of actions and reactions could be extended *ad infinitum*. Theory will forever chase after reactions to theory.[45,46] We may turn, then, to a final line of pragmatic defense.

---

[44] See also Henshel and Kennedy (1973) for a similar argument.

[45] For a more recent treatise on the problem of historical contingency in economic knowledge see Shackle (1972).

[46] Grünberg and Modigliani and others (cf. Buck, 1963) are quite aware of this problem, and argue that predictions and reactions may frequently converge—thus converting the problem of reflexivity to a technical matter. In a similar vein, Harris (1976) has argued that one should not be so concerned by the problem of infinite

Post Hoc Theoretical Accommodation

Within traditional science, the theorist generally attempts to develop abstract propositions within an "if . . . then" format. Scientific theories are thus conditional in that they treat phenomena under specified conditions only. From this perspective, the disconfirmation of a theory in a period of time subsequent to its initial substantiation does not necessarily challenge its validity. It may simply suggest that the conditions have been altered in such a way that a proper test is not being conducted (Nagel, 1961). Cross-time change in circumstances may prevent the investigator from establishing the conditions necessary for testing the theory as it was initially developed. It is in this vein that Manis (1976b) has proposed that when a theory loses predictive value over time, the theorist is presented with a unique opportunity. Such failure may provide an occasion for theoretical modification and elaboration. As new observations are made, ancillary "if . . . then" propositions may be added to the initial formulation, thus enriching and strengthening the formulation still further.

For example, consider the rather obvious proposition that the greater the ambiguity in a decision-making situation, the more susceptible the individual is to group influence. Surely it would be simple enough to furnish broad laboratory support for such a view. However, if future replications of such research failed to render support for this supposition, one needn't treat such failures as impugning its validity. Rather, one might be moved to compare the conditions under which positive versus negative results emerged. If one were to find, for instance, that there had been a subtle shift in the common beliefs about the function of remaining socially independent under ambiguous circumstances, one could simply augment the initial formulation accordingly. The initial proposition would remain steadfast, with the

---

regress. One may develop more general theories delineating the circumstances under which the changes in behavior of the system dictated by the nth cycle of the regress become vanishingly small. As he points out, game theorists have been concerned with such problems for some time. An equilibrium point could be reached, for example, between a pitcher and a batter, each of whom attempts to use their knowledge of the other's previous tactics to gain advantage over the other? In an attempt to solve this type of problem, game theorists von Neumann and Morgenstern have attempted to demonstrate that in the zero sum game, opposing players will reach equilibrium if they begin to think in terms of probabilistic strategies rather than restricting themselves to deterministic responses to the preceding move of the opponent. However, as we find, such arguments are only as strong as the conditions of choice are constrained. In the more common case, one possesses far wider latitude of choice than furnished in the typical experimental gaming situation or the limited economic model—including the choice of not choosing, or of creating entirely novel options not given within the initial norms of exchange. Even in baseball a pitcher may abandon concern with striking out the batter in favor of other ends (e.g., granting a base on balls to pitch to the opposing pitcher) or develop new goals (such as pitching balls that would cause the batter to loft easy catches into the outfield). In effect, people are seldom playing only one game with a fixed endpoint.

additional caveat excepting those conditions under which a high value is placed on independence under ambiguity. As additional research is conducted over the years, one's theoretical scheme would thus become increasingly precise, differentiating, and predictive.

Although this reasoning seems compelling enough on the surface, it is of doubtful merit, even from the traditional standpoint. First, the solution assumes that one is able to locate the factor(s) responsible for the receding validity of the initial proposition. Yet, as time passes an indeterminant number of variously interrelated changes occur. Essentially, history may be viewed as the unfolding confluence of inextricably linked events. As both historians and social indicators researchers are well aware, there is no means of isolating independent alterations in social circumstances. Hence, how is one to locate the particular circumstances responsible for the emerging impotence of a theory? If the monotonic function form relating situational ambiguity and social conformity ceases to predict, how does one begin to isolate the factor(s) responsible for change in conditions? Is it truly the shifting value of independence in society, or perhaps a reflection of increased feelings of middle class alienation, an increased suspicion toward social experimentation, a generalized cantankerousness provoked by the receding economic conditions, some combination of such factors, or what? All such changes are possible, hundreds of other possibilities may be advanced, and many such changes may be interdependent.[47]

More important, however, the pragmatic tactic of *post hoc* modification of theory is at odds with the logical empiricist assumptions that it is designed to salvage. If all failures at replication and all reversals in prediction occasion the development of new "if . . . then" qualifiers, the hypothetico-deductive system ceases proper functioning. Under such conditions no theoretical proposition could be denigrated or discarded through predictive failure. If all confirmations of a proposition contribute to its antecedent probability, and all disconfirmations eventuate in propositional qualification, the proposition is simply not open to test, even by traditional standards.

The Appeal to Theoretical Abstraction

As we see, the various attempts at pragmatic retrenchment are of limited value. More compelling for many are defenses relying on alterations at the level of theory construction. In this case one concedes that the particulars of daily life indeed

---

[47]Cherulnik (1981) has joined in the above defense of traditional experimentation by arguing that discrepancies among experimental findings, along with variations in mediating mechanisms, do not discredit the process of experimentation. Rather, each new finding represents a contribution to a more complex and more generally valid theory. As we shall see in the following chapter, what stand as experimental outcomes are not, in fact, objective data but samples of interpretive language. Thus, experiments do not essentially yield objective support for general theories. However, within the confines of the present analysis, the point is that virtually any social stimulus may be associated with virtually any form of subsequent activity, and with a potentially infinite range of mediators. Thus, which particular patterns

undergo continuous change. However, it is argued, it is the practitioner's task to deal with the transient idiosyncracies of the moment. It is for the scientist to discern amidst the flux the unchanging forms, dimensions, or processes (cf. Nagel, 1961). For example, there may be an infinity of different word combinations within the culture. However, most such combinations may conform to a few essential rules of grammar. It is to these "essentials" that scientists should direct their attention. The scientist essentially elucidates the contours of permanence through abstraction. One abstracts from the flow of particulars those qualities or characteristics that appear to remain the same or exemplify a common principle.[48] Let us examine several more specific forms of this argument.

Universal Experiences

At the most elementary level, many investigators draw sustenance from discovering similarities between contemporary ideas and works in other cultures or historical climes. Such discoveries suggest that there are universally shared experiences and thus a truly "human nature" upon which predictive formulations might be based. Thus, for example, when the investigator locates in the works of Aristotle a formulation of the attitude change process corresponding to contemporary theory, confidence is generated in the long-term predictive potential of the formulation. As Schlenker (1974) contends, thinkers such as Aristotle, Plato, Kant, Locke, Rousseau, and Hobbes continue to speak to present circumstances:

> Many of their hypotheses concerning human social behavior and cognitive processes appear as applicable today as the time they were made. Spinoza's *Ethics* contains numerous insights, some of which serve as fundamental postulates for Heider's (1958) balance theory. Machiavelli's sixteenth-century advice to his prince has served as the basis for theoretical work and systematic investigations in 20th century society (Christie & Geis, 1970). The list could go on indefinitely." (p. 5)

Yet, in spite of the compelling nature of these unanticipated affinities, they are not thereby to be elevated to the level of universals. For one, there may be diffusion of theory and related behavior pattern across time and culture. Some contemporary patterns of behavior resemble those of early Greek and Roman cultures because these cultures served as progenitors of the present. As Schlenker (1974) himself has commented, "The writings of . . . philosophers of more or less 'ancient'

---

and which particular mediators are operating in any given experiment at any given time is historically contingent. Thus, even if one grants the possibility of objective evidence, the very most an experiment could yield is a localized indication of the array of historically located dispositions.

[48] For refutations of the contention that all particulars can be viewed as "bundles of universals" or "collections of universal properties," see Armstrong (1978). However, Armstrong's counterthesis, that there are "objective" universals and that these are discoverable by science, seems, without advancing a means for such discovery, a vain hope in search of substance.

origin still affect contemporary conceptualizations of man" (p. 5). Thus, occasional resemblances between present theories and those of other times and cultures should not be wholly surprising.[49] The location of affinities may also represent the fruits of serendipity. Both the history of any given culture and contemporary life in any alien culture provide an enormous domain of events. If one searches carefully enough, one is apt to find certain points of convergence. In the same way that a psychiatrist or a clinician can look back into the rich and variegated events comprising a single life history to locate support for virtually any hypothesis, so will the investigator sensitive to similarities across time and space most surely find them. As it is said, cultures have always experienced wars, tyranny, conflict, prejudice, and so on, and one is titillated to think in terms of such patterns or tendencies as constituting "human nature." Yet with proper sensitivity one could as well generate evidence for the universality of sitting in the shade, gazing at the moon, and hopping on one foot. The mere location of occasional likenesses does not serve as an adequate basis for establishing universality.

Universal Dimensions

A second orientation to universals may be located in a variety of notable attempts to develop dimensional schemas of universal applicability. For example, Charles Osgood and his colleagues (Osgood, Suci, & Tannenbaum, 1957) have argued for universal dimensions of connotative meaning. Virtually all judgments of objects, persons, events, and so on are said to vary along the dimensions of evaluation, potency, and activity. Thus, people in widely differing cultures will evaluate any given stimulus according to whether it is good or bad, powerful or weak, and active as opposed to passive. Much the same orientation has been used by Foa and Foa (1980) in developing a series of dimensions for characterizing the patterns of resource exchange in various cultures. Although cultures may differ in their specific patterns of exchange, argue the Foas, virtually all such patterns can be accounted for along abstract-concrete and universalistic-particularistic dimensions. Similarly, Triandis (1977) has proposed that behavior in all societies varies along the dimensions of association-dissociation, superordination-subordination, intimacy-formality, and overt-covert.

Although such schemas have many compelling features, it is important in such cases to realize that the existence of universal schemas or dimensions is not synonymous with the presence of universal patterns of behavior. To assume the latter on the basis of the former is to engage in the fallacy of misplaced concreteness. Essentially the theorist is propounding a series of concepts or dimensions that may have universal applicability. However, the possibility for universal application rests on the cognitive skills of the theorist rather than in the world of observation. In the

---

[49] Toulmin (1972) attacks the assumption of universals of thought or mental process on the grounds that such an assumption is anti-evolutionary. As he demonstrates, many abstract concepts (including mathematical) once appearing to be universal were developed and abandoned according to historical exigencies.

case of rudimentary distinctions in presence or absence, precious little skill may be required. One can readily maintain that all cultures either possess or fail to possess hair ribbons, cottage cheese, or Frye boots. And, with sufficient skill, a theorist may raise more subtle dimensions such as shallow versus deep, polite versus impolite, or goal directed versus undirected to the level of universals. Such applicability rests in the ability of the theorist to negotiate the relationship between concept and observations in such a way as to make sense within a given system of communication. The ability to apply the schemas does not warrant their reification. In effect, virtually any conceptual distinction or dimension may have universal applicability; we learn nothing of universal behavior patterns as a result of the application.[50,51]

Universal Patterning

A third orientation, often coupled with the preceding pair, involves the empirical evaluation of hypotheses of universal scope. Exemplary of this orientation are behavioral scientists employing hologeistic analysis, that is, correlational analysis of data from multiple cultures (cf. Naroll, Michik, & Naroll, 1980). Using vast repositories of data (notably, the Human Relations Area Files), correlational studies have tested wide-ranging hypotheses relating, for example, family structure to food scarcity, residence rules to patterns of descent, aggression to economic status, romantic love and early weaning habits, population and social organization, and so on. Significant correlations suggest the presence of systematic functional relationships cutting across all cultures.

Yet the precautionary qualifications surrounding any given finding in this area are so numerous that the claim to universals must be limited to a whisper. Problems

---

[50] Relevant is Godow's (1976) observation: "It is hard to see what sort of evidence would clearly establish the existence of transhistorical laws" (p. 442).

[51] It is this problem that also confounds the numerous attempts to catalogue cultural universals. For example, in his attempt to enumerate cultural universals, Fox (1971) argues that all cultures, even if wholly isolated from one another, would be found to have language, laws about property, incest rules, myths, neuroses, and dancing. Such activities would be found, "because we are the kind of animal that does these things" (p. 284). Murdock (1945) lists seventy-three universal items, including bodily adornment, joking, family, trade, dream interpretation, and so on. Westcott (1970) offers a list of forty-eight human traits that are also shared by animals; Malinowski (1944) calls for "seven cultural imperatives" and Goldschmidt (1966) asserts that there are three essential universals of human cultures. It would appear that such lists may either be expanded indefinitely (in all cultures people use their index fingers, look into the air, do not remain forever in the same spot, etc.) or contracted, depending on one's skills in search and conceptualization. In the case of search, a single instance of an event could presumably qualify the culture as "in possession" (if the performance were solely that of a one-legged tap dance, the culture might be said to possess dance), and presumably, one could discount the vast percentage of the culture and the vast share of time in which the event was not in evidence.

stemming from the lack of reliable or standardized assessment devices, nonrepresentative samples from any given culture, inability to define the boundaries of a given culture, the lack of adequate control for cultural diffusion, and the lack of articulation between scientific classifications systems and relevant cultural systems of meaning prevail throughout such research.[52] Over and above these pitfalls, there is the insurmountable problem of extraneous variables. For the correlation researcher, the frequency, intensity, or character of any given behavior may be influenced by a variety of factors other than the one (or that group, in the case of multiple regression designs) currently under study. As a result, the nature of one's correlational results is inevitably dependent on the particular configuration of factors and their corresponding values existing in the various cultures making up the sample at the time of observation. Given the minimal assumption that the value of the extraneous factors may change over time, the magnitude (and direction) of the correlation coefficient is also free to fluctuate accordingly. In effect, the hologeistic method (and, by implication, any form of correlational hypothesis testing) may yield virtually any coefficient of correlation, depending on the particular time of observation and sample selection. To make inferences from such data regarding functional relationships of universal scope is without warrant.

An alternative to the hologeistic approach is that of the experimentalist (cf. Brown & Sechrest, 1980). Typical of this orientation is the replication of a standardized experiment in a variety of cultural settings. Thus, for example, investigators have explored the cross-cultural generality of hypotheses regarding communication in small groups, bargaining strategies, dissonance reduction, reactions to help, and so on (cf. Triandis & Brislin, 1980; Triandis & Lambert, 1980). The general hope is to emerge with theoretical principles of universal scope. Such pursuits have generally met with mixed success. Often a given experiment yields similar function forms across cultural boundaries, but failures at replication are quite frequent. The essential question is whether one may safely draw inferences of universal pattern, even when consistent findings are generated across a variety of cultures.

There are several obvious reasons for remaining cautious in this respect. For one, experiments typically employ very small samples. Inferences regarding an entire culture are often made on fewer than one hundred nonrandom cases. More fundamental is the extent to which ostensibly similar patterns of behavior substantiate the same theoretical formulation. Do identical experimental findings necessarily add confirmation to the same theory? The argument here may be illustrated by ref-

---

[52] In the search for universals, much has been made of the distinction between *emic* constructs (those of a culture under study) and *etic* ones (those used by the scientist to make generalizations across cultures). The emic constructs are thus viewed as culture bound, while the etic are employed to build universal theories (cf. Brislin, 1980). Yet, from the present perspective, the distinction may be viewed as spurious. Etic is essentially another name for the emic distinctions of the scientist. To argue that they are more functionally valuable in the building of science runs the danger of ethnocentrism.

erence to typical reactions to replication failure. When dissimilar patterns emerge, alternative explanations are typically sought in order to explain why the hypothesis of universality remains unthreatened. As Triandis (1978) has put it, in the face of replication failures,

> one needs to examine rival hypotheses for non-replication, such as unusual subject selection or sampling, inadequate controls of relevant variables (e.g., subject motivation to please the experimenter, or disrupt the experiment), nonequivalance of the response format, differential familiarity with the experimental treatments, and differential reaction to being a subject in an experiment. As long as such factors operate within a culture, it is not necessary to infer cultural differences for nonreplication. (p. 2)

Yet, it would seem wholly inappropriate to employ this full set of tactics to explain away cultural differences, while failing to apply them to successful replications. Ostensibly similar patterns of behavior may be found from one setting to another for entirely different reasons. Any given response in an experiment ultimately relies on a composite of preceding conditions, and differing composites may underly behavior that is phenotypically similar. In effect, with the same deftness that replication failures are explained away, one may also locate myriad explanations for patterns of similarity.

Finally, one must question the extent to which similar patterns of results are guaranteed by the manner in which the translation of experimental situations succeeds in evoking similar, commonsense interpretations across cultures. For example, if an investigator wishes to test a hypothesis concerning aggressive behavior, it is useful to arrange a stimulus situation in which aggression seems sensible and appropriate from the subject's point of view. Verbal means are often used to create the necessary stimulus conditions, but the same ends may be achieved through careful selection of a stimulus person, props, the experimental setting, and so on. In the cross-cultural replication of a prototypical experiment, one does not translate verbal materials literally, but attempts to capture the "underlying sense" or "proper meaning" of such materials. Yet the proper meaning of the materials is such that aggression, in this case, is an appropriate or commonsense response. Thus, in the translation of the original materials, one reinstigates the conditions under which aggression will again be the reasonable or appropriate behavior. Given sufficient latitude of methodological translation across cultures, the investigator may readily succeed in reestablishing the psychological conditions under which specified forms of behavior become acceptable or desirable.[53] In this light failures to replicate may often result when the experimental situation is highly rarefied (thus dispersing the

---

[53] If the investigator believes, for example, that it is human nature to defend oneself when attacked, the hypothesis may be universally sustained as long at the term "attack" (as in the research question, "How would you respond if attacked?") was always translated into the sort of terms for which "defense" was one of the few plausible responses.

range of commonsense interpretations that may be evoked) and little latitude of translation is available (e.g., an experimental game is completely structured, identical stimulus materials are used).

These particular issues hardly exhaust the discussion of universal pattern (cf. Lonner, 1980).[54] However, the discussion may be concluded by denoting two problems of cardinal importance in establishing universals, neither of which has yet been solved by those committed to such an enterprise. First, there is no intelligible account of the means by which knowledge of universals could be established. By what process can such knowledge be derived? The mere observation of people moving through space or emitting sounds would not appear to furnish grounds for concluding that they are engaged in a marriage ritual, a dance, or play, for example. Surely, one would not attempt to establish universals by locating precisely the same movement of the body in each culture.[55] This is to say that observation alone is not sufficient for developing such knowledge. And if knowledge of universals is not grounded in observation, what is its source? If the source lies within one's cultural meaning systems, surely the most reasonable answer to this question, then must we not reconceptualize the nature of the research inquiry? Rather than viewing the

---

[54] Some might wish to point to universals of language as grounding evidence for transhistorical lawfulness in human activity. To cite a major example, Greenberg (1966) lists 45 language universals. Among them, we find that, "In declarative sentences with nominal subject and object, the dominant order is almost always one in which the subject precedes the object" (p. 77), and, "If there are any gender distinctions in the plural of the pronoun, there are some gender distinctions in the singular also" (p. 96). Yet as these examples suggest, such uniformities are but poor support for a belief in the necessary patterning of human activity. In the first instance above we find not a true universal but a statistical tendency. Further, one rapidly recognizes the historical contingency of such universals by considering languages (either artificial or contrived) in which the rule is violated but communicative competency is retained. (In German one might make exclusive use of the S-O-V form as opposed to the more universally favored S-V-O sentence form and retain full linguistic efficacy.) As suggested by the second instance above, many of the so-called universals also seem to represent common modes of problem solving and not genetic necessities. People in virtually all climes may simply find certain solutions to practical problems more effective than others, and their languages thus acquire a family resemblance. To suggest that such resemblances were indicative of genetic programming would be similar to arguing that it is human nature for persons living near the water to employ means of flotation, or for all persons living in frigid zones to build shelters or dress warmly. People must surely share certain innate capacities in discerning classes of problems and reaching common solutions. In this case it seems clear that the innate mechanisms facilitate a broad array of possibilities, but fail to demand the endpoint. For a useful critique of Chomsky's (1968) concept of innate knowledge of language, see Cooper (1975).

[55] Murdock (1945) properly contends, "Universals are not to be found in a search for *exactly* the same habits around the world" (p. 142).

search for universals as a process of factual discovery, an objective assaying of "what there is," we must view it as the attempt to sustain a conceptual template while scanning immense variations in human activity. It is an activity of fitting one's preestablished interpretive network to a fluid, ever-unfolding sea of activity. Surely, by traditional standards of objectivity, this is a poor foundation on which to make truth claims.[56]

The second enigma besetting the investigator is closely related to the first. On the one hand, we have seen that the problem of building knowledge of universals is problematic; however, once an hypothesis has been established (by whatever means), on what grounds can one claim validation (or falsification) of the knowledge? To know whether one's theory is validated or not requires a set of correspondence rules enabling one to know when a given observation counts as support (or nonsupport). That is, the investigator must be capable of formulating rules connecting statements at the abstract level of universals with specific observables at various points in history. Without such correspondence rules, the concept of universals is without empirical content. Yet, if human activity is undergoing continuous change, if cultures develop novel patterns of action over time, then systems of correspondence rules are continuously threated by obsolescence. On what grounds is the reconstruction then to proceed? This tosses one again on the shoals of our initial problem of building knowledge. As will be demonstrated in the following chapter, there are impediments of intractable proportion blocking the route to the sound development of such rules. The linkage between modes of theoretical discourse and the particulars of daily life is itself historically contingent.[57]

---

[56] The position adopted within this section is far more congenial to philosophic nominalism than to realism, insofar as the former is committed to the existence of particulars while holding universals to be second order constructions. In effect, the present arguments place the burden of proof on those wishing to establish universals as matters of fact (cf. Armstrong, 1978). However, the present position is not to be equated with any form of nominalism that views person descriptors as standing in a one to one relationship with particulars, a point that will be clarified in the following chapter.

[57] Schlenker's (1974) argument for solution through abstraction holds that theories should be stated in sufficiently abstract terms that they can incorporate the particulars of any given historical period. However, theories of this sort are without empirical content. They fail to have predictive power, and remain essentially empty of implication until tied operationally to the specifics of a given era. One might, for example, imagine sets of alegebraic equations as forming the content-free abstractions. Such equations in themselves are unpredictive and uninformative. They gain power in each count only when tied to particulars, and it is on this level that the argument for historical dependency rests. For further criticism and commentary of Schlenker's position on abstraction see Godow (1976) and Hendrick (1976). For a general analysis of the incompatibility of seeking both generality and predictability in the same theory, see Thorngate (1976).

Defense through Reductionism

We may now explore one last line of potentially damaging defense. As we have argued, the prospects for developing objectively grounded principles within the natural sciences are far more optimistic than in the sociobehavioral sciences. However, it may be argued, given that the human body may conveniently be viewed as a physical system, its activities should prove amenable to natural science exploration. Exploration of the physical system should enable science to improve steadily in its capacity for prediction of human behavior. It is only a matter of time until the full range of human activity may be derived from more essential principles of chemistry and physics. Daily life may confront us with a highly complex and ever-changing array of behavioral particulars, but ultimately this array must be consistent with, and therefore amenable to, understanding through principles governing the physical system.

Despite the compelling quality of the reductionist argument, it is ultimately of little consequence. Several major difficulties emerge, the first of which is pragmatic. In particular, we must consider the implications of physical knowledge for establishing social knowledge. If we fully master the principles by which the nervous system operates, for example, do we position ourselves for the derivative understanding, prediction, and/or control of such common processes as verbal communication, gesturing, making and executing plans for a vacation, obtaining a divorce, or committing larceny? It would not appear so. The chief reason becomes apparent when we consider the analogy between the neurological system and the computer. The human system may form the analog to the basic hardware of the computer. Essentially, both systems serve to establish (1) the range of inputs or stimuli to which responses may be made, (2) the range of possible processing activities, and (3) the repertoire of available responses. In effect, both systems establish the *potentials* for action. Most importantly, however, in neither case does knowledge of the basic system tell us (1) which inputs will be made into the system, (2) which processes will be selected for employment (to the extent that these depend on the character of the inputs), and (3) which particular responses will be forthcoming on any particular occasion (to the extent that these depend on the events of the two previous stages). In short, knowledge of the "hardware" alone is insufficient to make predictions about the behavior of the machine on any particular occasion; such predictions inevitably depend on the data inputs and the selection of particular programs (or software).

It is in the latter domain that the arguments for historical change are most cogent. Inputs to the organism cannot be specified by an understanding of the physical processes alone. As we have also seen, the individual may be "programmed" to process information in an infinity of ways. Such programming is clearly susceptible to exogenous influences, and thus, largely beyond the bounds of physiological investigation. One may argue that this problem is in its most basic sense pragmatic. If control *could be* obtained over all inputs to the human being, including programming instructions, physical laws might ultimately yield reliable predictions concerning behavioral outcomes. However, that the problem is pragmatic does not make it less profound. Except in isolated circumstances, a society in which all inputs to the organism are systematically controlled is the stuff of science fiction. Further, variations in the manner of processing information (i.e., cognitive programming) would appear to depend on the entire history of the organism. To master the "software" would thus require control over social circumstances for the life span of the organism. To be sure, drugs may be injected for the activation or suppression of certain physiological systems, and certain behaviors may be controlled electrically or through cortical ablation. However, without complete control over the ever-emerging flux of daily life, the study of the human physical system could never furnish predictive or controlling power over the immense range of conduct of normal concern in the sociobehavioral sciences.

A second difficulty with the appeal to physiology is principled rather than pragmatic. However, its full explication must await treatment of person language in the following chapter. The critical problem is that of reductionism. Can a language for describing human action be reduced to the language of neurons? At the outset it is clear enough that knowledge of the physical system alone would be insufficient to derive forms of common understanding necessary for conducting daily affairs. That is, if scientists had complete knowledge of the brain, the hormonal system, the circulatory system, and so on, they could not derive an understanding of everyday terms such as shameful, fully qualified, legally separated, obligated, considerate, status conscious, and the like. Although they might be able to derive a system describing movements of the body, it is not to movements of the body that such concepts refer. In effect, the common vocabulary of person description does not generally appear to have physical referents. Without such referents, there is little means of reducing such description to the language of physics or chemistry.[58] Whether all person description thus invalidates the reductionist attempt, and the extent to which it must do so, will be of central concern in the next chapter.

In conclusion we find the sociobehavioral scientist confronted by subject matter capable of infinite variation, and in certain respects inclined against the steadfast perpetuation of singular pattern. Further, the very conduct of science in many respects may contribute to the alteration of existing patterns. Science is itself a life form that impinges on other domains of human activity. In this light the logical empiricist view of science to which the sociobehavioral sciences have largely been committed seems both misleading and unproductive. Alternative conceptions of the character and purpose of the sciences are required. Consideration of such alternatives must wait inquiry into the character of person description.

---

[58] As an analogy one might consider the relationship between the study of phonetics (speech sounds) and phonemics (the study of meaning systems). A full understanding of the former domain would not permit understanding of the latter and vice versa. The study of phonemics is required precisely because phonetic study is limited in implication.

Chapter 2

The Communal Basis of Social Knowledge

Thus far our analysis has failed to distinguish between experience and language, between the world as sensed and talk about the world. We have spoken about stimulus factors, psychological processes, and behavioral activities as if the words could furnish an adequate representation of events in nature. In effect, we have misleadingly treated words as if they could bear a point-to-point relationship to a prefashioned reality. Yet, if we extend our initial argument for continuous alteration of the experiential world, it becomes readily apparent that in adopting a language of entities the experiential world has been transformed. The language has created independent and enduring entities in an experienced world of prevailing fluctuation. It is the recognition of this discrepancy between experience and language that provides a useful departure point for examining the character of theory in the sociobehavioral sciences. As this analysis will demonstrate, the major functions assigned to theory within the traditional empiricist perspective are highly problematic. The attempt to establish theories subject to correction through observation would appear misguided. Yet, if the assumptions underlying the present analysis are extended, it is found that theoretical accounts of human action possess enormous potential that has been largely overlooked. When fully appreciated, these capacities may serve as the inspiration for a science of far greater potential than hitherto imagined.

The present chapter will primarily be devoted to the problem of identifying human action. On what grounds, it will be asked, can one determine into which theoretical category an observation falls, when one observation may be interpreted as the same kind of event as another, or when one can properly say that one event has ceased and another begun? As this analysis will attempt to demonstrate, that which is commonly viewed as theoretical description in the sociobehavioral sciences is fundamentally a product of linguistic convention and is neither guided nor corrected by behavioral observation. Observation thus serves as an excuse for theoretical work, but neither its source nor its sanction. This argument will lead us to consider the problematic character of various suppositions undergirding traditional inquiry in the sciences. Assumptions concerning the empirical evaluation of hypotheses, the accumulation of knowledge, and the application of theoretical principles will all be revisited. We shall then explore the basis for the particular dilemma in which the sciences find themselves. In this case it will be argued that because of the particular character of the subject matter, theoretical language of the kind that may be anchored by experience is virtually precluded in those sciences dealing with human behavior. Finally we shall begin to examine grounding assumptions for an alternative orientation to social knowledge. The positive functions of theory and research will be explored.

A Dilemma Solved and a Crisis Created

We may begin with a simple dilemma: If I see my good friends Ross and Laura approach each other at a social gathering, and Ross reaches out and momentarily touches Laura's hair, precisely what have I observed? What action has occurred before me? How am I to identify it? What does the action suggest about their relationship and the manner in which I should regard it if I wish to retain their friendship? Such dilemmas of identification are frequent; some might even conjecture that they are as numerous as there are discriminable social actions. And such dilemmas *must* be solved, it would appear, in order for us to carry on effective interpersonal relations. How, then, do we normally solve the essential problem of behavioral identification?

The problem is an especially vexing one, for it would appear that the action in itself can tell us little. Precise measurement might tell us that Ross' body moved at a certain velocity in a particular direction, that his hand moved away from the body for 1.62 seconds, and that his epidermis made contact at 9:02 P.M. with 23 strands of Laura's hair. Yet, with regard to social relations, this level of description is virtually uninformative. What does it *mean* to engage in such movements? Of what interpersonal significance is the behavior? This information cannot be derived from the observable movements themselves. No mensurational device, regardless of precision, can reveal the social significance (symbolic value) of the movements. And the capacity to carry on successful relations is virtually dependent on one's ability to label the activity with respect to its properties as a social signal. Clearly, then, if one is to identify the action in such a way as to "make sense," one must rely not on measuring instruments but on ancillary information. Principally, it would appear, we must turn to the social context in which the act is embedded in order to comprehend or identify it properly.

Let us consider first what may be termed the *retrospective context,* that is, the sequence of events occurring prior to the action in question. For example, if Ross informed me the week before that he was madly in love with Laura, this information might presumably solve my dilemma. I could confidently view his action as a signal of affection or attraction. If in later interaction with Ross I were to treat it as such, and not as a signal of derision, Ross and I might continue to maintain a smooth and unproblematic friendship. Yet, we must expand the retrospective context. Ross' announcement of the prior week may not be the only contextual constituent. Suppose I also learned from Laura several days ago that she told Ross she did not really believe he was a warm and affectionate sort of person. Rather, he was cold and unexpressive. At this point I might doubt the initial conclusion that the act was a signal of affection. Instead, I might consider it as an attempt on Ross' part to demonstrate that he is an affectionate, demonstrative person after all. In effect, the action is not quite so much an affectionate one as an act of self-presentation, or personal identification. Yet now consider the nasty bit of gossip to which I was just exposed: A mutual friend indicates that the night before the two lovers had a serious quarrel in which Laura accused Ross of being a prime egotist who believes the world revolves around him and that he can have any woman he likes. Laura has told him she wants nothing more to do with him; he is vulgar, insensitive, and intrusive. With this new information, I may wish to scuttle my previous interpretations and to reclassify the action. Perhaps it was an action of derision on Ross' part after all. Perhaps he was saying with this action that he, in fact, could have any woman he wanted, and that Laura would soon be his in spite of her abuse. Thus, to relate effectively with Ross at this point, it would be appropriate to treat the act as one of derision as opposed to attraction or self-presentation.

Yet, can one be so certain, after all, that derision is the proper identification of the action? Perhaps Ross was badly hurt by Laura's stinging accusation, and was making one last attempt to express his affection or to demonstrate finally that he was a most affectionate kind of person. More information is necessary to be confident. Thus far we have attended only to information within the retrospective context. We must turn for additional information to the *emergent context,* that is, to relevant events following the action in question. For example, immediately after the event I observe Laura breaking into a warm smile and gently caressing Ross' hand. Laura has clearly been touched by Ross' gesture, and feels contrite over the scolding she has administered. The stroking of the hair was a profound expression of affection after all. Or was it? Several minutes later, when I see Ross talking briefly with a friend, I notice that his posture and facial expressions are those of a man who is very proud of himself. I see him glance into a nearby mirror and smile contentedly to himself. Perhaps the gesture was not really an affectionate one, but Ross' final effort to present himself as a warmly expressive person. He is now quite pleased with himself that he has apparently succeeded. Ah, but the evidence is not yet complete. The following day I learn that later in the evening Laura asked Ross if she could borrow his car to run an errand. And, once the auto was in her possession, she scraped its body against a stone wall and thereupon abandoned the vehicle. Now the opaque becomes transparent. Laura saw that the stroking action was one of derision, yet treated it as an effective gesture in winning her love. This she did in order to gain Ross' confidence, whereupon she borrowed the auto in order to damage it, and thus achieve vengeance for the derisive action.

At last the dilemma appears to be solved . . . until the following week when Ross and Laura are spied in the park, speaking softly as they stroll arm in arm. . . .

From this turgid saga we may draw three propositions of substantial significance for both the processes of constructing theory and conducting human affairs.

1. *The identification of any given action is subject to infinite revision.* As we are exposed to events from both retrospective and emergent contexts, our manner of identifying the present action is subject to continuous modification. Theoretically, this process is without limit. This is initially so because the range of contextual indicators both past and present is without evident bounds. In the case of the retrospective context we must be prepared not only to account for all events in the lives of the individuals in question, but for all those events within the cultural history that bear on current meanings. For example, in the case of Ross' life, if we learned that he had been bitterly hurt in his last important relationship with a woman, we might have been less inclined to view the action in question as an expression of egoism (e.g., "I can have any woman I wish"). And, if we were to explore the natural history of the species to find that the male's touching of the hair of the female served as a mating signal, we might wish to reconsider all our previous interpretations. The emergent context is similarly without anchor point. The present action is subject to continuous redefinition as further events take place. As we saw, the final action cited in the present case, that of the couple walking happily together, appeared to throw the "ultimate definition" once again into jeopardy. Yet the latter event itself should scarcely be considered final. Nor are the future actions of the individuals in question the only ones bearing on the present definition. For example, if in light of later social history we learned that this particular era was one of great superficiality of emotional expression, we might retrospectively discount the sincerity of Ross' action. Perhaps it was simply a matter of artificial stylistics. We see, then, that the range of events relevant to the identification is without evident bounds.[1]

The potential for infinite revision of interpretation is dependent not only on the continuously unfolding range of contextual indicators, but on the unlimited possibilities for developing *intelligibility rules* linking contextual indicators to the event in question. To clarify, each event designated as a contextual indicator achieves this function by virtue of rules of agreement concerning the meaning of one event in relationship to a second. Ross' act of touching Laura's hair has no intrinsic relationship to his preceding proclamation of love. The proclamation bears on our interpretation primarily because of the widely shared rules in Western culture that encourage us to accept both proclamation and touch as signals of the underlying emotional state. Such intelligibility rules can be modified over time or be replaced by newly developed rules. For example, to many people it would seem nonsensical to argue that because Ross was weaned at an early age the act of touching Laura's hair was clearly one of devotion. There is no widely shared rule permitting people to employ the first event to interpret the second. Yet, within certain subcultures, and particularly those exposed to psychoanalytic thought, this connection is perfectly plausible. Through the development and elaboration of an alternative lan-

---

[1] Relevant is Heritage and Watson's (1979) attempt to demonstrate that participants in a conversation must frequently formulate what it is they have been saying as a way of attempting to settle on one of the many possible interpretations that may be made of their conversation.

guage of understanding, Freud succeeded in establishing intelligibility rules that enable the connection to be made and reinterpretation to occur. The limits to the range of possible intelligibility rules would appear to be those bounding the human imagination. In principle, any contextual indicator has the potential to be used in multiple ways in the service of interpreting or identifying any given action.

2. *The anchor point for any given identification is not fundamentally empirical, but relies on a network of interdependent and continuously modifiable interpretations.* This second proposition amplifies the first. As we see, there is no obvious way in which one can satisfactorily identify any given action *in itself.* The action in question does not furnish any empirical touchstone for proper identification. One is thus forced to consider the context of events both preceding and following. Yet, to extend the analysis, on what grounds are we to justify our use of the contextual indicators upon which we have placed our reliance? Are these not also actions the identification of which is problematic? In order to understand them properly, are we not forced once again into new contexts, both retrospective and emergent? For example, we were moved to interpret the stroking of Laura's hair as an expression of affection when we took into account Ross' previous declaration of love. Yet the declaration in itself is in need of interpretation. We must be certain that it is a declaration of real affection rather than a mere presentational attempt on his part to convince us of feelings he did not possess, for example, or perhaps an attempt at self-conviction, a whimsical gesture, or an act of self-deception. In order to determine which of the labels applies, if any, we are again driven to consider the ever-unfolding context of events both retrospective and emergent. What is Ross' previous history in making such statements? How casual are such statements within the culture more generally? What reasons might Ross have for convincing us of his ardor? What kinds of statements followed the present one? And so on. As we have seen, the range of indicators relevant to interpreting his statement, along with the range of intelligibility rules that might relate event and action, are without apparent boundaries.[2]

It follows readily from the preceding that events within these contexts are equally subject to the interpretive dilemma. Again we are cast outward by an ever-increasing expanse of events which are themselves in need of interpretation. In effect, we find that no single identification is fundamentally tied to a set of observables. Rather, the interpretation rests on a potentially immense array of interdependent interpretations. Further, any given interpretation is continuously subject to modification in light of a continuously altering context, and any event occurring within this array may wax and wane in its relevance as intelligibility systems evolve

---

[2] In a similar vein, Anscombe (1976) asks how one could correctly identify what an individual was doing if he were at one and the same time moving his arm up and down at the water pump, moving his muscles, casting a shadow, making clicking sounds with the pump, poisioning the members of the house into which the water is entering, and trying to rid the country of wicked leaders (the inhabitants of the house) so that better government will prevail. Is there one action, asks Anscombe, or as many as there are different descriptions?

over time. Thus, the contextual array cannot be viewed as static but as in continuous and reverberating motion.

3. *Any given action is subject to multiple identifications, the relative superiority of which is problematic.* Our third proposition extends the arguments developed in the preceding discussion. In the initial example, the touching of the hair, we took the perspective of a single observer of a given action. However, one may readily envision a wide range of observers, each of which differs in (1) the range of contextual events to which he or she is exposed, (2) the rules of intelligibility used to make sense of the present action vis a vis the various contextual indicators, and (3) the larger context of events and intelligibility rules upon which the immediately relevant context depends for its interpretive support. Given the ultimate lack of an empirical touchstone on which to rest any of these competing interpretations, we cannot easily argue for the superior validity of one as opposed to another.

One may contest this view on two grounds. First, it could be countered that an explanation based on multiple contextual inputs is superior to one that rests only upon a few. Yet, on closer inspection, this view is found to be without significant merit. At the outset, as the number of events believed relevant to a given identification increases in number, one does not move unproblematically toward clarity of definition. Rather, it would appear, one might anticipate increasing doubt in any given definition. As increasing numbers of events are considered, their contexts of interpretation appraised, and alternative intelligibility rules absorbed, confidence in any given interpretation might reasonably be expected to deteriorate. Thus, the most informed identification of any given action might be no identification at all. Although silence is philosophically defensible in this case, it does not enable one to solve the essential dilemma of ongoing behavioral identification. A second problem in seeking salvation through multiple indicators resides in the earlier argument that the number and range of events considered relevant to any given identification may vary from one individual to another. Thus, events that one observer views as particularly relevant to a given act a second observer may view as insignificant. As we have seen, many people would dispute the relevance of early childhood events to the proper definition of adult actions. Thus, one person's attempt to increase the number of contextual indicators may be another's exercise in inanity. Finally, since any given event may be subject to multiple interpretations, it should be possible for an observer to demonstrate how all events either support a preferred interpretation or are irrelevant to it. Once the individual has determined the plausibility of a particular interpretation, increasing the number of events lends no additional strength to the interpretation. With judicious selection of intelligibility rules it should be possible to employ almost any added event as support for the interpretation already secured. Adding new events as support for one's existing interpretation does not thereby increase its validity. Rather, it demonstrates the conceptual agility of the individual in generating coherence among interpretations.[3]

---

[3] The problem of defining standards of "correct" interpretation of written works has been of critical concern to historians, literary critics, religious scholars, and judicators. The major problem has been to make an intelligible case against cul-

The most powerful challenge to the argument for equivalidity of interpretation might be based on the claim that the *actor's* position is superior to any other. The actor, it can be argued, knows more about his or her own life history and about the internal state (intentions, motives, needs, etc.) giving rise to his or her actions. Actors essentially know what they are about, and if asked for a candid account in the present case, Ross could furnish the correct identification. Yet, when more fully considered, this rebuttal too is found unwarranted. First we find that it cannot be sustained on grounds that the actor knows more about his or her life history. This would be to argue that the actor's identification of his or her behavior benefits from taking into account a wider context of relevant events. Yet, as we have just seen, increasing the range of events bearing on a given interpretation in no way increases the validity of interpretation. In effect, as Ross considered more carefully the full complexity of his preceding life experiences, his cultural, historical, and genetic heritage, and so on, identification might only be rendered the more problematic. Or conversely, should he select an interpretation in advance of such considerations, he should be able to sustain it throughout the subsequent review.

More fundamental, however, is the problem of identifying internal states. Our analysis thus far has not revealed a means of objectively anchoring the identification of overt action. The problem is exacerbated manifoldly as we move to the covert level. In particular, we find ourselves without an intelligible explanation of how it is one might determine the accuracy of his or her identification of a psychological state. Several momentous problems confront the aspirant in this case. Four of these deserve special attention:[4]

---

tural and historical relativity of interpretation. In this author's view such a case has yet to be made. In the literary domain, one of the strongest advocates for validity in interpretation is E. D. Hirsch (1967). As he argues, accurate understanding is gained by reproducing for oneself the "object directedness" (or intention) of the author or speaker. However, Hirsch is unable to offer any convincing means for demonstrating superior validity (reproductive capacity) of one interpretation over another. He argues that interpretations that can explain more facts, and withstand attempts at falsification, are superior. Not only does this position fall heir to all the various attacks on neopositivism (see Chapter 1), but is rendered problematic by the present demonstration that with sufficient linguistic capability all interpretations can be elaborated so as to account for all descriptions of human action. Philosopher Maurice Mandelbaum (1967) has also attempted to combat relativism in interpretation in the case of historical knowledge. However, his account is premised on the assumption that behavioral events "possess an order, coherence and meaning independent of the activities of the human mind" (Mandelbaum, 1967, p. 205). Few would wish today to defend the position that meaning (to say nothing of order and coherence) are *independent* of the perceiver's interpretations.

[4] It should be noted that the present analysis also raises fundamental questions concerning the function and validity of "account taking" within the ethogenic tradition (cf. Harré & Secord, 1972). Early investigation in this domain was premised on the assumption that people can give accurate portrayals of the rules and intentions undergirding their behavior. Harré (1979) has since become more cautious

1. *Process in search of itself.* To say that one is "aware" of one's intentions, or can identify one's own psychological states more generally forces theoretical specu- lation to the border of incredulity. Such a conclusion would entail a concept of mind in which psychological process would be forced to turn reflexively upon itself and identify its own states. Rather than a single stream of consciousness, one would be forced into a mental dualism in which one level of process acted as a sensing and recording device and a second process furnished the stuff to be sensed and recorded. Such a dualism is sufficiently awkward that one is invited to consider how such a peculiar construction might have acquired such broad credibility. It seems most plausible in this case that the assumption of "internal perception" is a reconstructed form of the traditional metaphor for "external perception." The latter view is based on a subject–object dichotomy: A subject apprehending the character of the external object. The present model of "internal perception" ap- pears to represent a projection of this view into the covert world. A justification for this displacement is much in need.

2. *Internal perception as self-biased.* If one can perform the theoretical circum- locution necessary to justify an internal dualism, one faces a second problem of no less magnitude. Specifically, if both the sensing process and the sensed data are constituents of the same psychological structure, what safeguards (if any) could be placed over misperception? Could the processes one hoped to identify not hinder or distort the very task of identification itself? Freudian theory indeed posits just the kind of psychological processes that would obscure those entities (states, drives, intentions) one hoped to ascertain. On what grounds could one argue that internal processes do not operate in this way?

3. *The ambiguous properties of psychological states.* A third difficulty emerges when one inquires into the properties of mental states that would enable them to be identified. What is the size, shape, color, sound, or smell, for example, of an intention, a thought, a motive, a desire, a need, or a hope? Even the questions seem ill conceived. If one closes one's eyes, sits in silence, and turns one's attentions inward, what entities or states does one encounter? It is this fundamental ambiguity of internal states that stimulated the early work of Schachter and Singer (1962) on the social definition of emotions. Such work strongly suggested that the identifica- tion of emotional states is subject to wide-ranging contextual influences. Similarly, Nisbett and his colleagues (Nisbett & Bellows, 1977; Nisbett & Wilson, 1977) have argued that because of the opacity of mental states people must depend on socially derived scripts for determining the character of their internal world.[5] The extensive work on the reattribution of emotional states (cf. Harris & Harvey, 1975; Langer & Roth, 1975; Luginbuhl, Crowne, & Kahan, 1975; Mynatt & Sherman, 1975), along

---

regarding such possibilities. The present argument suggests that accounts are ill considered as mirrors of the subjective world. Their essential function would appear to be social (cf. Averill, 1980).

[5] Although the bases are disparate, the conclusions reached here regarding the social construction of psychological states bear a close affinity to those of Nisbett

with more extensive accounts of the social construction of emotion and motivation (Averill, 1980; Mills, 1940; Simon, 1973), further suggests that accounts of internal states are neither informed nor corrected by observation of the states themselves.[6]

4. *The infinite regress of recognition rules.* Finally, one is at a loss to understand how, if one did sense a mental state, it would be possible to identify a second instance of it. Typically it is said that recognition of this sort depends on the application of recognition rules. The rules essentially specify what properties must be present for one to conclude that a given state is being experienced. Thus, if one experiences the properties of "warmth," "pain," and a "pounding sensation," one could derive from the rules that an "alpha" state is being experienced. Anyone who experiences these qualities simultaneously can properly be said to experience "alpha." Yet it may be asked on what grounds is one to decide they have experienced the constituent properties of "warmth," "pain," and so on? One is thrown back once again on the logic of recognition rules. One knows one feels "warmth" when the following properties are present: (1) ＿＿＿, (2) ＿＿＿, (3) ＿＿＿ (one is at a loss to specify the particular characteristic of "warmth" in this case, lending further support to the preceding arguments for ambiguity.) Yet, should these qualities or properties be supplied, the question again emerges as to the process of recognition, and one is forced into an elaboration of third-order recognition rules. As is evident, one has entered into an infinite regress.[7]

As we find, then, one is left without any convincing account of how it is that an

---

and Wilson (1977). Interestingly, the Nisbett and Wilson case is constructed around evidence that deals with people's awareness of environmental effects on their actions, and not on their awareness of cognitive states themselves. As Sabini and Silver (1981) also add, ambiguity surrounds the concept of cognitive process, thus contributing to further confusion in understanding how it is one would make an inaccurate report of its character. Shotter (1981) is on target in viewing subjects' reports in the Nisbett studies as "avowels" or socially constructed "tellings" rather than reports on observations.

[6] Physiological psychologists may attempt to counter this thesis by arguing that research will one day become sufficiently advanced that one can differentiate among the physiological states that underlie what appear phenotypically as the same behavior, and can detect underlying states that may link phenotypically dissimilar activities. In this way, it may be maintained, one can truly identify the antecedent wellsprings of action. However, such a contention is shortsighted. There would remain the obdurate task of redefining brain state terms into the kind of vernacular that enable persons to orient themselves in daily life. Saying that an activity reflects a "lambda state" is virtually uninformative. In order to be applicable to daily life one must know whether "lambda" is, for example, an altruistic or a malevolent intention, and there are no logical or objective criteria for such a translation. As will later be demonstrated, motive language does not, in fact, refer to internal states but to behavioral effects or consequences. In this sense, the physiology of the actor is largely irrelevant to the descriptions of his or her activity.

[7] For an additional analysis of the problem of self-knowledge see Shoemaker (1963).

actor could "know" his own intentions, motives, or determining states. Yet to argue that all interpretations of Ross' action, or indeed any action, are equally valid is not simultaneously to argue that all are equally plausible. Thus, interpreting Ross' actions as "jumping in the lake," "performing a *jeté en l'air*," or "giving her a light" might seem difficult to justify in the present case. They are putatively untrue descriptions. Yet it is a mistake to confuse implausibility in such instances with empirical inaccuracy. Such descriptions seem implausible (or "untrue") because the rules of social usage do not immediately lend themselves to employing such terms in this case. However, given the common flexibility of such rules, it should be possible with further elaboration to justify their relevance in the present instance. For example, one might say of Ross, "Oh, oh, now he is really jumping into the lake," in referring to the likelihood that Laura will react angrily. Or it might be said, "This is really a jeté en l'air" in referring to the great risk Ross is taking in engaging in such an action after the argument of the preceding night. Or one might comment, "This action should really give Laura a light," in referring to the emotional arousal one believes will result. The critic might object that in each of these cases additional explanatory work was required in order to justify the descriptions. However, such work is required primarily because of the existing conventions of intelligibility in society. If in a slightly querulous condition, one might respond with puzzlement if it was said that the act was one of love, self-presentation or derision. Would a verbal declaration of two weeks ago really be a proper basis for labeling the act as love? Would a person truly attempt to demonstrate that he was an affectionately expressive person after being told he was an egotist? And is it terribly convincing, in fact, for one who has been called an egotist to validate the accusation? All are controvertible. In effect, the degree to which a given description seems empirically incorrect ("untrue") appears to be commensurate with the extent of justification required to demonstrate its propriety.[8]

---

[8] Putnam (1978) reaches conclusions similar to these, based on a different approach to the problem of interpretation. He asks how one would go about verifying a statement like "Jones is jealous." As he argues each piece of confirming evidence is subject to an indefinite number of alternative explanations. Thus, one could never justify the statement in isolation. One would have to verify an extensive psychological theory which covered a vast array of circumstances. Such a possibility seems impracticable. Putnam thus concludes that understanding others is carried out through a "practical knowledge" rather than through a scientific method (even an implicit one). As he argues, "If a historian reads documents, examines the public actions, reads the diaries and letters, how then does he decide 'Smith was hungry for power'? *Not* by applying 'general laws of history, sociology, and psychology' to the data as positivist methodologists urge he should! Rather, he has to absorb all this material, and then *rely on his human wisdom* that this shows power-hunger 'beyond a reasonable doubt' (as the court says). In effect, he uses himself as a measuring instrument; which is pretty much what Weber, Dilthey, etc. urged . . ." (p. 73).

Science and the Dilemma of Identification

We have now posed a dilemma, that of how one goes about identifying human action. We have attempted to solve this dilemma by elaborating on the manner in which both the retrospective and emergent context are employed in drawing tentative conclusions. In particular, it has been argued that in identifying any given action one must fall back on a network of understandings in the process of continuous erosion and reconstitution. Whether a given action counts as an exemplar of a given social category thus depends on the nexus of interpretive rules, along with one's skills in employing and modifying them in communicative exchange. We must now extend the implications of this discussion, for the several conclusions we have reached pose no small challenge to the traditional conduct of the socio-behavioral sciences. When the implications of these arguments are examined, the logical empiricist program for the sciences is placed in severe jeopardy. Consideration of alternative conceptions of scientific activity are invited. In the pages that follow we shall first explore several critical implications of the present line of argument. Particular attention will be given to the traditional assumptions of (1) empirical evaluation of hypotheses, (2) the accumulation of knowledge, and (3) the application of scientific principles. After then examining the underlying basis for the interpretive dilemma, we may finally consider the positive implications of the present arguments. Special emphasis will be given in this case to the function of theory and research in a reconstructed science.

The Assumption of Empirical Evaluation

Perhaps the chief assumption underlying contemporary behavioral research is that general theoretical statements are subject to empirical evaluation. During the hegemony of logical positivism the empirical validity of a given hypothesis was primarily linked to the frequency of its empirical confirmation. As we have seen, many feel this view has been supplanted by Popper's (1968) falsification doctrine. On this account a theory is scientific only to the degree that it can specify what range of observations would be incompatible with it, and a theory is proved superior as it withstands attempts at falsification. Yet, as also indicated, both "confirmationist" and "falsificationist" positions have come under heavy philosophic scrutiny in recent years (cf. Feyerabend, 1976; Kuhn, 1970; Laudan, 1977; Quine, 1951), and neither of these traditional criteria for theoretical evaluation is now viewed as wholly satisfactory. At the same time, it must be realized that most recent ("post-empiricist") critiques continue to struggle to substantiate some form of objectivity within the sciences. There remains a strong and understandable reluctance to sacrifice the doctrine of scientific objectivity. In this context, the present argument may prove disagreeably extreme. Yet, if we extend the line of thinking advanced above, we see that behavioral observations stand in a fundamentally equivocal relationship to theoretical statements. The extent to which any given datum either corroborates or falsifies a given theoretical statement is fundamentally ambiguous and open to continuous negotiation. Let us explore this conclusion more fully.

At the outset, there is little reason to believe that scientists stand in a privileged relationship to the world of social activity such that their capacity to identify behavioral particulars is in any way superior to others. Scientists, too, must inevitably rely on a series of intelligibility rules that, as we have seen, are without theoretical limit and permit continuous reconstruction. Initial indication of the magnitude of this problem in social psychology is encountered in most textbook or handbook treatments of major concepts within the discipline. In spite of the decades of research on such issues as attitudes, prejudice, attraction, personality, intelligence, aggression, altruism, person perception, morality, equity, and cognitive dissonance, for example, one can scarcely find either (1) a definition for any of these concepts about which there is widespread agreement or (2) a definition that ties the terms to concrete particulars or operations. Each of these fundamental theoretical terms remains in an ambiguous state, with various lines of research suggesting a wide range of possible meanings.[9]

However, let us examine the problem of empirical evaluation in more concrete circumstances. First, consider the most concerted attempt by psychologists to identify behavioral exemplars of given constructs, namely that of specialists in psychological testing. Such specialists have been most extensively engaged in the process of accurately sorting people's actions according to precise and objective standards. Measuring instruments are thus used to identify the intelligent, the schizophrenic, the authoritarian, the sex typed, the low in self-esteem, and so on. Yet, in light of the present arguments, we must give serious consideration to the possibility that *virtually any operational measure of any personal disposition may be*

---

[9]It is interesting to note that the present problems are not limited to scientists of human behavior, but pervade zoological and comparative study as well. Reynolds (1976) has, for example, compared the descriptive vocabularies used in various investigations of rhesus monkey behavior since 1942. As he demonstrates, there are numerous discrepancies in the descriptive categories used by various investigators. Some investigators may categorize monkeys as "fleeing," "playing," "making asocial gestures," "pushing," "molesting," or making a "haughty walk," while others do not recognize such activities as having an existence. As Reynolds (1976) concludes, "Students and their supervisors alike continue to work with behaviour types distinguished by verbal labels on a variety of bases and grouped together in a variety of ways. Problems of comparison between one person's work and another's still persist, and distortions of one kind or another have been part and parcel of all comparative work. . . . One discerns in some modern work an increasing trend toward "technological" rather than "human" data collection and mathematical rather than verbal methods of description, analysis and results. Does this signify the "new way forward" and if so how? Has the human mind with all its quirks been all but eliminated by the use of such techniques? Or are we merely being treated to a fashionable translation from one mode of attack to another? And if so, which is the more refined, which the cruder, which most productive of understanding, which the most able to generate and falsify hypotheses? I suggest we don't really know the answers to any of these fundamental questions, and rarely pause even to consider them for more than a moment" (p. 141).

satisfactorily treated as a measure of virtually any .lternative disposition. This is to say that any behavioral action purported to be an indicator of achievement needs, dominance tendencies, locus of control preferences, attitudes, a given level of moral development, and so on may be viewed as a potential indicator of virtually any other disposition. Responses said to be indicative of any one dispositional construct may in principle be interpreted as exemplars of almost any alternative construct.

The feasibility of this proposition may be demonstrated for anyone willing to engage in a demonstration that I have often employed with my own students. In this case students have been asked to select a trait that each felt was highly descriptive of self. A domain of approximately twenty different theoretical dispositions may thus be created in a class of twenty students. Students are then exposed to items from a standard measure from the discipline. For example, in one case students were furnished with four items from the widely validated measure of the *need for social approval* (Crowne & Marlowe, 1964). The students were not informed as to the source of the items, nor as to what they were purported to measure. Each student was then asked to demonstrate how *agreement* with each item would be an indication that one possessed the trait that each considered descriptive of him or herself. In effect, students were asked to explore the legitimacy of using each of the four items traditionally measuring approval needs as indicators of twenty different traits. In general, students experience little difficulty with such an interpretive task. In the present case, consider their approach to the standard item, "I always go out of my way to help others in trouble." As the scale constructors argue, agreement with this item is a way of gaining others' approval. It makes one seem very helpful and therefore likable. Yet for the subjects, agreement with this item could conveniently and compellingly be viewed as a measure of "conceit" (as one student maintained, people who agree with this item clearly have an overly high opinion of themselves), "patience" (the patient person would appreciate the needs of others and would spare the time to help them), "perception of internal control" (people viewing themselves as in control would believe that they could effectively help others), "hostility" (hostile people would help another because in giving help they are demonstrating the other's inferiority), and so on.

To press the illustration further, students have been asked subsequently to reconsider their interpretations of the response. Can they now find a legitimate reason for concluding that *disagreement* on each item is, in fact, a legitimate indicator of the trait disposition they have chosen for themselves? Although initially unsettled at such an ontological turnabout, students generally respond to this second challenge with a high degree of success. To reconsider the above example, people who indicated that they did *not* always go out of their way to help others in trouble were clearly indicating their "conceit" (it was argued in this case that conceited people are too self-centered to sacrifice themselves for others), "patience" (the patient person is one who believes that matters will work out over time and that one should not interfere with others' lives), "perception of internal control" (those who believe in internal control will assume that others are in the best position of helping themselves; to assert oneself in the situation is to threaten their control), and "hostility" (the hostile person dislikes others and therefore does not help them). All items selected for the illustration generally allowed such wide-ranging reinterpretations.

Of course, this is only a single illustration, and itself subject to many possible interpretations. However, the limits of the above assertion deserve careful consideration. What are the constraints, if any, on interpreting any dispositional response as both an indicator of any alternative disposition along with its opposite? If constraints can be located, what are their origin? For anyone concerned with the defense of an empirical science, such questions are of paramount importance.

If measuring instruments cannot in principle determine the objective identification of human action, what can be said of experimental outcomes? On what grounds can it be said that conclusions drawn from experimental data are objectively based? Experiments typically attempt to contrast the actions of groups of persons exposed to systematically varying conditions. However, in the preceding chapter it was advanced that people do not respond primarily to the raw physical circumstances of the experiment, but to the meaning of these circumstances for them. From this standpoint the concept of "systematically varied conditions" is thrown into jeopardy. The "experimental conditions" are subject to wide-ranging interpretation, and whether and to what extent the experimenter systematically manipulates the subjective realm remains moot.[10] Now if the stimulus conditions for an experiment are fundamentally ambiguous, and the subjects' actions "resulting" from exposure to such conditions are also quintessentially equivocal, we may conclude that the theoretical interpretation of experimental findings is highly vulnerable. There would appear to be no limits, save those of linguistic convention, over the ways in which experimental data may be described or explained.

In this context a second irreverent assertion may be ventured: *Virtually any experimental result used as support for a given theory may be used as support for virtually any alternative theory.* Of course, the practice of annexing the empirical support established by a competing theory by either demonstrating how the competing theory may be translated into one's own, or how the empirical results are consistent with one's own, has long been common within psychology. Early learning theorists were quick to show how competing theories, such as the psychoanalytic, could be translated into the more "scientifically" appropriate language of learning theory (cf. Dollard & Miller, 1950). Others have shown how both stimulus-response theories and cognitive–perceptual theories can subsume the empirical support gathered in the opposing domain. And, more recently, Lacey and Rachlin

---

[10] On occasion, investigators do express concern over whether their interpretation of the experimental manipulations agrees with those of the subjects. Curiosity is typically sated in such cases by asking subjects postexperimentally whether they agree with the experimenter's interpretation. Over and above the generalized hesitancy to probe myriad competing interpretations harbored by subjects, and the way in which questioning itself can create appropriate responses, it remains moot as to whether subjects' reports under such circumstances should be viewed as reports about their mental states. As the preceding analysis indicates, the assumption that people can furnish correct reports about the state of their concepts is highly problematic.

(1978) have argued that the claim of contemporary cognitive theorists for the superiority of cognitive theory over radical behaviorism (Fodor, 1975) is inappropriate. As they maintain, none of the behavioral exemplars cited by the cognitivists supplies unequivocal support for the cognitive orientation, nor are they beyond the explanatory power of the behaviorist.[11]

To explore the plausibility of a thoroughgoing intertranslation of empirical results, one may again replicate an exercise I have carried out on many occasions with advanced students in social psychology. In this case students are presented with a series of experimental findings typically used as grounding support for seven different theoretical models in social psychology (viz. dissonance theory, balance theory, Schachter's two-factor theory of emotion, self-esteem theory, social comparison theory, mere exposure "theory," and equity theory). At random, each student is given four of the seven results, and simultaneously furnished with four randomly selected theories from the above list. Each theory is randomly matched to one of the four empirical results (excluding the possibility of linking a given theory with the data originally gathered in its support). The empirical results themselves are presented in observation language, and the students are asked how the yoked theory could explain the findings.

This exercise again suggests that objective confirmation and falsification are chimerical goals for the science of human behavior. With few exceptions students accomplish the explanatory task with apparent ease. To consider only a single example, the Adams and Jacobson's (1964) classic demonstration of equity theory was described to one group of students. They were told that the subjects were to be engaged in a proofreading task and that in one experimental condition they were informed that they would be paid the wages of a well-trained professional proofreader. Other subjects were told that they would receive a rate of pay that was proper for someone with their skill. The first group subsequently demonstrated a higher degree of performance on the proofreading task than the comparison group. Initially such results were used to demonstrate that, when furnished with an inequitably high reward for their work, people would work more diligently in order to restore equity.

At the outset there was little difficulty in demonstrating how the result could be explained in dissonance theory terms. As Adams initially realized, equity restoration could be viewed as a form of dissonance reduction. However, the students also saw how the results were consistent with Schachter's theory of emotion (subjects who were told they were receiving higher pay were more aroused by the knowledge, and the arousal was channeled into task performance), balance theory (the task was positively linked to the high pay; the high pay was positively linked to the subject; thus, a positive link between the subject and the task could be forged by working hard), self-esteem theory (students receiving higher pay worked harder in order to support the positive image of themselves symbolized by the high-status wage), mere exposure theory (people are aroused by the unfamiliar, and the high-

---

[11] See also Gary Becker's (1976) claim that economic theory can be extended so as to account for *all* behavior.

pay condition was less familiar than the low-pay condition; high-pay subjects were thus more energized for the performance), and social comparison theory (subjects in the high-pay condition were induced to compare their performance with that of professionals, and performed more diligently in order to reduce the discrepancy between themselves and the target).

Again, one may argue that this illustration is itself subject to many interpretations. Yet it is difficult to discern what limits might be placed over the intertranslation of results from one theoretical domain to another. And, by the same token, one can well appreciate why there are virtually no critical debates among competing theories in social psychology that have yet been decided on the basis of empirical evidence. Virtually no theory has been discarded as clearly falsified, and no theory sustained because of the clarity of its support or its robust resistance to falsification. From the present perspective there is little reason to suspect future improvement in such matters.[12]

The Assumption of Accumulating Knowledge

As is readily apparent, if the validity of a given hypothesis about human behavior cannot readily be assessed through empirical means, there is little way in which the discipline can make good on the logical empiricist promise of accumulating knowledge. If one can neither verify nor falsify a given theory, then with respect to the traditional criterion of verisimilitude there is little way of emerging with superior knowledge. In this respect we must view the major generalizations contained within the traditional repositories of behavioral science knowledge, the text, the handbook, the research monograph, and the journal contribution, neither as objectively based knowledge nor the result of an empirical winnowing process. Rather, the theoretical conclusions or generalizations represent the commonly favored interpretations of the discipline. Research does not thus increase the empirical validity or predictive power of contemporary theory as opposed to its predecessors. Rather, it furnishes support for the "appropriate" or "reasonable" view of groups favoring a particular vocabulary of understanding or intelligibility system.

Two further implications of this line of thinking deserve attention. First, to the extent that empirical support is demanded, any theory may be sustained only as long as there is a community willing to interpret the data in its terms. The validity of the theory thus rests not on independently accumulated facts but on interdependencies among agents of interpretation. Should a vocal critic or a dissident minority take an interest in challenging the existing interpretations of the supporting evi-

---

[12] In light of the present analysis one can appreciate why even the most assiduous attempts to solve theoretical problems through empirical means are beset with frustrations. Consider Franz Samelson's (1973) comments on the concerted attempts of experimentalists to understand the risky shift phenomenon: "Over 10 years of ingenious manipulation of antecedent variables, almost 200 articles . . . filling our best journals, thousands of subject hours, and God knows how many dollars from how many research grants have not settled a limited 'empirical' laboratory problem, to say nothing about the issues of the 'real world' " (p. 1142).

dence, the theory can be debased. Thus, the social learning of aggression (cf. Bandura, 1973) is placed at risk when one begins to ask whether such actions as striking a plastic doll, delivering shock to a person upon instruction in a learning experiment, or selecting a gun or a tank for play as opposed to building blocks or toy cars are "truly" aggressive acts. After all, when children strike a plastic doll after viewing a model doing so, are their actions "aggressive," or are they simply copying the manner of *play* adopted by the model, demonstrating *acquiescence* to a socially desirable mode of responding, demonstrating *effectance,* manifesting *exploratory needs, showing off* to their peers, or any of a number of other equally intelligible possibilities? Similar questions can be raised about virtually any other measure of aggression. Thus, the viability of the social learning theory of aggression does not ultimately rest on "the data" collected on its behalf; rather, it depends primarily on the capacity of the theorist to interpret a series of actions in a way that will be agreeable (or at least, not disagreeable) to members of the relevant subculture.[13]

Second, it is important to consider the inherent tendency toward conservatism in sociobehavioral research implied by the present arguments. When any given research study is submitted for professional review, one of the major criteria by which it is typically evaluated is in terms of the availability of *alternative explanations.* Are there means of explaining the results other than those preferred by the investigator? If such alternatives are located, they are often used as grounds for rejection. As commonly argued, the research does not render unambiguous support for the underlying hypothesis. Yet the task of locating alternative explanations is clearly one in which the dilemma of behavioral interpretation is paramount. Essentially the evaluator asks whether there are alternative interpretations of the actions (constituting either the independent or dependent variables) that threaten the interpretation favored by the investigator. As the present analysis indicates, the number of alternative interpretations of any given action is virtually unlimited. All action may be viewed as fundamentally ambiguous, and open to a wide variety of interpretations, no one of which is objectively superior.

In this light the fact that many investigations do succeed in passing the crucible of the "alternative explanation" becomes a matter of puzzlement. Ruling out cases in which the evaluator harbors vested interests in the favored interpretation, along with cases of mental lassitude, why do some investigations pass muster and others fail? At least one compelling possibility is that those investigations supporting the commonly accepted intelligibility systems within the discipline will be favored in

---

[13] The implications of these arguments for the often-repeated admonition that what psychology most deeply requires is a full and proper taxonomy should be clear. No such taxonomy can or should be fixed in place. To the extent that people can continue to envision new functions or goals for human activity, such a taxonomy would always remain incomplete. Any new goal becomes a candidate for entry into the taxonomy, and with careful and intensive negotiation could principally be extended to cover virtually all observations. To the extent that any given taxonomy became fixed, the range of understandings that the science could make available would be concomitantly circumscribed.

the critical assessment over those that do not. Should the investigator's interpretation seem at odds with common sense, with what "any rational scientist" would conclude, then the research becomes a prime target for rejection. It becomes virtually incumbent on the evaluating agent, as a representative of a sane profession, to point out the "obvious alternative" interpretation. Deviant interpretations are thus relegated to oblivion. This rejection may be accompanied by a sense of self-righteousness, buttressed as it is by a view of proper scientific procedure. We now see that this view is a misleading one and that if steadfastly applied, little if any psychological research could pass muster. As it now functions, the review process generally ensures that the scientific literature will not deviate markedly from "what every reasonable scientist" already knows.[14]

The Assumption of Application

A third assumption central to the logical empiricist tradition is that behavioral theories, when properly corroborated, may be used for widespread social good. They may be employed in widely varied settings for purposes of prediction and control. Cartwright's (1978) tribute to the seminal work of Kurt Lewin captures the assumption, both as voiced by Lewin and as widely shared today:

> Lewin's treatment . . . was premised on the assumption that every field of science must be primarily concerned with theory, since it is theory that illuminates the causal structure of the empirical world. He (Lewin) then observed that, in social psychology, theory does more than advance knowledge, for it also provides the sort of understanding required for the solution of social problems. (p. 170)

It is largely on this basis that a common distinction is made between "pure" as opposed to "applied" social psychology, the former ostensibly generating sound principles of human interaction, and the latter making derivations from such prin-

---

[14] As this discussion should make clear, attempts to establish the objective validity of the historical arguments outlined in Chapter 1 are problematic (cf. Wolff, 1977). Because the relationship between descriptive terms and ongoing activity is open to continuous negotiation, one could not draw unambiguous conclusions with respect to whether change had occurred or not. For example, if one wished to test an hypothesis concerning task performance across temporal periods, one would confront the problem of determining what constituted task performance in a given instance. Since virtually all human activity (or conversely, no activity) can, with sufficient conceptual agility, be seen as "task performance," whether one believes such performance waxes or wanes over time is not an empirical matter but a matter of conceptual application. Seemingly stable empirical findings could be shown to be tapping different motivational (intentional) bases; unstable findings could be shown to reflect the same motivational base. This is also to point out the rhetorical rather than validating function of the research support employed in Chapter 1. However, the more general historical argument can be rested on an objective base in the traditional sense. Observations of the human body in continuous and infrequently recurring motion can be validated on traditional empiricist grounds.

ciples in solving ongoing problems. Too, because this model casts the pure scientist in the role of "fount of knowledge," while the practitioner becomes the "exploiter of knowledge," the latter has generally failed to acquire high professional status within the discipline.[15]

It seems clear that the traditional dualistic model of a pure and an applied science has outlived its value in the case of the sociobehavioral sciences, and must be replaced with an alternative conception (cf. Gergen & Basseches, 1980). However, it is useful to consider briefly the problem of application in light of the interpretive dilemma posed above. As we have seen, theories in psychology do not rest on unambiguous evidential grounds; rather, when empirical support has been garnered for a theory, it can remain "support" only as long as there is a willing cartel to support a line of interpretation. Further, as we have seen, because of the inherent ambiguity of human action, it is exceedingly difficult to furnish empirical definitions of key theoretical terms, that is, linkages connecting theoretical terms with ongoing conduct. In effect, then, *the theorist furnishes the practitioner with a set of abstractions for which there are no unambiguous particulars.* There is no clear means of knowing how the theoretical terms may be linked to the ongoing processes in which the practitioner is immersed, and thus, no means of knowing how effective predictions can be made.[16] If the practitioner is intent on "application," he or she must locate events that seem credibly related to the abstract terms. This search inevitably relies on the practitioner's inside knowledge of the common patterns of action and reaction within the application setting. In applying the theory, then, the practitioner is fitting the abstract theory to personal knowledge that he or she already possesses. The theory does not in this case furnish new knowledge; it primarily furnishes intelligibility for what is already known.[17]

---

[15] As Maslach (1975) has described the traditional view of application within social psychology, "Intervention is less prestigious than the purity of higher intellectual thought: 'Brilliant minds like ours should only be concerned with new ideas and new theories—their application should be left to the technicians.' . . . To the purist the practitioner is usually viewed as either a prostitute or a parasite. The prostitute is one who sells his or her knowledge and skills to the highest bidder. . . . The parasite is a consumer rather than a producer of knowledge. He or she takes the research findings of other psychologists, uses them in some sort of applied project, and personally profits from such use" (p. 240).

[16] Along similar lines Deutsch (1975) has said: "Social psychology as it now exists, is a peculiar discipline; it has much to say in general but little to say in particular. Many of us believe we know a good deal about how abstract man will behave in abstract situations but we know very little about how particular men will behave in a particular situation" (p. 8).

[17] See also Max Weber's (1949) discussion of the otiose character of nomological laws when applied to particularistic circumstances. As he maintains the choice of which situation and in which sense a general principle is applied to a concrete circumstance must be value guided. As Habermas (1971) has stated from a different perspective, "general interpretations do not make possible context-free explanations" (p. 273).

To illustrate, let us suppose an industrial psychologist in a manufacturing concern is given the task of increasing worker performance. Because many studies within the realm of equity theory (cf. Walster, Walster, & Berscheid, 1978) suggest that the theory should be relevant to such problems, this theory is selected for application. The theory maintains that by increasing worker rewards over what they believe to be equitable, they might increase their performance in order to achieve equity. How is this abstract theory to be realized within the factory setting? What constitutes an inequitable "over-reward" in this situation? The theoretical term itself stands mute. Should the workers be given tickets to the zoo, fresh salad during coffee breaks, new heels for their shoes? These possibilities are no less favored by the theoretical term than is a raise in salary.

One may rebut this line of argument by suggesting that the psychologist consult the workers themselves on the matter. They should be able to specify what "over-reward" means in this context. However, one again confronts the problem of negotiated interpretation, for in order to answer the question, the workers must know what the psychologist means by over-reward. The term itself is hardly free of ambiguity. The theory does not specify an operational definition for the term, thus preventing the psychologist from furnishing a referent. The term can only be defined, it would appear, by virtue of its use within the theory. Over-reward is that which causes one to increase performance to achieve equity. In effect, the worker is then asked what could he or she be given by the management that would increase productivity. At this level we see that the general theory has not served as an instrument for prediction and control, but as a device for motivating the practitioner to activate the forms of knowledge that are already possessed.

Descriptive Language: From Neurons to Nurturance

As we see, the interpretative dilemma poses fundamental and far-reaching problems for the traditional attempts to test hypotheses, accumulate knowledge, and enhance prediction and control in applied settings. Before examining the constructive implications of the present arguments, we must explore more thoroughly the particular condition of the sociobehavioral scientist. One may be inclined at this point to argue that the problems confronted by investigators of human conduct are no different in principle from those experienced by natural scientists. Theories of chemistry, physics, and biology also stand in an ambiguous relationship to the entities under study; such entities do not appear with labels attached, and they may be interpreted in a wide variety of ways. Surely this is the implication of Quine's (1960) demonstrations of the indeterminacy of reference and of Wittgenstein's (1963) analysis of the contextual dependency of language use. Yet, so the argument might proceed, these sciences have also achieved immense success. Their by-products are everywhere in evidence and have vitally enhanced the quality and duration of human life. Thus, although the interpretive problems outlined above are surely very sticky, the sociobehavioral sciences might reasonably continue to model their activities on those of the natural scientist.

Although such arguments offer substantial comfort, their fruits would appear ill gained in the present instance. First, if the problems of the natural scientist are as severe as those developed above, either a new account of natural science achievements is demanded, or the assumption of natural science progress must be challenged. To be sure, both of these inquiries have been pursued within recent years. In the case of alternative accounts of scientific progress, for example, Feyerabend (1976) has argued that advances in the natural sciences do not depend on any of the procedural rules advocated by traditional empiricist accounts (viz. deduction and empirical test). Feyerabend's solution in this case is to recommend methodological anarchy. Others such as Kuhn (1970) and Laudan (1977) have raised far-reaching questions concerning the character of progress itself. It remains moot as to whether natural science theories have demonstrated progression over the centuries; theories have been discarded, but the superiority of their replacements in terms of correspondence with evidence remains undemonstrated. To be sure, modern technology enables humans to achieve ends heretofore unimagined. Yet the extent to which these advances depend on accretions in theoretical accuracy remains to be established.

However, it is in neither of these directions that the present analysis will press. Rather, there is important reason to believe that the problems faced by the sociobehavioral scientist are of a different magnitude than those confronted by most natural scientists. In particular, there appear to be means of developing empirical constraints over theoretical language in most natural science domains that are not generally available in the case of human conduct. As we shall see, an analysis of the problems confronted in the two domains suggests that the sociobehavioral sciences are essentially nonempirical. That is, theory within this domain is neither engendered, stimulated, sustained, corroborated, nor falsified by observation. Justification for this presumptive conclusion is obviously necessitated.

We may begin by considering the grounds by which theoretical statements can ever be corrected or verified by observation. Essentially theoretical constructions are linguistic performances, and outside of social convention or aesthetic preference, there would appear to be little reason for employing one language form as opposed to another on any given occasion. On this account John Smith could justifiably claim that he could "fly" on the basis of his capacity to jump five centimeters off the ground. The only clear grounds by which such an account could be challenged is that of social convention. Others can argue, "No, you cannot fly by our standards; that particular jump is not what we call flying." In effect, the theoretical proposition that "John Smith can fly" cannot be verified or falsified unless one is willing to enter into the language conventions of a particular group.[18]

We may push further, however, to ask how it is that participants in a given language community can reach accord with regard to Smith's claim. Without acceding to logical positivist conceptions of meaning or truth, it is here that one must grant to the positivists the importance of ostensive definition. That is, by using linguistic

---

[18] Also see Donald Campbell's (1973) analysis of word–object relations and the limits of relativity in the language of observables.

terms to refer to a range of observables, and restricting the use of the terms to these conditions, a given community can develop a linguistic convention that will enable them rapidly to determine through observation whether others are employing the term properly. In this sense they may justifiably say of Smith, "The proposition that you can fly is incorrect." They may do so because his performance does not fall within the range of observables to which the term "fly" is typically used within the community. In this sense, theory can be corrected or verified through observation. If Smith joins the community of language users, he will readily discern that he cannot fly, but birds and Boeing 727s can do so.

Let us further inquire into the grounds for ostensive definition. What must be the case regarding the observable world in order for conventions of denotative language to develop? It would appear that a minimal requirement would be the availability of *continuing or recurring properties* available to public scrutiny. Thus, for example, we may establish the meaning of the term "automobile" by referring to relatively enduring patterns of experience. (These patterns might commonly be referred to as "wheels," "engines," "seats," and so on.) Broad agreement may be reached primarily because the relative stability of the experiences allows them to be recorded in memory and shared with others. To be sure, there may be generalized unclarity with respect to what constitute the components of the proper automobile. People may disagree with respect to which components or characteristics are required before an object may be called an auto (e.g., Must the object possess an engine to count as an auto, and if the engine were a jet, would we continue to call the entity an auto?). In this sense all object words may include a "fuzzy set" of constituents. Yet, for most practical purposes, a social group may develop agreement as to what constitutes an automobile, an embryo, velocity, temperature, and the like by a pointing procedure. One may single out an observable composite and announce, "That's what I mean by a temperature of 68 degrees, and if you will agree to use that term whenever the gauge is at this level we can proceed to agree for most practical purposes as to when a temperature of 68 degrees is present and when it is not."

Let us consider, in contrast, experiences that are either momentary or nonrecurring. From the present standpoint, such experiences are poor candidates for establishing referential meaning. We have an impoverished vocabulary with which to speak of variations in ocean waves, for example, primarily because any given wave formation is of brief duration and nonrecurring. The relevant experiences do not remain sufficiently "fixed" that we can be certain when we have an exemplar of a given category and when we do not. We can speak of such gross properties as "wave height" or "white caps" because both terms refer to properties that are relatively fixed or recurring. In the same way we can speak of "candle flames" in general, while we do not have agreeable classes of flame types; variations in flames occur so rapidly and with such little recurrence that scant agreement could be reached in matching terms with experience.

It is within this context that we must confront the problem of describing human behavior. Let us consider two continua of experience, the first representing variations in the endurance and the second in the recurrence of phenomena. Viewing these continua in tandem we see that for events approaching the upper end of both continua (enduring for lengthy periods and continuously recurring), ambiguity in identification becomes minimized, while events toward the latter ends of the continua are subject to a high degree of confusion in identification (if not its complete inhibition). Of cardinal significance, it is clear that the vast share of human activity falls toward the latter end of the continua. Human activity furnishes the observer with a continuous and ever-changing array of experience. Eyes, facial muscles, limbs, voice, fingers, torso, and so on may all move simultaneously, and stability of pattern may be retained for only the briefest instant. Further, few patterns are recurrent. Seldom does an individual furnish others with precisely the same stimulus confluence over time. On what grounds is the process of ostensive definition to proceed?

To clarify further, consider the problem of assigning linguistic labels to the actions of a machine. If the machine possesses a single lever the movements of which are circumscribed to a single vertical plane and a single velocity, one would encounter little difficulty in employing ostensive identification to speak of the machine's actions. At t_1, it might be said, the lever was at 48 degrees, moving in a descending direction and at t_2 it was at 98 degrees and in ascent. Such characterizations of the lever's actions could yield a high degree of agreement within a language community, and enable the participants to rule on the accuracy or inaccuracy of a subsequent description through observation. However, let us now increase the number of levers and allow each to move in multiple planes at multiple speeds. As we do so, verbal characterization of the machine's state during any given period becomes increasingly difficult. Given six levers each moving in six planes would require at least twenty-four terms (specifying lever, plane, speed, and direction). Each microsecond's duration might require an additional description of the same magnitude. As can be seen, communication among people regarding the continuous state of the machine would become quite arduous.

Now let us consider a machine with no precise boundaries among parts, all sectors of which might move at varying speeds through all planes. Further, the various confluences of movement are seldom duplicated. At this point we find that both the potential and the utility of ostensive definition are fully obscured. The infrequent recurrence of any particular configuration discourages the attempt to develop such definitions at the outset. What, it may be asked, is the utility of such definitions if there will be no subsequent occurrences to which they will apply? Further, because of the compounded characteristics of the configurations, any attempt toward precision in descriptive terminology would rapidly tend toward Byzantine complexity. And, as a result of the continuous alteration in configuration, one would be at pains to determine precisely when one configuration was terminated and another begun. Finally, it would appear that the demands placed upon the human system for storing and retrieving a vast, complex, and seldom repeated descriptive language are simply beyond its capacity. The number of referential units required to describe all movements, sounds, and smells of a single subject in a single minute of a single experiment might well approximate the storage capacity of a small computer. Given the continuous alteration in configuration, what goal might possibly be achieved in attempting ostensive description?

Even in cases where behavior patterns are highly circumscribed and a strong emphasis is placed on replicability, it is often very difficult to tie descriptive terms unambiguously to action patterns. Perhaps the most concerted effort of this variety has been made not by behavioral scientists but by choreographers. In spite of the long-standing attempt to formalize the dancer's movements in classical ballet, it remains exceedingly difficult for a choreographer to communicate his or her conception other than by direct demonstration. Verbal description of the choreography is seldom sufficient to enable others to carry out the dance as initially envisioned. Attempts at a formal language of dance movements (e.g., Laban notation) have been constructed, and can enable others to approximate roughly the original choreography. However, even in this case it is impossible to communicate precisely how the dancer is to execute an *arabesque* or move from a *jeté* to a *tour en l'air*. In modern dance, where a premium is placed on developing new forms of movement, an easily adopted language of description has proved an insoluble task. In this case, repetition is infrequent; with neither constancy nor recurrence in movement, precise classification is exceedingly difficult to accomplish. The conduct of daily life is a far closer approximation to modern dance than classical ballet.

It is at this point that the grounds for the enigma of behavioral identification with which we began this chapter become transparent. The identification of Ross' hand moving through the air to make contact with Laura's hair cannot be identified through observation of the act itself because the vocabulary of ostensive terminology for person description is so impoverished. Because of the intractable difficulties of developing such a language, one's capacities for identification through observation are delimited. And, as we saw, as one moves to the context of actions surrounding the conduct in question, one generally fails to improve the capacity for identification by recourse to observation. Because there is little way in which any given characterization or description can be judged correct or incorrect by virtue of observables, continuous renegotiation of accounts may be considered the rule.

The Emergence of Motive Language

Given the necessity of a language for describing persons, and the enormous impediments to developing a denotative language for such purposes, on what grounds is person description to proceed? How can we account for the immense repository of person descriptions within the culture? Closer inspection suggests that this latter achievement depends on abandoning concern with overt movements as such and focusing rather on their effects or results. What general end is achieved by this or that physical movement? Thus, for example, in saying that "Marya is brushing her hair" we are not describing a particular set of physical movements per se, but an end point of these movements, namely the brushed hair. Marya might thus engage in an infinitely varied array of actions, but if their accomplishment were always the same (i.e., the well brushed head of hair) the phrase "brushing the hair" would be an appropriate designata. By the same token, precisely the same physical movements designated as "brushing one's hair" on one occasion might be referred to as "brushing the fly away" on another. It is not thus to the movement themselves that such terms refer but to their accomplishments. In the same way, if a person's activity results in the improvement of another's condition, the activity eventuating in this end may be designated as "help" or "support." If the composite activities carried out by the individual results in one's receiving pain, this end point may be employed to label the general tendency of the other's action as "aggressive."[19]

This is not to say that person descriptors do not contain important information. That is, they do furnish an indication of the describing agent's vocabulary of end points. If a man is described as "argumentative," we know nothing of his precise activities. However, we do know that many of his activities result in what the agent of the characterization designates as an argumentative end point. Similarly, to say that a person X is trying to kill Y tells nothing about X's precise movements; however, the description does indicate that as a collection their end point is what would be termed the demise of Y.

Yet shifting the focus from the transient particulars of ongoing activity to its accomplishments does not fully solve the problem of person description. The results of an actor's conduct can be described without reference to the actor him or herself. One may say in the above examples, "I am helped" or "I am put in pain," and thus refer to the results of another's activity with reference to the other's actions. In effect, a vocabulary of end points would not in itself solve the problem of describing persons (other, perhaps, than one's own subjective states). Required, then, is a means of solidifying a relationship between the actor and the designated end points, of using the vocabulary of end points to describe the actor. This task would appear to be achieved by the simple mechanism of shifting the designation of the descriptive term from ends to means. That is, the vocabulary of ends is used *as if* it referred to the actor producing the effect. Through this relocation in designatum, "I was helped" as a description in the language of ends becomes

---

[19] Along similar lines Dennett (1978) has pointed out that predictions about physical objects are often made on the basis of either their design or their physical properties. However, as physical objects become highly complex, as in the case of complex or sophisticated machines, these common predictive modalities cease to function adequately. As he says: "The best chess-playing computers these days are practically inaccessible to prediction from either the design stance or the physical stance; they have become too complex for even their own designers to view from the design stance. A man's best hope of defeating such a machine in a chess match is to predict its responses by figuring out as best he can what the best or most rational move would be, given the rules and goals of chess. . . . Put another way, when one can no longer hope to beat the machine by utilizing one's knowledge of physics or programming to anticipate its responses, one may still be able to avoid defeat by treating the machine rather like an intelligent human opponent" (Dennett, 1978, p. 5).

"he helped me"; "I was put in pain" becomes "he aggressed." Through such a displacement in referent the language comes to function as description of persons in motion. The result is a language that appears to describe observable actions but does not in fact do so.[20]

This alteration in the descriptive locus is of critical significance in understanding the character of person description and the limits and potential of the sociobehavioral sciences. The by-product of this relocation is essentially the emergence of a new domain of discourse. For convenience we may term this a domain of motivational discourse (although for various purposes one might substitute such terms as intentional, telic, dispositional, or directed state). This result would seem a necessary derivative of the preceding arguments. As we have seen, the normal vagaries of human conduct do not lend themselves to the development of a vocabulary with observable referents. Thus, when end-state terms are reassigned to the person, they have no obvious referent. In saying of a person, "he is eating," "he is friendly," or "she is hostile," one is not referring to the specific spatiotemporal movements of the target. Rather, one transcends the particulars of the ever-changing surface and treats the descriptive terms as if they referred to internal tendencies or motives. Thus, the ostensible referents for person descriptors generally lie "within" the

---

[20] One may wish to object to the thrust of this analysis on the grounds that end points of activity do meet the criteria of intersubjective agreement. People can all agree on what the act achieves, even if they cannot agree on the underlying motive or intent. We may all agree that a given set of movements culminates in the "buying of a car," although we cannot ascertain what the individual himself is "trying" to do in this instance. However, this rebuttal falters on several counts. First, there is no apparent means by which end points can be clearly differentiated. By what means is one to distinguish when an end point has or has not been reached (or was in the process of being reached when the action was terminated)? How is one to dissect the ongoing stream of action and announce, "Ah, now here is an end point"? To specify end points, one must freeze the ongoing process, and there are no objective guidelines for carrying out such a task. Second, and closely related, is the problem of means versus ends. Any action that figures as an end point in one account may serve as a means in an alternative account. People do not generally describe the various end points achieved by the hand carrying the spoon to the mouth (viz. "It has now achieved an altitude of 14 centimeters from the plate," "It has now covered an arc of 62 degrees") because all such movements are counted as means toward the end point of eating. Third, the specification of end points is highly dependent on the social conventions governing what it is that people are reasonably about. We do not have a rich vocabulary dealing with movements of the spoon while eating primarily because it is not reasonable that people would be trying to move their spoon 14 centimeters from the plate or covering an arc of 62 degrees. They are simply eating. In effect, the specification of end points is derived from the more general "grammar of motives" operating in the culture at the time. Finally, the specification of end points is frequently reliant on the observer's evaluation of what the action achieves for him or her. The same action may thus be seen as "aggression" or "defense," depending on whose ox is gored. Such disputes cannot be settled by recourse to observables.

individual. It is this inner world that is typically granted the power to originate and control the goal-directed actions of the person.[21]

In effect, we confront a language of person description that does not refer to observables but to hypothetical dispositions or motives within the person. The language of motives operates essentially as an autonomous domain of discourse, which may be used at will to account for virtually any observable configuration of human activity. In the same sense that students could quickly discern how wide-ranging verbal statements could be the result of a diversity of motives, human movements approximate blank slates upon which others can carry out exercises in discourse. Thus, today we may speak of behavior as aggressive, altruistic, intelligent, loving, or dominating chiefly because contemporary linguistic practices enable one to speak as if people possessed motives of this variety. We cannot easily speak of behavior as meiotic (seeking understatement), ophidian ("snakist"), chartering, diuretic (seeking to promote the secretion of urine), flexional (seeking to be bent), four-seeking, and so on primarily because it is not intelligible within contemporary conventions to speak as if people possess such motives. In broad terms, it may be said that the "contents of psyche," those powers, motives, intentions, needs, wants, urges, tendencies and so on, that are endowed with the capacity to direct human behavior have no ontological status, but appear to do so because they are objectified through linguistic practice. They are essentially reified by-products of human communication practices.[22,23]

---

[21] It is for this reason that person descriptions are virtually interchangeable with accounts of underlying motivation. For example, to see an infant "reaching" for a bottle of milk is at once to specify an end point of the action *and* its intent. (One can scarcely "reach" if one does not have this end point seemingly in mind.) Or, in different form, it might be said of the infant's actions, "Look, he wants milk." The descriptive termonology now functions as a motivational term. In short, virtually all dispositional terms simultaneously designate an end point and a motive or energizing source. The implications of this argument for the long-standing debate over whether reasons can be viewed as causes of behavior (cf. Ayer, 1967; Davidson, 1963; MacIntyre, 1970) as opposed to the position that reasons are only logically and not causally related to behavior (cf. Louch, 1969; Melden, 1961; Peters, 1958) is worthy of note. On the present account when a behavior is named (viz. reading, playing, helping), one has simultaneously specified its motive or reason. It is superfluous at this juncture to multiply ontological levels; because the descriptor stands simultaneously for both goal-directed behavior and intention does not warrant the positing of two realms of activity, the behavioral and the intentional. To ask whether a reason could have caused the action is to mistake one's conception of the goal of the action for its causal (or intentional) source.

[22] Embedded in the present thesis is perhaps the most significant argument against the possibility of physiological reductionism in psychology (see Chapter 1). If the language of person description inherently refers to internal dispositions (motives, intentions, etc.), then the physiologist's contribution to understanding human action is vitally dependent on the capacity to link specific physiological conditions to particular dispositional states. This has indeed been the hope of many neobehaviorists attempting to anchor various hypothetical constructs (e.g., drive, drive reduc-

It is the creation of an "inner world of motives" through the relocation of reference that enables us to appreciate a family of frequently recurring distinctions over the past four centuries of Western thought. As argued in widely disparate contexts, it is exceedingly difficult (if not impossible) to describe or explain human behavior without recourse to an "inner realm." For Descartes, it seemed possible to account for most animal activity in terms of the physical system. Yet, while a system of physical reference was sufficient to describe animals, it did not seem adequate on the human level. For Descartes, humans seemed unique in their capacity for "reasoned" action. In effect, a living human could be defined in part by the capacity for mindful decisions. A similar argument is captured in Kant's distinction between *noumena* as opposed to *phenomena,* the former pointing to action based on ratiocination and the latter to responses determined by environmental conditions.

More recently such distinctions have come to figure in discussions of the character of the sociobehavioral sciences. Dilthey, Weber, Rickert and many others have argued that the special feature of "the human studies" is their "concern with a world which has meaning for the actors involved" (Rickmann, 1967, p. 23). As it was maintained, the natural science (Naturwissenschaft) attempt to develop and apply general laws is inapplicable to the problem of human understanding. A different form of science (Geisteswissenschaft) is required, one that focuses on people's attempt to understand the meaning beneath others' actions. A similar line of argument was reflected in R. G. Collingwood's (1966) influential work, *The Idea of History.* As Collingwood maintained, "Unlike the natural scientist, the historian is not concerned with events as such at all. He is concerned with those events which are the outward expression of thoughts and is only concerned with these so far as they express thoughts" (p. 217). To illustrate, if a stroller is suddenly struck from behind and barely escapes a calamitous fall into the street, how might he respond to the individual who had administered the blow? His reaction will not depend on the

---

tion, stimulus generalization) to the physiological system. Yet, as we now see, terms for internal dispositions are generally displaced terms for end points or goals of the activity in question. Thus, they are ill-considered as "hypothetical constructs" open to assessment through inference. Rather, they derive their existence from the rules of discourse regarding meaningful end points of human activity. Physiological linkage is thus obviated. To put the argument more sparingly, physiology might ultimately hope to gain predictive power over bodily movement; however, as we see, person description does not (and cannot) generally refer to bodily movement. Physiology is thus irrelevant to most frameworks of understanding human action. See also Peele (1981).

[23] As Dennett (1978) has argued: "Deciding on the basis of available empirical evidence that something is a piece of copper or a lichen permits one to make predictions based on the empirical theories dealing with copper and lichens, but deciding on the basis of available evidence that something is (may be treated as) an intentional system permits predictions having a normative or logical basis rather than an empirical one, and hence the success of an intentional prediction, based as it is on no particular picture of the system's design, cannot be construed to confirm or disconfirm any particular pictures of the system's design" (p. 13).

physical properties of the blow itself. Rather, he would be concerned with the meaning of the action for the actor. For example, was the blow an act of aggression? If the individual who administered the blow now seemed to be laughing at his plight, he might presume that the act was designed to harm him in some way, and consider various means of retaliating. However, if it appeared that the seeming assailant was leaning backward to avoid an errant cyclist, he might conclude that the act was not intended as harmful. It was not "meant as aggression," but was "accidental movement."[24]

Much the same argument is reflected in Peter Winch's (1958) searching work,

---

[24] Attempts have been made in philosophy to reinstate intentional language as observational language, that is, as allowing reference through empirical pointing (cf. Brodbeck, 1971; Feigl, 1961; Taylor & Walton, 1971). Perhaps the central argument to emerge from such analyses is that mental state terms (intentions, reasons, motives) can be redescribed as behavioral dispositions, and that behavioral dispositions are observable. As Feigl (1950) puts it, "The designata of the mentalistic language are identical with the descripta of the behavioristic language" (p. 623). In a similar vein, but from a different perspective, Ryle (1949) argues, "when we describe people as exercising qualities of mind . . . we are referring to those overt acts and utterances themselves" (p. 25). From the present standpoint, however, this line of argument is unwarranted. On the present account, neither movements of the body through space and time nor moment-to-moment vocalizations count as instantations of most person descriptors. Precisely the same movements or sounds may count as instances of a potentially infinite variety of person descriptors, and the infinite array of varied movements may occasion the use of the same descriptor. Bodily movements frequently furnish the occasions upon which person descriptors are employed, but most such terms refer to an imagined impulse, motive, or intention lying behind the movements themselves. In this sense, such terms correspond to natural science concepts such as gravity or electricity. However, in the latter case, the concepts are used principally as explanatory devices for observed events (movement of particles, increments in luminosity), and it is the events themselves that stand as the ultimate focus of prediction and control. In the case of behavior, the descriptor does serve an explanatory function, as indicated, but the physical movement of the body is virtually inconsequential. Taylor (1964) takes a different route in arguing that purposive explanations are subject to empirical verification. Within his framework it is permissible on objective grounds to state that an individual possesses an intention X (e.g., "to eat") when (1) the state of his system and/or the surrounding context favor a given goal (e.g., the person is hungry), and (2) the behavior in question will achieve this goal (e.g., cooking an omelette). However, this analysis suffers on the grounds that the identification of its components are themselves unverifiable. On what grounds can one justify accepting the individual's report about the needs of his or her system, and perception of means–ends relations? What data base would the individual consult in answering such questions? Anscombe (1957) abandons altogether the attempt to use observations as the basis for knowledge about one's dispositions or intentions. She maintains that knowledge of one's intentions is not justified through observation but is a form of *practical* knowledge, which in the end, only the individual can declare. The grounds for such declarations remain obscure.

The Idea of a Social Science. However, Winch goes on to maintain that physical description, unlike person description, is primarily concerned with events that we may presume to exist outside the language of description. Disputes may exist over how the event (or set of observations) is to be named, what theory is relevant, or whether a theory recognizes them as events. However, the occurrence in itself is not generally disputed. In contrast, when describing human action, that which is named has no ontic status; it has no existence independent of the language. To illustrate, consider Winch's (1958) distinction between an act of obedience with a clap of thunder:

> In the case of the latter, although human beings can think of the occurrences in question only in terms of the concepts they do in fact have of them, yet the events themselves have an existence independent of those concepts. There existed electrical storms and thunder long before there were human beings to form concepts of them or to establish that there was any connection between them. But it does not make sense to suppose that human beings might have been issuing commands and obeying them before they came to form the concept of command and obedience. (p. 122)[25]

These arguments also find their parallels, and in some degree were informed by numerous accounts of person description within ordinary language philosophy. Perhaps the most relevant line of argument to emerge in this context is that distinguishing between reasons and causes as explanations for human conduct (Ryle, 1949). As argued by Richard Peters (1958), Charles Taylor (1964), and others, ordinary language use makes an important distinction between behaviors that are produced by forces or elements acting on the individual and over which he or she has no control, and those that are motivated by the individual's goals. If a man steps from the edge of a precipice, his downward movement would occur regardless of his state of mind. One might say that the gravity *caused* the behavior in question. However, if the man makes his way to the top of the mountain, we would be more inclined to attribute his actions to his reasons or goals (i.e., to use motivational language). He is ascending "in order to" see the view, to gain exercise, or to throw

---

[25] Influenced by the writings of Winch, Collingwood, and others, along with early Verstehen psychologists, many have argued that behavioral scientists must confine themselves to the study of indigenous meaning systems. Because social life is determined by meaning systems, such meanings must be the focal concern of the sciences. However, from the present perspective, such an exclusive focus seems unwarranted. First, as we have seen, there is no satisfactory means of determining what an actor means (intends) by his or her acts; one's study is thus limited to account giving. Second, the scientist's analysis is itself an account, and not an "accurate portrayal" of the actor's meaning. If the scientist is communicating an account, and this account cannot reflect the actor's intention in any case, the scientist is essentially free to construct virtually any intelligible theory of the actor. In a sense the scientist is not thus engaged in "studying meaning," but in creating it. For other arguments with conclusions congenial to the present, see Menzel (1978), Brown (1963), and Thomas (1979).

himself off the precipice. In effect, the action is carried out for a reason rather than a cause. Further, it is argued, most of the actions with which the social sciences are concerned are of the latter variety.[26] The social scientist is not chiefly concerned with actions that are propelled by physical forces, but with those based on the person's reasons. Social scientists would be unintelligible if their accounts of human conduct were limited to a description of the physical conditions preceding an action (decibel level, temperature, state of the neurons) and their relationship to the physical properties of the action itself (e.g., its velocity, direction, number of morphemes emitted).[27] Instead, in order to communicate intelligibly about human action, the social scientist must typically be concerned with people's intentions. Thus, for example, an analysis of communication that confined itself to vocal utterances would not enable one to make sense of such action; clarity is achieved only when one comprehends the meaning (intention, or motive) of the speaker.[28,29]

---

[26] There is abundant criticism (cf. Brown, 1963; Fodor, 1968) of the psychologists' use of intentions, dispositions and reasons as forms of explanation. The major point of the present argument is not to defend against such critiques (which are lethal enough) but to demonstrate the virtual incapacity of the scientist to identify behavioral acts independent of reference to such internal tendencies.

[27] For a superb satire of the futility of the experimental, causal approach to understanding human action see Pencil's (1976) discussion of salt passage research.

[28] The equation of meaning, as used in the present context, with intention is hardly unique to this treatment. See, for example, Grice (1957) and Searle (1970).

[29] Radical behaviorists may wish to argue that their scientific program does not make use of intentional or directed-state terms. However, as a variety of critics have pointed out, such terms are essential and implicit in Skinnerian theory. In Dennett's (1978) picaresque phrasing, "The claim is . . . that once the animal has been trained, a law-like relationship is discovered to hold between non-intentionally characterized events: controlling stimuli and bar-pressing responses. A regularity is discovered to hold, to be sure, but the fact that it is between non-intentionally defined events is due to a property of the Skinner box and not of the occupant. For let us turn our prediction about mathematicians into a Skinnerian prediction: strap a mathematician in a Skinner box so he can move only his head; display in front of him a card on which appear the marks: 'How much is seven times five?'; move into the range of his head-motions two buttons, over one of which is the mark '35' and over the other '34'; place electrodes on the soles of his feet and give him a few quick shocks; the controlling stimulus is then to be the sound: 'Answer now!' I predict that in a statistically significant number of cases, even before training trials to condition the man to press button '35' with his forehead, he will do this when given the controlling stimulus. Is this a satisfactory scientific prediction because it eschews the intentional vocabulary? No, it is an intentional prediction disguised by so restricting the environment that only one bodily motion is available to fulfill the intentional action that anyone would prescribe as appropriate to the circumstances of perception, belief, desire. That it is action, not merely motion, that is predicted can also be seen in the case of subjects less intelligent than mathematicians. Suppose a mouse were trained, in a Skinner box with a food reward, to take exactly four

The latter distinctions have come to occupy a critical role in recent philosophy of social science, and have stimulated many to view the social sciences primarily as an interpretive discipline (cf. Giddens, 1976; Taylor, 1971). Such a conclusion is, of course, quite compatible with the arguments of the present chapter. What has essentially been added by the present treatment is an account of the origins of the ordinary language distinctions, grounds for concluding that the sociobehavioral sciences could not easily take an alternative path, and an argument against the objective anchoring of such description.[30] To summarize, a denotative language is favored to the extent that experience is stable and reliable. However, because of the difficulties posed by the infinite alteration of action to the human processes of recording, recalling, and communicating, accounts of human activity are typically framed in terms of the end points of activity. However, as these abstract end points are attributed to the actor, they take on a secondary meaning; they come to name the motivation for action. They appear not only to describe, but simultaneously to explain. Description in terms of general tendencies appear to be a virtual requirement in the attempt to "make sense" of human action. As previously argued, there are no objective yardsticks by which one can judge the true motive, intent, or goal of an activity. There is no means by which observers can objectively specify the end point of an activity. And, as we have seen, the actor does not occupy a superior position in this respect. He or she is also forced back on linguistic conventions concerning the range of reasonable motives possessed by people of the culture and historical period. In effect, the nonobjectivity of theoretical terms would appear to be an inherent characteristic of the sociobehavioral sciences.[31]

Science, Hidden Process, and the Problem of Pseudo-operations

At this point in the analysis many may wish to form a final line of resistance based once again on the manifest success of the natural sciences. As it may be argued, the natural sciences are vitally concerned with nonobservable processes. As Bhaskar (1975) and others of the realist school maintain, such generative processes are of focal concern to the development of scientific knowledge; laboratory prediction is

---

steps forward and press a bar with its nose; if Skinner's laws truly held between stimuli and responses defined in terms of bodily motion, were we to move the bar an inch farther away, so four steps did not reach it, Skinner would have to predict that the mouse would jab its nose into the empty air rather than take a fifth step" (p. 14).

[30] For further discussion of the nonobjective character of person description see Abelson (1977).

[31] "Indexical" terms within the ethnomethodological domain are terms not applied to observables via correspondence rules. Rather they are terms that acquire utility within particular circumstances in which an observable is encountered. Such terms require "contextual information" in order to be understood. As we see, from the present exercise, most terms of person description are thus indexical, rather than referential. Those sciences engaged in descriptions of human action are thus dealing primarily in indexical language.

of secondary importance. And, to extend the argument in its traditional form, if the natural sciences have made such impressive gains by employing such concepts, why should the sociobehavioral scientist not anticipate similar achievements? Concepts of motive, intention, plan, mental association, and the like in the psychological realm are analogs to concepts of gravity, force field, electricity, and black holes in the physical.

This line of defense has a long history in psychology, and its elaboration has been critical in the solidification of neobehaviorism. However, there has also been general agreement in both the philosophy of science and in the sciences themselves that the positing of unseen forces, processes, or entities is legitimated through a process of establishing connectives between the unseen and the seen. That is, at various points the scientist must be willing to specify a range of observables, the activities or properties of which may be used to substantiate (or falsify) the hypothesized construct. Thus, the concept of gravity is useful, in part, as a conceptual tool for unifying diverse observations of the observed movement of bodies through space; principles of magnetism are useful in predicting the activity of a gaussmeter as one changes latitude. Without any implications for the world of observation, it is generally maintained, hypothetical processes or entities would have little scientific utility. In more radical form, it is said that empirically empty concepts are injurious to the science; they are the stuff of the occult and the romantic.

In psychology this line of thinking is generally realized in the normative procedure of operational instantiation. The experimenter exploring "short-term memory processes," for example, will develop operations standing as putative indicators of such processes. Essentially the subject under study must perform an observable act, and this act is used as the basis for making inferences regarding the "hypothetical" process of concern. In similar fashion one may measure or operationalize "concept learning" in terms of a particular type of verbal performance, the capacity for "cognitive conservation" in terms of responses to questions about a variety of stimulus objects, dissonance reduction in terms of verbal evaluations of a stimulus object, "self-esteem" in terms of agreement or disagreement with self-referent statements, and so on.

Although the traditional rationale for employing hypothetical processes or entities in the sciences may seem persuasive enough, demanded in this case is a more careful assessment of the capacity of the behavioral sciences to realize its aspirations. In particular, we must ask whether the typical attempts to operationalize the hypothetical construct do indeed succeed in linking the construct to an observation base. It is the present contention that this procedure, as commonly practiced in the sociobehavioral sciences, yields only *pseudolinkages*—that the connection between the hypothetical and the observed is only an apparent one. When closely examined, we find the investigator to be making linkages only between hypothetical constructs and generally unable to make exit to a field of observable referents.

This contention follows quite readily from the arguments of the preceding section. There it was maintained that ostensive or denotative terms of person description were scarce, and that intractable impediments stood in the way of a flourishing vocabulary of this variety. And, as we saw, many terms appearing to describe ongoing behavior are found, on closer examination, to refer to the motivational source of the activity. These arguments lead one to suspect that the referent for operational or behavioral terminology is not an observable datum, as demanded by the traditional rationale, but a hypothetical construct. In effect, the hypothetical construct of concern is not tied to an observable in the typical instance, but to *another hypothetical construct.*

To illustrate, social psychologists have devoted immense research to understanding principles of attitude change. Many hold the concept of "attitude" to be the critical fundament in the cultivation of a general theory of social conduct. Commensurate effort has been devoted to the development of operational or behavioral realizations of the underlying construct. Although there are elaborate procedural rules for attitude scale construction, the vast majority of attitude measures require respondents to indicate their degree of agreement or disagreement with a number of evaluative statements. Thus, for example, one who agreed with the statement, "The Republican Party represents only the interests of Big Business," might be said to harbor a negative attitude toward the Republican Party. Public agreement furnishes an operational definition of the hypothetical construct. But let us examine more closely the referent for the term "public agreement." What is the observable activity denoted by the term? To the extent that one observes at all, he or she might be exposed to the subject's hand moving through space at a given velocity as it places assorted marks on paper. It further seems clear that this particular movement of the hand is not the referent for the ostensible observation term, "attitude agreement." If people were trained for many hours to make precisely these same movements, it would *not* be said of them that they were demonstrating attitude agreement; and, if a subject in an attitude study chose to employ a far different movement to administer marks to paper (e.g., holding the pencil between clenched teeth), it might well be said of him that he *was* demonstrating attitude agreement. In effect, the term "attitude agreement" does not refer to the movement itself but to what the individual is "trying," "intending," or "is motivated" to do. The latter terms, as we have seen, are hypothetical constructs on a par with the concept of "attitude." Attitude theory, on this account, is an abstract system, a set of linguistic conventions, with no empirical coordinates.[32,33]

---

[32] This same line of argument applies to research in widely variegated realms. For example, research on obedience behavior is not concerned with the movements that go into pressing the switch that delivers shock. The subject could press the switch with his nose and it would be inconsequential to the description. What does matter to all concerned, however, is the subject's intention. Thus, if a subject's elbow accidentally pressed the switch as he was grabbing his coat to depart, the investigator would be disinclined to count the action as throwing the switch. The subject in this case was "leaving the experiment," it might be said; he did not "intend" to press the switch, and therefore the action does not count as "pressing the switch." In contrast if the subject "tried" to press the switch but was prevented from doing so by a petit mal seizure, he could satisfactorily be counted in this case as "pressing the switch." His situation (aim or motive), not his actual behavior, is the essential referent for judging whether there has been "an occurrence."

Is this to argue that future research in the sociobehavioral sciences should confine itself to observables? Should a premium be placed on the development of a denotative language? It would not appear so. Critical problems would emerge if the sciences confined themselves to observable movements, sounds, smells, and the like. We have already seen that, at least with respect to human activity, there may be an infinity of variations and no particular configuration need be repeated. The attempt to build a predictive science concerned with the movements, sounds, smells and so on, of physical bodies in motion would thus seem of limited utility—even more futile than consigning physicists the task of predicting the course of dust particles in a hurricane. This is not to say that such concerns are wholly without merit. Research concerning physiological states, performance incapacities, and certain skills, for example, may usefully confine itself to the occurrence or nonoccurrence of recurring bodily movements. However, such a focus would fail to speak to the preponderance of societal concerns.

A second problem with confining the sciences to observable movements is closely related to the first. The problem in this case is that of professional significance within the culture more generally. If the scientist fails to take account of the meaning of actions to persons, research can easily become remote from matters of common concern. This state of affairs did indeed seem to exist during the late 1960s when great demands were made on sociobehavioral sciences for "relevant" research. When the laiety consulted experimental research on aggression for answers to problems of international and domestic conflict, for example, the experiments themselves seemed generally palid and irrelevant (Rosnow, 1981; Sarason, 1981). Pressing shock buttons and striking plastic dolls might be called aggression by laboratory investigators, it was argued, but it did not appear to be "real aggression" of the kind faced by the society more generally. It was merely artificial aggression, bearing little resemblance to what people typically mean by the term. In effect, if the sciences do not speak to the problems of culture, they run the risk of losing public support, and if they are to speak to such problems, they must link their theoretical work to the common behavioral vernacular. This vernacular seems incontrovertibly welded to a motivational base.[34]

----

[33] Relevant is the manner in which investigators such as Tedeschi, Smith, and Brown (1974) and Mummendey (in press) have shifted the focus from the study of aggression as a behavior to the way an act comes to be defined as aggression. As the former authors have put it: "Analysis suggests that definitions of aggression founder in the problem of attribution of intention. There is a subtle shift in meaning depending upon the particular problem faced by the theorist, from a simple notion of nonaccidental behavior to a more complex attributional problem of determining the motivation behind an actor's behaviors" (p. 559).

[34] In this regard, Argyris (1980) has pointed out that in the attempt to develop rigorous measures, gaps are typically created between what investigators think they are measuring and the "theory in use" meanings of people in actual situations. The rigorous study of the bargaining process using the prisoner's dilemma game, he argues, has virtually nothing useful to offer those engaged in what is understood as interpersonal bargaining on the level of daily life.

The Revitalization of Theory

As we see, the problem of human change poses a lethal challenge to the traditional conception of the sociobehavioral sciences. The function of theory as a means of describing and predicting human action and the role of research in the assessment of truth claims are all called into serious question. Many will hold that such arguments are too pessimistic, and may be moved to develop means of escaping the present assault. Such attempts are indeed to be welcomed. However, as will be shown in Chapter 5, the present line of argument may be viewed as but a single instance of a generalized disenchantment with traditional empiricist methatheory. The present critique must be viewed within the context of broad-scale criticism both in philosophy and adjoining disciplines concerned with understanding human conduct. It would appear that if defenses are to be erected, they might strive for greater solidity than the present line of inquiry alone might recommend.[35]

In the meantime, it would seem a propitious time in which to undertake serious consideration of alternative conceptions of the science. In fact, much groundwork for such an enterprise has been laid over the past several decades, and a variety of derivative movements have gained increasing audibility in psychology. The contours of such work will be traced in Chapter 5. In preparation for such treatment it will benefit us now to consider more carefully the positive implications of the present

---

[35] One counter to the present thesis is that if behavioral theory can make no legitimate truth claims, then the present thesis is equally subject to such a critique. It, too, can make no claims to truth, and therefore may be disregarded. However, this line of rebuttal is problematic on several counts. First, to the extent that it is legitimate, the argument is no less applicable to the positivist–empiricist metatheory that the present thesis attempts to dislodge. There is no means, for example, by which one can empirically falsify the hypothetico-deductive model of scientific progress. To do so would in itself invalidate the very grounds upon which the falsification rested. Second, to discount an analysis such as the present on the basis of its lack of empirical proof would be to engage in a form of what Weimer (1979) calls justificationism—the identification of knowledge with proof and the identification of proof with authority. The legitimacy of such justification has yet to be adequately demonstrated. There are numerous instances in which one may be in possession of knowledge, but chose to ignore it in reaching decisions about the best course of action (viz. one stricken by an illness known to be fatal may simply wish to disregard this knowledge in planning for the future; the optimism of ignorance may furnish greater fulfillment than the pessimism born of truth). Third, it is important to distinguish among the kinds of empirically based statements that have been used to support the present thesis. In certain cases, the objectivity of such statements should be discounted. Data have been used in such cases as means of vivification, to be discussed shortly. However, in other cases (viz. the discussion of alterations in bodily movement), the truth claims stand in no less a legitimate relationship to observation than do theoretical statements in the natural sciences. For much of the argument, then, ostensive reference can be established. Finally, in selecting this means of discounting the present thesis, one must implicitly accept the thesis. To demonstrate the falsity of the thesis one would be obliged to embrace its truth.

critique. The present arguments are themselves premised on a complex set of assumptions, and when more fully articulated, these assumptions may furnish preliminary grounds for a transformed science. As we shall see, the transformation emerging in the present case can properly dispel the residual pessimism left by the above analysis, and replace it with promise of far more significant dimension. There is reason to believe that the traditional account of the sociobehavioral sciences has greatly underestimated their potential. When properly understood, the sciences may be viewed as a pivotal force within the culture.

Let us first consider the character of theory. As we have seen, it is unpromising to view theoretical work as a form of behavioral description, a reflection of ongoing behavioral events. Rather, it seems preferable to consider theory principally in its linguistic aspects. The theorist is fundamentally a source of linguistic activity. This is to say that the chief product of the vast attempts at manipulation, control, assessment, and quantification are essentially word systems. In this sense the behavioral sciences are similar to the humanities; both possess certain forms of linguistic expertise.[36] It may further be advanced that these forms of expertise are not fundamentally different from other skilled activities of the human being. Just as people learn to do things with words, they may also learn how to use their feet for dancing, their hands for sculpting, or their eyes for surveying the safety of their surrounds. Just as the artist manipulates pigments, the juggler his pins, or the fencer the rapier, the scientist selects and juxtaposes words.[37]

---

[36] A useful analogy may also be made between the behavioral theorist and the mathematician. Each possesses expertise in the formulation of symbol systems, and in each case, such systems stand as abstract and autonomous structures unto themselves. At the same time these systems, floating independent of the observation world, may be selectively employed in such a way as to alter one's relationship with that world.

[37] The view of science developed here may be usefully compared with Derek Phillips' (1977) analysis of Wittgenstein's implicit theory of knowledge. While sharing many points in common, they differ importantly with respect to the issue of demarcation between science and nonscience. Phillips wishes to use Wittgenstein to blur this distinction, thus retaining a unity between natural and social science study. The present analysis attempts to demonstrate differential problem forms separating the vast range of study in the two domains. To be sure, there is an important sense in which the ontology of the natural world is also a social construction. (See, for example, Latour and Wollgar's [1979] analysis of the social processes involved in sustaining natural science theory.) Although the emphasis on the social construction of scientific fact is thus common across domains, there appears to remain a fundamental distinction between the major forms of study in the two scientific realms. In the natural sciences one does confront an empirical world that exists independent of theoretical forms of description, and scientific theory can be used to increase one's prediction and control of this world. However, as advanced in the present case, descriptive terms in the sociobehavioral sciences are, by and large, observation free; it is not a spatio-temporal world independent of the theoretical language with which the scientist is concerned. Theories are not thus "underdetermined" by observation; there are essentially no observations that would stand as correctives,

Yet, unlike certain other human skills, linguistic proficiency cannot be evaluated outside of the social sphere within which it is embedded. One may learn to play a musical instrument in ways that give pleasure solely to oneself; however, linguistic expertise can only be determined within the framework of others' activities. The autistic production of sounds does not constitute language. Intelligibility or "sense making" is essentially a social product; if others do not agree that one's words are sensible, they are simply nonsense. To adopt Wittgenstein's (1963) metaphor, one may usefully view words as pieces in a game played with others. If it is to function at all each language move must be accepted as a move, and, once accepted, has implications for one's outcomes in the game. In this sense, theories of human activity are more like dance steps than they are mirrors, more akin to checkers than to cameras. In effect, social knowledge is a product not of single individuals acting autonomously, but of social collaboration.

Yet it is also important to realize that the game of language is far more profound in consequence than most others, primarily because of its manifold implications for the remainder of one's activities.[38] Unlike dance steps or checkers, language moves can be intimately related to other moves in the "life game." This is so primarily because language is easy to perform (in a way that other activities such as dance steps are not), it is differentially articulated (in a way that gross bodily movements are not), no physical artifacts are essential for performance (in a way that would be untrue if the bass viol were the major instrument of communication), it takes place with a relatively high degree of speed (in a way that semaphore does not), and there is an unlimited potential for the production of novel integers as new circumstances develop. Through language one may truncate other interpersonal processes of longer and more arduous duration. For example, one may furnish verbal directions for baking a cake, conducting a wedding, or touring the Amalfi coast without leading the listener by the hand through the requisite motions. Or one may verbally instruct a child about forms of desirable activity and thereby circumvent innumerable instances of mutual discomfort. As is apparent, language is one of the most powerful tools available to human communities; linguistic expertise may vitally affect the composition of the community.[39]

---

referents, or empirical anchors to most person description. Theories cannot be employed to predict or control a world independent of such theory, as it is not spatio-temporal events to which such theories refer.

[38] Also see Ricoeur's (1976) distinction between language as saying something (a locutionary act), as doing something in saying (an illocutionary act), and as producing effects in saying (a perlocutionary act).

[39] This latter line of argument may initially appear to violate the preceding discussion concerning the lack of objective referents for behavioral language. Earlier we found that terms appearing to refer to human activities do not generally refer to specific movements. However, in the above argument we have spoken of the intimate relationship between language and other forms of activity. How is it possible to speak of such forms of activity if the description cannot refer to objective movements? Indeed it cannot. However, as we have also seen, given certain linguistic conventions, "descriptive" terminology can properly refer to the full range of

In this light we may consider the position of the sociobehavioral scientist. If language can serve as a means for altering or sustaining others' actions, and if the capacity to create such effects is equivalent to power in relationships, then we must conclude that scientists can occupy a position of considerable power in society. There would appear to be three major contributions to this elevated position. First, power accrues to scientists by virtue of their years of education, along with their continued practice and development of linguistic skills through writing, teaching, consulting, and/or curing. In addition to the possession of substantial skill, the professional also occupies a position of enhanced credibility. Increasingly, within the past century large segments of the culture have turned to the scientist for understanding and guidance. People wish to know how to raise their children, learn more effectively, relieve emotional distress, fight crime, reduce traffic fatalities, build environments for human satisfaction, construct effective organizations, treat the deranged, and so on. It is to the sociobehavioral scientist and to few others that the culture turns for answers to such questions. Finally, the scientist has substantial access to the mass media. Through books, television, radio, periodicals, and newspapers the effects of the scientist's words penetrate the culture at large. In contrast, the power base of the common citizen is limited to the face-to-face relationship.[40]

In the broad sense, scientists are furnished with the skills and station for creating and/or maintaining the social order. It is the scientific account itself that has the potential for altering the character of human activity. This situation may be contrasted with the traditional view of the scientist as technocrat (Habermas, 1971). On this account the scientist serves as society's mensurational device. The scientist's activities provide society with an accurate indication of "what leads to what." The society is then free to employ the scientist's results as it sees fit. The scientist's activities *qua* scientist are terminated when the technical information is supplied. As we now see, this account vastly underestimates the potential of the science and the extent to which scientists may realize their hopes for society. The effect of scientific accounts does not await the ancillary policy decisions of existing institutions. Rather, the effects may be as immediate as the act of comprehension. And the policy maker is not the arbiter of social ends in this case; scientific accounts are ends impregnated.[41]

---

activities that may eventuate in a given end point. Thus, in furnishing instructions for baking a cake, one is using conventional terms that refer to end points or consequences, and not to the specific activity or means by which such end points are reached. In certain cases, those in which certain bodily movements are reliably repeated (conditions approximating, let's say, classical ballet), the terms of description or instruction may refer to observable composites of behavior (e.g., "now march," or "now sit").

[40] For conclusions similar to the present see London's (1977) useful discussion of historicity and the altering effects of theory on society.

[41] It appears that many professionals avoid confronting the valuational biases in their work, or the potential for using their work as implements of value expression, for fear of ignorance in the realm of values. As Brewster Smith (1969) counters, "the psychologist has *as much* right to posit values as anyone else, in some impor-

Given this position of enhanced power, the critical question concerns its use. To what ends is the scientist to employ his or her skills? As we have seen, for the scientist to announce that he or she is "merely reporting the facts" is both misleading and manipulative. The chief question confronting the theorist is not, "How accurate is the description?," but rather, "What function is the selected theoretical language to play within the human arena?" What forms of activity is a theoretical account designed to sustain, create, or destroy? How is the linguistic account to be employed within the society, and for what ends? Viewed in this light there is no essential distinction to be made between theory and praxis: *Theoretical work constitutes a form of praxis.* It is a form of activity with broad human consequence.[42]

In this context we may usefully distinguish between two major arenas of theoretical work, those that are *external* as opposed to *internal* to the discipline. In the former case theoretical language may serve ends that lie beyond the boundaries of the discipline itself. The theorist may actively employ his or her theoretical language to influence the existing order. Economics and political science both furnish plentiful instances in which theory has been of broad exterior consequence. Marxist and capitalist economic theories, along with centralist and participatory theories of political decision making, have essentially furnished the grounding suppositions for political and economic policies of broad impact.[43] As we saw in Chapter 1, outside the therapeutic domain most psychological theories have been insensitive to such consequences. It is partly for this reason that most such theories have failed to have substantial impact.

As should be apparent from this account, questions of value are thrust into a position of cardinal significance in the sociobehavioral sciences. If objective fidelity is obviated, and theory is viewed as a form of activity that may be employed in achieving various purposes, then the central criteria for evaluating theory are gener-

---

tant respects more. It is time to dispel the shopworn bromide that the humanist (or moralist or philosopher) has a corner on pronouncement about values, while the psychologist (or sociologist or scientist generally) must restrict himself to fact" (pp. 183–184).

[42] Ollman (1971) has expressed a similar view: "the value of [Marxist] theories must be measured by utility rather than truth. . . . It is in this sense that philosophical systems are never exploded, but instead, like styles of clothing, simply go out of fashion, usually because other interpretations are found more useful or because the group whose interests these ideas serve itself disappears" (pp. 232–233). Yet, it is also important to note that the concept of utility, as employed by Ollman and in the present work, does not offer a means of establishing an empirical yardstick for assessing progress in the sociobehavioral sciences. Utility is essentially a statement of personal value and thus fully normative. In this sense, the present arguments are congenial with what Bartley (1962) has called "comprehensively critical rationalism." From this standpoint, one holds all beliefs, including one's basic philosophical position itself, open to criticism.

[43] For an examination of the use of political language in maintaining the sociopolitical system see Mueller (1973).

ated by questions of purpose. The chief grounds for such appraisal would appear to be valuational. One goal stands superior to its broad field of competitors chiefly in terms of the value one places on its goals. Of what value to self or society are the various forms of change or stasis? Once the value of theoretical purpose has been established, a series of second-order criteria can be brought to bear. These concern the degree of success achieved by the theoretical language in achieving the specified ends. In this case, one might rely on such traditional criteria as logical coherence, parsimony, clarity, and formal elegance. Essentially, these traditional criteria for theoretical comparison stand as guides to effective rhetoric. To be logically coherent, simple, and clear is to increase the potential impact of the theory within the culture.

From the present standpoint it is not illegitimate for a theorist to restrict his or her aims to increasing intelligibility, pleasing clients, or making money. One is free to place value in such goals. It is left to others to demonstrate the impoverishment of such goals and to elucidate alternatives. For this reason it is essential that the disciplines nurture a critical wing. Required are individuals whose chief concern is with the broad consequences of various theoretical viewpoints and with the elaboration of alternatives. Such individuals not only furnish necessary prophylactics against oppressive univocality, but their work can also provide the first step toward the creation of fresh perspectives.

Let us turn from externally oriented theory to the function of theory within the discipline itself. Although the above concern with valuational ends is no less relevant in this case, additional factors must also be taken into account. As we have seen, theoretical languages are equivalent to many other activities that vary with respect to performance skill. In this regard some theoretical languages are feats of daring magnificence, while others are clumsy and barren of potential. As an analogy one might compare the languages of the child and the adult in terms of the range of accomplishments that may be achieved. The child's vocabulary is limited and the grammatical structure simple. As a result the efficacy of the child to achieve ends through linguistic means is restricted. In contrast, the adult often possesses a richly differentiated vocabulary and the ability to execute such grammatical forms as the subjunctive and counterfactual conditional. The result is an increased capacity for achievement. In this light we see that it is of fundamental significance for the discipline to support and sustain theoretical inquiry, the chief aim of which is to enhance the skills of the discipline more generally. Required is theoretical work enabling the discipline to improve the capacities of its theoretical languages. For example, the early attempt to explain behavior patterns in terms of instinct (cf. McDougall, 1908) was not replaced by environmentalist or learning accounts because instinct theory was inaccurate. Rather, the number of instincts tended toward unbridled expansion and the theory thus became increasingly clumsy. Given sufficient theoretical development nativism has since been able to reestablish itself in the form of sociobiology. And, in developing the concept of "generic rules of grammar," Chomsky (1968) was not replacing Skinnerian theory of language development with a more accurate or more predictive account. Rather, given contemporary descriptions of children's language development, Chomsky's theory provided an intelligibility that Skinnerian theory did not.[44]

It is in this capacity for developing interior skills that psychologists may be more sanguine with respect to past accomplishments. For example, cognitive theorists have furnished a rich vocabulary with which to speak about human thought processes and their implications, behaviorists have been successful in demonstrating theoretically how the vast share of human activity may be accounted for in terms of environmental contingency, trait theorists have demonstrated the intelligibility of seeing human activity as the product of acquired dispositions, and so on. Yet, for all its conceptual productivity, the discipline has yet to begin systematic inquiry into the advantages and shortcomings of such accounts as linguistic devices. The vast share of critical attention has been needlessly directed toward the predictive accuracy of competing accounts. Necessitated at this juncture are analyses of theoretical forms in terms of their contribution to the capacities of the discipline more generally. What limitations are inherent in various forms of understanding or explanation? Should certain theoretical forms be revitalized? Are there needed forms that have yet to be elaborated?

To distinguish between the external and internal functions of theoretical language is not to argue that a theory should exclusively be devoted to either one end or the other. The functions may be considered orthogonal, such that any given theory may be evaluated with respect to both simultaneously. In this regard, one of the most remarkable theories of the past century is that of Karl Marx. Marxist theory is wholly indeterminate with respect to accuracy. However, with respect to external functioning, the theory has served as the essential means by which entire social and economic structures have been altered. Much of the theoretical language was developed for just such purposes. At the same time, Marxist theory has had a broad impact on economic and social theory more generally. Scholars in wide-ranging areas have been able to incorporate or extend aspects of the initial theory in numerous ways. Within social psychology the opportunity for developing theories that simultaneously fulfill both systemic functions would also appear considerable. Traditional areas of scholarly concern, such as attitude change, prejudice, attraction, aggression, and altruism, are also those of the marketplace. One who can offer invigorating ideas to the discipline can frequently anticipate a broad audience within society.

The Significance of Empirical Research

Given this orientation to theoretical inquiry, what can be said about the place of empirical research? Thus far we have treated theories as forms of discourse related in various ways to other language forms, as well as various forms of nonlinguistic

---

[44] The present arguments for multiple theories are congenial with Nelson Goodman's (1978) advocacy of multiple worldviews. However, the present analysis differs from Goodman's in its focus on the social effects of "worldmaking" and the implications of these effects in establishing criteria for theoretical evaluation (see Chapter 3).

activity. In this light it becomes apparent that empirical research in the sociobehavioral sciences does not furnish observations. That is, the audience for research reports is never exposed to ongoing events; one never gains first-hand experience with the research process itself. Rather, the chief product of research is language. Research reports essentially furnish linguistic accounts or interpretations. To be more specific, the researcher typically furnishes two levels of discourse, one that is said to be theoretical and a second that is often termed "observation language." The latter frequently borrows heavily from ordinary language of the culture (a "profane" language), while the former is typically a more rarefied guild language ("sacred").

Typically the observation language is treated as a report of "what really happened" in the research setting while the theoretical language is seen as more hypothetical. Yet, as we saw in our discussion of operationalization, this view is misleading. Both linguistic forms are equally hypothetical; their major difference is that they are based on differing linguistic conventions (the one used within the sacred society of the discipline and the other by the profane, or general culture). For example, the term "obedience" may be featured at the theoretical level of interpretation, while "throwing a high voltage switch" may be used to describe the "actual behavior" of the subject. Yet as our previous analysis makes clear, neither the description "being obedient" nor "throwing a switch" possess empirical referents. They are both forms of motive language. Similarly, descriptions of persons "pressing a shock button," "giving money to a confederate," "completing a life-events checklist," "running for help," "reporting a crime," "turning a crank," "running a maze," "memorizing a word list," "agreeing with a group," "recalling early experiences," "committing suicide," and so on are not, as they have been treated, descriptions of ongoing behavior. They are essentially forms of interpretive language, for which the referents are nonobservational.

If the constraints placed upon the two languages of research are not fundamentally empirical, then what are the sources? Extrapolating from our previous discussion we find that they derive from two major sources. The first constraint is furnished by the matrix of language conventions governing the domains from which the discourse samples are drawn. On the theoretical level one cannot speak, for example, of "memory as a function of the magnitude of Holy Spirit," or "concept formation as influenced by centrifugal energy displacement," not because these are untrue descriptions; they are merely nonsense within the contemporary language conventions of the discipline. And, on the level of observation language, one cannot easily say that when "the subject was asked whether, she agreed she emitted three different phonemes at 75 decibels," or, "after the subject moved her right shoe 18 centimeters in a direction of 180 degrees, her partner let the curl in the front of her forehead drop 4 centimeters." Such descriptions are simply opaque or irrelevant to the ordinary language for understanding ongoing activities.

Although the domain conventions furnish substantial constraints over the "empirical" research report, it is the second basis of constraint that is critical to understanding the central function of research in a transformed science. We have seen that empirical investigation yields two language samples—one "theoretical" and the

other "empirical." This condition furnishes the second major constraint over the
reporting process, for in order to make sense as a coherent communication the two
forms of discourse must be compatible. Given one form of discourse, the other
must be sensibly derivative. This means that once a theoretical language is selected,
there are certain constraints placed over what may be said about the empirical
operations; or once the investigator has selected what it is he or she wishes to study
(in the ontological system of ordinary language), there are constraints placed over
the theoretical interpretation.

To illustrate the effects of theoretical language, if one's theory deals with the
problem of obedience, then one's research language must be consistent with talk
about obedience within the confines of contemporary convention. The researcher
would not thus speak about the movements of the subject's mandible, the number
of uttered vowels, or the number of times subjects tilted their heads by $47°$ during
the research procedure. Language of this sort would appear to border on nonsense
because it is not generally related to talk about obedience in contemporary life.
The investigator might, however, speak of the number of times subjects laughed
nervously, looked away from the experimenter, or pressed the switches demanded
by the experimenter. Such terms are intelligible within the context of modern
talk about obedience. It is not research that determines what the theorist can say,
but the theorist's selection of theoretical terms that determines what can be said
by research.

Constraints over theory are also generated by the common vernacular of event
description. If research is stimulated by a concern with ongoing events, one almost
inevitably borrows from the common terms of understanding to frame the question.
One may study "war," "loneliness," "rape," "burnout," "depression," "opinions,"
"memory loss," and so on not for theoretical reasons, but because the common
language has objectified such "entities." However, once the common language has
been used to frame the question for study, constraints are placed over the form of
theoretical understanding. For example, if one wished to study "the historical
development of slavery in the United States," one could scarcely adopt a stimulus-
response model. If one understands life in terms of a long-term trajectory, it is difficult (though perhaps not impossible) to employ a theory that focuses on discrete,
short-term events. Stimulus-response theory is both clumsy and ill equipped for the
task. If one selected, however, a discrete incident for study (e.g., an 1842 lynching
in Alabama), a stimulus-response model could be rendered sensible (cf. Dollard,
Doob, Miller, Mowrer, & Sears, 1939). Similarly if one wished to study "the influence of pornography on the incidence of rape," a rule-role formulation might not
be favored. One cannot easily imagine how the rapist could be following a role
prescription or "rules of rape" (although such an analysis is not fundamentally
precluded).

In this light let us reconsider the functions of research. If it is agreed that theory
has little value until it is successfully communicated, and that theoretical utility
(external or internal) is enhanced to the degree that others incorporate, adopt, or
apply this theoretical language to the course of their activities, then research must
be viewed primarily as a rhetorical implement. Its chief function is to lend power

(persuasive impact, appeal, felicity) to the theoretical language. Research fulfills this function for two major reasons. First, it enables the theorist to borrow from the apparent objectivity of the observation language. The theorist is confronted with the essential problem of making truth claims for an uncommon, explanatory language. Its very unconventionality underlies the common conception that such language is "more interpretive" than observation language. Observation language stands in contrast as that "which everyone knows to be true." Thus, to the extent that the theorist can demonstrate a fit or coherence between the theoretical language and the more "objective" language of observation, the former appropriates the credibility of the latter. People may be cautious in accepting a theory of dissonance reduction. At the same time, the description of subjects changing their attitudes for little reward seems eminently persuasive. In using the ordinary language as an instantiation of dissonance theory the seeds are sown for the objectification of the theory.[45,46]

The second means by which the research process lends rhetorical power to theoretical interpretation is by enabling the theorist to render the more rarefied theoretical terms sensible in terms of ordinary language. Such terms as "cognitive schemata," "mands," "anomie," and the like fail to communicate until they can be linked to existing linguistic conventions. In the research report the observation language furnishes the appropriate medium. One learns to see "what is meant" by the theoretical terms. In effect, the research report trains the reader in how to employ the theoretical language. Observation language is the *lingua franca* that solidifies intellectual communities and links the scientist with the surrounding culture. A discipline without any form of translation into such language remains remote and impotent.[47]

In its extreme this argument suggests that the significance or vitality of theory is not fundamentally dependent on the actual conduct of systematic observation. In principle, compelling theories may be sustained without laboratories, interviews, statistics, and the host of other modern research accoutrements. The theorist could succeed in furnishing the necessary linkages with observation language by simply

---

[45] As can be seen, the present proposal is at considerable variance with Merton's (1948) classic statement regarding the bearing of empirical research on theory. From the present standpoint, observation in itself cannot, as Merton maintains, verify, falsify, initiate, reformulate, deflect, or clarify theory. However, observation languages (not themselves reliant upon observations) may serve these functions at the rhetorical level.

[46] Older psychologists can recount the early days in the animal laboratory when they would watch with rapt attention to see if rats would "turn" right or left in a T-maze. If the rat would but select the proper turn, it would validate the belief that people possessed cognitive maps rather than their being mere pawns to stimulus-response connections. As described, the drama of such occasions was as intense as to evoke cheers and applause if the rats' activities were supportive.

[47] In part, the sociobehavioral sciences may attribute their remarkable expansion of the past century to their success in linking theory to observation language. Philosophers have generally eschewed this process with a concomitant loss in centrality.

drawing selectively from the storehouse of "what everybody knows." In this sense, no observational research is necessary to sustain a theory of obedience and its relationship, for example, to various social conditions. Such theory may be rendered fully compelling by dipping into the repository of examples within the common language. The popularity of Erving Goffman's (1959, 1961, 1963) writings amply illustrates the point. Goffman's work has had an impressive impact, both within sociology and the literate society more generally. Yet, its so-called data base is generated by a collection of homely accounts from everyday life.

However, it would be an unfortunate error for the sciences to univocally adopt the latter research posture. To abandon experiments, surveys, field studies, and the like would be to destroy some of the most effective rhetorical implements available to the theorist. As rhetorical technique it is far more impressive to demonstrate how one's theory applies in a large number of randomly selected cases than it is in a few preselected instances. As one multiplies the instances in which the theory seems to make action intelligible, and does so regardless of the case selected, the theory gains substantially in persuasive impact. Similarly, if the investigator can, at will, establish replicable conditions under which his or her theory seems applicable, it argues strongly for both the theorist's depth of understanding and the broad significance of the theory. In a broad sense, the empirical researcher is in an enviable position. He or she may possess the skill to generate illustrative materials of great vividness, and that may stand as compelling support for the broad-scale applicability of the theory.[48]

It should be noted that the chief concern of these arguments is with the development and sustenance of the academic or intellectual tradition. The interest is in the creation of more significant and challenging theoretical work. Yet there are many scientists whose chief concern is with matters of prediction. As employees of government, industry, or educational institutions, for example, their concern is ascertaining in advance the probability that a new welfare program will function adequately, a product will gain popularity, college alumni will respond generously to a fund raising program, and so on. There is nothing that has been said thus far to denigrate the potential of such work. Patterns of human conduct may change with time, but during any period of history one may anticipate a certain degree of reliability. Within delimited periods of time, probabilities can be assigned to certain events. At the same time this is not to reify the names given to such events. One may develop actuarial formulas for predicting the number of "auto accidents."

---

[48] Other forms of empirical pursuit are also favored by the present analysis. In particular need of development are methods of research attempting to edify the research participant, enhance the participant's skills or engender reflexive concern, all of which goals stand in contrast to the alienating and objectifying effects of the major research forms currently in use. Such newly developed methods might thus impart a "knowing how" in the sense of enabling the participant to broaden the range of his or her capacities rather than being used to vivify a "knowing that." Similarly Argyris (1980) also describes means by which research may be used to demonstrate to people the limits of their skills, and enable them to articulate their tacit but unverbalized programs and defenses.

However, one should not thereby conclude that what is being predicted are actual "accidents" (and not intended suicides, negligence, aggression, depression, etc.).[49]

It is also important to realize that while theorists cannot, as we have seen, furnish abstract principles from which practitioners can make predictive generalizations in such cases, they can serve as agents of intelligibility and sensitization. One who is concerned with actuarial prediction cannot simply measure all antecedents of the class of events to be predicted. One requires an ontological scaffold specifying the range of antecedent "events," and a theoretical understanding sufficient for selecting certain of these events for study and not others. It is in these domains that the theorist may be of inestimable value. For example, the practitioner assigned the problem of developing programs for reducing juvenile drug consumption begins with a prefashioned entity (juvenile drug consumption) and a rudimentary ontology of antecedents furnished by the common language (e.g., "drug pusher," "gangs," "racial differences"). On this basis alone one could develop and test a simple ameliorative program. However, existing theory also creates a range of additional antecedents, including "achievement needs," "anomie," "identification," "deterioration of the family unit," "group cohesiveness," "social comparison," "uniqueness striving," "reactance," and so on, each of which may enrich the range of the investigator's concern. Theory thus stands available to expand the scope and sophistication of the practitioner's program.[50]

Finally, the present arguments should not be construed as saying that the concept of accumulation is irrelevant to social knowledge, or that the texts or handbooks of today do not represent advances over previous treatments. As the conceptual weaknesses or ambiguities are elucidated within various theoretical domains, as alternative views or conceptual distinctions are developed, as research challenges previous ways of thinking or pricks the public conscience, and as new means are found for increasing the accuracy of broad-scale social prediction, the attention paid to older work may be appropriately reduced. Advances may be generated primarily through criticism, novel theory generation, unsettling predictions, and new means of solving present problems within the society. In this sense advances in the sociobehavioral sciences may parallel those found in philosophy or

---

[49] As Toulmin (1961) has demonstrated, the process of explanation in the sciences does not stand in any logically necessary relationship with prediction. The scientist may develop highly useful forms of explanation with little predictive value (e.g., Darwin's theory of evolution), or develop sensitive predictive formulae (e.g., the predictive systems of the insurance actuarial) on little but rudimentary and unarticulated theoretical grounds.

[50] The present analysis of the relationship between theory and actuarial prediction is realized in certain degree in contemporary economics. On the one hand there exist an array of general economic theories (Keynesian, monetarist, etc.) that make no exact predictions, but are valuable in making economic policy intelligible. Quite separated are economists whose major concern is with the development of predictive formulae. The latter are not particularly concerned with the validity of one general theory as opposed to another; however, the general theories do often point to factors that may enter into the actuarial formulae as potential predictors.

the arts.[51] Philosophic schemas serve as important devices for making the world intelligible at a given period. Their implications may then be explored and shortcomings examined. Although any given corpus of philosophic work may grow into disuse, it remains available as a discourse of understanding to be employed or exploited during later periods (e.g., as in the "rediscovery" of Vico). Progress is inherent in such a process. One need not struggle once again to lay out the tenets of a Platonic or Cartesian world view, or to elaborate and critically examine them. Such tasks have been accomplished by previous thinkers and enable contemporary inquiry, thus informed, to be directed toward new problems and to fashion new solutions. In the same way, artists need not recreate the ideas underlying Realism, Impressionism, or Expressionism. Such aesthetic styles are the products of previous generations; they remain available to serve human needs in the present. And their existence liberates the artist of today to probe new modes of expression. Accumulation is thus achieved.

In effect we find the scientist poised at the threshold of the future. As languages of understanding are developed and disseminated, the scientist crosses the threshold and enters not as a pawn to an impersonal and autonomous unfolding, not as a dispassionate spectator of the inevitable, but as an active agent. No longer is it necessary for the scientist to entertain the dim hope that one day a particular finding, a measure, or function form will be employed by some unknown person for purposes of public good. Rather, through the conduct of science itself one can hope to achieve directly the benefits of value-sustaining effort. No longer is it necessary to answer existential challenges of life's purpose with murmurs of contribution to an ultimate truth. Rather, the settlement can be accomplished in the immediate, concrete renderings of understanding. To communicate one's understanding is to make a small investment in the creation of the future.

---

[51] The functions of theory outlined here are not dissimilar to those which Northrop Frye (1971) attributes to literary renderings. As he says, "There is a reality out there, a reality that is given and has in itself no moral significance, and there is a reality which does not exist to begin with, but is brought about through a certain kind of creative activity" (p. 95). And, for what Frye views as the function of the poet, one may equally substitute the behavioral scientist: ". . . poetry, in its totality, is in fact society's real myth of concern, and . . . the poet is still the teacher of that myth. He may be an unacknowledged legislator, but he is (a) lawgiver of civilization . . ." (p. 95).

Chapter 3

Generative Theory and Degenerative Metatheory

When inquiry is made into the function of theory, the traditional response points to its essential contribution to "understanding, prediction, and control." If one were to inquire further into what is meant by "understanding" in this case, the answer might well be framed in terms of the scientist's role in "apprehending clearly the character, nature or subtleties" of human conduct (Urdang, 1968). From this standpoint, social conduct is granted a preeminent ontological status: It furnishes the essential mysteries for the scientist to unlock. Yet, there is a contrasting sense in which one may understand, a sense that does not take nature for granted. Understanding may also entail the assignment of "meaning" to experience; in this case understanding is a product of ratiocination and experience merely furnishes the raw material upon which it operates. The former sense of understanding finds its roots in empiricist philosophy, where one typically commences with the assumption of a fundamentally ordered nature to be reflected with accuracy by scientific theory; the latter form of understanding may be traced to rational-idealist philosophy in which the mind is generally granted powers of organizing and synthesizing sense data. Rational-idealist views, while long vital in European intellectual life, have gradually given way in the sciences to the empiricist view. The former sense of understanding has generally obscured the significance of the latter.

This distinction in orientations may furnish an important insight into what appears as an ironic discrepancy between the seminal theoretical contributions of earlier years and the relatively pallid offerings of contemporary behavioral science. In spite of the vastly expanded professional ranks and far superior resources within the latter context, theoretical contributions have seemed far less impressive and provocative in their effects. Few modern investigators have been able to match the intellectual ferment furnished by such figures as Adler, Adorno, Dilthey, Durkheim, Freud, Fromm, Jung, Köhler, Levi-Strauss, Lorenz, Mannheim, Marcuse, Marx, Piaget, and Weber, among others. American social psychology is characterized by the same discrepancy. Most modern treatments of theory in the field typically devote primary attention to Freud and Lewin; for many, Fritz Heider's richly suggestive work is deserving of equal status. All have deep roots in continental (rational-idealist) philosophy. In terms of general theoretical perspective, learning theory may be the only broadly significant contribution to emerge within the empiricist context. In effect, the strength of contemporary investigation does not seem to lie in its capacity for engendering theory of broad scope and challenge. More generally, it may be ventured, correspondent with the hegemony of the logical-empiricist orientation to understanding has been a diminution in catalytic theorizing.

As many would agree, modern theoretical work primarily serves to stimulate empirical research within an elite, professional circle. In contrast, the theories of Freud, Marx, Durkheim, and others often challenged the assumptive bases of social life, with profound catalytic effects both within and outside the profession. The primary debates emerging from contemporary social psychological theory, for example, are generally limited to questions of generalization range, methodological adequacy, and the availability of alternative explanations (cf. Bem, 1972; Cartwright, 1971). In contrast, the earlier offerings often fostered colloquy about fundamental issues among scientists of diverse origin along with philosophers, historians, theologians, politicians, and so on. As Asch wrote in 1952: "It has to be admitted that social psychology lives today in the shadow of great doctrines of man that were formulated long before it appeared, that it has borrowed its leading ideas from neighboring regions of scientific thought and from the social philosophies of the modern period. It is paradoxical but true that social psychology . . . has as yet not significantly affected the conceptions it has borrowed" (p. viii). And as Tajfel (1972) has more recently commented, "Social psychology has certainly not succeeded in creating an intellectual revolution in the sense of deeply affecting our views of human nature . . ." (p. 106).[1] One might wish to defend contemporary theory by pointing to its superior testability, and its related capacity to yield reliable bodies of social knowledge. Yet it is difficult to distill from the immense contemporary effort at hypothesis testing a body of highly reliable propositions (cf. Cartwright, 1971; Greenwald, 1975); nor can one fault the earlier theories for the lack of research which they have generated (cf. Blum's 1964 summary of empirical research on psychoanalytic theory). As we have seen in the preceding chapter, empirical validity with respect to the description and explanation of human conduct is a highly problematic criterion in any case. In effect, the contemporary alternatives do not appear demonstrably superior in other respects.

This discussion furnishes a useful departure point for considering a more general criterion for theoretical comparison. We have seen in previous chapters that the chief criterion for theoretical evaluation (by traditional standards), namely empirical validity (or its close associates, "truth value." "empirical content" and "resistance to falsification"), is inappropriately applied to theories of human conduct. What replacement might be adequate to a science sensitive to the issues raised in the present treatment? Let us propose as a chief contender that competing theo-

---

[1] Berkowitz (quoted in Smith, 1972) echoes the lament for significant theory: "We seem to be somewhat at a loss for important problems to investigate and models to employ in our research and theory" (p. 86).

retical accounts be compared in terms of *generative capacity, that is, the capacity to challenge the guiding assumptions of the culture, to raise fundamental questions regarding contemporary social life, to foster reconsideration of that which is "taken for granted," and thereby to generate fresh alternatives for social action.* It is the generative theory that can provoke debate, transform social reality, and ultimately serve as a stimulus to reordering social conduct. Let us examine more fully the goals and rationale for generative theorizing.[2]

First consider Feyerabend's (1976) commentary on conventional ways of thinking about physical objects. As he points out,

> we typically say "the table is brown" when we view it under normal circumstances, with our senses in good order, but "the table seems to be brown" when either the lighting conditions are poor or when we feel unsure in our capacity for observation. This habit expresses the belief that there are familiar circumstances when our senses are capable of seeing the world "as it really is" and other equally familiar circumstances, when they are deceived. It expresses the belief that some of our sensory impressions are veridical while others are not. We also take it for granted that the material medium between the object and us exerts no distorting influence, and that the physical entity that establishes the contact-light carries a true picture. All these are abstract, and highly doubtful assumptions which shape our view of the world without being accessible to direct criticism. Usually, we are not even aware of them and we recognize their effects only when we encounter an entirely different cosmology: prejudices are found by contrast, not by analysis (Feyerabend, 1976, p. 31).

It would appear that Feyerabend's example holds true for virtually any descriptive or explanatory statement concerning human behavior. All contain a host of unstated and unwarranted assumptions, and the prejudicial grounds for such assumptions may be realized primarily through contrast. The fruits of nurturing contrasts should also be substantial. To be more specific, we first find that *Commitment to any given form of interpretation may truncate one's capacities for problem solving.* To the extent that patterns of human action are undergoing continuous and often unsystematic change, novel threats to personal well-being are continuously encountered. Any given interpretation, whether of the fragmentary, commonsense variety or of the fully articulated science, furnishes but a single myopic view of such experience and a concomitant limitation in problem solving modes. To think of individual behavior as "stimulus controlled," for example, is to close the door on solving problems with a vocabulary of personal volition or responsibility; to account for behavior solely in terms of rule following is to abandon the possibility for describing actions as "beyond one's control." Likewise, a psychology focused solely on individual processes is unable to offer ways of think-

---

[2]It should be clear that one may also speak of "generative research." As we have seen, research is essentially a device for vivifying interpretations, and such interpretations may vary considerably in the extent to which they sensitize the culture to alternatives. See also Smith (1980).

ing about superordinate units; a sociology concerned with social structure alone cannot speak to the vicissitudes of personal experience. A premium is thus to be placed on theory that may reduce the myopia of univocality; as one opens new theoretical vistas, the options for adaptive behavior are increased.[3]

In addition to this rationale for challenging common conceptualizations, every form of behavioral interpretation, whether informal or systematic, *serves as a potential form of social control.* In the broadest sense gaining other's understanding is simultaneously to secure their participation in a language system, frequently with broad implications for what else they do. In a narrower sense, selected forms of description and explanation are often employed by those wishing to sustain a social order in which they possess control. It is within this arena that theorists such as Habermas (1971), Apel (1967), and others in the critical tradition (cf. Jay, 1973) have argued for *emancipatory theory.* When theoretical analysis reveals inconsistencies in the dominant conceptions of an oppressive society, such analysis may serve to free those who are victimized by these conceptions.[4] On purely humanistic grounds, one may also argue that *conventional interpretation limits the range of human potential.* As existing theories specify the range of "reasonable" actions, they also reduce the potential options for experience, limit one's sensitivities, and stifle the imagination. As conventional theory is challenged, human potential may be enhanced.[5]

---

[3] Stephen Toulmin (1981), along with many others, has despaired of the theoretical devisiveness in psychology along with the tendency of many theorists to extend their theories to cover vast domains of activity. Toulmin challenges the discipline to work toward a common language of understanding. In contrast, the present analysis attempts to demonstrate: (1) the grounds for the existing devisiveness (viz. the lack of empirical touchstones for person description), (2) the grounds for the aggressive extension of theory (viz. there are virtually no empirical limits to such extensions), and (3) the value of retaining conflict rather than seeking communion among theories (viz. the necessity of defending multiple valuational orientations along with the flexibility of multiple theoretical languages). The present arguments extend the implications of Warr's (1977) adversary model in the sciences, and in this particular sense are congenial to the spirit of critical rationalism.

[4] As Bauman (1976) has said in another context, "Science continues to supply reliable knowledge . . . only so far as those men whose conduct it describes remain objects, i.e., thing-like, due to the unbroken hold of the habit-enforcing routine conditions of life . . . Emancipation starts, however, when those conditions cease to be seen 'as they really are'" (p. 93). In a broader sense, it may be said that the key characteristic of human life is changing activity. If methodically repetitive, human activity is considered aberrant; if the body is wholly static it may be viewed as lifeless. In this sense, the more fully do persons seek to achieve their potential, the more dispensable traditional science. See also Sampson's (in press) useful discussion of "transformative psychology."

[5] Congenial with this argument is Nietzsche's view of the potentials of historical study. These lie "in inventing ingenious variations on a probably commonplace

Finally, on the pragmatic level it is not clear that the sciences may sustain themselves if their major theoretical outcomes primarily perpetuate the commonsense understandings of the culture. Neither will the intellectual issues be sufficiently engaging to capture the interests of intelligent professionals, nor will the research appear of sufficient importance to merit public funding. The sciences may wither out of ennui, and their efforts may be curtailed because of the impoverishment of insight. Such problems are hardly new ones in social psychology. The criticism that the field too often duplicates common sense has long been echoed, and from the present standpoint, such criticism may continue as long as the traditional mold for "doing science" prevails. With the loosening of such strictures and the development of generative theory, avenues for significant challenge may be opened. To borrow from Schumpeter, needed in the realm of theory are "gales of creative destruction."

It is the principal aim of this chapter to examine a range of significant constraints on theoretical development within the sociobehavioral sciences. In particular, we shall be concerned with the impact on theory of the long-standing commitment to logical empiricist metatheory, or theory of science. This commitment at the metatheoretical level, it will be argued, has severely limited the theoretical capacity of the sciences. The concern with the effects of metatheory on social knowledge is derived from a more general view of the development of theoretical languages, the seeds of which were planted in the closing pages of the last chapter. There it was maintained that there is an interdependent relationship between theoretical language and observation language such that a commitment on either level constrains what may be said at the other. We may now expand this view to take into account both scientific metatheory and its associated methods. Talk about the nature of science and those methods appropriate to it are forms of discourse. If one is to maintain coherence in understanding, a choice of discourse mode at either the metatheoretical or methodological levels must be consistent with one's form of talk about persons or why they behave as they do. For example, without generating mischief, one can scarcely commit oneself to an empiricist orientation on the metatheoretical level while simultaneously arguing on the theoretical level for principles of phenomenological organization. Likewise, one cannot easily adopt a rule-role orientation in describing persons and simultaneously commit oneself to a form of laboratory experimentation denying the concept of intention.[6]

As more formally depicted in Fig. 3.1, the scientist is confronted with four levels of discourse, all of which stand in an interdependent relationship with each other. One may enter the system at any level, from metatheory to observation language. However, any commitment made upon entry is likely to have pervasive effects through the full range of discourse domains. Ample illustration was furnished in the

---

theme, in raising the popular melody to a universal symbol and showing what a world of depth, power and beauty exists in it" (p. 59; 1909-11).

[6] For a general analysis of discourse rules and the relation among systems of discourse see Foucault (1972).

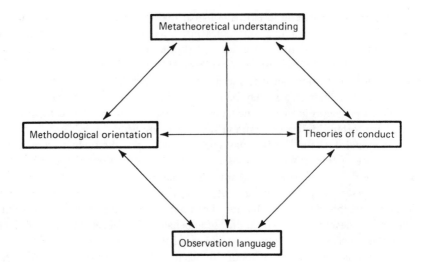

Fig. 3-1. The interdependence of discourse domains.

preceding chapter of the relationship between theory and observation language. There we saw how one's theory determined what could be said about one's observations, and how one's observation language constrained one's choice of theoretical description and explanation. The present chapter will focus on the limiting effects of both traditional metatheory and its associated methods on contemporary theory.[7]

Discussion will be divided into four parts. In the first we shall explore the ways in which assumptions made at the metatheoretical level have guided the choice of constructs at the theoretical level. In this case it will be shown that descriptive and explanatory content are metatheoretically saturated. Second, beyond its influence over the range of theoretical ideas open to consideration, metatheoretical commitment guides the conception and selection of methods. At the same time, this methodological commitment has resonating effects on theoretical development. Of particular concern in the present chapter will be the detrimental effects on theory of the long-standing romance with experimentation. Finally, we shall turn our attention more directly to the problem of generative theory. In this case we shall see that certain aspects of logical empiricist metatheory directly diminish the likelihood of generative theorizing. The traditional metatheory is itself an impediment to significant theoretical advances. This discussion will set the stage for exploring a variety of means by which generative vistas can be opened.

---

[7]It is only for expository purposes that this analysis is restricted to the language domains within the science. As Chapter 1 makes clear, each of these domains is also dynamically related to a wide range of ideological, economic, political, and other influences within the culture (cf. Bloor, 1976; Brandt, 1979; Buss, 1979c; Unger, 1975).

The Impact on Theory of Logical Empiricist Metatheory

Within recent years behavioral scientists have become increasingly sensitive to the ways in which their constructions of knowledge are influenced by their cultural surrounds. It has become progressively and sometimes painfully apparent, that in formulating the basic inventory of behavioral events, selecting particular events for study, developing means for observation, and explaining the resulting observations scientists can be vitally influenced by the normative assumptions and value investments of the surrounding culture. Because scientists participate in the assumptive base upon which the meaning of their conduct is premised, it is difficult to forge a body of knowledge independent of this base. Yet, as also outlined in Chapter 1, the relationship between scientist and society must be viewed as a reciprocal one in which scientific undertakings also influence the collective assumptions of the surrounding culture. It would appear that if intervention into this mutually supportive system could be effected, it might reduce the dependency of the scientist on existing normative assumptions. At the same time it might increase the discipline's capacity to enrich the society through innovative insight. In suspending a particular set of normative assumptions, the scientist may be moved to search anew, to further increase the range of theoretical lenses, to reanalyze and resynthesize, and to emerge with conclusions of greater challenge to the prevailing system of understanding. One means of reducing the dependency on a set of particular influences is through expanding cognizance of them and their effects on the science. By understanding the forces shaping contemporary scientific thought, one may escape their inertial hold over the future.

The chief contention of the present discussion is that the primary model of psychological functioning within the behavioral sciences, one that has dominated inquiry for over fifty years, represents the simple recapitulation of a long-standing conception within the culture. Further, with a flowering of empiricist philosophy in the twentieth century, this conception received an official "stamp of approval." When scientists embraced the logical empiricist program for scientific conduct, they simultaneously absorbed the underlying conception of psychological functioning. As a result, relevant disciplines have been significantly limited in the range of their concerns, in the types of behavior selected for study, in the choice of explanatory constructs, and in their vision of human potential. In the following pages we shall first review several key assumptions within the logical empiricist tradition, and the psychological model presupposed by these assumptions. We shall then examine the manner in which these same assumptions appear to shape theory and research in an explanatory domain, namely that of social psychology.

Psychological Assumptions Underlying the Logical Empiricist Program

Twentieth century empiricism, along with its particular realizations in logical positivism and critical rationalism, withstands any simple characterization. Many conflicting views have been championed within this general domain, and considerable modification in emphasis and outlook has occurred over the years. However, as outlined in Chapter 1, certain recurring lines of thought have been incorporated into the rationale for behavioral science. As commonly maintained within the science there is a world of palpable entities (behavioral events) that may be explored and understood through proper employment of the human faculties. Such exploration requires potential agreement among persons as to the character of their sense data at a specified time. Thus, the same behavioral observations should be available to all persons of normal constitution under similar conditions. On the basis of initial observation, the scientist may proceed to formulate more general statements. These statements typically take the form of "if . . . then" propositions. As seen, ideal scientific conduct would include the mounting of new and more systematically controlled observations. The latter observations would be based on logical deductions made from the initial theoretical formulation. Such observations would ideally take place within the context of experimental tests of specific hypotheses representing the conclusions reached through the deductive process. Observations validating the hypotheses serve to enhance one's confidence in the general theoretical network. Invalidating observations may be used to alter the initial theoretical construction or to invalidate initial conclusions altogether. This, the hypothetico-deductive process, is thus held to be self-corrective. If systematically followed the ultimate outcome will be a repository of fundamental, objective knowledge.[8]

Most of these suppositions are virtual truisms for a broad sector of the discipline. However, it is important for present purposes to adumbrate several key psychological assumptions embedded within this line of argument. In general, it may be said that most philosophical positions harbor theories, typically unstated and incomplete, of psychological functioning.[9] In the present case, it appears that beneath the hypothetico-deductive program lie important conceptions about the nature of human functioning, both in its common and ideal forms. A complete analysis of such assumptions would take us beyond our current needs. For present purposes we may confine ourselves to three central clusters:

---

[8] Also see Koch's (1959) analysis of the guiding suppositions of what he terms the "age of theory." As he argues, in spite of their manifest dysfunctionality, these suppositions continue to guide the vast share of contemporary inquiry in psychology (Koch, 1981).

[9] Inherent in the present analysis is a reversal of the traditional relationship holding between philosophy and the science of psychology. Typically the psychologist has looked to the philosopher for a viable definition of knowledge and an account of those procedures essential for its attainment. The received view thus establishes a rationale for scientific comportment. From the present standpoint philosophic analysis itself is seen to rest on a prior set of assumptions about human psychology. In effect, philosophic metatheory harbors an implicit psychology that itself stands open for study by the psychologist. Required at this point are more detailed and definitive studies of the implicit psychology of philosophic systems: a *psychology of philosophy*.

1. *Dualism and the mind as mirror.* At the outset, an essential dualism is proposed that distinguishes between the experiencing individual and objects of experience. Ideally, psychological processes should provide a veridical representation of the empirical world. To the extent that psychological functioning acts *upon* the input supplied by the existing phenomena, it may disrupt the process of recording. Ideal psychological representation thus occurs when the individual acts as a passive recording device.

2. *The centrality of cognitive processing.* A class of psychological processes can be singled out that may be designated cognitive in character. Among those cognitive capacities essential for proper understanding are those of abstraction and logic. Through conceptual abstraction the individual may remove him- or herself from the press of immediate sense data; generalizations cutting across isolated circumstances may be developed. Through logic (both inductive and deductive), the individual can draw systematic inferences from a body of sense data. Through logic one may make predictions regarding future events.

3. *Affect as interference.* Cognitive processes may be distinguished from those that are noncognitive. Among the most significant of the noncognitive processes are those generally viewed as affective. Emotions, values, desires, and motives would all be included within this latter domain. Processes in the affective domain may properly serve as a motivational base for seeking knowledge (cognitive processing), but once the latter process has begun, they may be viewed as deterrents to proper cognitive functioning. To the extent that affect enters into the process of observation, such observations are said to be biased and untrustworthy. When affect guides the process of abstraction or determines the end point of logical analysis, such processes are defective.

Of course, these particular assumptions did not spring anew from the soil of logical empiricist thought. In fact, many of their roots are as deep as the Western intellectual tradition itself (cf. Pepper, 1972; Randall, 1956). Logical empiricist philosophy has essentially captured a number of important elements within this tradition and provided sophisticated reinforcement. Other conceptions have been available to psychologists, and some of these conceptions have been adopted by various minorities within the profession. However, the embodiment of the above conceptions within the logical empiricist program has virtually ensured their perpetuation by psychologists accepting the program as a guide to proper scientific conduct.

Metatheoretical Suppositions and Psychological Theory

As we have seen in earlier chapters, derivations from logical empiricist metatheory furnish the guiding rationale for the vast share of current behavioral inquiry. We have also had reason to question certain aspects of both the metatheory and its resultant practices within the discipline. Our present concern, however, is with the effects of adopting the metatheory not on the process of doing science but on the content of psychological theory. In adopting the program, far more has been acquired than a set of rules for appropriate scientific conduct. Simultaneously, one tacitly accepts the underlying conception of psychological functioning and its optimal state. To "do science" in the logical empiricist mold is to accede to the underlying assumptions concerning the nature of common psychological functioning and to its optimal utilization. Social psychological study will again furnish the necessary illustrations.

The Study of Attitudes

For over thirty years attitude change research has been guided by two competing theoretical orientations. The initial approach was developed by Carl Hovland and his Yale colleagues, and dominated the literature on attitude change roughly between 1940 and 1960 (cf. McGuire's 1968 review). Fundamental to this model is first the dualistic perspective: Real-world events serve as inputs to psychological functioning. As Hovland, Janis, and Kelley (1953) put it, "Characteristically an individual is bombarded with a host of diverse and often contradictory points of view which must somehow be integrated in arriving at an opinion" (p. 286). In effect, opinions are built up out of incoming stimuli in the same way that the classic philosophers argued that the mind is a product of incoming sensations (see Robinson, 1976). By the same token, opinions will not change until they are exposed to new information inputs. In Hovland, Janis, and Kelley's (1953) terms, "opinions, like other habits, will tend to persist unless the individual undergoes new learning experiences" (p. 10). In effect, the generally accepted model of psychological functioning appears to be that of the rational individual acting adaptively to environmental events. In keeping with this model of the person *qua* empiricist, it is argued that a credible communicator, one who provides more reliable and trustworthy information, is more effective in changing opinions than one who is not credible (Hovland, Janis, & Kelley, 1953; Insko, 1967). Surely, it would be irrational by traditional standards to change one's opinions when exposed to an untrustworthy and unreliable communicator. Similarly, any factor indicating that communication may be biased (by virtue of the communicator's membership in an alien reference group, through forewarning that one is attempting to persuade, or by realizing that only one side of the issue is being presented) is said to decrease the impact of a given message (at least, for educated or cognitively sophisticated people). Again, the implicit assumption of a rational being striving for maximum adaptiveness to the exigencies of the environment is apparent.

With the waning of operationism and the emergence of the cognitive movement in psychology, attitude theorists have explicated more fully the rational basis of attitude change. In particular, the currently fashionable expentancy value models now serve as the analog of proper scientific activity from the traditional standpoint (cf. Ajzen & Fishbein, 1972; Fishbein & Ajzen, 1975). As Jaeger (1981) points out, such models "assume that individuals use information in a reasoned and rational manner in order to come to terms with a complex world. Hence, attitudes toward an object are determined by the information one has about that object" (pgs. 2-3). Values furnish a motivational source for action, just as they may legitimately serve as the basis for a scientist's concern with curing cancer or increasing the world's grain supply. However, given a particular set of goals, it is one's expectation, based on rational assessment of probability, that determines one's final action.

A second major line of research within the Hovland tradition has attempted to demonstrate that various factors may interfere with rational processing of environmental information. Consistent with the guiding metatheory, such research primarily places the blame for such disruptions on various emotional factors. For example, concern has been registered over the advantage of a physically attractive or ethnically desirable source in changing attitudes (Kelman, 1968; Mills & Aronson, 1965). To change one's attitudes on the basis of the communicator's beauty or skin color is to be inappropriately influenced. Research into emotional biases becomes most clearly articulated in research on personal dispositions and attitude change. In particular, people whose feelings of regard or esteem for self are either very high or very low are virtually condemned for their irrationality in processing incoming information (cf. Janis et al., 1959).[10] Similarly, those who are extreme in their feelings on an issue are singled out for their inaccuracy in processing incoming information (Sherif & Hovland, 1961). As it is argued, emotional involvement in an issue has distorting effects on one's ability to perceive incoming information. Assimilation and contrast biases are more extreme under these conditions (Sherif, Sherif & Nebergall, 1965).

Given these two types of research endeavors, the one demonstrating the adequacy of rational processing, and the other isolating emotionally based interferences with such processing, we can better understand the existence of certain long-term controversies within the Hovland tradition. For example, Irving Janis (1967) and his colleagues have maintained that strong threats of danger associated with certain objects or lines of action evoke a high level of fear. Fear, as a fundamental emotional reaction, interferes with rational processing, and the individual is likely to respond dysfunctionally. High fear may thus reduce the likelihood that the individual will change his or her attitudes in such a way that the source of the fear will be avoided. For example, people made to feel highly fearful over the consequences of poor care of their teeth are shown to be less caring of their teeth than those who are made to feel less fearful. Emotion within this framework thus plays its traditional role in reducing rationality. However, the particular fashion in which it does so also implies that rationality is ultimately a victim of the emotions. The argument thus proves disagreeably extreme from the metatheoretical stance because, by implication, there is reason to doubt what appear to be rational (properly scientific)

---

[10] For example, Cohen (1959) reports that persons with very high self-esteem "appear to take on early in life a defensive mode which handles challenging experience by a strong self-protective facade. They repress, deny, ignore, or turn about their potentially disturbing impulses . . ." (p. 116). With respect to the person who is easily persuaded, Linton and Graham (1959) conclude: "he is likely to guide his behavior by external standards in other situations as well, to have values that favor comformity, to have an immature and weak concept of himself, to be unimaginative, and to have a limited range of interests" (p. 93).

decisions. It is within this context that we can appreciate the emergence of theorists such as Howard Leventhal (1970), who do not wish to see rationality thus subdued. As Leventhal (1970) says, "Our paradigm views the organism as an active decision maker" (p. 180), rather than the pawn to emotional dynamics. Operating from the same logical empiricist base, it is argued in this case that emotional arousal need not diminish rational capabilities. It does so only under specialized conditions. One of the most important occurs when the individual cannot cope with fear or danger. On this account rational problem solving of the traditional sort is less in evidence among defective people. Those persons with normal coping capabilities can "execute protective recommendations" (Leventhal, 1970, p. 143). In this case fear motivates rational processing rather than interfering with it. In effect, the local disagreements over the function of fear in attitude change serve to recapitulate the dual view of emotions in the underlying metatheory: They may properly undergird theory, but should not affect one's rationally derived conclusions. In the light of the singular image of human functioning to which both enterprises are committed, it seems unlikely that the controversy can be resolved through additional research. At base, both lines of investigation are essentially in accord. Both render support for the empiricist vision, but emphasize contrasting functions of emotional or motivational dynamics within this perspective. To foreclose on either approach would be to cast doubt on the prevailing metatheory.

With the emergence of cognitive consistency models in the 1960s, interest in the Hovland paradigm began to wane. From the present perspective, such models (including dissonance theory, and the balance models of Newcomb, Heider, Abelson and Rosenberg, Osgood and Tannenbaum, Cartwright and Harary, and others) have commanded broad attention within the field primarily because they appeared at first to challenge the prevailing positivist–empiricist vision of human functioning. In contrast to viewing the individual as a rational animal whose proper functioning could occasionally be undermined through emotional arousal, the consistency models suggested that forms of rational processing could themselves eventuate in illogical or dysfunctional ends. For example, dissonance theory (Festinger, 1957) is based on the assumption that the presence of inconsistent cognitions is unsettling or dissonance arousing. Although this assumption is quite compatible with the positivist–empiricist image, Festinger and many others went on to argue that, in the quest for dissonance reduction, the individual is often moved to irrationality. The presence of an illogical or dissonant thought can lead to denial of the thought, closure to inconsistent evidence, increased preference for the belief that was challenged by the dissonant information, or increased attraction for an object or person denigrated by the dissonant information (cf. Brehm & Cohen 1962; Wicklund & Brehm, 1976).

Various formal theories of balance led to similar conclusions (cf. Abelson et al., 1968). Such models were based on notions of preferred psychological states. Such states led to conclusions often at odds with the accepted position regarding the positive role of rationality. The rational being does not change his or her attitudes or behavior in the absence of empirically based justification. Yet, from the balance perspective, such changes may occur simply to achieve a state of psychological harmony. For instance, there is no logical reason for changing one's attitudes toward person P when he or she criticizes a painting that one has long admired. These actions *in themselves* do not provide rational grounds for attitude change. Yet virtually all balance models predict a negative change in attitude toward P in order for the state of balance to be achieved. As in the case of dissonance theory, change is born of internal strivings for a desirable end and without rational regard for the character of impinging reality. In effect the consistency models, if carried to their logical end point, would replace empiricism with some form of rationalism at the metatheoretical level.

Yet, in spite of its apparent challenge to the traditional views, and in spite of the immense effort of researchers in this realm, interest in the family of balance models has also waned. This decline of interest can scarcely be traced to the entry of some novel or compelling alternative, nor to the ultimate vitiation of the basic suppositions. From the present perspective it may be ventured that the alternative image of human functioning represented in the family of consistency models was forced to abdicate by existing metatheoretical presuppositions. To accept these models would be to undermine the metatheoretical "deep structure" of the discipline. Initial attempts were made to settle the matter on empirical grounds. However, intrinsic shortcomings in experimental methodology generally barred the way to such resolution. To be more specific, although the dissonance formulation was exciting in its seeming capacity to predict the counterintuitive, the psychologist was still faced with the vast range of behavior that seemed intuitively appropriate, and objectively reasonable. An uneasy suspicion could thus be nurtured that the theory might be restricted to rather limited circumstances. In a sense, aberrant reasoning of the variety celebrated by dissonance researchers could be viewed as analogous to the emotional intrusions documented within the Yale tradition, that is, "possible but not probable."

Given their heavy reliance on experimentation, it was virtually impossible for dissonance researchers to quell this suspicion. Experiments invite the researcher to preselect settings that will ensure support for his or her hypothesis. One can never be certain that alternative settings of greater numerosity would not yield findings to the contrary. The heavy reliance on laboratory manipulation proved additionally troublesome. Particularly within the dissonance paradigm, the existence of many counterintuitive results motivated other investigators to attempt replications. Replicating the initial results often proved difficult, and the conclusion slowly emerged that one's experimental results often relied on a subtle complex of factors often specific to a particular laboratory or investigator.

However, the major prophylactic against this alternative vision of human functioning took the ever-reliable form (see Chapter 2) of the alternative interpretation. In the case of dissonance theory, Chapanis and Chapanis (1964) first documented important methodological flaws inherent in many of the relevant studies. Essentially, their critique suggested that the commonly accepted view of rational functioning was being subverted through methodological artifice. Subsequently, two additional interpretations emerged, both strongly buttressing the traditional view of rational functioning. First, Janis and his colleagues (cf. Janis & Gilmour, 1965) argued that many of the dissonance findings could be explained through a modification of the Hovland framework. Experimental findings were used to document the claim. More persistent was the research of Daryl Bem (1972) and his colleagues, who showed how many of the dissonance findings could be explained through a modified form of Skinnerian behaviorism. Except for its eschewal of mind–matter dualism, Skinnerian theory is virtually a caricature of the logical empiricist image of human functioning. Its primary assumption is that the behavior of organisms represents an optimal adjustment to real-world contingencies. All behavior may thus be seen as rationally appropriate within its particular circumstances. As Bem (1972) maintained, "Individuals come to 'know' their own attitudes, emotions, and other internal states partially by inferring them from observations of their own overt behavior and/or the circumstances in which action occurs" (p. 2). Thus, for Bem, dissonance results could be derived from the logical analysis of observed data. The empiricist metatheory was thus vindicated.

The internecine battles that raged between dissonance advocates, on the one hand, and the Janis and Bem forces, on the other, ultimately revealed that there was no way in which the psychological basis for behavioral events could be unequivocally demonstrated. As discussed in Chapter 2, any experimental result could properly "be explained away" through careful analysis by the opposition.[11] Thus, the chief means offered by the hypothetico-deductive program for selecting between competing theories, that is, the controlled experiment, had failed the challenge. Essentially, there was no way in which the counter-normative vision of human functioning could be sustained, and the model of human functioning embedded within the metatheory remained obdurate.

Social Cognition

Research in social perception and attribution have played conceptual counterpoint with the attitude change domain. Although the psychological structures or processes often bear different labels, the underlying model is much the same. Both traditions are intertwined, certain studies speak to both domains, and with respect to basic assumptions about human conduct, each provides continuing support for the other. The cognitive dimension of the attitude is thus represented in the perceptual domain by such terms as "concept," "attribution," "percept," or "cognitive element." Such constructs are said to serve as internal representations of real-world events. This dualistic orientation has generally dominated investigation for over four decades.

As in the case of attitude research, major disagreements have emerged over the extent to which conceptual or cognitive activity represents a rational accommodation to the contours of the "real world." And, similar to the metatheoretically invested resolutions witnessed in the attitudes domain, the literature on social perception has tended over time to be cleansed of "antiscientific" processes. Perhaps the classic case of such cleansing took place in response to Solomon Asch's (1946)

---

[11] As Greenwald (1975) has demonstrated in a very careful analysis, neither dissonance theory nor self-observation theory is, in principle, disconfirmable.

research on impression formation. Asch was essentially trained in the rational idealist tradition and thus favored a view of perception in which cognitive processes
took priority over the stimulus in determining outcomes. For Asch the individual
performed mental operations on incoming stimuli, such that the latter were organized and reshaped by psychological process. Yet to extend such a view to its
logical conclusion would preclude an objective science; it would suggest that scientific knowledge is shaped by mental processes rather than the contours of nature.
In this light it can well be appreciated why Asch's argument that certain traits (such
as "warm" and "cold") served a central, organizing function in impression formation could not be sustained. No more congenial replacement could be found than
the associationist doctrines so central to early empiricist writings. As Locke, Her-
bart, and James Mill had all reasoned, the relationship among mental events is
cemented through frequency of association, and such frequencies are based on the
observation of real-world events. Thus, mental structure can legitimately be said to
correspond with real-world arrangements. It was this line of thought that was
represented in Wishner's (1960) reanalysis and extension of Asch's research. As
Wishner argued, Asch's analysis could be replaced by a learning view of impression
formation. Of course, the belief in some form of "glue" that holds ideas together is
no more justified than faith in the "magnetic" qualities of certain concepts. Neither
associationist principles nor Gestalt organizing principles can ultimately be dis-
lodged by evidence. However, given the metatheoretical context in which the field
has developed, associationism came to replace the Gestalt orientation favored by
Asch with little more than a whisper of contention. And this view continues into
the present to serve as the guiding metaphor for a wide range of research (cf.
Rosenberg & Sedlak, 1972).

Further insinuation of metatheory into theory is exemplified in the place assigned to emotional and motivational processes. Such processes have typically been
considered independent of cognition and a potential threat to proper perception.
The classic research on perceptual defense illustrates the prevailing disposition. This
line of work was based on the assumption that desires (wants and fears) could bias
perception in such a way that people are more likely to see what they desire and
less likely to register undesirable events (cf. Jones & Gerard's 1967 summary).
Thus, motives were experimentally manipulated or isolated within extreme groups
(repressors, sexual neurotics, etc.), and the attempt was made to show how heightened arousal or extreme motivation biased perceptual judgments. Affect in the
traditional sense is thus considered injurious to perceptual fidelity. Research into
prejudicial stereotyping has followed much the same path. In this case, the central
interest has been in demonstrating the affective basis of such biased cognitive activity. In particular, numerous demonstrations have been used to show that negative
affect toward a given group engenders stereotypic perception (cf. Harding, Proshansky, Kutner, & Chein, 1969). Such ventures reached their extreme in theory
and research on the authoritarian personality (Adorno, Frenkel-Brunswik, Levinson,
& Stanford, 1950). Here, an elaborate psychodynamic basis was provided for cognitive biases. Adult problems in perceiving and understanding were attributed to
problematic emotional patterns established at an early age.

he separation of cognition from the emotion, along with the denigration of the
ler in favor of the former, has continued relatively unchanged into the present
/a. One of the most interesting of contemporary cases is furnished by inquiry into
causal attribution. The traditional conception of emotional dynamics as bête noire
is retained, as wide-ranging investigations attempt to demonstrate that the assignment of causal responsibility may be "erroneously" or improperly influenced by
people's desire to see a just world, to obtain an enhanced social image, or to reduce
criticism from others (cf. Bradley, 1978; Lerner, 1970; Weary, 1980). As widely
argued, attribution processes often suffer from "self-serving bias" (Bernstein,
Stephan, & Davis, 1979; Schopler & Layton, 1972; Snyder, Stephan, & Rosenfield,
1976). Of equal interest, however, we find that research into causal attribution has
undergone a fate similar to that of consistency theory in the attitude change domain: Although the initial thrust was rational idealist, basic conceptions have been
transformed over time so as to correspond with the dominant empiricist metatheory. In Heider's (1946) initial work the central focus was on the manner in
which psychological tendencies determine the locus of cause in human action.
From Heider's perspective, phenomenal causality could not be derived from sense
data, but was viewed as a product of intrinsic cognitive tendencies. Thus, inherent
cognitive tendencies could be said to lie at the heart of interpersonal relations, a
condition that Heider believed separated perception of natural objects (in the
logical empiricist model) from social perception (Heider, 1958). In his concern with
the intrinsic tendencies of cognition, Heider was manifesting the assumptions embedded in the rational idealist orientation of his German mentors, Meinong and
Lewin. And, in this assumption of autochthonous perceptual processes, Heider was
maintaining a position the implications of which could threaten the dominant metatheory within the discipline. To the extent that the perceptions of persons is guided
by psychological processes that cannot be factually grounded, and to the degree
that causality is a product of psychic functioning, one faces problems in justifying
metatheoretical arguments for an objective science of cause and effect. Scientists,
it could be maintained, are susceptible to the same intrinsic tendencies of cognitive organization.

In this context one can readily understand the broad enthusiasm that greeted
both the Jones (Jones & Davis, 1965; Jones & McGillis, 1976) and the Kelley
(1967, 1972) models of causal inference. From Jones' standpoint the perceiver
operates as a computer-like information processing agent who identifies the common and noncommon effects of various actions, assesses the social desirability of
these effects, and maximizes his or her outcomes. Similar to the ideal scientist as
traditionally conceived, the perceiver not only relies on incoming information in
determining the fundamental dispositions of the actor, but also on expectations
(category and target based) built upon past observation (Jones & McGillis, 1976). In
effect, the Jones model shifts the image of the social perceiver from one who is
driven by transcendental demands of experiential organization to one who proceeds
to construct increasingly reliable expectations (hypotheses) about the world on the

basis of observation and deduction. Kelley's transfiguration of the Heider formulation is even more outspoken in its reinstigation of empiricist metatheory. For Kelley, "the ideal perceiver is a *social scientist*" (Shaver, 1975), who employs James Mill's method of difference to determine whether the source of a given action is to be found in the person or the environment. As Kelley points out, the chief function of developing attributional schemas is to aid in the "prediction and control" of behavior. Attributional schemas thus serve the function traditionally assigned to scientific theories. Such schemas are said to be built up inductively through the observation of co-occurrences. A given social stimulus is judged to be the cause of an action to the extent that its presence is followed by the action, and the action fails to occur in its absence. For Kelley, the ideal scientist employs an identical process of locating cause–effect relations with the help of systematic observation and sophisticated analysis of variance techniques.[12] With such reinstigation of metatheoretical assumptions, Heider's early view has been all but obscured. Contemporary attribution theory reinstigates traditional empiricism.

The prevailing metatheoretical assumptions are also manifest in Jones' highly influential work with Nisbett (Jones & Nisbett, 1971) on actor and observer discrepancies in causal attribution. As argued in this case, while actors tend to see their actions as responses to external conditions, observers are likely to attribute the same actions to internal processes or dispositions of the actor. If one views attributional processes as inductively generated, a reflection of real-world cause and effect, it is then appropriate to inquire into the differential accuracy of these discrepant attributions. Who is the more objectively accurate in assigning cause, the actor or the observer? Jones and Nisbett do indeed address themselves to this question and, although demurring from exacting criteria, do express a strong preference. This preference may again be traced to the prevailing metatheory. If the external world drives sense impressions, if theory is built inductively from sense data, and if behavior is essentially a response to the stimulus world—all interdependent assumptions—then attributions placing the locus of human action in the environment are to be preferred over those that look to the individual as the source of his or her activity. It is thus to the actor that Jones and Nisbett give approbation in the partitioning of causal sources. The actor sees correctly that the environment determines action. The Jones and Nisbett preference for external causes of behavior becomes a fully articulated principle in Ross' (1977) treatment of "the fundamental attribution error." For Ross, observers systematically "overestimate" the importance of internal processes or dispositions in accounting for others' actions. In keeping with the empiricist metatheory, it is the environmental situation that determines human processing and resultant behavior, and not intrinsic demands of psychological functioning.

In summary, it appears that the logical empiricist image of human conduct has

---

[12] The close connection between much contemporary attribution theory and logical empiricist metatheory is also elaborated in McClure (1980).

played a key role in shaping theories of attitude change and social cognition. It is manifest in the dominant conceptions of human functioning, the interpretation of research findings, the reinterpretation of alien theories, and the insulation of the discipline from alternative theories. The influence of the metatheory is hardly limited to these areas. In group psychology, for example, much effort has been devoted to improving group decision making. The prevailing assumption is that optimal, rationally based decisions may be formed and it is to such decisions that groups should aspire. However, various extraneous factors are said to interfere to misguide or obfuscate the process. Research is typically dedicated to isolating these various forces of irrationality. Group size, structure, composition, leadership characteristics, and so on have all figured in the attempt (Davis, 1969; Janis, 1972). Before perishing of its own weight, the risky shift literature was similarly oriented (Cartwright, 1971). For many, the drama of such research lay in the possibility that irrational forces were unleashed within the context of group discussion, and such forces lead groups to riskier decisions than were reasonably merited. Similarly, much research on race relations demonstrates the same fundamental assumptions. In this case, Harding, Proshansky, Kutner, and Chein's (1969) comments in the *Handbook of Social Psychology* are informative. As they point out,

> The norm of rationality is basic for the definition of prejudice proposed by Powdermaker (1944), Lippitt and Radke (1946), Allport (1954), Kelman and Pettigrew (1959) and Simpson and Yinger (1965). The norm enjoins a persistent attempt to seek accurate information, to correct misinformation, to make appropriate differentiations and qualifications, and to be logical in deduction and cautious in inference. (Harding, Proshansky, Kutner, & Chein, 1969, p. 5)

One may also discern the recapitulation of the prevailing metatheory in many of the assumptions made within social exchange theory. Essentially exchange theory is lodged in the assumption that individuals employ real-world evidence (in the form of positive and negative payoffs) to reach rational decisions (i.e., maximize rewards and minimize costs). Like the scientist, they may be motivated by many diverse goals; however, once the goals are established, people operate functionally by taking into account (e.g., developing and testing expectancies or hypotheses) the feedback supplied by the surrounding environment.

Finally George Kelly's (1955) theory of personal constructs must be noted for the singular clarity with which it links the empiricist metatheory and psychological functioning. As Kelly says, "When we speak of *man-the-scientist* we are speaking of all mankind and not merely a particular class of men who have publicly attained the stature of 'scientist'" (p. 4). And this view of the scientist is the now-familiar one: "each individual man formulates in his own way constructs through which he views the world of events. As a scientist, man seeks to predict, and thus control, the course of events. It follows, then, that the constructs which he formulates are intended to aid him in his predictive efforts" (p. 12). To reiterate a theme developed in Chapter 1, one may view therapeutic intervention based on such theory as a grass-roots education in epistemology.

Metatheory and Theoretical Foreclosure

As we see, a single, overarching model of human functioning appears to prevail throughout mainstream social psychology, a model that is derived from and sustained by prevailing metatheoretical commitment. One might wish to defend this commitment on the basis that it has provided a certain degree of unity across a variety of highly diverse enterprises. It has furnished a paradigm within which the science could demonstrate progression. Yet, if the central product of the science continues to be an elaboration and extension of a singular world-view, the science would seem to abnegate what many view as its fundamental aim, to expand understanding. Social psychologists have done a great deal to further understanding within the logical empiricist framework. However, such work has primarily expanded or elaborated on the accepted belief system rather than providing a significant challenge to normative assumptions. As we have seen, out of an apparent commitment to metatheory, theoretical attempts to challenge common assumptions have typically encountered strong interest, then criticism, reinterpretation, and finally rejection.

The extent of such intellectual foreclosure is difficult to assess. However, it is of some interest that the field has witnessed virtually no extensive elaboration of prominent alternatives to the view of humans as miniaturized scientists. Psychoanalytic theory has proved immensely stimulating within other domains of social science and the humanities. However, the theory is virtually disregarded by the contemporary research community. Symbolic interactionism has suffered a similar fate. Extensions of this outlook, including labeling theory, ethnomethodology, and dramaturgical analysis, have played an immensely rich and stimulating role within the sociological domain. Yet it would appear, because of the inimical implications of this line of thought for traditional assumptions of an objective science (cf. Wilson, 1970), that they have scarcely figured in the psychological research literature. Further, dialectic theory has had an exhilarating effect on the social sciences more generally. It is also a form of thinking that many view as antithetical to the aims of traditional behavioral science. The virtual absence of dialectically oriented contributions within the major periodicals of the field should not be surprising. Again, metatheory would appear to obfuscate theory.

One may be justifiably concerned over the lack of intellectual ferment and development within itself. However, there are further repercussions for the well-being of the profession. For many the discipline has lost intellectual challenge; fundamental questions of human conduct seem tangential. One must further consider the standing of the discipline within the intellectual community more broadly. The smug self-satisfaction that developed in the 1940s and 1950s, based as it was on a faith that the assiduous application of empirical methods would engender superior knowledge, appears to have fostered a form of intellectual insularity. In the case of social psychology, there has not only been a bifurcation between psychological and sociological branches, but there is also little indication of significant interchange with colleagues in other intellectual spheres. With little but patchwork communications across disciplines, the potential for significant theoretical departures in psychology seems further diminished. Let us turn now from the influence of metatheory on theory to the theoretical ramifications of method.

Methodological Selection and Theoretical Constraint: The Controlled Experiment

Embedded within the conception of proper scientific comportment lie ancillary dispositions toward method. Claims concerning what the scientist is attempting to do are often linked to conceptions of how it might be done. In the previous discussion we centered on the dualistic assumptions embedded within empiricist metatheory and their implications for theory construction. In a broad sense this form of dualism, granting nature preeminent status in guiding or fashioning mental process, commits the discipline to some form of stimulus–response theory. As indicated in our preliminary analysis, such a metatheoretical orientation also carries with it strong implications for preferred forms of methodology. In particular, if the stimulus world is superordinate and antecedent to psychological process, and the latter is responsible for behavior, required is a methodology that precisely traces the connections among the stimulus–response elements. And, because elements within the psychological and behavioral sphere are fundamentally dependent on the conditions within the preeminent sphere of the stimulus world, the most sensible course of research is to alter stimulus conditions systematically and to observe the resulting repercussions. The favored methodology can thus be none other than the controlled experiment. Metatheory, theory and method are interlocking and mutually reinforcing.

It is within this context that one can well understand why the practice of psychology has become increasingly identified with the experimental method. For many this development has been welcomed, and much effort has been devoted to sustaining its hegemony. Through experimentation it was believed, one could move from sheer speculation to the level of empirically grounded theory. No longer was it necessary to rely on the wholly unreliable accounts of a single observer, nor was the scientist fettered by correlational techniques and their shaky grasp of causal sequence. Through experimentation it seemed possible to test precise ideas about cause and effect against actual events, and thus to accumulate a repository of fundamental knowledge. In addition, experimentation ensured that behavioral scientists could lay claim to the respectability increasingly enjoyed by their colleagues in the natural sciences. Psychology could link itself securely with the positivist-empiricist orientation and its underlying commitment to the unity of science (Koch, 1959).

The results of this line of development are widely apparent. For example, in social psychology the percentage of experimental studies appearing in the *Journal of Personality and Social Psychology*, the most prestigious voice in the field, increased from approximately 30% in 1949 to 83% in 1959, and then to 87% in 1969 (Higbee & Wells, 1972). *The Journal of Experimental Social Psychology* and the *European Journal of Social Psychology* are commonly viewed as competitors in respectability. Their contributions are almost entirely experimental. Even in the more peripheral journals such as the *Journal of Research in Personality* and the *Journal of Applied Social Psychology*, the vast majority of the present contributions rely on experimentation. Simulation methodologies are rarely employed in these journals; survey research is almost exclusively limited to the field of sociology and political science (Fried, Gumper, & Allen, 1973); and in Weick's (1968) review of observational methodology in social psychology, only 15% of the three hundred references are taken from the four major journals of the field and less than half of this group from the five-year period prior to publication of the review. The one elite organization within the field is aptly named the *Society for Experimental Social Psychology*. Within psychology the pursuit of social understanding has become virtually synonymous with the experimental method.[13]

Criticisms of the experimental approach have emerged over the years. Classic is Bakan's (1969) largely unheeded criticisms of null hypothesis testing. Discussions of demand characteristics within the laboratory setting (Orne, 1962; Alexander & Sagatun, 1973), along with the closely related work of Rosenthal (1966) and others on experimenter bias, have been widely heralded. However, the primary effect of this work has been to enhance experimental rigor; experimenters now take special precautions so as to reduce or nullify experimenter effects. Numerous critics have called attention to the artificiality of the laboratory setting and to the failure of experiments to generate knowledge about common social life (Bickman & Henchey, 1972, Harré & Secord, 1972; Kelman, 1972; McGuire, 1967; Proshansky, 1972; Tajfel, 1972). Such criticisms have given rise to a plethora of experiments in field settings, but, as McGuire (1973) has argued, the field experiment has operated as a "tactical evasion" of more basic problems. The ethical suppositions and implications of experimentation have also been seriously questioned (cf. Kelman, 1968), and critics such as Jourard and Kormann (1968) as well as Harré and Secord (1972) have argued that the experimentation is limited to the study of superficial and highly defensive relationships among virtual strangers. Ring (1967) has attacked experimentation on the grounds of its trivial outcomes. Argyris (1980) maintains that because experiments require the development of unilateral control over subjects' behavior, experimental results are of questionable validity in the more open circumstances of daily life. Hampden-Turner (1970) has further taken experimental research to task for the misleading picture it paints of human motives and action.

Yet, in spite of the emerging doubts, the experimental tradition has continued

---

[13] Even in 1961 M. B. Smith, editor of the *Journal of Abnormal and Social Psychology*, wrote: "There are occasions when I have the unpleasant fantasy that psychology has become so enamored of method that techniques become an independent matter and our substantive problems are reduced only to dependent ones" (p. 462). As Darwin Cartwright reiterated in 1979, "the fascination with statistics seems all too often to have replaced a concern for substantive significance . . . One might think our journals would have to go out of business if the use of analysis of variance were to be prohibited" (p. 87). And as Silverman (1977) has noted, "Social psychology . . . grew in its own peculiar way from a commitment to a method" (p. 357).

relatively unabated. To be sure, greater sensitivity to potential biases and to ethical improprieties has been generated. And doubting graduate students may have paused fitfully before pushing on with an experimental thesis that would ensure passage to a secure professional niche. However, with the lack of convincing alternatives to experimentation, in combination with immense institutional inertia, experimentation remains the central research vehicle.

It is the present contention that the romance with experimental methodology has vitally constrained the range of theoretical explanations admitted to the relevant disciplines. The possibility for such effects were established in Chapter 1. There we saw that in the selection of methods for studying human action the investigator also favors certain theoretical assumptions about the nature of knowledge and how it is best acquired. In effect, the researcher reveals the rudiments of a theory of human understanding in the process of acquiring what he or she takes to be such understanding. Thus, to constrict the range of methods is simultaneously to reduce concern with alternative views of understanding. Further, as indicated above, various forms of stimulus-response (or S-O-R) theory, favored by logical empiricist metatheory, are also congenial to experimental methodology. Thus, to fasten upon the experiment is virtually to ensure the perpetuation of stimulus-response conceptions of human functioning. In another context, McGuire (1973) has also discerned a link between methodological commitments and theoretical potential. As he has argued, the emphasis on experiments has diminished any interest in complex theories involving mechanisms of parallel processing, bidirectional relationships, and feedback circuits. In this context he encourages the development of techniques of computer simulation, multivariate time series designs, and path analysis. As Pepitone (1981) has also demonstrated, methodological doctrines in social psychology have militated against the development of "relational" concepts that might be used in understanding social interaction.[14]

We must now extend such concerns in a variety of important directions. If an alternative to logical empiricist metatheory is to be developed, it too must rely on a conception of human functioning. Several aspects of such an alternative conception have been implicit in our previous analyses. These aspects shall become more fully articulated in the present discussion, as it is this alternative conception that is largely closed to consideration through exclusive reliance on experimentation.

Stimulus Events as Contextually Embedded

One rich intellectual heritage, provocative in social implication but fallow in terms of elaboration in the discipline, has been termed *contextualist* (Pepper, 1972; Sarbin, 1977). From the contextualist standpoint, understanding of events (including people) depends on one's taking account of the expanded network of events in which the focal event is embedded. A contextualist might thus argue that behav-

---

[14] See also London and Thorngate's (1981) discussion of the insufficiency of experimental methods for studying phenomena in a process of "divergent amplification," i.e., displaying multiple forms in transformation.

ioral events typically occur within and are intimately related to a highly complex network of contingencies. Casting the argument in stimulus–response terms, it may be said that few stimulus events considered independently have the capacity to elicit predictable social behavior; responses to most stimuli seem to depend on a host of attendant circumstances. For example, a clenched fist has little inherent stimulus value. Responses to the fist alone would be extremely varied and difficult to predict. However, as additional features are added to the situation, response variability is typically decreased. When one knows the age, sex, economic, marital, educational, and ethnic characteristics of the person whose fist is in question, when one knows about what others are present in the situation, the surrounding physical circumstances, and the events preceding the raising of the fist, one is able more accurately to predict reactions to the stimulus. From the contextualist perspective, it is only by taking into account the range of attendant circumstances that the stimulus gains "meaning" for members of the culture. If the fist is that of a three-year-old in response to his mother's admonishment in the privacy of their own home, the stimulus has far different meaning than if the fist is that of a thirty-year-old Puerto Rican on a street in Spanish Harlem. In effect, social stimuli are typically embedded in broader contexts, and conduct within this complex depends importantly on the cultural meanings assigned to them.

Contextualist thinking is essentially antithetical to the rationale underlying experimental methodology. The power of the experiment, it is argued, lies in its capacity to document relations among isolated stimuli and responses. To accept a methodology premised on such a belief is to remove contextualist theory from serious consideration. To elaborate, the ideal experimenter delimits his or her concerns to independently delineated variables. The rigorous experiment is the one that "disembeds" the stimulus from its surroundings, and examines its independent effects on a given behavior. On this account, one may examine the effects of noise level on helping, jury size on the harshness of the verdict, communicator credibility on attitude change, the presence of weapons on aggression, and so on. To the extent that a particular stimulus may be decomposed into more discrete units, the research may be denigrated and further studies mounted in an attempt to form a more precise statement regarding necessary and sufficient conditions. For example, if "crowding" serves as one's independent variable, and crowds also tend to generate a higher noise level and greater heat, the rigorous experimenter will attempt to control the latter factors. Crowding is thus disembedded so that its effects may be ascertained independent of noise level, heat, and other "extraneous" factors. Although the logic of this practice is compelling, its ultimate effect, from the contextualist perspective, is to obliterate the meaning that "the crowd" possesses in modern life.

In general the contextualist would argue that in the attempt to isolate a given stimulus from the complex in which it is normally embedded, its meaning within the common cultural framework is often obscured or destroyed. When subjects are exposed to an event out of its normal context, they may engage in behavior that is unique to the situation and has little or no relationship to their conduct in normal settings. It is in this respect that Harré (1974) has concluded that "experiments are largely worthless, except as descriptions of the odd way people carry on in trying to make social sense of the impoverished environment of laboratories" (p. 146).[15]

Yet, if this line of reasoning is plausible, it may be asked, why is it that so many laboratory experiments yield findings that are plausible, that do seem fully consistent with what we know of everyday life? Although one answer to this question may be derived from the preceding chapter's discussion of the indeterminant relationship between observation and interpretation, it is also apparent that, in order to achieve sensible results, the experimenter covertly re-embeds the stimulus of interest into a context that is meaningful for the subject. The experimenter does not thus manipulate a single variable in isolation from the remainder of the stimulus world. Rather, he or she alters an event within a context that renders the alteration meaningful, and without which the alteration would be inconsequential. Such re-embedding occurs as the experimenter makes choices of experimental setting, the stimulus materials, the experimenter's gender, and so on. Such decisions contain a host of assumptions that are left wholly unarticulated either at the level of observation language or theory. To illustrate the point, the social psychologist interested in effects of communicator credibility on attitudes can scarcely usher a prominent scientist into the experimental chamber and have him or her speak in support of a randomly selected topic—all that is demanded by a consideration of "communicator credibility" as an abstract variable. Rather, the experimenter must prepare the subject in special ways, ensuring that the subject anticipates the message, will attend to the communicator, and will not be frustrated by doing so. Care must also be taken to see that the message is relevant to the subject's realm of interest or knowledge, and does not personally offend the subject, that the subject is in no way threatened by the presence (or absence) of the communicator, that listening to the message is a meaningful act, and so on. Such circumstances are wholly obscured in the concentration on the disembedded stimulus, and yet appear essential to the effects of communicator credibility. From the contextualist standpoint, what passes for knowledge within the discipline may thus rest on an immense number of unstated assumptions and obscured conditions. Knowledge in the form of independent statements of relationship among isolated variables is largely misleading.

Stimulus Events as Diachronically Embedded

Historically oriented thinkers often join the contextualists in arguing that social events are integral parts of sequences occurring over time. Such events acquire their particular meaning from their special placement within a diachronic sequence.[16] The exchange of smiles at a first meeting is of a far different character than that occurring after a bitter fight, primarily because the sequence in which an event is

---

[15] Also see Mishler's (1979) critique of context-free laws and the use of context-stripping methods in traditional psychology.

[16] As John Dewey (1931) argued, "Behavior is serial, not mere succession. It can be resolved—it must be—into discrete acts, but no act can be understood apart from the series to which it belongs" (p. 253).

embedded is of utmost importance in understanding its social significance. However, to engage in rigorous experimentation is to reduce theoretical consideration to temporally truncated sequences occurring in the early stages of a relationship.[17] Elaboration of the point is required.

In the application of fundamental standards of rigor, the experimentalist attempts to ensure that variations in the dependent variable can be traced unequivocally to variations in one or more independent variables, each of which can be isolated independently or considered in combination with others. Such strictures demand that investigators limit themselves to very brief behavioral sequences, as the greater the interval separating the manipulation of the independent variable from the assessment of the dependent variable, the greater is the difficulty in interpreting one's data. As the period intervening between the onset of the stimulus conditions and the assessment of the effects is increased, the number of uncontrolled processes or extraneous factors that can intrude to cloud the chain of causality responsible for the results is increased. For this reason most research in social psychology takes pains to ensure that, after exposure to the major manipulation, subjects do not speak with anyone whose behavior is not standardized. It is partly out of the same interest in rigor that the psychology of group process has floundered (cf. Steiner, 1974), and well-trained social psychologists often avoid research on programs of social change. In both cases it has proved impossible to trace accurately the connections among independent and dependent variables, and the research is thus considered opprobrious.

It is out of similar concern for rigor that social psychologists have largely confined themselves to the early stages of relationships. To the extent that experimental subjects have already established a relationship, experimental results may be contaminated by events outside the experimenter's control. The experimenter who hopes to explore the effects of competition, for example, may find that the meaning of competitive instructions for friends of long standing is different from that of strangers. Since the experimenter cannot control the many different meanings that such a concept would have among long-term friends, they are simply disregarded for purposes of experimental rigor. With such intensive concentration on brief sequences, extended patterns of social interaction are virtually nonexistent in the social psychological literature. Similarly, the discipline has almost nothing to say about the development and breakdown of friendship, professionalization, career trajectories, alterations in family interaction, or the development of extended negotiations or armed conflict. All would require an analysis of interaction patterns across extended periods. All are disregarded to the degree that experimentation is given preferential status.[18]

---

[17] See also the historical-contextual arguments of Moscovici (1972), Tajfel (1972), Secord (1976), and Gottlieb (1977).

[18] Noteworthy exceptions to this general conclusion have begun to emerge in recent years. The work of Harré (1979), Levinger (1980), Rosnow (1978), Gadlin (1978), Albert and Kessler (1978), Altman and Gauvain (1981), Simonton (1979), Martindale (1975), and Veroff, Depner, Kulka, and Douvan (1980), for example, all mani-

The Individual as Self-Directed

In contrast to those who wish to understand human behavior as the product of multiple determinants, others are concerned with developing voluntarist accounts of human action. Yet the presumption of experimentation places restrictions over this line of thought of no less magnitude than those placed upon contextualist and historical orientations. Let us consider the position of the potential voluntarist in light of two common assumptions undergirding the experimental paradigm. First, as the experimentalist will argue, the laboratory experiment enables one to manipulate a single variable of interest while holding other variables constant. In this manner the effects on behavior of variations in a single variable may be traced with precision. We have already seen (Chapters 1 and 2) how the assumption of single-variable manipulation is misleading. However, the major point in the present case is that, to the extent that investigators assume that they manipulate or control specific factors in the investigation, they implicitly deny the capacity of subjects to decide how they wish to interpret, conceptualize, or treat the same configuration. As the experimenter lays claim to control, he or she simultaneously deprecates the assumption that subjects may choose what they wish to see or do, that is, that they are creatures of choice.[19, 20]

To illustrate, many investigators have wished to explore the effects of social density on various forms of human behavior and have arranged experiments in which the number of persons in a given space (or the amount of space for a given number of persons) has been manipulated. Typically the experimenter assumes that a single variable has been manipulated for subjects in the experiment while others have been held constant. The investigator must assume in this case that it is density that has been manipulated and subjects are not free to select another interpretation. Indeed, if subjects were free to attend to whatever they wish or to assign whatever meaning they desire to the situation, then the conception of manipulation and control is obviated. In this case, the investigator would have done nothing more than furnish differing opportunities for subjects to interpret and behave as they wish. Such a conclusion would virtually obliterate the traditional function of experimentation. This problem is hardly a trivial one, as researchers in the area of population

---

fest a strong diachronic perspective. In each case, investigators have also been willing to break with the experimental tradition. Also see Armistead (1974) and Hendrick (1977) for discussions of the way in which the romance with experimentation has smothered the interests of social psychologists in developmental processes.

[19] Elucidating in this regard is Rychlak's (1978) account of the way in which his experimental findings have been systematically rejected from relevant journals because of the employment of a *telic* (or voluntarist) theoretical interpretation as opposed to the more widely accepted mechanistic forms.

[20] As Brewster Smith (1974) has lamented, the behaviorist orientation does not encourage active planning of the future. If one's actions are controlled by contingencies, as the behaviorist would have it, planning behavior must also be contingency determined. Therefore, one is not moved on this account to plan alternatives. If planning were warranted, it would occur automatically.

density have become painfully aware (cf. Freedman, 1975-1976; Griffitt, 1974; Stokols, 1977). To the extent that subjects do not wish to perceive an increase in the number of people as crowding their space, but choose to view them as a something else (e.g., greater opportunity for entertainment, greater interest value, greater opportunity for fantasy), then the precise function of such experimentation becomes obscured.

As we have also seen, traditional scientific metatheory invites the researcher to view behavioral events as the lawful consequences of antecedent conditions. Experimentation within this context is said to involve the rigorous manipulation of antecedents. Thus, one typically speaks of manipulating an "independent variable," and observing "resultant" changes in a "dependent variable." The experimental model is, in this sense, a deterministic one where responses are driven by stimuli. On what grounds should one accede to such a view? Surely it does not derive from experimental evidence itself. There is little reason to believe that such common experimental antecedents as the presence of weapons, the presence of a mirror, an erotic film, an equitable wage or the like *drive* or require anyone to do anything. When cut away from the language of the experimental paradigm, it may be argued, people are free to behave in virtually any way they wish under such conditions. However, when one enters the realm of institutionalized understanding of experimentation, this vision of human freedom is largely obfuscated. Experimental findings do not vitiate the voluntarist view; it is the common understanding of the experimental process that does so.[21]

As we see, a commitment to the experimental paradigm has broad implications for the kinds of theories that are likely to be elaborated in the discipline. To commit oneself to a given methodology is to place a range of significant restrictions over the kinds of theories that are likely to be developed and sustained. As argued here, theories emphasizing contextual embeddedness, diachronic sequence and voluntaristic action are all discouraged in the commitment to an experimental orientation. As we shall explore in Chapter 5, it is just such views of human functioning that furnish the groundwork for an alternative to logical empiricist metatheory.

Metatheoretical Constraints on Generative Theory

Thus far we have examined a variety of ways in which a commitment to a form of empiricist metatheory has saturated the contents of theoretical description and explanation, and how a commitment to the methodology favored by the metatheory has placed restrictions over theoretical development. We may now return to the topic with which the chapter began, that of developing generative theory. A generative theory, it was said, is one that unsettles common assumptions within the culture and thereby opens new vistas for action. The paucity of such theorizing in contemporary science was also noted and questions raised concerning the origins

---

[21] See also Rychlak's (1980a) illuminating discussion of the confounding of mechanistic theory and the experimental method.

of this condition. It is the present contention that major constraints over generative theorizing may be traced in significant degree to traditional metatheoretical commitments. The dominant conceptions of the process of science have operated in important ways to restrict the potential for theoretical challenge. After examining three major metatheoretical assumptions and their inimical consequences for generative theory, we can turn to the problem of theoretical liberation.

The Preeminence of Objective Fact

As outlined earlier, it is traditionally held that the scientist's task is to document with accuracy the systematic relationship among observables. On the basis of preliminary observation it is said, the scientist may build inductively toward general theoretical statements describing and explaining the phenomena in question. Classical astronomy is often considered exemplary in this respect. The science commenced, it is said, when systematic recordings were made of the movements of the heavenly bodies. On the basis of such records general theories were developed and subsequently tested against continuing observation. The general acceptance of the traditional position within contemporary social psychology is widely evident. As Shaw and Costanzo (1970) state the case,

> Modern social psychology has largely been empirical in nature, basing its propositions and conclusions upon observations in controlled situations. . . . As a result of the empirical approach, a considerable amount of data about social behavior has accumulated. To be useful, such data must be organized in a systematic way so that the meaning and implications of these data can be understood. Such systematic organization is the function of theory. (p. 3)[22]

In keeping with this orientation, graduate training is commonly centered around the process of systematic observation. Extensive knowledge of methodology and statistics is normally required, and the thesis typically ensures that the candidate has mastered the skills of sound observation. Training in the process of theory construction is a rarity. The primary journals of the field are also devoted almost exclusively to the establishment of fact. Freedman's (1975-1976) comment on the state of the art appears to capture the modal thinking of the discipline:

> Since research [on crowding] has only been going on for a few years, and since the findings are rather inconsistent and confused, it seems that people should be doing research rather than worrying about theories. The idea that there could already be a review of the theories in the field is certainly depressing. It is perfectly alright for people to offer hunches or tentative explanation or what might be called mini theories of any area of social psychology, but to start presenting theories when we don't even know what the facts are is an exercise in futility.

---

[22] Similar sentiments may be found in Broadbent's (1980) discussion of general and applied psychology.

Yet, the common belief that scientific theory should ideally be premised on sound fact seems to have continued undaunted by significant misgivings within the philosophic realm. As discussed in Chapter 1, it is apparent that the scientist cannot approach nature as an unsophisticated or unbiased observer of the facts. Rather, he or she must already harbor conceptions of "what there is to be studied" in order to carry out the task of systematic observation (Hanson, 1958). From this perspective scientific astronomy did not begin with the process of documenting fact. Required were preliminary conceptual distinctions between the earth and the heavens, and among entities existing within the heavens. In effect, "it is the theory that determines what is to count as a fact and how facts are to be distinguished from one another" (Unger, 1975, p. 32). It has further been recognized that canons of inductive logic are inadequate to describe the process by which the scientist typically moves from the concrete to the conceptual level. The most careful observation and cataloguing of all the stone formations on earth, combined with the most assiduous employment of inductive logic, would not yield contemporary geological theory (cf. Medawar, 1960). Neither the facts nor the logic can furnish the questions to be asked of the data or a metaphor for conceptual organization. Concepts such as "the ice age" or "geosynical stage" appear to require some form of creative or intuitive act that is as yet poorly understood. Again, it appears that a premium is to be placed on theoretical imagination, and that a preeminent commitment to establishing "the facts" is inimical to such investments.

The implications of the traditional homage to the fact are particularly potent with respect to generative theory. If "commonsense assumptions" concerning, for example, the units of behavior, their labels, or their relationships, are allowed unconsciously to guide one's research, then the resulting theoretical accounts will inevitably reflect such assumptions. The theoretical accounts will unwittingly approximate "common sense," a problem with which psychologists have been struggling for several decades. When one "begins with the facts," one has already incorporated the common consensus, and the potential for a generative outcome is thereby reduced. Or, as Moscovici (1972) has more forcefully concluded in the case of social psychology, "social psychologists have done no more than to operationalize questions and answers which were imagined elsewhere. And thus the work in which they are engaged—in which we are all engaged—is not the work of scientific analysis but that of engineering" (p. 32).[23]

The Demand for Empirical Evaluation

From the traditional perspective, a close relationship should ideally be maintained between theory and data. Not only should theories emerge from initial observation, but once developed, they should be subjected to thorough and systematic empirical test. Through empirical assessment, theories of high predictive validity may be sustained and those that fail to correspond with fact excluded from the corpus of

---

[23] For an analysis of the extent to which scientific knowledge is premised on untested propositions in the domain of daily life see Campbell (1978).

"acceptable knowledge." Yet, as previous chapters have attempted to demonstrate, the assumption that hypotheses can be tested in the sociobehavioral sciences is ill conceived. As we saw in Chapter 1, in confirming or challenging an hypothesis the investigator is typically faced with such a broad range of intelligible instantiations of any theoretical variable that, with careful selection of cases, theoretically congenial results are ultimately inescapable. Further, theoretical interpretation can itself alter society in such a way that the location of apparent confirmations or disconfirmations is facilitated. In Chapter 2, we found that actions are identified according to their meanings and that meanings are infinitely negotiable. Thus, observations of human activity approximate blank slates on which the theorist can inscribe his or her ideas. One cannot in this sense test whether a given principle is correct or incorrect by traditional empirical standards. The major battles are to be fought over the consequences of taking a given interpretive position for what else is to be said or done.[24]

The implications of these various arguments for the development of generative theory should be apparent. As long as the discipline remains committed to the view that the chief criterion for evaluating theory is its correspondence with fact, the vast share of scientific effort will be directed toward empirical work and the investment in theoretical speculation minimized. As investments in improved methodology are increased, interests in creative theorizing diminish. To the degree that the key to the gates of intellectual expression is the statistical confirmation, then we may anticipate little beyond a handful of self-evident if . . . then propositions. When the major share of professional training is devoted to statistics and methods,

---

[24] Henshel (1980) agrees that too much emphasis has been placed on the laboratory experiment as a tool for verification, and suggests that, instead, such experiments be used for "discovery" purposes—to locate regularities that are not discerned outside the laboratory. However, from the present standpoint, the experiment cannot legitimately be used for such a purpose. The major outcomes of experiments are linguistic interpretations, and the content of such interpretations is not observation driven. In effect, the discovery precedes the experiment; the process of discovery takes place at the theoretical level and furnishes the implement for rendering experimental results sensible. The rudiments of much theoretical language in psychology may be traced to forms of ordinary discourse within the culture. In this sense, psychological theory has served to articulate and formalize the ambiguous and the informal. However, this process of fleshing out ordinary understanding could be accomplished far more efficaciously without the arduous demand for experimental justification. For example, McGuire's (1968) review of the attitude change literature in the Hovland tradition reveals some 30 factors that may influence the amount of attitude change. The 30 years of experimental research used to justify these various theoretical distinctions is largely inconclusive (and fundamentally rhetorical). However, after plying with wine a laywer friend with no background in psychology, he agreed to list all the factors he believed to be important in influencing attitudes. In an hour's time he listed 35 factors, many of which overlapped with the traditional literature and many that were both novel and interesting. Essentially, rich theoretical scaffoldings could be constructed by using articulate resource persons from the culture . . . amply supplied with a properly aged Médoc.

degree requirements are built around the production of data, upward mobility in the field is dependent on contributions to the empirical literature, and funding is reserved exclusively for those engaged in empirical evaluation of propositions, then we can anticipate the maintenance of a discipline that will offer little of significant intellectual or social challenge for the community of the whole.[25]

The Assumption of Enduring Fundamentals

Much has been said in the first two chapters concerning the alteration in patterned activity, and the implications of such change for a science buying time with a promissory note of behavioral prediction. Little need be added on this score. As we also saw, however, one traditional way of avoiding confrontation with continuous change is to argue that ongoing conduct represents the continuous manifestation of a limited number of generic and universal determining mechanisms. The transient is equated with the superficial, and the scientist's task is said to be that of looking beyond the superficial, to the underlying, enduring characteristics of human nature. We have already examined a number of serious problems confronting such a view, most notable among them the fact that the putative, observation languages with which the "abstract," "universal," or "hypothetical" constructs are to be linked are equally hypothetical.

Now in question is the debilitating impact on generative theory of the more general assumption of enduring fundamentals. To accept such an assumption in itself constrains theoretical activity. Of particular concern, it would appear that to the extent one believes deep-seated psychological mechanisms constitute the core of "human nature," and such mechanisms must be revealed in all one's conduct, then it is to the present that one may reasonably direct the major share of attention. It is the controlled study of today that can be heralded as the key to unlocking the riddles of human nature. There is little reason either for studying the past or constructing alternative futures. In contrast, if the theorist considers current patterns of action as fragile, temporary, and capable of alteration, theoretical analysis need not be circumscribed by a consideration of "what now exists." The theorist may usefully direct attention to differences between past and present. What forms of conduct have been abandoned? What has developed anew, and with what functional consequences? Most important, the theorist may be invited to consider alternatives to the present and to explore the advantages and disadvantages of patterns as yet unseen.[26]

---

[25] As Robert Nisbet (1977) has said in another context, "none of the great themes which have provided continuing challenge and also theoretical foundation for sociologists during the last century was ever reached through anything resembling what we are today fond of identifying as 'scientific method'" (p. 3). Nisbet goes on to contrast sociological theory development with artistic imagination.

[26] For an attempt to free theories of social organization from the "myth of the given," see Dachler and Wilpert (1978). As they cite Israel (1972) in their analysis, "The empiricist doctrine . . . has been developed in intimate contact with natural

To illustrate, traditional theory of aggression has confined itself largely to making sense of existing patterns of action. Concepts such as frustration, modeling, generalized arousal, the presence of models, the presence of weapons, and so on (cf. Bandura's 1973 review) have all been applied primarily to contemporary patterns of conduct. The result is that such patterns come to be seen as essentially fixed. Yet, if we take seriously the individual's capacity for wide-ranging change, then we may begin to consider alternative patterns and to evaluate their comparative assets. To apply the view that frustration leads to aggression or that aggressive models lead to aggressive activities of the observer is to sanction the continuation of behavior interpreted in those terms, and to close the door on alternative possibilities. The generative theorist might, in contrast, develop theories specifying a range of intelligible alternatives that one might adopt when frustrated (e.g., relaxation, altruism, rationalization) or when exposed to an aggressive model (e.g., punish the model, self-examination, humor). In elaborating such alternatives the theorist operates generatively to undermine common assumptions about human conduct. The theorist thus breaks the hammerlock of what people accept as "human nature" and opens consideration of alternative arrangements.

In a similar fashion, by positing fixed and fundamental processes the theorist also discourages people more generally from autonomous consideration of alternatives. Traditional theorizing essentially sanctions the status quo by implying its immutability. For example, Freudian theory depicts the common individual as floundering in a state of neurosis created by early childhood repression. Repression of basic impulses, for Freud, is essential for the existence of organized society. Once accepted, the viewpoint can be used to interpret wide-ranging forms of conduct, and, outside of years of psychoanalytic probing, there is little one can do to relieve his or her basically "sick" condition. Had the theory been constructed otherwise, such that it permitted the employment of libidinous impulses for the creation of new and more fulfilling social patterns, it might stand as an invitation to a more promising future. Much the same may be said of theories that posit the inevitability of war, view all behavior as a function of minimax strategies, or argue that inactivity is the result of helplessness. To the degree that one believes contemporary patterns of behavior to be fundamentally enduring, he or she may be little motivated to attempt reformation. If one believes observed patterns to be historically limited, the invitation for generative theorizing is intensified. The theorist is invited to view him- or herself as a potential contributor to the historical situation and thus capable of its alteration.

In summary, it appears that in the commitment to various empiricist assumptions, the discipline has substantially curtailed its capacity for generative theorizing. The attempt to build theory inductively from "what is known," the demand for

---

science . . . Therefore the problem of 'world order' has not acquired any special prominence . . . [Empiricism] acquires a value-bias when it is applied to the social sciences . . . [in that] it accepts the 'world order' as *given*, and therefore has direct social and political implications" (p. 158).

empirical evaluation of theoretical ideas, and the disregard for the temporally situated character of human activity all seem detrimental to catalytic theorizing.[27]

The Development of Generative Theory

Given the relative paucity of generative theory in contemporary inquiry, and the inimical effects of traditional metatheoretical investments, we may finally turn to the question of the future of theory. Are there means by which the generative capacity of the discipline may be enhanced? From the present standpoint, it is apparent that the greatest strides toward generative theory lie within the development of an alternative metatheory. That is, the development of fresh theoretical perspectives may depend importantly on the availability of alternative views of the process of doing science. To the extent that challenges can be made to the scientist's self-conception, he or she may be stimulated to think anew the character of human functioning more generally. The two preceding chapters have begun to lay out the rudiments of one such alternative, and we shall examine this perspective further in Chapter 5. However, putting aside the question of alternative metatheory, what other possibilities can be discerned? Let us suppose that the press of logical empiricist theory were removed. How could one facilitate the task of generative theorizing?

The theorist faces a peculiar irony at this juncture. If one's understanding inevitably depends on existing forms of interpretation, how can one create interpretations that violate these forms? If common conventions of making sense are employed as the instruments of understanding, then how can one develop or comprehend an argument that violates common convention? Would such arguments not appear as patent nonsense? Clearly, however, commonsense interpretation is undergoing continuous alteration and upheaval over time. Yesterday's nonsense often becomes tomorrow's profundity. Means must exist for accelerating this process in a productive way. Let us consider, then, four avenues available for generative theorizing. In each case we shall also indicate a relevant mechanism for overcoming the

---

[27]See also MacKenzie's (1977) thesis that the adoption of the logical empiricist orientation in behavioral psychology has impeded theoretical growth. As he says, "What united behaviorists was their conviction that the methodology of science, rather than its content, was what constituted an activity specifically scientific, and that methodological principles provided a sufficient basis on which to build scientific systems" (p. 23). This fallacious belief in the inductive building of theory from method of observation left the field unprepared for the self-conscious elaboration of theoretical viewpoints. While MacKenzie's argument seems well taken, the present analysis attempts to demonstrate that logical empiricism supplied more than a belief in method. It also supplied the rudiments of a theory of human behavior, and these rudiments become progressively elaborated in later theoretical developments.

seeming inability of conceptual systems to yield ideas that are antithetical to the systems themselves.[28]

The Articulation of Minority Interpretation

At the initial level an investigator may act on behalf of individuals or groups that do not share majority group perspectives or assumptions. Frequently those who believe themselves to be oppressed by majority views share interpretive conventions that have neither been fully articulated nor understood by members of the majority. By attempting such articulation, the scientist may first galvanize the minority group by enabling it to achieve common understanding, and second, undermine or reorder the views of the majority. Precisely this form of organized audacity has sparked the rise of most major social movements in recent American history. The black power movement, the antiwar movement, and the women's liberation movement, for example, are all indebted to individuals who have been close enough to the shared experiences of such groups to elaborate their assumptions, and to redefine the world of human relations in such a way that the majority framework of interpretation was discredited. Although the vast majority of such interpretive efforts have not been undertaken within the sciences, social scientists have participated in significant measure. For example, the attempt to redefine the motives of black ghetto rioters in such a way that they appear justifiable reactions to an oppressive society, to characterize the antiwar protester as intelligent and highly principled, and to redefine common heterosexual practices as sexist have all served to fortify the groups in question and undermine existing views of the majority.[29]

How are minority interpretations rendered intelligible to those who would otherwise view them as nonsense? At least one major mechanism would appear to be that of the *recontextualized referent*. That is, the theorist in this case lifts various terms from their conventional context, and by placing them in alternative contexts, alters their meaning. The scientist thus relies on existing terms of understanding, but shifts the context of their usage. For example, to remove the concept of gender from its traditional placement within discussions of biological differences, and to treat it within the context of social constructivism (cf. Kessler & McKenna, 1978) is to challenge the meaning of gender differences in society. Gender becomes a

---

[28] Also see McGuire's (1980) listing of heuristics for theory construction. The present account differs from McGuire's primarily in its emphasis of generativity in theory construction. While McGuire is concerned with promoting theory construction in general, the present analysis argues for a more instrumentalist approach to theory generation: The contours of theory should be governed by one's purposes vis-à-vis the science or the culture more generally. Helpful in this context is also Wicker's (1981) discussion of means to creative theorizing.

[29] The concept of "minority" in this case should not be restricted to demographic divisions. Of great importance are also intellectual minorities—individuals or groups whose ideas have been obscured by history, linguistic barriers, or disciplinary exclusion.

product of social systems, a novel and exciting possibility, as opposed to biology. In such an analysis the conceptual components remain intact, only the context of usage is altered.

Extension to the Borders of Absurdity

A second means of achieving theoretical generativity is to extend an acceptable set of commonsense assumptions to the borders of absurdity, that is, a point at which the assumptions prove audacious but not offensively contrary. Perhaps the most dramatic example of this form of theorizing is furnished by Skinnerian behavior theory. In its modest form, the theory captures many elements of commonsense reasoning. Most people would probably agree that environmental contingencies do have important effects on behavior: "Obviously, people are responsive to reward and punishment." If such theoretical assumptions had been left unextended, behavior theory might long ago have slipped into obscurity. Yet Skinner has continued to elaborate and extend the interpretive bounds of the theory in ways that many consider disagreeably extreme. For one, Skinner and his colleagues have demonstrated how the theory may encompass virtually *all* forms of human action. Further, the manner in which the theory may serve as the basis for a utopian society (Skinner, 1948) has been explicated, and demonstrations made of the way in which cherished ideals such as "freedom" and "dignity" stand in the way of achieving such ends (Skinner, 1971). It is in just such arguments that the theory became generative, and as a result, has continued to play a highly catalytic role in intellectual and social life.

Much contemporary theory could be extended in this manner but has not. Such extension must perhaps await an eroding of the traditional belief in theoretical testability, for as long as one's ideas move only minimally ahead of one's data base, little of challenging intellectual interest is likely to result. Dissonance theory (Brehm & Wicklund, 1976; Festinger, 1957) contained many elements of common sense (most people would probably agree that they do not prefer to hold inconsistent ideas). It also began to acquire generative strength when it was argued that in the attempt to achieve consonance people will engage in irrational actions. Yet the immense research effort devoted to verification (and falsification) of this claim virtually garroted the theory in terms of generative potency. If less attention had been devoted to the misguided process of empirical evaluation, and a greater investment had been made in considering, for example, the use of dissonance in social control, the valuational implications of dissonance reduction, the class and educational biases reflected in the demand for dissonance reduction, and the limitations of analytic processing implied by the theory, the theory might continue to be of widespread interest. The rule–role orientation captures many elements of commonsense interpretation (e.g., few would disagree that people frequently follow rules or play roles). This orientation long remained moribund in social psychology until theorists began to extend its implications to the point of threatening traditional models of cognition (cf. Shank & Abelson, 1977), along with deep-seated conceptions of science (cf. Harré & Secord, 1972).

In contrast to the mechanism of reconstituting common convention, the present vehicle for enhancing generativity relies primarily on *extending the inherent logic of an existing set of assumptions.* Thus, in the Skinnerian case, one moves from the commonsense assumption that *some* activities are controlled by environmental contingencies to the audacious extreme: Virtually *all* human interaction is controlled by environmental contingency. In the case of the rule-role orientation, one moves from considering the assumption that commonplace actions are governed by rules to arguing, for example, that both passion and disorder are rule constrained. The recipient of such arguments is essentially moved by his or her acceptance of relatively timorous assumptions to extreme positions initially unanticipated.

The Search for Antithesis

One may also foster generative theory by searching for an intelligible antithesis to commonly accepted understandings. For example, in arguing against a spiritualist account of the emergence of the human species, Darwinian theory once served in this capacity. Sociobiologists have similarly attempted to replace social accounts of human institutions with genetic accounts, and much useful controversy has resulted. In miniature, this orientation is often employed throughout the experimental domain. Support for a given hypothesis stimulates others to propose an antithetical position for which support is then amassed. For example, a demonstration of the commonsense assumption that increased similarity has a positive effect on attraction has stimulated others to propose that increased similarity can produce the opposite effect (see Chapter 2). Yet, too often the generative capacity of the latter demonstration is diminished in the subsequent attempt by theorists to locate a commonsense rationale enabling both positions to be incorporated. One simply reverts to the position that under X conditions the phenomenon will be found but that under Y conditions its reverse (or absence) will occur. Neither the original allegation nor its apparent reversal are beyond the agreeable understandings of the culture. Infrequently does one find the leap to antithesis employed as a means of unseating the initial assumption. To propose a "fear of success" in the face of a commonly assumed belief that most everyone seeks success, to propose a search for intrinsic reward in the face of the behaviorist emphasis on extrinsic rewards, and to propose that there are no distinct emotions but only distinct interpretations all represent generative gains in contemporary theory.

However, much needed are ambitious attempts to sustain more general theories countervening current beliefs. Might it be possible, for example, to argue convincingly that most social behavior reflects the individual's search for moral imperatives or for pleasing artistic form, that the vast share of human activity cannot accurately be accounted for by antecedent conditions but is based on spontaneously developed impulses, or that consciousness represents a form of ignorant onlooking of no consequence to human action? The elaboration of any of these positions would contradict much that is widely accepted within the culture, and if the present analysis is correct, each of these positions should be capable of intelligible articulation.

A third mechanism appears to play an important role in the case of developing antitheses. In this case, prime reliance may be placed on the *reorganization of existing conventions*. The theorist knits previously held assumptions into a novel amalgam that itself violates a set of major assumptions in the culture. Consider, for example, the common belief in the spontaneity of developing relationships. How could it be argued that there is no true spontaneity on such occasions, but rather what appears as spontaneous is the result of highly constricting rules? If this position were applied to the unfolding of heterosexual relations, the theorist might make use of several component arguments, each of which could contribute to a convincing unity: (1) most heterosexual interaction appears to have a limited number of end points, and thus behavior of the participants is not spontaneously varied but relevant primarily to these end points; (2) young people do not know how to achieve success in heterosexual relationships without exposure to peers, to television, the cinema, etc., and thus it makes sense that their behavior in such relations is not spontaneous but a form of modeling; and (3) most people can tell us what forms of heterosexual activity are prohibited by the "rules of the game" just as they might in soccer or tennis—again suggesting that they are following rules in such relationships rather than acting spontaneously. Thus, the antithesis is sustained in this case by the theorist's search for a series of component arguments, each of which "makes sense" within itself and the combination of which serve to undermine the prevailing thesis.

The Search for Alternative Metaphors

Many commonly accepted explanations for human action are tied to prevailing metaphors within the culture. One frequently speaks of anger, for example, as "an explosive," marriage as "warfare," heterosexual infatuation as "disease," friendship as "bonding," eating meat as "beastiality," eating fully as "piggishness," and so on. At times, such metaphors appear to have highly significant influences over social action. For example, the metaphor of falling dominoes seemed to possess a mesmerizing influence over policy-making bodies of the United States during the 1960s. If one nation falls to Communists, it was argued, that nation's fall would precipitate the demise of its neighbor, and the end point of this process over time would be the collapse of democratic society. To be sure, such a theory could exist without the metaphor, but so convenient and compelling was the visual image that very little attention was given to alternative perspectives. Similarly, it appears, many executives carry into the world of work the metaphor of the "dog pack" or the "football match." To view their colleagues as out "to maul" or "to vanquish" them, a conclusion favored by such metaphors, may sustain particularly brutal forms of activity that would not be encouraged in the absence of the metaphor.

Theories within the social sciences often employ metaphors as the central integrative mechanism. Lewin's "field theory" borrowed heavily from the image of electronic fields of activity in physics, dissonance and balance theories both employed the metaphor of bodily homeostasis, social exchange theory depends heavily on the metaphor of the marketplace, and so on. Although such metaphors have proved highly compelling, very little attention has been given to their use in unsettling common ways of thinking within the society, that is, to their generative capability. Should it not be possible to formulate alternative metaphors for the world of work, for example, such that the prevailing views are undermined? For instance, could one view work as a form of "mutual entertainment" in which various participants are performing for the delight of each other? Rather than the football field or the dog pack, is work not more like a circus? Or, might one consider work as a form of religious order in which participants are attempting to find spiritual significance in their investment? Or is work not more like a form of dance, in which the participants are attempting (with unequal success) to create beauty?[30] In each case, the metaphor informs one of an alternative way of viewing the work experience, and in doing so, reduces the pervasive and potentially debilitating effects of the prevailing form.

Unlike the previous mechanisms for generative reinterpretation, the metaphor does not rely so much on concept manipulation as on *visual substitution*. The theorist attempts to create a novel visualization that may unify a range of diverse concepts. In many ways, this manner of unseating common knowledge may be difficult. For one, people commonly recognize the difference between metaphor and action (e.g., work is *like* a football match; it is clearly *not* the match itself), while it is not always so easy to distinguish between words and actions (e.g., to say "he hit me" is a form of verbal reification). Thus, the theorist who relies on metaphor asks others to join in what seems to be a form of "make-believe" (Cohen, 1978). Second, to be effective, a high degree of secondary theoretical elaboration may be required. To illustrate effectively how the world of work is like a circus might require myriad linking definitions (e.g., working interdependently is like a trapeze team, selecting one's clothing is like costuming, some people are high-wire experts while others serve as clowns, and so on). Because of the burden of linking multiple metaphorical components to other concepts, the use of metaphor as a generative device may be delimited.

Yet, if a compelling metaphor can be effected, there is much to gain. Metaphors often seem more accessible to cognition in daily relations than abstract schemas. We can look at an individual and instantaneously see him or her as a clown, an infant, or a field marshal. Yet the formal propositions of the theorist often seem remote from the moment-to-moment fluctuation of daily relations, even for the theorist who has propounded them. The generative metaphor also lends itself to creative elaboration on the part of the recipient. After accepting the "football match" as an apt metaphor for the world of work, one can independently think of one's own resemblance to various heroes, or how certain individuals are "captains" and "coaches," while others are "second stringers." Such elaboration individualizes the metaphor and thus gives it a special potency.

In conclusion, we have found that the traditional adherence to positivist–empiricist metatheory has insinuated itself into all aspects of scientific activity. Of particular concern has been the extent to which theoretical content reincarnates metatheoretical assumptions, the manner in which the method of experimentation

---

[30] See S. P. Turner's (1977) treatment of complex organizations as savage tribes.

has delimited theoretical considerations, and the constraints placed over generative theorizing by traditional metatheory. The generative criteria for theoretical comparison, as a replacement for truth value or verisimilitude, are favored by the basic condition of the sciences—confronted as they are by continuous change. However, the achievement of generative theorizing will ultimately depend on whether the scientist is willing to withdraw from the comfort of convention and play dangerous games with accepted truths.

Chapter 4

The Turning Point in Life-Span Study

Previous chapters have attempted to elucidate major deficits in the traditional empiricist model of behavioral science and to sketch significant contours for an alternative orientation to both theory and research. Yet, although the present arguments are intended to traverse the full range of sociobehavioral sciences, they have been applied chiefly to theory and research in social psychology. The attempt of the present chapter is to underscore the generality of the various lines of reasoning by extending them in more detail to a second arena of inquiry, namely that of life-span development. The attempt in this case is not to advance a new base of argumentation. Rather, earlier proposals will be elaborated within a contrasting context.

There is ample reason for selecting the life-span arena for such treatment. A questioning attitude toward tradition has been a hallmark of inquiry in this domain. Within the life-span arena, vigorous debates are encountered at every level of the scientific process, including the metatheoretical (cf. Datan, 1977; Reese & Overton, 1970; Weiss, 1978), the theoretical (cf. Brim & Kagan, 1980; Freedle, 1977), and the methodological (cf. Hultsch & Hickey, 1978; Labouvie, 1975; Nesselroade & Reese, 1973). The querulous condition in the life-span arena may be traced in part to the context of the field's inception, a context of grave doubt over the adequacy of traditional developmental theory to deal with problems of adulthood and aging. If the long-revered theories of development could have led so many for so long to believe that human development was being fully portrayed, then what other traditional premises might be amiss? Too, because the field has also been vitally concerned with cross-time change, it has captured the interests of dialectical theorists whose orientation opposes that of the traditional empiricist in many significant ways (cf. Riegel, 1975). Finally, as Baltes and Cornelius (1977) argue, life-span study is unlike other fields in psychology in its focus on long-term change. With such a focus it often stretches the boundaries of existing assumptions at both the theoretical and methodological levels.

Because of its singularly intense reassessment of tradition, life-span study may also form a weathervane for future developments within the field of psychology more generally. The enhanced degree of self-consciousness, the openness to fresh alternatives, and the high degree of sensitivity to the metatheoretical bases of the science suggest that developments within the life-span domain may presage future concerns within the more conservative areas of the discipline. It is a central thesis of the present chapter that a major crisis in the function of general theory is emerging within life-span study and the results may have substantial implications for the psychological sciences more generally. We shall first examine two major lines of inquiry giving rise to this critical condition. In particular, we shall consider developing concerns with the historical relativity of individual life-span trajectory, and the evolving image of the individual as autonomously self-determining. Based on these lines of work, traditional beliefs both in the testability of general theory and the utility of such theory for purposes of prediction and control are thrown into jeopardy. In light of the problems raised with traditional assumptions, we shall inquire into the alternative employment of life-span theory. In particular, we shall examine the use of theory for altering action patterns and sustaining value systems.

From the Stable to the Aleatory in Developmental Trajectory

It is initially useful to contrast the dominant theoretical orientations governing traditional developmental research with the view currently emerging within the life-span arena. Two traditional orientations may be isolated, the first of which deserves specialized attention.

The Stability Account of Human Development

For many years the dominant theoretical form within developmental psychology placed greatest emphasis on the stability of behavior patterns over time. In this case the overarching theoretical template essentially registers stability and eschews the transitory. In certain respects, Freud's theory of character formation provides the classic exemplar of the stability orientation. As Freud maintained, the first six years of life are critical in determining adult personality. As a result of early psychosexual history, and particularly the configuration of repression, the foundation for adult psychodynamics is firmly established. Without massive intervention through psychoanalysis the same psychobehavioral patterns will relentlessly repeat themselves throughout the life cycle. Much the same view was adopted by early learning theorists. Here it was maintained that the effects of early learning experiences are of greater strength than later experiences. Early learning thus provides the basic orientation toward later experience. Whatever exists tends to endure. A similar orientation has been more recently represented by Sterns and Alexander (1977) in their argument that living systems are designed to resist or minimize change. Alterations in the environment do cause organismic change they argue, but such change is always "intended to provide *higher order* stability for the organism" (Sterns & Alexander, 1977, p. 110).

Over the years an immense wealth of data has been amassed favoring the stability orientation. Case studies number in the thousands; longitudinal research is typically dedicated to the discovery of continuity; animal experimentation has often demonstrated the long-term effects of early learning experiences; studies of adult psychopathology often reveal systematic differences in early experience between hospitalized and normal populations; and so on. So immense is the volume of supportive data that in spite of the current hegemony of the ordered-change orientation (to be discussed shortly), the stability orientation has remained relatively free of direct assault. It may fairly be said that contemporary culture has almost fully incorporated the assumption that early experience is vital in shaping adult behavior. The range and depth of this incorporation has been examined elsewhere (Gergen & Benack, in press). For now, however, it is important to note the broader social implications of this belief that the early years serve to "bend the twig." In particular, it would appear to make a substantial contribution to the maintenance of traditional sex-role differentiation. If the basic character of the child, and thus its long-term future, is crystallized during the early years, it would be the irresponsible parent who would willingly entrust important caretaking functions to, for example, a day-care center or a surrogate family. And, it is the female who is chiefly reprehensible should the traditional role be abnegated. To challenge the account is thus a means of weakening the institutions it serves to sustain. Such an attack is possible, in this case, on the same grounds typically used for substantiation, namely, empirical grounds. Given the broad adherence to the account, and the societal implications of this belief, it is useful at this juncture to take the brief detour required to demonstrate how the premises may be unsettled. Through interpretive analysis it is possible to demonstrate that the stability account is highly misleading.

First, it is important to realize that the major share of evidence for the stability assumption takes the form of case studies. Psychoanalysts, psychiatrists, and clinical psychologists have all attempted, as did Freud, to show how adult disorders can be traced to events long since removed. Yet, if the case study is a valid indicator of events in nature, it should be possible to use early case material to predict adult behavior. If one begins with the hypothesis that early socialization has a strong effect on adult character, it is very easy to find validating evidence in anyone's life history. Life histories are very rich affairs, and it is possible to find support for virtually any hypothesis in the welter of available detail—along with support for antithetical hypotheses. One might be far more sanguine if, provided with the early life history material, one could predict the outcome. Knowing about an individual's childhood, could one tell whether he or she was likely to end up a criminal, a minister, a psychotic, or just an average bloke? Freud himself remained diffident in this matter. However, it is interesting to consider several actual cases in this light. For example, the following is from a biographical account of some importance.

> My father (was) a conscientious employee of the (government), my mother, occupied with the household, and above all was devoted to us children with loving care. . . . How it happened, I cannot now say, but one day it was clear to me that I would be a painter, an artist. . . . The only curious thing was that, as I grew older, I took an increasing interest in architecture. . . . Along with music, I thought architecture the queen of the arts. . . .

Was this individual to become hero or villain? As it happened he later became perhaps the most roundly castigated human being of the century, Adolph Hitler (1943, p. 4). Alongside this account, we must consider a few details from the life of Charles Wilson. Wilson was a big, handsome boy who grew up in a small Texas town. He starred in football, basketball, and track, and managed at the same time to achieve high academic marks. He attended a Methodist church near his father's small grocery store and gas station. In his junior year of high school, Wilson was voted outstanding member of his class. How was Wilson to develop during the college years? In this case, we find that within two years of leaving his hometown, Wilson was an active participant in the notorious Manson gang. Together, the group slaughtered almost a dozen persons without any significant motive; Wilson's specialty was carving initials in the corpses. Let us consider a final autobiographical account:

> I was a coward. I used to be haunted by the fear of thieves, ghosts, and serpents. I did not dare to stir out of doors at night. Darkness was a terror to me. It was almost impossible for me to sleep in the dark. . . .

Therapists might be duly concerned by such an account; most would never suspect that this young man of little promise grew up to be Mahatma Gandhi (1958, p. 7).

These various cases are not unusual; many others could have been supplied. And to be sure these particular cases prove very little; they were, after all, selected for the occasion. The major point is that case study materials can be employed effectively in the service of virtually any hypothesis.

More compelling to most investigators are those studies that systematically examine individuals as they develop over time. Because of the immense demands placed on the researcher, such longitudinal studies are indeed rare. However, perhaps the most significant study of this sort was conducted at the Fels Institute, Yellow Springs, Ohio. In this study, some eighty individuals were followed from soon after their birth until after their thirtieth year of life. In each of four testing periods, some sixty to one hundred different tests were made. Assessments were made of tendencies toward passivity, aggression, dependency, achievement, sexuality, compulsivity, conformity, and so on. The major results of this work are published in Kagan and Moss' (1962) now famous work, *From Birth to Maturity*. This volume has been widely cited for its compelling evidence that traits developed early in life persist into adulthood. Indeed, a number of intriguing correlations do emerge from the study. For example, there is a significant correlation of .39 between aggression shown by boys to their mothers between the ages of 3 and 6 and the aggression they display toward the mother in early adulthood; females displaying marked independence in the teens also do so as adults.

However, the results of the study deserve more careful examination. Rather than concentrating only on those findings that support the stability supposition, one must consider the entire data set, the confirming findings as well as the disconfirming. Several interesting facts emerge from such an analysis. Looking at the various traits measured during the infancy to three-year-old period and the same traits as assessed during the thirty-year-old period, we discover virtually *no* significant findings. Of the one hundred twenty correlations computed, only six reached statistical significance; by customary standards of significance, exactly six should have emerged. If we then look at the relationship between the traits as measured during the three- to six-year-old period and early adulthood, we find almost no improvement in predictive ability. Out of approximately two hundred correlations, only twenty emerged as significant; ten of these would have done so by chance. It is not until we examine the 10- to 14-year-old group that we begin to discover results that approach significance. Here, some 25% of the correlations are beyond chance. However, at this point, we also find that the average magnitude of correlation hovers at approximately .23. In effect, even when reliable predictions can be made from the early period (in this case, adolescence), the predictions are generally trivial in the amount of variance in adult characteristics for which they account. When closely examined, the Kagan and Moss findings simply do not stand as substantial support for the stability assumption.[1,2]

Results from infrahuman research are equally questionable. Perhaps the most frequently cited evidence supporting the stability assumption is that of Harlow and Harlow (1965) on maternal deprivation in the infant monkey. As the Harlows so dramatically demonstrated, when a rhesus monkey is deprived of all social contact during the first six weeks of life, and then reintroduced into the monkey colony, the deprived animal is permanently debilitated. The animal continues indefinitely to display aggressive, antisocial, and otherwise aberrant characteristics. Of course, the extent to which infrahuman research such as this should be applied on the human level remains problematic. However, even if we do accept the implications of this work for human functioning, research by Suomi and Harlow (1972) indicates that these effects need not be permanent and are easily reversed. A six-week retraining program in which the deprived monkey continuously associates with a somewhat younger animal is sufficient to obliterate the ill effects of early deprivation.

Additional research within social psychology strongly suggests that whatever habits are acquired during development do not generally seem to persist across diverse circumstances. For example, because of their extensive cultural training, most people do not believe they could be induced to torture another human being to the point of death; most would loathe the thought and believe their socialization had insulated them against such heinous behavior. Yet, as Milgram's (1974) classic work suggests, adults of all ages and from diverse backgrounds can be coerced rather easily into delivering the most painful shocks to an innocent victim of cir-

---

[1] In another telling illustration, Nesselroade, Jacobs, and Pruchno (1981) administered two standardized measures of anxiety to subjects on four separate occasions within a fourteen day period. On each occasion the measures were intercorrelated. However, for neither measure did the correlations from one testing period to another approach significance. Some correlations were slightly negative. The largest correlation (.32) was found between the *first* and *last* testing session for one form, and it was not statistically significant. See also Buss and Royce's (1976) discussion of the temporality of trait constructs over historical periods.

[2] Kagan has since modified his views considerably. See Kagan (1980).

cumstance. Other research of this kind indicates that when exposed to selected stimulus materials male university students can develop searching doubts as to their longstanding sexual preference (male or female) within twenty minutes (Bramel, 1962). Further, people who are marked by their meager contributions to group discussion can with twenty minutes of systematic encouragement effectively take over group leadership roles (Hastorf, 1970). And, with only the encouragement of a darkened room, complete strangers will voluntarily choose to engage in forms of physical intimacy typically reserved for romantic partners of long acquaintance (Gergen, Gergen, & Barton, 1973). Such studies as these are only illustrative of a massive volume of research in social psychology that stands as an interpretive obstruction to the widespread assumption of stability.

In summary, we see that the stability account of human development cannot easily be justified by an appeal to empirical evidence. What stands as relevant evidence can be marshalled with equal force for purposes of vitiation. There are many arguments both for and against sex-role differentiation. However, as we see, traditonal justification for tying the female to the domestic sphere—namely, that the children's long-term future is at stake, cannot be sustained on empirical grounds. After touching on a second traditional account of human development, we shall consider the emergence of a viewpoint wholly antithetical to stability theory.

The Ordered Change Account

The second major orientation to human development centers on change as opposed to stability. In particular, it is assumed that development is constituted by patterned or orderly change across time. Typically, such change is said to be invariant both across the human species and throughout history; development is essentially constituted by the unfolding of ontogenetic trajectories.[3] Again, Freud provides the initial exemplar of this orientation; the theory of psychosexual development elaborates a natural history of libidinal development. Although Freud's theory is limited primarily to the first six years of life, revisionists have fruitfully extended the theory to account for later developmental crises. Erik Erikson (1963, 1968, 1980) has been seminal in this respect. With the possible exception of Loevinger's (1966) work on ego development, such psychodynamic interests have largely been shunted aside in recent years as concern with cognitive development has taken center stage. The impact of Piaget's account of cognitive growth cannot be underestimated. It may fairly be said that the ordered-change orientation in general, and Piagetian theory in particular, has become the guiding paradigm within contemporary developmental psychology. For the present it is unimportant to distinguish among contributions emphasizing quantitative as opposed to qualitative change, or change through accretion as opposed to crisis. It is sufficient for now to recognize a class of theories similar with respect to their focus on orderly, replicable change in human development.

---

[3] For a more general treatment of the metaphor of ordered change as it has functioned since classical antiquity see Nisbet (1969).

Although less central to our concerns, it is also useful to realize that the data used to support the ordered change account are no less equivocal than in the case of stability. The more extended exercise carried out in the latter case need not be repeated in the present context. However, it is useful to keep in mind the fact that, for example, continued study has done little to increase confidence in Freud's particular characterization of psychosexual development. And, with respect to theories of cognitive development within the more general Piagetian framework, what are traditionally viewed as ontogenetically based styles of thinking appear to be subject to a host of environmental influences (see summary in Dasen, 1972). Attempts to link stage theories of cognitive development to chronological age have also proved less than promising, as great variability is evidenced in the cognitive capabilities manifested within any given age group. And ample evidence for "regression" or reversals in the expected sequences has been generated, evidence that has been used to argue that sequences in cognitive orientation are environmentally contingent (Bandura & MacDonald, 1963; Cowan, Langer, Heavenrich, & Nathanson, 1969; Prentice, 1972). In effect, just as in the case of the stability account, ordered change theory is empirically indeterminant.

The Emergence of the Aleatory Account

In part because the stability and ordered change accounts have raised few interesting questions concerning conduct over the life span, we find that investigation in this latter realm has been relatively unrestricted in its acceptance of new forms of data, its vigorous pursuit of new methodologies, and its consideration of alternative theoretical perspectives. Although the full range of such work defies tidy summarization, one can discern amid the numerous empirical findings, and just beneath the theoretical veneer, an alternative to the stability and the ordered change accounts. Central to this orientation is the assumption that there is little about human development that is "preprogrammed"; that is, people enter the world with a biological system that establishes the limits of their activities but not the precise sequence of activities over time. For many it seems that the human continuously confronts a confluence of changing and potentially interacting factors, and precise prediction of developmental trajectory is hazardous. In the broadest sense, development is *aleatory* or chance dependent. For any individual the life course seems fundamentally open-ended.[4] Because of the close affinity between this view and the thesis outlined in Chapter 1, it is useful to touch on several investigations undergirding this view.

First, much interest has been taken in accounts of human development in other eras of history (Borstelmann, 1976; Demos & Demos, 1969; Gadlin, 1978). To the extent that people in earlier periods of history manifest developmental patterns

---

[4] Congenial to this account is John Dewey's (1929) statement, "Man finds himself living in an aleatory world . . . The world is a scene of risk; it is uncertain [and] uncannily unstable. Its dangers are irregular, inconstant, not to be counted upon as to their times and seasons" (p. 41).

different from those posited by contemporary theories of stability or ordered change, doubt is cast upon such theories, and one must consider the possibility for the historical relativity of developmental trajectory. Particular interest has thus been taken in child development, that period which, by most traditional accounts, should demonstrate transhistorical stability. In perhaps the classic investigation of this type, van den Berg (1961) has examined the concept of "childhood" and "maturation" across widely disparate time periods. As he points out, from the fifteenth to the seventeenth century no strong distinction was made in Western culture between the child and the adult. The child was simply viewed as an adult in miniature; maturity was largely achieved with changes in quantity not quality of thought. Thus, Montaigne wrote placidly of a child who read Greek, Latin, and Hebrew when he was six years old and translated Plato into French when he was not yet eight. Girls could typically read the Bible before they were five. Six-year-olds were often confronted with the most serious discussions of death, sex, and ethics. From the perspective of contemporary theories of cognitive and emotional maturation, such capacities would fall beyond the pale of reason. As van den Berg concludes, contemporary society has essentially "created" the character of today's child and the stages of development that he or she must traverse.[5]

Much the same message is reiterated in comparative studies of sex role development. Clear developmental patterns of male as opposed to female behavior over the life span are exceedingly difficult to locate. As the literature suggests, males and females can adopt wide-ranging patterns of behavior, and these patterns may be radically transformed at any point in life. As Neugarten (1968) argues from her research, the manner in which the "female personality" unfolds is importantly dependent on existing demands for labor. For example, the proportion of women in the labor force at various stages of adulthood has undergone dramatic alterations between 1870 and 1966, with consequent alteration of the adult female life pattern, her needs, and prevailing dispositions. As Neugarten and Datan (1973) conclude, "Changes in the life cycle (such as these) have their effects upon personality, and it is likely that the personalities of successive age cohorts will, therefore, be different in measurable ways . . ." (p. 68). Consistent with this theme, David Gutmann (1975) finds current sex role patterns potentially dangerous to the nuclear family, and argues for an alteration in social conditions so as to reinstate earlier sex role patterns. Not all investigators are willing to abandon the possibility of ontogenetic sex role patterning. However, as one of the more reluctant investigators, Walter Emmerich (1973), concludes on the basis of his review, "many ontogenetic changes in sex-role behavior will continue to occur only as long as diffusion of changed sex-role norms to all age-graded environments remains incomplete" (p. 143). In effect, historically contingent role conceptions may overpower whatever ontogenetic proclivities may be discerned.

This emphasis on shifting sociohistorical circumstance is amplified by studies of mental health over the life span. As Lieberman (1975) maintains, emotional mal-

---

[5] See also Verhave and von Hoorn's (1977) analysis of the changing concept of the self over historical periods.

adjustment appears far less dependent on intrinsic patterns of development than on environmental stressors, wherever they happen to occur in adult life. Explorations of Pearlin (1975) and of Schlegel (1975) into the environmental sources of the often-observed differences in depression between males and females reach much the same conclusion. The onset of depressive symptoms in males as opposed to females does not primarily result from genetic programming; rather, such patterns seem to depend on the differential configuration of demands placed on men and women in contemporary culture. Klaus Riegel's (1975) research into people's accounts of their own development extends this conclusion into the domain of normality. As Riegel demonstrates, people typically see change in their life not as the result of smooth and orderly unfolding, but in terms of crises or disruptions largely stemming from a concatination of unique circumstances. Additional re-search has concentrated on potential disruptions or marked deviations in life-span trajectory that may occur at virtually any point in the life cycle. Depending on insinuating circumstances, previous developmental directions may be wholly revised (Baltes & Labouvie, 1973; Birren, 1964; Botwinick, 1970). Or, as the individual is exposed to various training experiences, whether by accident or systematic social intervention, previous trajectories can be modified, halted, or reversed (cf. Birren & Woodruff, 1973; Hooper, 1973; Montada & Fillipp, 1976). Similarly, life crises may disrupt otherwise stabilized life styles and shift trajectories, sometimes drama-tically (Dohrenwend & Dohrenwend, 1974; Riegel, 1975).

The most extensive support for the aleatory position has been furnished by the exploration of cohort differences in life-span development. As cohort research indicates, differing developmental trajectories are almost invariably found among cohorts born in different historical eras within the same culture. Depending on the sociohistorical circumstances, differing age-related trajectories are found in value commitments, personality characteristics, mental capabilities, political ideology, communication patterns, and so on (cf. Baltes & Reinert, 1969; Baltes & Schaie, 1976; Huston-Stein & Baltes, 1976; Nesselroade & Baltes, 1974; Woodruff & Birren, 1973). Elder's (1974, 1979) closely detailed analysis of the life-span effects of growing up in the Great Depression does much to elaborate on the many interacting factors that may shape development within a given historical period. As Matilda White Riley (1978) argues in the case of the aging process, each new generation "differs from earlier cohorts because of intervening social changes of many sorts: in education, in nutrition, in the occupational and income level at which people begin their careers. . . . There is no pure process of aging. . . . The life course is not fixed, but widely flexible" (pp. 39-41). Echoing this view, Allan Buss (1974) maintains, "Each new generation interprets reality without the years of commit-ment of a previous ideology and thereby transforms that reality" (p. 66). And, as Looft (1973) has concluded, "No longer should developmental psychologists focus so exclusively on ontogenetic age functions; each new generation will manifest age trends that are different from those that preceded it, and thus, previous empirical endeavors are reduced to exercises in futility" (p. 51).

The practical implications of such findings have also been disconcerting to inves-tigators attempting to develop dependable programs for social intervention. For example, an educational reform that proves highly serviceable in one generation may lose its potency in the next, only to be discarded at a point when it once again might be effective. As Baltes and Schaie (1973) conclude, "it is questionable whether behavioral scientists will ever be able to demonstrate the type of treatment and prevention effects that characterize much of the classical biological and medical sciences" (p. 380).[6]

In summary, the theme that is continuously reiterated in life-span research is that human developmental trajectories may be virtually infinite in their variation. In contrast to the stability account it is maintained that adult behavior pattern is little fashioned by early experience. Further, the applicability of ordered change accounts seems limited largely to early periods of physiological maturation. This does not mean that human conduct is essentially chaotic or that continuities may never be found in developmental trajectory. People may ensure that their environment remains reasonably well ordered at any time, and over time they may find a stable behavioral niche. However, precisely what patterns are maintained or changed over time is not recurrent in principle. In the main, developmental trajectories might be characterized in Meehl's (1978) terms:

> a human being's life history involves . . . something akin to the stochastic process known as a "random walk." . . . At several points that are individually minor but collectively determinative, it is an almost "chance" affair whether a person does A or not A. . . . Luck is one of the most important contributors to individual differences in human suffering, satisfaction, illness, achievement, and so on . . ." (p. 811).[7]

As we shall see, the aleatory view has substantial ramifications at the metatheoretical level. However, treatment of these issues must be postponed briefly for consideration of a second theoretical turn in life-span study.

---

[6] As demonstrated in Chapter 2, it would be a mistake to view the various research results described in this section as justifying the aleatory view. Such research is essentially rhetorical, and is used in the present case to indicate a contemporary shift in the preferred paradigm of understanding.

[7] Brim and Kagan's (1980) summary of their fourteen-chapter volume on constancy and change in human development is fully synchronous with the present account. They write: "The conception of human development presented in this volume differs from most Western contemporary thought on the subject. The view that emerges from this work is that humans have a capacity for change across the entire life span. It questions the traditional idea that the experiences of the early years, which have demonstrated contemporaneous effects, necessarily constrain the characteristics of adolescence and adulthood. As the other thirteen chapters in this volume show, there are important growth changes across the life span from birth to death, many individuals retain a great capacity for change, and the consequences of the events of early childhood are continually transformed by later experiences, making the course of human development more open than many have believed" (Brim & Kagan, 1980, p. 1).

The Emergence of Autonomous Self-Direction

Coupled with the emerging view of developmental patterns as historically contingent, one may also discern within life-span study a shift in theoretical conception of human functioning. At base, the conception has its origins in rational idealist philosophy, and particularly the work of Kant. As Theodore Mischel (1975) has described,

> Central to Kant's analysis . . . is his claim that human beings can have a *conception* of what it is they want and what they should do in order to get what they want, and that their conceptions—the meaning which situations and behaviors have for them in virtue of the way they construe them—can make a difference to their actions. Rational beings "have a faculty of taking a rule of reason for the motive of an action" (Kant, 1788, p. 151), they have the capacity to formulate plans, policies, or rules, and they can follow these rules—they have the power to act from the "mere conception" of a rule (pp. 144–145).

This view of the individual as an active agent may be contrasted with the traditional view of individual action as a determined product of environmental inputs. As discussed in previous chapters, from the behaviorist (positivist–empiricist) perspective, behavior is said to bear a lawful relationship to stimulus conditions. The scientific search is thus for the necessary and sufficient conditions producing various forms of activity.[8] However, if the individual is viewed as an active agent who may construe the environment in an infinity of ways, he or she remains fundamentally independent of the impinging environment (with the exception of physical constraints). If the individual conceptually constructs the environment, the environment is essentially the product of the individual, not the artisan of the individual's activity.

Neo-behaviorist attempts to discredit this analysis typically replace the agentive ingredients of the neo-Kantian analysis with intervening mechanisms or structures. Mental associations, stimulus–response connections, habits of self-reinforcement, natural categories, and cognitive schemata have all been used in this capacity. Yet, it is countered, such replacements are unconvincing, as each falls victim to the individual's capacity for reflexive conceptualization. In each case, the individual may turn to review his or her own patterns of conduct, and whatever their basis, alter

---

[8] The present arguments amplify the concerns of the preceding chapter with the effects on theory of metatheoretical commitments. The positivist–empiricist metatheory, with its emphasis on knowledge as a mirror of nature and laws connecting observable antecedents and consequents, essentially establishes the mold for stimulus–response psychology in general and the theoretical accounts of developmental stabilization in particular. The ordered change orientation does run counter to the stability account, but is not at fundamental variance with the traditional metatheory. The account simply shifts the locus of the stimulus from the environment to the genetic program. For an expansion of these arguments see Gergen and Benack, in press.

them according to some standard. The result of such reflexive capacities, then, may be self-generated curtailment, modification, or accentuation of internal tendencies. The internal system may thus continue to operate on itself without benefit from environmental input; it may undergo autonomous transformation.

One of the most important contributions to the developing conception of the autonomous organism is contained in Reese and Overton's (1970; Overton & Reese, 1973) distinction between *mechanistic* and *organismic* models of development. In the former case the dominant metaphor of human functioning is said to be the machine. Here the investigator sets out to identify the individual components or mechanisms within the individual; their interrelationships are plotted and their operations are traced to systematic alterations in antecedent conditions. For example, in the case of learning theory the strength of internal stimulus–response connections may be based on the number of preceding reinforcements; in modeling theory the tendency to emulate a model is said to be a joint function of the model's attractiveness, power, and outcomes; and in psychoanalytic theory the strength of the superego is believed to depend on the intensity of castration threats. Thus, from the mechanistic perspective, human behavior is held to be fundamentally predictable, and thus subject to highly general descriptive laws. As can be seen, the mechanistic view of human development is largely embedded in the stability orientation discussed above; behavior patterns at any given time are based on preceding environmental inputs (e.g., socialization), and such patterns are assumed to remain stable until the individual is exposed to differing stimulus conditions.

This view is contrasted with what Reese and Overton term the organismic model of human functioning. From this standpoint the individual is seen as "the source of acts, rather than as the collection of acts initiated by external (peripheral) force" (Reese & Overton, 1970, p. 133).[9] In this case, a major emphasis is placed on change, and such change is not itself explicable by efficient, material cause, but by formal cause. That is, organismic change must be traced to the properties or form of the entity itself rather than to antecedent events. For Reese and Overton, this view of the organism is tied to several correlated assumptions. For one, a commitment to wholism as opposed to elementarism is implied; if the organism is autonomously operating as a complex organization, then any given action must be seen in relation to the full state of the organization. Thus, for example, a smile as an isolated action cannot be properly interpreted. Interpretation will optimally depend on knowledge of the total state of the individual's psychological system at the time. The same action may imply pleasure, pain, insight, defensive rigidity, and so on, depending on the full psychological context. A commitment is also made to a structure–function orientation as opposed to one emphasizing antecedents and consequents. The task of the scientist is said to be that of discovering the function or goals of various interacting components of the organismic system rather than tracing the relationship among componential states. From the organismic stand-

---

[9] See also Hollis' (1977) distinction between the "plastic" and the "autonomous" models of man, the former holding behavior as the result of impinging events and the latter as the result of internally directed states.

point the individual may be viewed teleologically, as striving toward certain systemically necessitated ends. It also follows from these assumptions that primary investigatory emphasis should be placed on change in the overall organismic structure as opposed to discrete behavioral acts. One is thus primed to explore qualitative changes in the total organization of the system over time, a view that lends itself to theories of stages of development. As Overton and Reese (1973) indicate, the developmental theories of Piaget, Werner, and Erikson all embody certain essentials of the organismic model.

One is inclined at this point to seek a parallel with the earlier association drawn between the mechanistic view and the stability account. If the mechanistic world view favors the stability account, does the organismic orientation not favor ordered change theory? And if it favors ordered change, is it not then opposed to the conception of the individual as an autonomous agent? This point deserves closer scrutiny as the Overton and Reese treatment contains elements favorable to both conclusions. It is the present contention that the central thrust of their thesis has served to stimulate concern with autonomous agency and historically contingent pattern. It is only in the elaboration of the correlated assumptions that the aleatory account is obscured. To elaborate, the organismic view is chiefly concerned with the individual as an active participant in social interchange as opposed to a passive respondent. As an active participant, the individual is in motion, continuously changing, and such change can be internally originated. This emphasis is clearly consistent with the above described image of the autonomous actor. And, as we saw, if the individual is capable of self-direction, and may through symbolization direct his or her activities along an infinity of varying paths, then the likelihood of universal life-span trajectories is considerably diminished. Reese and Overton (1970) are also intrigued with this possibility, as they state: "[the organismic] position results in a denial of the complete predictability of man's behavior" (p. 134). Yet, in adding certain associated corollaries, the image of the self-directed, voluntary actor is obscured. In particular, this possibility is diminished when Reese and Overton suggest that there are certain necessary or systematic ends to which organisms generally strive, and that these ends are reached through a series of sequential stages. As Looft (1973) points out, this particular addition to the organismic model holds the individual to be a "closed system," and in this sense is unnecessary to the mechanistic–organismic distinction.

The image of autonomous self-direction also surfaces within many of the dialectic contributions to the life-span literature. The primary emphasis of dialectic theory is cross-time change, and such change is typically traced to the ongoing conflict between being and negation, between an entity and its obverse (located either within itself or extraneously). Clearly, the dialectic emphasis on ongoing change is antithetical to the mechanistic, stability orientation. And, for many, it is also supportive of the autonomy argument. However, a distinction must be made in the latter case between what may be viewed as a materialistic–deterministic form of dialectic theory and a rationalist–autonomous orientation. In the former case, change over time is viewed in part as the result of material determinants. An interaction is posited between the individual and both the social and material context: The individual both shapes and is *shaped by* the context. For example, Riegel (1972, 1975) posits an ongoing set of mutually interacting relations among inner–biological, individual–psychological, outer–physical, and cultural–sociological factors. Thus, self-direction is only partial; one is also influenced systematically by external forces. In some instances, dialecticians tend to view the interchanges as being fundamentally lawful. Hook (1957) speaks, for example, of laws of dialectic change, and Reese (1977) has argued for a dialectic theory of discriminative learning that may be subjected to empirical test. In effect, dialectic theory is sometimes treated as a form of the ordered change orientation. It is the latter view of a dialectic determinism to which Popper (1968) has devoted critical attention. As he argues, dialectic theories of societal transformation are not fundamentally scientific; rather, they are fatalistic. They do not admit to conditions under which their premises could be falsified, and are thus nonconditional in their predictions. As we see, the same argument may be applied as well to the closed system of ordered developmental change.

However, coexisting with this deterministic emphasis, certain forms of dialectic theory adopt a rational idealist perspective that lends itself substantially to the image of the self-directing organism. In this case the emphasis is placed on internal processes operating upon themselves; the individual is viewed as self-reflexive and thus capable of autonomous change. What is seen as the objective material world by the more deterministically oriented dialectician is now a world that is subjectively construed. From this standpoint, inputs into the psychological system from material, the sociocultural, and the biological world are all psychologically constructed by the individual. As these constructions may be altered from within the psychological domain over time, there is no means of testing dialectic principles through recourse to observables. And, if such constructions may be altered from within, as the individual engages in self-reflection, then one cannot presume the existence of a stabilized observation base upon which universal, deterministic principles might be based. It is this view of dialectic theory that is favored, for example, by Kvale (1977). As he describes the process of memory, "The formal structure of the stream of consciousness consists of a *now*, constituted through an impression and joining a train of *retentions* and a horizon of *protentions*. As the retentions refer to the 'just gone,' the immediate memory, the protentions refer to the 'not yet' of the immediate future. . . . The flux of consciousness constitutes its own unity" (p. 168). Similarly, Meacham (1977) adopts the subjective form of the dialectic orientation in his transactional model of memory. Fundamental to the transactional view, "both the perceiver and the world-as-perceived are products of the processes of perception" (Meacham, 1977, p. 265). From this perspective, then, we are confronted with an organism in the state of conceptually based, self-initiated change.

Finally, in her integrative synthesis of research on the development of individuality, Leona Tyler (1978) lends strong support to the image of the autonomously directed individual. Central in her view of development is the role of active, cognitive processing in the selection of behavioral alternatives. As she argues, people "deal actively with possibilities, recognizing, selecting, combining, organizing the voluminous raw material of experience and incorporating the patterns of individuality . . . More than on anything else, one's individuality depends on the choices one makes" (Tyler, 1978, pp. 204-205). And, reiterating our present theme of open-ended development, Tyler concludes her review by saying,

> each individual represents a different sequence of selective acts by means of which only some of the developmental possibilities are chosen and organized. No one individual can ever be considered typical of the human race. . . . As Whitehead pointed out, the fundamental realities are actual occasions in which indeterminate possibilities are transformed into determinate actualities. . . . Individuals create themselves (1978, p. 233).

Science and Historically Situated Self-Direction

Having explored two major developments within the life-span arena, let us consider their implications when viewed in tandem. First, it is becoming increasingly apparent to investigators in this domain that developmental trajectories over the life span are highly variable; neither with respect to psychological functioning nor overt conduct does there appear to be transhistorical generality in life-span trajectory. To be sure, there may be certain ontogenetic maturational sequences at the physiological level, as well as certain biological deterioration in the later years. And there may be eras of relative stability in which life-span trajectories are similar across groups and across generations. Yet, the individual seems fundamentally flexible in most aspects of personal functioning. A virtual infinity of developmental forms seems possible, and which particular form emerges may depend on a confluence of particulars the existence of which is fundamentally unsystematic.

The emphasis placed on the individual's processes of interpretation are further consistent with the argument for flexibility. One of the major capabilities of the human organism, and that upon which its malleability seems centrally reliant, is that of symbolization. In particular, the possibilities for multiple symbolic translations of the same experiential conditions, and for singular translations of multiple and varying conditions, enable the individual to move in any number of directions at any time (or, conversely, to remain stable over a variety of seemingly diverse circumstances). Further, the possibility of securing prediction through assessment of cognitive styles is rendered problematic because of the individual's capacity to reconceptualize the styles themselves. Processes of self-reflexive activity may themselves generate alteration in decision-making preferences. We find, then, a considerable affinity between the arguments for the relativity of developmental trajectory and the capacity for autonomous self-direction.

As outlined in the preceding chapter, there is an important relationship between metatheoretical and theoretical accounts within the science. In the case under study, we find theoretical accounts emerging that have not been derived from the logical empiricist metatheory undergirding the stability and ordered change paradigms. Further, if these various contributions to an aleatory account of life-span development do come to guide theory and research, certain critical assumptions of traditional metatheory must be reassessed. In the latter respect let us consider briefly the implications of current theoretical trends for the metatheoretical assumptions of predictive regularity and of empirical validation, both of which are sufficiently central to the tradition that their elimination would demand a profound reshaping of the concept of science.

The Assumption of Predictive Utility

From the positivist–empiricist perspective, one of the chief outcomes of theory is enhanced prediction. However, as we have also seen, the promise of increased power of prediction is dependent on the reliability of the phenomenon of interest.[10] When the focal phenomena are either stable or recurring, one may hope to develop a theoretical description at t_1 upon which accurate predictions can be made about the state of nature at t_2. Should either the stability or the ordered change account of human development form an accurate template across historical periods, a certain degree of successful prediction might be anticipated. The stability template assumes that life patterns are determined at an early period, and thus adult dispositions may at any time in history be predicted from accounts of early socialization. The ordered change template generally assumes the existence of universal, ontogenetic trajectories in development, and is even more optimistic with respect to prediction. The course of development may not only be predicted in the present era, but barring major changes in human genetics, predictions may be made with respect to developmental trajectories in the distant future.[11]

Yet, as our earlier analysis has demonstrated, both of the latter positions are thrown into question by the emergence of the aleatory account. If development is importantly related to the peculiar confluence of historical circumstances as construed by the individual, and these perceived circumstances may be in a continuous state of unfolding, then we can anticipate neither a high degree of cross-time stability nor much in the way of universally recurring developmental sequences. Theories attempting to account for trajectories occurring during any particular era may have limited predictive value. Given a subject matter that seems to offer little in the way of an inherently recurring observation base, the hope of a unidirectional path to increasingly precise prediction in the science is considerably reduced. Theories that appear to make reliable predictions in one era may lose their relevance for prediction in the next. To hold prediction as a central goal of theory thus appears misguided. With respect to research, small-scale observational or experimental studies testing various hypotheses and reaching publication long after execution are problematic. As Bell and Hertz (1976) have commented, "phenomena

---

[10] As should be apparent from the discussion in the preceding chapters, one must be exceedingly cautious in speaking about "phenomena." Nowhere in the present thesis is there an attempt to deny experience of an existing world. By "phenomena," in this case, reference is being made to the experiential world and not to linguistic objectifications within theoretical accounts.

[11] As Neugarten (1979) argues, the rate of change in patterns of life-span development has increased over the years. Major life events are becoming increasingly less predictable, age is losing its customary meaning, and the trend is toward an age-irrelevant culture.

are changing faster than scientists have been able to produce useful conclusions about them. . . . If developmental psychologists can offer only obsolete research findings to the public then why should the research be carried out?" (p. 7).[12] If prediction is the aim of research, required are problem-oriented studies designed for rapid and efficient analysis of data and dissemination of the results. Such research would function as a handmaiden to more general societal ends rather than posturing as a contribution to fundamental or enduring knowledge.

The Assumption of Empirical Evaluation

A second major assumption underlying traditional developmental psychology is that properly formed hypotheses are subject to empirical evaluation. Theories should be subject to correction, modification, or abandonment in light of systematic observation. However, this quest for establishing increasing correspondence between theory and fact cannot easily be sustained in light of the emerging view of development. At the outset, if a theory is based on a given range of phenomena existing at t_1, and the phenomena are no longer existent at t_2, then the empirical evaluation of the theory at t_2 is rendered problematic. This point has been sufficiently elaborated in Chapter 1 that no more need be added at this juncture. However, given the alteration of pattern across time, it is also clear that what may be taken both as confirmation and falsification of any theory may typically be secured by judicious selection of historical context. In the same sense that case histories furnish such an immense array of material that virtually any theory of development may be sustained, cultural history offers such a welter of developmental exemplars that investigators may select as needs or interests dictate. In effect, whether a theory appears to be confirmed or falsified importantly depends on the tactics of observational selection. At the same time, once a given subculture is located within which support for a given theory may be found, such confirmations can be generated *ad infinitum*.

A final shortcoming in the assumption of empirical evaluation in developmental research must be briefly outlined. As we have seen, there is a growing consensus in the discipline that developmental trajectories are fundamentally indeterminant. Much the same argument would appear germane to human conceptual activity. That is, one may conceptualize the world in an infinity of ways, and existing conceptual preferences may be seen as historically situated. Further, one's employment of a given conceptual repertoire must typically be supported by the community of others with whom communication is necessary for personal well-being. Without agreement in the way terms are used, communication is obviated. This dependency of conceptualization and communication on historical context raises fundamental questions concerning the capacity of the investigator to falsify a given theory of development. If any given observational pattern is subject to multiple conceptualization over time, each one of which may be rendered valid through social inter-

---

[12] In the same vein, Washington policy makers quip that sociology is "journalism in slow motion."

change, then there is little way in which the investigator can confidently identify any given phenomenon across time. For example, what counts as an observation of "prosocial" activity in one era may be seen as "egotistical" or "conforming" in the next; what is taken as an indicator of "volition" in one historical period may later be viewed as "habit" or "achievement motivation." In effect, one's contemporary array of exemplars for a given theory is subject to continuous reinterpretation, any one of which may suggest that previous theories were misguided.

In similar manner, an investigator can seldom be sure whether a given pattern of action should be counted theoretically as the "same" or "different" from a pattern documented earlier in the life of a given individual. A given pattern of harsh and abrasive language may be viewed as "attention seeking" when adopted by a young person, but an indication of "social disengagement" when used by the elderly. Sexual questions posed by the adolescent may be classified as "healthy inquisitiveness"; for the middle-aged adult the same activity may be termed "prurient." And, as investigators into life-span continuity are painfully aware, it is exceedingly difficult to recognize consistency or continuity in pattern when measures of the same construct (e.g., aggression, dominance, gregariousness) over the life span rely on different measures for different developmental periods. The primary result of historical variation in conceptualization and communication is that one can never be certain when a given set of observations either confirms or falsifies a given theoretical claim about human development.

Consistent with this argument is Paul Meehl's (1978) observation: "It may be that the nature of the subject matter in most personology and social psychology is inherently incapable of permitting theories . . . to yield the kinds of strong refutations expected by Popperians, Bayesians, and unphilosophical scientists in developed fields like chemistry" (p. 828). Surely for many scientists Meehl's conclusion is an unhappy one. Yet such pessimism issues primarily from the distress at falling short of the traditional goal of truth through science. Should other goals be sought, such pessimism would prove unwarranted. It is toward an alternative orientation to the role of theory that we now turn.

The Functional Utility of Life-Span Theory

When serious credence is given to the argument for the historical relativity of the developmental trajectory, along with the companionate view of the self-directed organism, the traditional views of the nature and functions of scientific theory are critically challenged. These various arguments confront the traditional scholar with difficult problems indeed: Should the primary theoretical focus be turned toward historically delimited descriptions of immediate utility but low transhistorical value? Of what value is general theory if it neither possesses long-term predictive utility nor is open to convincing empirical evaluation? What reasons save those that are self-serving can be offered for the continued elaboration of developmental theories such as those of Freud, Piaget, Werner, or the dialecticians, no one of which is sufficiently unambiguous that empirical assessment can be compelling?

Should the developmental discipline shift its orientation sharply, then, toward historically centered description relevant to specific societal needs?

To answer such questions requires inquiry into the positive functions of general theories of development. If we abandon the traditional theoretical goals of establishing empirically valid theories for purposes of prediction and control, what rationale remain to sustain the general theorist? One may argue that no rationale is required; theorists may continue their conjecture for the sheer intellectual joy of doing so. This argument cannot be refuted on any fundamental level. There is little reason to abandon the search for intellectual stimulation, whether in the form of the parlor game or the professional journal. However, for many, such self-centered pleasures lack nourishment; they simply do not furnish sufficient motivation for a life investment. Nor, on the wholly pragmatic level, can one anticipate the fiscal support of major institutions, both academic and governmental, should the sole concern of the theorist be self-stimulation. Other rationale must be explored. In particular, there are three major functions of developmental theory over and above those of prediction and control.

Theory as the Creation of Intelligibility

Nothing within the present analysis militates against the central function of theory within traditional science, namely that of explaining the vagaries of experience. Given the press of an ever-changing sea of ambiguous events, the individual may frequently search for a means of determining "what there is" and "why." Theory offers a means of dissecting the flux; through theory the rough and tumble of passing experience is rendered orderly. Theory furnishes an essential inventory of what there is and ideally satisfies the individual's quest for why the units of the inventory are related as they are. In this way theory furnishes a satisfying sense of understanding, along with terms enabling the individual to communicate this understanding to others. Thus, Freudian theory is highly useful in its capacity to demonstrate how seemingly diverse behavioral events across the life span are all expressions of a constant psychodynamic pattern. The chaotic and the bizzare are thus transformed into a seemingly inexorable pattern, and psychological sources are posited to make intelligible their existence and to suggest a cure. In the same way, other theorists rely on the concept of developmental stages to transform the immensely complex range of experiences into an orderly progression. In tying these stages to genetic sources or to social context, the theorist indicates "why" these stages occur as they do. And, in each case, the theorist furnishes terms of discourse, so that communication about experience is possible. The most broadly potent theories of the past century, including those of Darwin, Freud, Marx, and Keynes, have all served in this capacity. Not one is falsifiable; not one contains a strong predictive capacity. Yet all have been immensely important in furnishing intelligible understanding and associated language for communication.

Although these arguments are elementary, there is a far more complex issue lingering in the wings. If such general theoretical structures are essentially untestable, then how is one to select among competing theories? Or, to rephrase the question, given a single compelling system of intelligibility, for what reason should one quest for a second? This question gains increasing impact in light of the earlier arguments concerning contextual interpretation. As we saw in Chapter 2 there is a fundamental ambiguity in linking abstract conceptual terms to empirical referents. Because patterns of human action are in continuous motion, and seldom repeated with precision, the vocabulary of person description does not generally refer to observables. Observation may occasion the use of description, but it does not constrain it. Thus, virtually all behavioral observations might be rendered intelligible from any coherent, abstract system. The point seems well demonstrated in the case of psychoanalytic theory, a theory that has long proved satisfactory as a means of comprehending the immense range of experiences reported within the analytic process. In effect, the theoretical structure does not appear to have been vitally challenged by any set of phenomena reported to analysts during the past five decades. The theoretical terms appear capable of convincing application within highly varying experiential contexts. Other general theories of development should fare no worse. Thus, we find ourselves faces with the dilemma of selecting among theories, none of which may be subject to empirical test, and each of which may be extended so as to explain wide ranges of human activity.

At this point one might turn for help to the traditional but seldom used arsenal of comparative criteria for scientific theories. One might, for example, inquire into which formulation is the most parsimonious, the most logically coherent, the least ambiguous, or the most heuristically potent. However, when the dust is removed from these venerable criteria, we find little of useful substance. With increments in parsimony are frequently associated decrements in differentiation; as differentiation often increases the range of sensitization, parsimony comes with an attached cost. Reinforcement theories of development, for example, are highly parsimonious; however, in their failure to distinguish among various forms of reinforcement and the specific problems or promises attached to each, they lose their capacity for sensitization. Logical coherence is clearly an asset, but few available theories are obvious candidates for illogicality. Clear differences do exist among competing theories with respect to ambiguity, but, again, clarity carries with it associated costs. The ambiguous theory, like the ambiguous poem, is often more evocative or suggestive. Further, with increments in ambiguity, theoretical terms are frequently rendered more flexible with respect to applications; terms that are tied precisely to a given context cannot easily be generalized across domains. Finally, the traditional criterion of heuristic potency loses its edge in light of the weaknesses of the falsification assumption. If empirical evidence cannot satisfactorily add to or subtract from the validity of abstract theoretical accounts, then theories spurring researchers into activity can scarcely be viewed as superior to those inviting lassitude. Thus, the innumerable attempts to test Piagetian theory cross culturally may attest to the heuristic value of the theory. However, such research does not fundamentally strengthen or weaken the evidential grounds of the theory, and one might reasonably be suspect of the abundant research activity stimulated by the theory. This is not to argue that the traditional criteria are irrelevant or dysfunctional; rather, each is problematic, and together they do not take us far enough.

It appears, then, that traditional criteria offer little means for selecting one intelligibility system over another, nor is it obvious at this juncture why additional theoretical work is required of the discipline. Existing theory can, with skilled negotiation of conceptual meaning, account for virtually all life-span experience. A satisfactory answer to the question of "Why multiple theories?" hinges on discussion of the two additional functions of developmental theory.

The Generative Function of Theory

At the outset, there appears to be no adequate means of assessing the degree of fit between a theory of human development and the presumed contours of nature. If the individual is in continuous motion, altering patterns, abandoning old patterns, creating new ones, it indeed becomes hazardous to speak of the "contours of nature." In attempting to describe such fluctuations, one is fitting a language that, by virtue of its structure, demands a world of discrete entities to a world in which there are no "entities," but continuous emergence. Under such conditions the scientist essentially renders experience intelligible by creating its identity. The theory serves as a lens for structuring momentarily what is fundamentally unstructured. Yet, as analytic lenses, all theories have significant limitations. Each lens serves to blind as it illuminates. In observing a large crowd of people, one encounters an immense array of ever-changing stimuli. However, if one begins to search for the red pattern embedded in the crowd, he or she soon begins to observe a dominant red form, and other color variations recede into the background. When a second color is considered, and one's attentions are redirected, the color red recedes into oblivion and the new color looms into view.[13]

In a similar way, a developmental theory of attachment creates a way of understanding ongoing mother–child relations. Given the theory, one has a means of analyzing action, answering questions, and formulating plans. At the same time, a theory of attachment furnishes only a limited way of understanding, and thus, a limited range of possible implications. To call a differentiated pattern of activity "attachment," for example, suggests the manner in which one should respond, both conceptually and behaviorally. The term implies, in this case, a positive and interdependent relation between individuals. Such a relationship would not be implied if a common indicator of attachment, such as the tendency of the child to remain within close physical proximity to the mother, were described as "power retention" (referring to the desire on the child's part to keep in view those objects over which he or she feels power is possessed). Similarly, the term "attachment" implies that one might look positively on such activity during the early developmental years but negatively as "maturity" is reached. Such evaluations are implied by the widespread cultural belief that mother and child should be "attached" during the "formative years" but that "independence" is necessary for maturity. In effect, a premium is

---

[13] This must be viewed as a metaphorical example or run the risk of replicating Hanson's (1958) problematic argument that theory actually alters the character of sense data.

to be placed on multiple theoretical perspectives. Each serves to correct the restrictions inherent in its competitors.

From this perspective, the potential of the theorist to influence the course of society may be immense. The theorist who creates compelling theory is engaged in a form of ontological education. Further, when sensitivities are thus educated, patterns of conduct within the culture may be altered as well. As one learns how to understand, one absorbs a logic for action. As we have seen, available theory frequently teaches one not only to perceive patterns of attachment, but to value such patterns in early stages of development and to view them skeptically at later points. The theorist thus intervenes in the life of the culture. Prior to the theory there is relatively undifferentiated flux and little demand for action; with the emergence of theory there are discernable patterns and desirable actions.

Given the power of theory to shape both understanding and action, we must raise the question of criteria. What forms of theory may be viewed as desirable? When should a theory be discarded? One major answer to such questions hinges on a distinction between theory that is consistent with or reflective of common assumptions within the culture and theory that is inconsistent with these assumptions—theory that duplicates existing lenses or supplants them. In the latter case we may speak of generative theory (see Chapter 3). Generative theory is that which challenges the guiding assumptions of the culture, raises fundamental questions regarding contemporary life, fosters reconsideration of existing constructions of reality, and, by so doing, furnishes new alternatives for action. Let us consider more closely two central components of generative theorizing along with arguments supporting such formulations.

The Generation of Doubt

As we have seen, any given theoretical view simultaneously serves to sensitize and to constrain; one sees more sharply, but remains blind to that which falls outside the realm of focus. Thus, it may be argued, any theory that commands widespread belief, that serves as the univocal view of reality within a given culture poses a threat to the culture. As one's actions are often consistent with one's comprehension, then the companion to partial comprehension is a delimited range of action. Where there exists a single, widely shared, commonsense construction of reality, one is likely to encounter inflexibility of action. When a theory is used generatively, it will challenge the commonly shared construction of the world; it will generate doubt in such constructions and thereby engender flexibility. When used generatively, theory may increase the adaptive potential of an individual or a culture.

On this account Freudian theory serves as an outstanding example of generative theorizing. Initially the theory did much to unseat Victorian assumptions regarding the sexlessness of the early childhood period, and the antiseptic view of the relation between parent and child. More important, the theory called attention to the possibility of unseen and virtually impenetrable, unconscious connections between seemingly disparate events over the life span. Events that were phenotypically dissimilar and temporally dissociated could be related dynamically within the unconscious. In an important sense, Freudian theory was the reincarnation of romanticism: it invited one to suspend belief in the phenomenal givens of contemporary life and to accept the reality of unseen forces. One could scarcely ask a theory to provoke greater doubt in the "commonsense givens."

At the same time, as Freudian theory becomes absorbed into the assumptive bases of the culture, there is an associated ossification of understanding and a reduction in adaptive capability. Thus, at any point in time there is a vital need for theory that challenges the shared assumptions of the times. The capacity for Freudian theory to generate doubt may now be largely exhausted. Much of the theory has entered the fund of common knowledge. As such knowledge is solidified, it is necessary to develop bold new theories of development that again thrust the culture into doubt.

The Formation of Alternatives

Closely allied with the generative function of creating doubt is that of furnishing alternative courses of action. Not only should generative theory give one reason to pause and reconsider current modes of activity, but ideally should point to other forms of actions and their potential results. One may here discriminate among generative conceptualizations that (1) succeed only in instigating doubt, (2) generate doubt and also *imply* alternative courses of action, and (3) fully articulate alternatives to current investments. It would be difficult to locate pure exemplars in these various categories. However, generatively oriented analyses do differ in the relative emphasis given to these various ends. A methodological critique, such as that mounted by Kurtines and Grief (1974) against Kohlberg's theory of moral development, does succeed in generating doubt in Kohlberg's analysis, but little is offered or implied by these investigators with respect to an alternative formulation. In contrast, Riegel's (1973) analysis of the cultural and economic underpinnings of current developmental theory, Sullivan's (1977) critique of Kohlberg's theory of moral development (1969) and the liberal social science ideology on which it is based, and Buck-Morss's (1975) assessment of the socioeconomic bias underlying Piagetian theory all function both to generate doubt in the relevant theoretical scaffoldings while implying alternatives. All might represent proper exercises of what Horkheimer (1972) has termed the "critical attitude," and particularly so in their argument that an acceptance of contemporary theorizing can favor exploitative relations among persons. By implication, one is challenged to consider alternative theoretical forms that might favor the reconstruction of society along less exploitative lines.

Freedle's (1977) attempt to employ Thomian topological theory in building a developmental theory enabling both *p* and *not p* to be simultaneously true, along with his proposal for using nonclassical or nonmodal logics to understand certain forms of development, not only generates doubt in the currently existing theories of development, but succeeds in laying the scaffolding for important alternatives. However, Freedle's analysis falls short of the full generative demand inasmuch as it does not clearly elaborate alternative forms of action related to the orientation.

Models are proposed but their behavioral implications left ambiguous. In contrast, Runyan (1980) has outlined a "stage-state" framework for describing the life-course which is specifically designed to enable people to exercise conscious control of their life-trajectories. The framework may thus be used for purposes of "visualizing an array of possible paths and outcomes, designing plans and strategies for the pursuit of desired goals, and for making decisions in light of expected short- and long-term consequences of alternative courses of action" (p. 960).

Most desirable from the present standpoint are theoretical forms that enable one to perceive the shortcomings of existing positions and elaborate alternatives. For example, if one were invested in the reconstruction of social institutions, what view of human development would most favor such an end? If one seeks reforms in social policy vis-à-vis the aging, could the process of aging be reconceptualized in such a way that alternatives to the present policies might be favored? As argued elsewhere (Gergen & Basseches, 1980), such formulations are particularly needed by practitioners and others whose major investments are in social change. Theorists who uncritically set out to describe contemporary patterns of development typically lend implicit support to the status quo. For those concerned with social change, compelling theoretical rationales are required to legitimate alternative forms of action at the conceptual or intellectual level.

The Value-Sustaining Function of Theory

The preceding discussion furnishes ample prelude to a final role to be played by general theories of life-span development. To speak of the capacity of theories to create doubt and to foster new patterns of action clearly implies that any given theoretical commitment is to be negatively valued, and that the capacity to engage both in a pattern of activity and its antithesis is superior to either one of these options alone. This position cannot be justified either on logical or empirical grounds; its basis is fully valuational. Essentially, it is being argued, one may justifiably dislodge a theory for valuational purposes. In this case, the value behind the theory is adaptive flexibility; however, other valuational criteria may be proposed with equal legitimacy.

One can argue that if values come to serve as the chief motivating force for theoretical development, the discipline will rapidly become a podium for ideological partisanship, and abnegate its responsibility for rendering value-neutral accounts of reality. Should value investments be allowed to determine theoretical description, then one could no longer claim to be doing science; rather, such activity would become a form of secular religion. Yet, as elaborated in Chapter 1, it is naive to believe in the existence of theoretical accounts that do not favor certain forms of action over others, that do not add to the power, pleasure, fortune, or life chances of certain groups in society at the expense of others. As increasingly numerous accounts have shown, even the most technical and innocuous theoretical accounts of human activity harbor numerous value implications. They do so in the selection of phenomena for study (thus lending such phenomena an importance not granted to potential competitors), the selection of terms enumerating these phenomena (theoretical terms indicate the value to be placed on various states and conditions), the selection of explanations (explanations place the locus of blame on varying persons or institutions), the image of the human functioning which they convey, and the choice of research methods. We are not speaking here of the extent to which theorists' value investments have actually played an instrumental role in fashioning theory, nor of the extent to which personal values have guided the selection of method or data. Rather, the important point is that in numerous ways even the most disinterested theory conveys value implications. Theories insinuate themselves into culture in such a way as to alter the culture, to disrupt, or to fortify certain cultural patterns, and such effects are of valuational importance to those who are so affected.

It is elucidating in this context to consider the three basic forms of developmental theory outlined in the beginning of this chapter. First, with respect to the stability template, we find normal behavior defined as that which is stabilized or consistent across time. Inconsistent behavior, on this account, may be viewed as improper, maladjusted, immoral, or neurotic. To the extent that one appears to change plans, goals, or life investments, he or she may be considered, from this perspective, to be abnormal or defective. Such terms as "shifty," "shallow," "lacking strong character," "two-faced," and "directionless" all serve as cultural epithets for individuals failing to measure up to the implied ethic. In effect, the stability orientation lends support to those within the culture whose moral values favor consistency or coherence in comportment (cf. Gergen, 1968).[14]

Within the ordered change orientation, three prominent evaluative biases are evident. The first is that change *should* occur. The individual who is stabilized at a given stage is typically viewed as a deviant, subject to special attention, if not veiled contempt. The Freudian concept of "fixation" provides the boldest statement of the bias. Fixation, in Freudian terms, is a serious form of neurosis, subject to cure through analysis. However, being arrested in a Piagetian preoperational state or Kohlberg's second stage of moral development would carry with it the same pejorative implications. The second prominent bias is that the individual should not return to previous behavior patterns. Change should be unidirectional. The Freudian concept of regression serves as the evaluative cornerstone for subsequent theorizing. Regression in psychoanalytic terms is a defensive maneuver through which people avoid realistic confrontation with their problems. Regression within the schemas of Piaget and Kohlberg is viewed as a special anomaly and requires extensive justification. When one has transcended an inferior status, how is return to be justified?

Both of these prescriptive biases must be qualified by a third, the "middle adulthood prejudice." Although forward change is generally viewed as positive, this

---

[14] Such valuational ends are widely supported in other areas of psychology. For example, personality theorist Prescott Lecky (1945) maintains that the normally functioning person strives for consistency in all aspects of life. Emotional imbalance is equated with blockage of the need for consistency, and therapy is largely envisioned as a tool to remove such blocks. Carl Rogers (1947) also equates comfort and freedom of tension with the achievement of cross-time coherence in behavior.

demand is attenuated once the individual has reached "maturity." Generally speaking, within Western culture middle adulthood provides the model for optimal comportment, and the more remote one's behavior from the optimum, the more questionable it becomes. Thus, if an adult regresses to adolescent behavior, he or she may be tolerated (if such behavior is limited to specific periods set aside for "immaturity"); however, to behave like an eight-year-old is more deplorable, and to act childishly is wholly culpable. Such differential approbation cannot be accounted for in terms of simple age grading (i.e., everyone should act their age). If a child begins to demonstrate adult characteristics, the parents are typically congratulated for either the rich environment they have provided or their genetic constitution. The preference for middle adult behavior patterns is again manifest when one considers models of aging. Generally, the more removed one's behavior from the middle adult norm, the more inferior its evaluative status. For example, a negative value is thus built into the process of disengaging from society (Cumming & Henry, 1961; Neugarten, 1968). Indeed, the very concept of development, with its intimations of "forward" movement, is applied with hesitancy to the later years.

Finally, with respect to the aleatory orientation, we find an account that would legitimize variation in human outlook and differentiation of behavioral pattern across the age spectrum. It would favor stability for those age cohorts in which this pattern seemed organically coherent, ordered change in other cohorts, and radical alteration in still others. Virtue is thus embodied in variation. In a broad sense, the orientation also invites conflict, favoring as it does the existence of multiple groups with varying investments. However, it simultaneously eschews hierarchies in society; it stands as a rationale against the domination of certain subcultures by others. Finally, the aleatory account grants the individual the fundamental capacity for choice. It invites one to suspend belief in the past as a prison, an anchor, or a directive power, and to consider oneself as inherently free to change the trajectory of one's life. And, by granting choice, the aleatory account restores the concept of personal responsibility to the repertoire of evaluative terms. Because there is choice people may be properly praised or condemned for their conduct.

Given the inevitability of value-loaded theory, and the insurmountable problems of establishing empirical validity, it would appear altogether appropriate to consider the value-sustaining potential of theory not as an inadvertent *hazard de parcours*, but as a critical ingredient of theoretical development. If theories do not adequately meet the traditional criteria of the positivist–empiricist paradigm, we may consider those ends toward which they are most efficacious. We need not consider theories the less scientific for achieving these ends; rather, we must reconsider the concept of science as it is applied within the human sphere. In the present case, it would appear that theories properly function as implements for the sustaining of value positions. They may thus be judged according both to their effectiveness in this capacity, and with respect to their agreement or disagreement with one's personal commitments. Theories that carry out the task poorly (e.g., those seen as mere sentiments masquerading as theory, purely ideological, or propagandistic) may be judged the more harshly. And should a theory be found personally disagreeable, the way may be opened for critical reexamination and synthesis.

Chapter 5

The Historical Context of Transformation

As indicated at the volume's outset, discontent with the positivist–empiricist program for accumulating behavioral knowledge is becoming increasingly apparent. Many of the concerns voiced within these pages are echoed throughout the socio-behavioral sciences.[1] In many instances these concerns have been stimulated by significant developments within various sectors of philosophy. In effect, the present arguments are nurtured by a context of generalized ferment and must be located within an historical process. Although previous chapters have touched on various facets of this process, the time is at hand for a more coherent elaboration of both the process and the place of the present arguments within it. Three specific tasks are to be undertaken. First, we shall scan several developments of the past century forming the grounding context for the present theses. This analysis will locate a critical antinomy, the dynamics of which have shaped a number of major colloquies both within philosophy and psychology, and the recapitulation of which we are witnessing in contemporary debate. Second, we shall focus on the current attempts of scholars (and particularly psychologists) to explore alternative orientations toward science. We shall review the efforts of a variety of heterodox schools and assay their progress to date. This analysis will set the stage for a consideration of the future. In particular, we shall be concerned with locating metatheoretical suppositions that form a basis for unification among the dissident encampments. If such a metatheory can be charted, it may serve as a phalanx for the future. As in previous chapters, we shall again devote particular attention to social psychology as the elucidating case.

---

[1] As Sarason (1981) has described it: "There is a creeping sense of malaise in psychology about psychology. But that malaise is not peculiar to psychology. It is suffusing the atmosphere in all the social sciences. Indeed, in some of the social sciences, like economics, there are those who not only believe that the emperor is naked but also that he has a terminal disease" (p. 836).

The Pivotal Conflict: Exogenic versus Endogenic World Views

Wilhelm Wundt is often considered a founding father of experimental psychology in general and social psychology in particular. If one surveys the vast corpus of Wundt's contributions, one is struck by what appears to be a significant evolution in orientation. In his early work, such as the *Principles of Physiological Psychology* and *Lectures in Human and Animal Psychology,* Wundt helped to chart the terrain that was later to become the private reserve of American experimental psychology. It is to this work that Boring's (1929) classic history devotes such singular attention. Yet, during the culminating years of his career, Wundt turned from the task of isolating biologically based mechanisms of psychological functioning to the problems raised by social pattern. The bases of such patterns do not lie primarily within the nervous system, argued Wundt, but are essentially social creations. Patterns of religious activity and governance, for example, along with such culturally significant concepts as honor or truth, are products of people at particular points in history. As such, they demand forms of exploration that differ from those of the experimentalist (Blumenthal, 1977, 1979; Mischel, 1976). *Völkerpsychologie,* the ten-volume work that was to occupy Wundt for the last twenty years of his career, represents his exploration into this alternative form of inquiry. As is apparent from the history of American social psychology, it is Wundt the experimentalist, and not the author of *Völkerpsychologie,* to which the discipline turned for a model of investigation.

Wundt's concept of social psychology is an interesting one and much deserving of contemporary scrutiny. For Wundt the guiding metaphor for social psychology was not that of natural science, but rather that of historical analysis (*Geschichte*). Rather than searching for general laws of psychological functioning, the task of the social psychologist was to render an account of contemporary behavior patterns as developed from the culture's history. Toward this end the laboratory experiment could contribute very little. Rather, the method for social psychology was to lie in the documentation and explanation of historical patterns as they emerged over time. The function of social psychology was not that of making predictions. Consistent with Popper's (1957) views of behavioral science, Wundt did not believe in the inevitability of social patterning. Rather than prediction, the goal of the social psychologist was to render the world of human affairs intelligible. And, like Darwin, this task was to be carried out by examining the etymology of contemporary patterns.[2]

Yet, in spite of the enticing implications of this line of thought, it is Wundt's conflict between fundamental conceptions of science that furnishes the proper base for examining subsequent developments in psychology and the complexion of current conflict. This is so because the bifurcation in Wundt's career is but a localized instance of an antinomy of long-standing and profound consequence both within the intellectual sphere and without. Like many of his contemporaries, Wundt was

---

[2] A significant movement toward the establishment of a diachronic form of social psychology has begun to emerge in recent years. See footnote 18 in Chapter 3.

grappling with competing metatheoretical assumptions concerning human knowledge and its relationship to the natural world.[3] Although these competing assumptions may be characterized in many ways, it will prove useful to center our attention on the critical conflict between environmental- versus person-centered theories of knowledge. On the one hand, human knowledge in ideal form may be viewed as a reflection of the real world or a map of nature's contours. From this standpoint empirical entities are granted preeminent status in the generation of human knowledge; the human mind best serves the interests of knowledge when it operates as a pawn to nature. In contrast, the human mind can be viewed as the origin of knowledge, a fount of conceptional construction, or a source of thought forms that frame both the questions that may be put to nature and the answers derived therefrom. It is the former view that spurred Wundt's concern with the physiological mechanisms driven by or reliably dependent on variations in the natural environment; it is the latter view that sustained Wundt's inquiry into the historically relative patterning of ideas.

It is the present thesis that Wundt's conflict continues to pervade the discipline and for the past hundred years has played a critical role in shaping and reshaping the discipline at the theoretical, methodological, and political levels. Further, there is reason to believe that we have not only witnessed a profound shift in the balance of power between these antagonistic views, but are currently on the threshold of moving beyond them. The redistribution of power is one to which social psychologists have indeed contributed, and if the impending transformation continues social psychology will be thrust into a pivotal position vis-à-vis the broad intellectual community. The first task will be, then, to sketch out an account of the role played by this conflict over epistemic assumptions during the past century, both in psychology more generally and social psychology in particular. This historical resumé will function as a necessary prolegomenon to our assessment of the critical shift taking place in contemporary psychology and the amalgamation of dissidence.

To appreciate properly the historical context of the antagonism, a brief précis is required concerning the protagonists. Let us first employ the term *exogenic* to refer to theories of knowledge granting priority to the external world in the generation of human knowledge, and *endogenic* to denote those theories holding the processes of mind as preeminent.[4] Although one can scarcely locate a pure exemplar of either variety, many philosophic writings may be singled out for the inspiration they have furnished to those of one or the other persuasion. Surely John

---

[3] For further analysis of Wundt's paradigmatic conflict see Blumenthal (1957) and Danziger (1980). Wundt's attempt to distinguish two forms of psychological science, one concerned with natural process and the other with human artifacts, was paralleled by many others, including Dilthey, Rickert, Troeltsch, and Windelband.

[4] The distinction between the exogenic and endogenic views may be usefully compared with other analytic distinctions including mechanistic versus organismic (Reese & Overton, 1970), plastic versus autonomous (Hollis, 1977), structuralist versus functionalist (Rychlak, 1977), and mechanistic versus person centered (Joynson, 1979).

Locke's arguments against innate ideas, along with his analysis of the means by which elementary sensations give rise to the development of complex ideas, has played a major role in the history of exogenic thought. Similarly, Hume's tracing of compound ideas to the association of simple impressions and James Mill's view of the mind as an accumulation of sensations driven automatically by physical inputs have contributed substantially to the exogenic position. Although one may draw a meaningful parallel between traditional empiricist philosophy and what is here termed exogenic thought, the relationship between endogenic thinking and both rationalist and idealist philosophy is more clouded. However, certain rationalist arguments, including Spinoza's attempt to derive knowledge not from experience but deductively from propositions, and Kant's theory of *a priori* constructs of time, space, causality, and so on, must surely be viewed as seminal contributions to endogenic thought. However, lodged against these rationalist arguments and sustaining the endogenic line are Schopenhauer's later tracing of knowledge to the wellsprings of will, and Nietzsche's arguments for knowledge as a product of one's motives for power.[5]

Lest this metatheoretical antagonism seem pallid, let us glimpse a number of localized conflicts of more pungent familiarity. As an ideal typification the following may be ventured:

1. Those who favor an exogenic world view are likely to argue that because the external environment drives the senses in predictable ways, objectively grounded knowledge about this environment is possible. In contrast, those who take an endogenic perspective are likely to argue against the possibility of objective knowledge. Because knowledge is primarily a product of the processing agent, traditional criteria of objectivity are rendered suspect.

2. The exogenic thinker tends to believe that because there are objectively correct and incorrect answers about the world, people of sound mind should reach common agreement. Science should thus ideally strive for consensus among practitioners. For the endogenic thinker, however, multiple interpretations of experience are usually held to be both legitimate and desirable. Thus, if total accord exists within a group, it may be a signal either of oppressed minority views or shallow conformity. The process of generating knowledge, from this standpoint, holds conflict to be superior to consensus.

---

[5] Some may feel that the close association between rationalist and idealist forms of philosophy signified here is unwarranted. Rationalist thought is usually identified with the belief that knowledge must be gained through some form of rational process, thus allowing many rationalists to argue that such processes may be applied to evidence given to the senses. Idealism, in contrast, is usually identified with the position that reality is essentially the manifestation of an idea, a position that cannot so easily be reconciled with the kind of dualism many rationalists find acceptable. However, the two positions are linked in the present case inasmuch as thinkers typically (though not always) identified with them have been set against various

3. The exogenic thinker, holding that reality is independent of the observer, may frequently argue for scientific neutrality. If the scientist allows his or her values to guide the course of observation, the result may be a faulty recording of the state of nature. For the endogenic thinker, however, recordings of reality are not so much correct or incorrect as they are creations of the observer. If scientific statements are not data driven, but psychologically generated, then in what sense can one be neutral or independent of what is known? The possibility for scientific neutrality is thus obscured.

4. For the exogenic thinker, it is often argued that the empirical world impinges on the senses and may thus be considered the determinant of psychological states. Such environmental determinism may be direct, in terms of immediate sensory input, or indirect, as in the case of the continuing effects of previous learning experiences. The causal locus for human action is thus placed in the environment; human behavior is dependent on or determined by antecedent environmental events. In contrast, for the endogenic thinker, the individual is often viewed as free to construct or interpret sense data furnished either from the environment or from memory. The causal locus of human action thus tends to be placed within the individual; for the endogenic thinker environmental determinism is often replaced by voluntarism.[6]

5. Because of the emphasis on environmental determinism, and the related belief in a separation of fact and value, the exogenic theorist is likely to view questions of moral value as beyond the scope of the discipline. From the endogenic perspective, with its emphasis on personal constructions of reality and the inseparability of fact and value, moral issues often seem inescapable. To declare them irrelevant may itself be morally culpable.

6. The exogenic thinker is likely to place strong emphasis on methods of measurement and control, as it is through such methods that one may obtain unbiased assessments of the facts. For many endogenic thinkers, however, "correct assessments" are suspect. Thus, empirical methods may be seen as means of sustaining theoretical positions already embraced. Given a particular theoretical standpoint, methods may be anticipated that will yield support. Methods thus furnish rhetorical rather than ontological support for the scientist.

With the lines of battle thus drawn let us follow Wundt's example and strive toward understanding the present complexion of the discipline by examining its historical development.

---

empiricist doctrines. See Robinson (1976) for a lucid account of the empiricist and rationalist foundations of contemporary psychology.

[6] It should be noted that the endogenic orientation does not inherently commit the theorist to voluntarism. For example, mechanistic theories of cognition are endogenic, but deterministic. However, a voluntarist commitment does require an endogenic viewpoint. To the extent that the voluntarist employs concepts of intention, decision making, rules, plans, or heuristics, he or she is relying on an endogenic language.

Exogenic-Endogenic Détente: The Reality of the Internal

It is no intellectual accident that psychology as a science was given birth at the close of the nineteenth century. One might indeed ask if it was not a sign of lassitude that its beginning was so late in arrival. The foundations had long been laid. The concept of an empirical science had been well developed since the time of Newton, and the function of laboratory experimentation had been impressively demonstrated by Lavoisier, Berzelius, the Curries, and Rutherford. Coupled with this self-conscious attempt to unlock nature's secrets through systematic empirical study was a long-standing belief in mind as an empirical entity. Thinkers from Plato to Descartes had granted the mind ontological status, and by the late nineteenth century, philosophers such as John Locke, David Hume, David Hartley, and James Mill had supplied rather detailed theories of mental processes. For almost a century German thinkers had also given careful thought to the relationship between mental elements and the physiological system.[7] In effect, there existed in the 1900s an auspicious conjunction between the exogenic and endogenic perspectives: Mind was an empirical entity that could be studied with no less rigor and precision than the surrounding environment. There remained only the task of welding the belief in the palpability of mental entities with the experimental orientation of the natural sciences to give birth to the science of psychology. This was fully accomplished in late nineteenth century Germany.[8]

Yet, while the late 1800s were optimal years for the growth of psychology as a science, they were simultaneously unfavorable to the development of a social psychology. If the mind was the focus of empirical study, and if mental operations and their biological coordinates furnished the essential questions, there was little obvious role for a uniquely social psychology. Social stimuli had no distinctive

---

[7] Kirsch (1976) has argued that the emergence of psychology as an empirical science can largely be attributed to developments in German psychology, where attention was being directed to the physiological basis of experience. MacKenzie (1976) maintains that the development of Darwinism was an essential catalyst for the emergence of an empirically oriented psychology. Ben-David and Collins (1966) trace the impetus to the shifting structure of German academic institutions of the time.

[8] The concept of a détente between the exogenic and endogenic views falls far short of representing the full range of opinion during this period. Indeed, the concept of an empirical science of mind was hotly debated in many circles. Dilthey, Windelband, Rickert, Hensel, and others all carried out strong attacks against the empiricist position. In the same way, pockets of strong endogenic thought continued to exist during the hegemony of American behaviorism. In the latter case, for example, Havlock Ellis' 1923 volume, *The Dance of Life,* presents science as an aesthetic creation, no more objectively valid than religion, dance, or literature. As Morawski (1979b) points out, Ellis (1923) here followed Vaihinger's doctrine of fictions: "Matter is a fiction, just as the fundamental ideas with which the sciences generally operate are mostly fictions, and the scientific materialization of the world has proved a necessary and useful fiction, only harmful when we regard it as a hypothesis and therefore possibly true" (pp. 91–92).

properties; they were essentially patterns of light, sound, and so on to be processed like any other stimuli. Nor was it necessary to develop a special category for social as opposed to nonsocial behavior. An understanding of all behavior patterns should ultimately be derived from thorough knowledge of basic psychological processes.[9]

As a result, to develop his *Völkerpsychologie* Wundt had to begin an entirely separate enterprise. Virtually none of his experimental work, nor the contributions of Fechner, Helmholtz, Weber, and the like, made their way into his account of the historical emergence of social institutions. Likewise, when the first two American texts on social psychology appeared in 1908, one by William McDougall and the other by E. A. Ross, neither drew significantly from the empirical study of mind. McDougall's book relied heavily on an evolutionary perspective, while Ross' work drew sustenance from earlier sociological thinking. For neither of them was it possible to discern useful connections between social activity and the laboratory study of mental process.[10]

It was William James who essentially carved out a niche for social psychology within the domain of psychology proper. As he reasoned, there might be certain psychological processes that were distinctly social in their implications. His discussion of the basic senses of self along with his formula for determining the individual's self-esteem (dividing success by pretension) thus informed later generations of social psychologists that if they wished an independent place in psychology, they must identify mental processes that are uniquely social in their function.[11] From

---

[9]The exogenic–endogenic détente is also evident in Comte's analysis of the social sciences. As Samelson (1974) points out, in *la morale* ("the sacred science") the subject and the object coincide. In this composite is reached what Comte believed to be the definitive stage of human reason, a full subjective synthesis. And, consistent with the endogenic position, Comte saw a close relation between value and science. Science was to be used in the service of reforming society. In the United Stages, Hugo Münsterberg was also attempting to synthesize the laws of nature with social idealism (Hale, 1977). Münsterberg wrote in his diary of 1900 that his aim was the harmonization of a positivistic study of human life with an ethical idealism consistent with Kant's and Fichte's philosophy.

[10]Texts are, of course, only one marker for an emerging discipline. However, even in the publication of the journal *Zeitschrift für Völkerpsychologie und Sprachenwissenshaft* during the 1860s and the French "protosocial psychologies" of the mid-nineteenth century (along with the later works of the Tardes), virtually no mention was made of developments in experimental psychology (Apfelbaum, 1979; Lubek, 1979).

[11]It would be a mistake either to view James as a full proponent of the exogenic-endogenic détente or to assume that the détente was enthusiastically endorsed in all circles. For James, along with Josiah Royce, Henri Bergson, and others, the central intellectual problem of the age was to identify "a transcendental source of values and purpose in a world where science had transformed nature into the blind interaction of atoms and history had relativized all cultural standards of beauty, morality and truth" (Hale, 1977, p. 150). For James this search ultimately led to his severing connections with psychology and to the publication of *Varieties of Religious Experience* (1936).

this standpoint, the very most social psychologists could anticipate was a small piece of the mental pie. As we shall soon begin to see, however, there is good reason to believe that social psychology may serve a far more pivotal role in understanding human action. Indeed, the mental pie may be viewed primarily as a social creation.

Exogenic Succession: Toward Public Reality

The conjunction between the exogenic and endogenic perspectives that gave birth to early psychology was not to last. Within the robust realism of the American climate, assumptions concerning the character of "the mind" soon became targets of attack. American culture, faced with the zesty promises of an expansive environment, was yielding up a philosophy of its own, namely pragmatism. For the pragmatist nothing was considered real unless it made a difference in practice. With such major thinkers as John Dewey, William James, and Charles Pierce contributing both to the philosophy of pragmatism and to theoretical psychology, American psychology could hardly remain unaffected. There were also seemingly insoluble theoretical squabbles emerging in German circles regarding the nature of mind, and the introspective method allowed no hope of solution. Simultaneously there were the impressive experiments of Pavlov demonstrating systematic behavioral changes without reliance on experiential analysis. Finally, the mentalistic concerns so strongly represented in German psychology must surely be counted among the casualties of World War I.[12]

It was thus in 1924 that J. B. Watson could boldly contrast the "old psychology" that viewed "consciousness" as its subject matter with the "new" psychology of behaviorism, holding that, "the subject matter of human psychology is the behavior or activities of the human being. Behaviorism claims that 'consciousness' is neither a definable nor a usable concept; that it is merely another word for the 'soul' of more ancient times. The old psychology is thus dominated by a kind of subtle religious philosophy" (Watson, 1924, p. 6). This shift toward an exogenic psychology was further stimulated by the rise of logical positivist philosophy. Based on the writings of Schlick, Neurath, Ayer, Frank, and others, behaviorist psychologists could draw sustenance from the early positivist argument that assertions closed to empirical evaluation are without positive function in a mature science. Thus, concepts of psychological process, whether driven by environmental stimuli or autonomously sustained, were all subject to disapprobation. Further, the psychologist could draw comfort from the logical positivist arguments for the unity of science. If all theoretical statements in psychology could be linked to an observation language, and all observation language could ultimately be translated into the language of physics, then psychology could anticipate ultimate assimilation into the family of natural sciences.

Social psychologists of the time had much to gain by joining the exogenic succession. Social activity was, after all, publicly observable and could therefore be placed at the center of scientific concern rather than serving as a peripheral deriva-

---

[12] For amplification see Blumenthal (1977).

tive of mental process. Social psychology had also been criticized as "hopelessly speculative and verbose,"[13] and a shift of emphasis to observable entities held out promise for greater scientific respectability.[14] It was thus in 1924 that Floyd Allport wrote in the preface to his important text, *Social Psychology,* "there are two main lines of scientific achievement which I have tried to bring within the scope of this volume. These are the *behavior viewpoint* and the experimental method" (p. 12). It was largely through Allport's efforts that the scattered social experimentation of Triplett and others became amalgamated into a "scientific discipline."[15]

Exogenic Liberalization: Personal Reality as Hypothetical Construction

The hegemony of radical empiricism proved short lived within psychology. As positivist–empiricist philosophy flourished and became extended in the 1930s and 1940s, it became increasingly clear that the demand for science without reference to unobservables was far too stringent. In physics, concepts such as "energy," "wave," and "field" were usefully employed, none of which could be directly represented by empirical operations. There appeared no good reason for excluding such terms in psychology. Terms not referring to immediate observables thus came to be viewed as "hypothetical constructs" (MacCorquodale & Meehl, 1948). They were to be admitted into the science, provided that one could ultimately tie them, through a series of linking definitions, to public observables. Under these conditions it was possible to readmit internal or psychological states into proper study as hypothetical constructs. Personal experience once again had scientific credentials—only on a hypothetical level.[16]

This loosening of the criteria for mature science was enthusiastically received in many quarters of psychology. Many influential thinkers, including Woodworth, Tolman, Cattell, and Gordon Allport, had never been moved by radical behaviorism and had continued to place a major emphasis on psychological process.[17] The 1940 publication of *Mathematico-Deductive Theory of Rote Learning,* reflecting the

---

[13] See E. B. Holt's 1935 essay on the "whimsical condition" of social psychology.

[14] In his 1930 review of "recent social psychology," Sprowls argued that the establishment of prediction and control of human behavior as chief aims of social psychology was largely in response to the demands of American politics, philanthropy, industry, and other social institutions. He also agrees with the dominant view of the time that "behavior patterns" should take "first place" among the concerns of the profession. See also Murchison (1929) for a reiteration of the behavioral viewpoint in social psychology.

[15] In their challenging analysis of the Triplett study Haines and Vaughan (1979) argue that, contrary to common belief, the research does not occupy a unique place in the history of social psychology, and that the claim for Triplett's being the first experiment functions only as an "origin myth."

[16] Koch's (1959) analysis of this liberalization is perhaps definitive.

[17] Critical reactions to the inception of the behaviorist movement have been nicely documented by Samelson (1978).

efforts of Clark Hull and his colleagues in both psychology and philosophy, also demonstrated the seeming precision with which such hypothetical terms could be used. And finally, the 1930s exodus from Germany of such Gestalt thinkers as Köhler, Wertheimer, and Koffka sparked an innervating romance with endogenic thought. To the extent that autochthonous psychological processes enabled the organism to create figure, ground, form, groupings, and movement from a stimulus array that did not itself contain such properties, then a concept of self-directing, internal process seemed inescapable. The liberalization of the positivist–behaviorist orientation was in full force.[18]

Had the exogenic liberalization not occurred, Kurt Lewin might today be an obscure figure. Arriving in the United States in 1933, Lewin was indeed in treacherous waters. With philosophers Husserl and Cassirer as his intellectual forbears, his endogenic commitment was not easily reconciled with the dominant empiricist temper of the times. For Lewin the chief subject of attention was the mental world of the individual, not the world of surrounding nature. Empirical reality of the positivist variety indeed occupied a nebulous position in Lewinian theory—never quite absorbed but not entirely rejected. This ambivalence was also reflected in Lewin's use of the term "external reality." At times the concept referred to public observables, but at others to the internal or psychological construction of the world (Deutsch, 1958). This ambiguity in the status of empirical reality is nicely illustrated in Lewin's 1935 essay on environmental forces. At times he argues for an independent reality capable of altering the psychological field. As he points out, "The mere knowledge of something (e.g., of the geography of a foreign country . . .) does not necessarily change the child's life-space more than superficially. On the other hand, psychologically critical facts of the environment, such as the friendliness of a certain adult, may have fundamental significance for the child's lifespace . . ." (Lewin, 1935, p. 74). But are these "critical facts" to be viewed as existing entities? Lewin's (1935) explication is equivocal, "The environment is for all its properties (directions, distances, etc.) to be defined . . . according to its quasiphysical, quasi-social, and quasi-mental structure" (p. 79). Further comment proves equally ambiguous: "Environment is understood psychologically sometimes to mean *momentary situation* of the child, at other times to mean the *milieu,* in the sense of the chief characteristics of the permanent situation" (Lewin, 1935, p. 71). To further complicate the argument, Lewin (1935) then speaks as if the psychological world is the empirical world: "These imperative environmental facts—we shall call them valences—determine the direction of the behavior" (p. 77). As the present analysis makes apparent, Lewin's classic equation stating that behavior is a function of the personal construction *and* the environment $(B = f(P, E))$, represented his attempt to conjoin two fundamental epistemologies. In tracing behavior to psychological process he revealed his long-standing immersion in endogenic thought; in

---

[18] For an analysis of the Gestalt movement as a revolt against positivist science see Leichtman (1979).

tracing behavior to environmental determinants he catered to the exogenic interests that dominated the American scene.[19]

It was left to Lewin's students, Back, Cartwright, Deutsch, Festinger, Kelley, Pepitone, Schachter, Thibaut, and others to reconcile fully Lewin's endogenic leanings with mainstream empiricist psychology. This was accomplished first by the adoption of the hypothetico-deductive form of exposition so impressively represented by Hull and his colleagues. Within this mode, the task of the scientist is that of developing and testing hypotheses about the world of observable fact. Festinger's (1954) widely heralded theory of social comparison furnished an impressive model for social psychology. Here Festinger laid out a series of formal assumptions, each accompanied by supportive research findings. The reconciliation with empirical psychology was further achieved through the virtually exclusive adoption of the experimental method.[20] Importantly, this *modus operandi* also resembled that developed by the major competition—the Hullian satellites, including Hovland, Doob, Dollard, and others.[21] Thus, the theories and experiments of the Lewinians, along with such monographs as *Frustration and Aggression* (Dollard, Doob, Miller, Mowrer, & Sears, 1939) and *Communication and Persuasion* (Hovland, Janis, & Kelley, 1953) furnished a univocal model for scientific conduct. It was in this mold that social psychological inquiry was contentedly, if not enthusiastically, cast until recent years. In effect, by the late 1960s social psychology had witnessed the apotheosis of neobehaviorism.

But let us carefully note the fate of the endogenic perspective during this period. Clearly the scientists themselves were following positivist–empiricist doctrine with

---

[19] For further discussion see Miriam Lewin (1977).

[20] Social psychology was hardly independent in the development of its central paradigms. In fact, its form may be viewed as an emulation of mainstream, experimental psychology, which by 1938 was characterized as *empirical, mechanistic, quantitative, nomothetic,* and *operational* (Bills, 1938). In their review of the preceding fifty years of social psychology, Bruner and Allport (1940) largely agree that such a designation had also come to be applicable to the social domain as well. The only important deviation appeared to be in the concomitant concern of social psychologists with research on social problems.

[21] The Yale group, with its close attachment to the exogenic roots of learning psychology, tended to place a strong emphasis on the manipulation and measurement of observables with a secondary emphasis on mental processes, while the endogenically oriented Lewinians tended to emphasize mental process and place secondary emphasis on accounting for a multiplicity of stimulus or behavioral variables. This difference in epistemological orientations explains McGuire's (1980) description of convergent versus divergent forms of research. However, the differential emphases were not sufficiently radical to prevent relatively easy transition from one camp to the other. Lewin's student Harold Kelley could thus become an important contributor to the Hovland program in attitude change (cf. Hovland, Janis, & Kelley, 1953) and to later accounts of attribution processes (cf. Kelley, 1967).

respect to their own conduct. From the guild standpoint, they were attempting to map reality as accurately and systematically as possible, and to test such maps against reality in dispassionate fashion. However, the endogenic perspective so strongly represented in Lewin's orientation remained. Where? Essentially it became embodied in the theories under empirical study. People other than scientists were said to be dominated by cognitive constructions, motives, needs, and so on. *They* lived in a world of intrinsically generated mental process. It is this ironic duality—the scientist employing an exogenic theory to guide his or her own conduct, while assuming an endogenic basis for others' actions—that now returns to haunt the discipline.[22]

Deterioration of the Exogenic World View

In order to appreciate recent developments in psychology, it is again necessary to take account of the intellectual ethos. As we have seen, there has been an important interplay between psychological theory and contributions to exogenic and endogenic thinking more generally. Sustaining the thesis developed in Chapter 3, existing metatheoretical assumptions have played a key role in determining the direction and form of scientific inquiry. The recent past is no exception. In particular, one cannot but be impressed with what appears to be a broad-scale disenchantment with exogenic assumptions in philosophy. This disenchantment appears to be highly correlated with (1) the cognitive revolution in psychology, (2) the general malaise with respect to traditional scientific inquiry, and (3) what has been termed "the crisis" in social psychology. Let us deal first with the deterioration of the exogenic position in philosophy and the growth of cognitive psychology. We may then turn more directly to the critical condition of contemporary psychology.

The generalized disenchantment with exogenic assumptions may be traced to three important developments in philosophy. The first, as touched on in Chapter 1, is the *broad reassessment of the positivist-empiricist* paradigm. At the outset, those philosophers most closely identified with the founding of logical positivism themselves retreated over time from the bold and invigorating promise of certainty in science. By 1932 Neurath was prepared to argue that verification is a relation between propositions and not between propositions and experience; Carnap ultimately gave up his early argument that meaning in the sciences was to be identified as translatability into experience, and Ayer (1940) finally admitted that sense data cannot be conclusively used to prove assertions about the physical world. In the

---

[22] It is of interest in this context to note Festinger's early resolution of the exogenic-endogenic conflict. In his theory of social comparison, Festinger (1954) reconciles the opposing epistemologies by distinguishing between a "physical" reality and a "social" reality, the latter being essentially psychological. As Festinger argued, when people cannot obtain proper information for decisions in the former domain, the subjective process of social comparison commences.

meantime Karl Popper (1957) argued persuasively against the classic view that scientific knowledge can be built up from pure observations (Popper, 1957, 1968), and against the positivist view that empirical confirmation of a theory constitutes a proper means of accumulating knowledge. Yet, even Popper's falsification thesis has not resisted deterioration. As Quine (1953) demonstrated, falsification is a problematic process. For one, the defender of a given theory can typically locate auxiliary theoretical assumptions to discredit or absorb the disconfirming evidence. And as argued by Hanson (1958), because what counts as data relevant to a theory's falsification cannot easily be specified outside the language of the theory itself, the range of potential threats to a theory may be severely truncated. In effect, what counts as a fact cannot be separated easily from theoretical premises.

The break with empiricist philosophy of science became fully apparent with Kuhn's (1970) account of scientific progress. As Kuhn argued, shifts from one major theoretical paradigm to another in the sciences do not generally depend on either confirmation or falsification. Rather, what appears to be "progress" in science represents a shift in perspectives based on a confluence of social factors, along with the generation of anomalies that are simply irrelevant to previously favored theories. The new theories are not improvements over the old in terms of predictive power; they primarily represent differing frameworks of understanding. More polemically, Feyerabend (1976) has argued that rules for induction and deduction, along with methods of hypothesis testing, are basically irrelevant to scientific progress. Necessary for a flourishing science is procedural anarchy, argued Feyerabend, where hypotheses contradicting well-confirmed theories should be championed, and social and ideological persuasion should be given equal footing with evidence. To be sure, brisk argument continues in virtually all these sectors. The major point is that the weight of the argument has shifted substantially over the past forty years, so that the chorus of lusty voices that once sang hosannas to positivist–empiricist rules of science has now been replaced by a cacophony of dissidents.

A second major contribution to the erosion of the exogenic commitment has been made by analytic or *ordinary language philosophy*. Stimulated largely by the work of Moore, Russell, and Wittgenstein, concern shifted away from the problem of relating experience to knowledge to the way in which claims about knowledge and experience functioned within the language. As it was argued, problems within both philosophy and everyday life are often created by the language, and their solution may thus require an analysis and possibly purification of that language. Of particular concern for the behavioral sciences, increasing attention was given by philosophers such as Ryle, Anscombe, Hamlyn, and Austin to the language of person description. As such concepts as mind, motivation, intention, and behavior were scrutinized, increasing attention was paid to the forms of discourse used in the behavioral sciences. From such analyses a fundamental critique of the empiricist–behaviorist orientation emerged. As discussed in Chapter 2, it was argued that human action cannot be rendered intelligible in strictly physical terms (Hamlyn,

1953; Hampshire, 1959; Peters, 1958; Taylor, 1964, Winch, 1958). By referring to the physical properties of the stimulus, physiological process, or resulting behavioral events alone, human action is not intelligible. To take account of the temperature, the wind velocity, the pitch and magnitude of vocal tones, and so on to which John Jones is exposed on a given occasion, and relate these systematically and precisely to subsequent movements of his arms, legs, mouth, and so on is not to "make sense" of his behavior. Such an account would indeed leave one mystified. However, this form of empirically based discourse, often termed *causal,* may be contrasted with another, which enables immediate comprehension. If we simply point out in this case that John Jones is "greeting his neighbor," we have informatively explained his actions. This level of discourse, often termed *reasoned,* typically requires that reference be made to reasons, motives, purposes, or intentions. When we know what the person is trying or intending to do, his or her actions are typically made intelligible. Thus, it could be concluded that endogenic concepts of reason, intention, motive, and so on were fundamentally indispensable to a behavioral science. Concomitantly, the role of environmental stimulus and response became increasingly unclear. If intention is built into our language of understanding, then environmental stimuli cannot easily be viewed as the cause of action. And, if action can only be identified by knowing its intentional basis, then behavioral observation plays an ancillary role to symbolic interpretation.[23]

Coupled with these two important philosophic movements has been a third force antagonistic to the traditional exogenic commitment in behavioral science, that is, the *flourishing of "the critical stance"* within the social sciences. As a result of the widespread political and international tensions of the 1960s, a wide variety of potentially culpable institutions such as government, industry, and education underwent strong critical scrutiny. Included among these was the scientific establishment. Of particular importance, trenchant questions were raised concerning the ideological implications of what appears, on the surface, to be value-free description. Various facets of this work have been discussed in Chapter 1. In neighboring fields, the ideological underpinnings of historical accounting (Zinn, 1970), along with behavioral theory in political science (cf. Surkin & Wolfe, 1970), were examined. Such queries also kindled deeper interest in the writings of Habermas, Adorno, Horkheimer, Marcuse, and other members of the Marxist-oriented, Frankfurt school (Jay, 1973). As the critical model became increasingly well developed, it also became apparent that the empiricist assumption of a value-neutral social science was deceptively misleading (cf. Unger, 1975). Social science knowledge is not an impartial reflection of "the way things are," as the empiricists would have it, but inherently reflects the vested interests, ideological commitments, and value preferences of the scientists themselves.[24]

Each of these movements, then, has succeeded in undermining major assump-

---

[23] See von Wright (1971) for a discussion on the implicit antipositivism of analytic philosophy and the affinity between the latter and hermeneutic philosophy.

[24] Leo Marx (1978) has argued that the current era is witnessing a "neo-romantic" revolution against the cold formalism of "science" more generally.

tions of the positivist-empiricist model of science, along with the exogenic world view with which it is allied. As is also clear, many of the themes developed within these divergent contexts are reechoed in the particular concerns with historical change and descriptive relativism of the previous chapters. Before turning to the present "crisis-like" atmosphere of the sciences, however, we must briefly consider an important theoretical spin-off generated by the disenchantment with the exogenic view.

The Cognitive Revolution and the Return to Endogenesis

It is difficult to ascertain precisely how and where the foregoing shifts in philosophic perspective influenced the course of psychological thought, or even whether such influence was unidirectional. However, it does seem clear that the three major developments outlined above constitute the generative context for the "cognitive revolution" in psychology. Several reasons may be offered for this compatibility. Among them, the philosophy of science ceased to offer encouragement and guidance to those who wished to purify the language of psychology of mentalist terms. The door was open for what has now become a wholesale reification of mental process.[25] Terms such as "concept," "memory," and "decoding" have come to acquire an ontologic status similar to that granted to the "facts of consciousness" by the nineteenth century German mentalists. A second fillip to cognitive study was furnished by the philosophic shift toward linguistic analysis and its relationship to thought. Such work furnished a basis for useful interchange between philosophers and psychologists, often obscuring the boundaries between the disciplines. In the work of Noam Chomsky (1968), for example, one finds the reincarnation of the nineteenth century philosopher-psychologist. And, as the present analysis makes clear, the debate between Chomsky (1959, 1964) and Skinner (1957) was not only a scientific disagreement over which theory best fits the data (cf. Dixon & Horton, 1968). It was also a recapitulation of the fundamental conflict between exogenic and endogenic world views—Chomsky, the self-styled neo-Kantian, against Skinner as radical empiricist.[26]

The shift from the exogenic to the endogenic perspective is evident throughout the cognitive domain. Ittelson (1973) has nicely traced the subtle but significant change in the concept of stimulus in the history of perceptual study. As he shows, the traditional view is one that holds the stimulus to be "physical energy outside the organism which, when it impinges on the organism, initiates processes, the end product of which is a response wholly determined, and predictable from the nature of the stimulus" (Ittelson, 1973, p. 8). Exogenic thought could have no clearer

---

[25] As Mueller (1979) describes the return of the subjective in recent psychology, "By the 1970s the . . . return to the earlier mode of thinking had grown to the point that a popular textbook dealing with the psychology of sensory coding stated that psychology is a science whose proper content is . . . inner awareness . . ." (p. 22).

[26] For a more detailed analysis of the empirical incommensurability of the Chomsky and Skinner positions see Lacey (1980).

exemplar. However, this line of argument has gradually been eroded. Thus, for example, Gibson (1950) stated that "the term 'stimulus' will always refer to the light change on the retina" (p. 63). Yet, by 1966, he had reconsidered this position, and stated that his early definition "fails to distinguish between stimulus *energy* and stimulus *information* and this difference is crucial" (Gibson, 1966, p. 29). In effect, information is a concept that recognizes the autonomous processing capacities of the organism; it assumes an organism that is in search and uses stimulation to fulfill its goals. The quandary over exogenic and endogenic views has now become a focal point of discussion. In his popular text on cognition, we find Neisser agonize: "No choice is ever free of the information on which it is based. Nevertheless, that information is selected by the chooser himself. On the other hand, no choice is ever determined by the environment directly. Still, that environment supplies the information that the chooser will use" (Neisser, 1976, p. 182). Finally, we must consider the work of Piaget (1952, 1974). From the present perspective we find Piaget undertaking the titanic challenge of integrating both the exogenic and endogenic world views in a single theory. He wished simultaneously to accept a real world about which true knowledge could be obtained, along with an active organism that formulates and interprets. Thus, Piaget's concept of accommodation yields to exogenic assumptions, while the concept of assimilation emphasizes his commitment to endogenic thought. Development in Piagetian terms is an epistemological seesaw.

To be sure, social psychological thinking has been much influenced by the shift toward cognitive formulations in the field more generally. However, social psychologists were amply prepared. As we have seen, early formulations of the Lewin group planted important seeds for endogenic thought within the discipline. The more general deterioration of the behaviorist–empiricist orientation furnished a context in which such thought could reach fruition. Thus, with Schachter's two-factor theory of emotional labeling (Schachter, 1964; Schachter & Singer, 1962), cognitive processes replaced biological determinism as the basis of behavioral explanation. Festinger's (1957) theory of cognitive dissonance, which began with the supposition that people's actions are driven by inherent cognitive tendencies, became the battle cry for a small army of social psychologists (cf. reviews by Brehm & Cohen, 1962; Wicklund & Brehm, 1976). Yet few investigators bothered themselves with the earlier empiricist demand for an independent behavioral anchoring of hypothetical constructs. Balance formulations (Abelson et al., 1968; Heider, 1946; Newcomb, 1961) also came to demand equally wide attention. Again, such formulations assumed the existence of autonomous tendencies toward cognitive equilibrium, tendencies that were not obvious products of previous environmental influences.[27] This variety of formulation continues to the present day. Reactance

---

[27] It is of historical interest to note the shift from exogenic to endogenic assumptions in the Yale volumes on attitude change. Although early volumes were largely concerned with isolating external determinants of attitude change, with the 1960 publication of *Attitude Organization and Change* (M. S. Rosenberg & C. I. Hovland,

(Brehm, 1966; Wicklund & Brehm, 1976), equity (J. S. Adams, 1965; W. Walster, & Berscheid, 1978), self-awareness effects (Duval & Wicklund, 1! uniqueness striving (Snyder & Fromkin, 1980), and many similar concepts have all been added to the arsenal of cognitive tendencies.

Heider's (1958) theory of causal attribution also demonstrated its origins in German endogenic thought. For Heider the experience of causality was not given in the movement of relationships among environmental entities; it was rather a phenomenological necessity inherent in mental functioning. Although an over-whelming number of studies were inspired by Heider's formulation, much of this work has attempted a reconciliation with the empiricist roots of experimental social psychology. That is, the inherent mental tendencies so fundamental to the endo-genic basis of the theory gave way to traditional exogenic thinking (see Chapter 3). In the Jones and Davis (1965) and Kelley (1972) formulations, both pivotal to attribution inquiry, internally driven cognitive tendencies are largely eschewed. Instead, the perceiver becomes a rational being weighing the evidence supplied by the senses. Indeed, the Kelley formulation uses as its basis James Mill's canons of logical inference, long a mainstay in empiricist philosophy.

In adopting a cognitive basis of explanation, social psychologists have also been successful in linking their interests with adjacent domains. The attempt of disso-nance researchers to account for biological motives (cf. Brehm & Cohen, 1962), along with later research on helplessness, and coping and health (cf. Glass, 1977; Glass & Singer, 1972; Rodin & Langer, 1977; Seligman, 1975), helped form the basis for what has become behavioral medicine. And, with the more recent work on cognitive processes in social decision making (cf. Nisbett & Ross, 1980) and person memory (Hastie et al., 1980), social psychology has allied itself once again with traditional experimental psychology. So enthusiastically have such enterprises been pursued that many have come to fear that concern with fundamental social process may be relegated to a secondary status. Social psychology may become an ancillary discipline whose concerns will be dictated either by applied or experimen-tal psychology.

The Struggle toward a New Science

Thus far we have seen that the breakdown of exogenic metatheory has been a congenial context for the flourishing of cognitive theory. However, of greater im-portance for present purposes, this breakdown has fostered critical reconsideration of the nature of behavioral inquiry. As previous chapters have attempted to demon-strate, positivist–empiricist metatheory engenders and sustains a particular theoreti-cal orientation toward human action. As faith in the metatheory erodes, support

---

Eds.), the endogenic metamorphoses was virtually complete. In the latter volume concern had shifted almost entirely from external determinants to internal process.

also recedes for its theoretical and methodological counterparts in the science. The initial result, as we have seen, is the flowering of the cognitive revolution. Yet, if the implications of the cognitive orientation are extended, we find the traditional concept of science is threatened. The flourishing of endogenic theory so acts as to erode belief in exogenic metatheory. For example, as shown in Chapter 1, if one accepts the view of the individual as an agent of conceptualization, then the assumption of "standardized stimulus conditions" in experimentation is rendered untenable. The result of this generalized shift in the endogenic direction has been the development of widespread uneasiness with the promise of traditional science and a groping toward an alternative metatheory. In the remainder of this chapter we shall assay the range of discontent and attempt to elucidate the common bases for an alternative metatheory.

Observers of the science frequently comment on what they take to be a deep and pervasive discontent with the outcomes of traditional research pursuits (cf. Sarason, 1981). With increasing outspokenness, investigators of high visibility and lengthy research experience have begun to raise sobering questions concerning the promise of traditional science. Meehl's (1978) critique of traditional hypothesis testing along with the Popperian view of science, Bruner's (1976) view of psychology as in its "winter of discontent," Cronbach's (1975) lament over the cumulativeness of experimental findings, Sarbin's (1977) argument for a contextualist orientation to understanding human action, Neisser's (1976) misgivings about the predictive capability of cognitive research, Bronfenbrenner's (1977) concern over the ecological irrelevance of much developmental research, Argyris' (1975, 1980) elucidation of the manipulative and misleading implications of traditional empirical research, Riegel's (1972) attack on the ahistoric character of traditional developmental psychology, Sarason's (1981) examination of the social and ideological roots of psychological theory, Fiske's (1978) dismay with the meager progress of personality research, Mahoney's (1976) assessment of the damaging effects of the professional reward system, and recent portrayals of research on learning and memory as both ideologically and historically bound (Kvale, 1977; Meacham, 1977; Schwartz, Lacey, & Schuldenfrei, 1978) are all indicative of a major evolution in thinking. It seems fair to say that such generalized ferment has not taken place in psychology since the advent of radical behaviorism in the 1920s.[28]

It is also apparent that what has been termed "the crisis" in social psychology (Cartwright, 1979; Duck, 1980; Elms, 1975; Graumann, 1979; Lewin, 1977;

---

[28] Such citations are only representative of a much broader array of critical self-appraisals within recent psychology. Sigmund Koch's (1959) work may be viewed as prophetic in this regard. However, many others must be added to the list, including Allport (1975), Bakan (1969), Bhagat (1979), Campbell (1969), Chein (1972), Deese (1972), Finkleman (1978), Gordon, Kleiman, & Hanie (1978), Hermann (1979), Holzkamp (1976), Hudson (1972), Israel and Tajfel (1972), Kendler (1981), Lorenz (1967), McKeachie (1974), Mishler (1979), Morawski (1979a), Newell (1973), Palmonari (1976), Petrinovich (1979), Rosnow (1978), Rychlak (1975), Sampson (1978), Secord (1977), Shotter (1975), and Ventimiglia (1978).

Mertens & Fuchs, 1978; Sherif, 1977; Silverman, 1977) is not a matter of localized dyspepsia. Within the manifest discontent with the experimental method (cf. Gadlin & Ingle, 1975; Gergen, 1978; Harré & Secord, 1972; McGuire, 1973), misgivings concerning the capacity of present research to solve pressing social problems (Helmreich, 1975), arguments against the generation of transhistorical predictions (Gergen, 1973; Hendrick, 1976), arguments for breaking the link between understanding and prediction (Thorngate, 1976), the critical exploration of the human image implied by social theory (Shotter, 1975), doubts about the cumulativeness of programatic research (Cartwright, 1973; Smith, 1972), and concern with the ethical foundations underlying psychological research (Kelman, 1972; Mixon, 1972; Schuler, 1980; Smith, 1974), social psychologists are critically confonting the logical–empiricist tradition. Further, in the questioning of the value bases implicit within descriptive theories (Apfelbaum & Lubek, 1976; Archibald, 1978; Hampden-Turner, 1970; Sampson, 1977, 1981), in the growing concern with the effects of social context on social psychological knowledge (Buss, 1979a), in the probing of the extent to which scientific theory creates social phenomena (Gergen, 1979), the exploration of the rule following basis of social action (Ginsburg, 1979; Harré, 1979; Harré & Secord, 1972), the elucidation of the dialectic orientation (Buss, 1979b; Cvetkovich, 1977; Rappoport, 1978), the inquiry into the interpretive bases of social life (Gauld & Shotter, 1977), the questioning of the extent to which people may voluntarily escape the predictive efforts of the science (Scheibe, 1978), the search for biases underlying the discipline's history (cf. Baumgardner, 1977; Morawski, 1979a; Samelson, 1974), and the various conferences and colloquies devoted to the nature of the discipline and its potential (cf. Armistead, 1974; Israel & Tajfel, 1972; Strickland, Aboud, & Gergen, 1976), social psychology is breaking clear of a tradition that, for all its solidifying capacities, had become strangulating in its singularity. Such self-conscious concern may be viewed, then, as a salutory sign that the field is healthily linked to the broader intellectual community and is making a serious attempt to reach solutions in its own terms.

Yet many social psychologists have grown weary of the soul-searching appraisals of recent years. They are hostile to "attack without alternatives," and demand from their seeming assailants a fully developed model for an "improved science" along with compelling exemplars.[29] Although emotionally sustaining, there is little to

---

[29] Based on a survey of two hundred thirty social psychologists concerning the "crisis" in social psychology, Zwier (1980) contends that two cultures have emerged in the profession. One group is engaged in examining the bases and potential of the field; it is theoretical in orientation and concerned with application. This group tends to believe that experiments are used as implements largely to demonstrate the obvious, that fads and fashions govern research enterprises, that social knowledge is historically contingent, and that knowledge is ideologically based. A second group is primarily engaged in hypothesis testing, and tends to reject the beliefs of the former group. It is also a group that typically responds positively to the statement, "I am sick of hearing about a crisis in social psychology." The groups do not differ, however, in their capacities to acquire grant funds, to communicate with others in

recommend such a defense. Its parallel would be to disregard criticisms of astrology because the critics' capacities for prophecy failed to be superior or because the critics failed to furnish alternative pastimes. Yet, on both pragmatic and intellectual grounds, there is manifest demand for an alternative metatheory. A fully developed rationale is required for the development and flourishing of alternative forms of inquiry. With the elaboration of an alternative metatheory, one may begin to establish viable end points or functions for investigation, and to examine forms of academic training, journal policies, and professional gatekeeping of more substantial promise.

In major degree the preceding chapters have attempted to establish the rationale for a new way of thinking about scientific activity. However, the contours of an alternative metatheory may also be detected among the constituents of what may be viewed as a critical vanguard. As we shall see, central elements of the emerging scaffold for an alternative science are highly congenial to the conclusions reached in the preceding chapters. At present, the constituents of this dissident "counter-culture" dwell in relative independence; lines of metatheoretical agreement have not been elaborated. Yet, with respect to the politics of knowledge, it is these lines of fundamental agreement that may begin to furnish a basis for disciplinary transformation. It thus becomes useful to consider the broad-ranging developments within four heterodox constituencies: the hermeneutic–interpretive, the dialectic, the critical, and the ethogenic. Finally, we may examine the extent of agreement among these perspectives with respect to metatheoretic fundamentals.

The Hermeneutic–Interpretive Movement

Prior to the eighteenth century hermeneutic study was concerned with the interpretation of Biblical scriptures. Hermeneutic scholarship served as the handmaiden of philosophy and historiography in their combined search for the proper or most accurate interpretation of early religious writings. By the end of the eighteenth century, however, hermeneutics began to take on the more difficult tasks of accounting for the nature of interpretation itself (Palmer, 1969). In attempting to locate proper interpretations of scriptural passages, one must presumably be able to ascertain the writer's intentions, or the meanings that he or she wishes to convey. On what grounds can such a determination be made? The question indeed demands inquiry into the nature of communicative acts, along with a viable account of social knowledge more generally (cf. Gadamer, 1975, 1976; Ricoeur, 1974, 1976). Students of history, literature, and jurisprudence have been no less immersed in the complicated question of how accurate renderings can be made of the meaning of early historical accounts, literature, poetry, and judicial opinion. And, during the twentieth century, it has become increasingly clear that if a science of human behavior is to develop, it, too, must face these same difficult questions. One is ill

---

the field, or to publish. As Zwier argues, the fundamental difference between these groups is a difference in world view—including the conception of human beings and of knowledge. Also see Nederhof (1978).

equipped to conduct a science in the traditional sense without the ability to identify or classify behavioral acts; yet such identification must seemingly depend on the complicated question of how one can with certainty assess an actor's intentions.

The latter issue becomes acute in light of a conclusion emerging with increasing but painful clarity among hermeneutic theorists themselves: The major criterion by which the validity of a given interpretation may be judged is the extent to which it accords with the prevailing rules of communication within the culture. In effect, interpretations may be rendered acceptable or unacceptable to the extent that they meet currently adopted standards of intelligibility. This view, amplified in Chapter 2, has always been an unhappy one for theologians, literary critics, and historians, inasmuch as it implies a thoroughgoing social relativity in interpretation. From this standpoint, scriptures, literary masterpieces, and judicial opinions may be interpreted differentially across time and culture with no means of discriminating between "correct" and "incorrect" interpretations. Such a conclusion is not a sanguine one for most behavioral scientists, as it suggests that the meaning of social actions is generally created by scientists themselves. Aggression, altruism, conformity, and the like are not "out there to be classified or studied," as the traditional empirical view would have it, but are by-products of the rules of intelligibility existing within the sciences. They are essentially created by the prevailing forms of interpretation within the sciences and may change as meaning systems evolve in the culture. Attempts to rescue the process of interpretation from the shoals of social relativism have as yet proved less than compelling outside the behavioral sciences (cf. Hirsch, 1976; Mandelbaum, 1967; Ricoeur, 1976). As seen in Chapter 2, it remains highly problematic as to whether such a rescue effort is possible within the sciences.[30]

This concern with the conventionalist character of social interpretation has served as a catalyst for two significant lines of inquiry in the social sciences. The first line of inquiry has been into existing forms of social interpretation. Such exploration proves quite consistent with the hermeneutic emphasis on social production of meaning. Thus, the hermeneutically informed writings of Alfred Schutz (1962), along with the symbolic interactionist contributions of Cooley (1902), Mead (1934), Thomas (1966), Blumer (1969), and others, set the stage for contemporary study of socially shared meaning systems. Perhaps the most visible of the earlier investigations were those falling under the general rubric of "labeling theory" (cf. Becker, 1963). Such investigations were particularly challenging in their argument that various forms of deviance are not essentially empirical in character, but are created through systems of socially shared labels. The deviant is thus a product of those who label.

The epistemological challenge implicit in labeling theory has become more

---

[30] It is important to note the significant influence of Wittgenstein's work, along with the previously mentioned work within ordinary language philosophy on what is here being characterized as hermeneutic–interpretive inquiry. Rules of interpretation in the latter domain closely correspond to the grounding suppositions for person description elucidated within ordinary language analysis.

fully articulated within the field of ethnomethodology. As envisioned by Harold Garfinkel (1967), ethnomethodology is essentially concerned with the methods by which people generate and sustain common sense, and render "visibly reportable" their understandings about the world. Thus, for example, it is commonly taken for granted that certain deaths are suicides, while others are caused by natural occurrences. From an empiricist standpoint, one should be able, in principle, to record the number of suicides within the culture at any given time. Yet, as Garfinkel (1967) attempts to show, suicide is a product of social rules, the application of which must be continuously negotiated. To commit suicide one must presumably "intend" to do so. Yet intentions are not observable, and the rules for determining the presence and absence of intention are diffuse. In the same vein, Cicourel (1968) has demonstrated how systems of social understanding must be sustained by police, probation officers, and other officials in converting the immense complexity of an ever-shifting reality into ordered units such as "offenses," "family units," and "harmless behavior." In their extensive analysis of gender identifications, Kessler and McKenna (1978) have argued even more dramatically that gender is also a social creation. Men and women do not exist as two distinct social types. Biologists, medical practitioners, lawyers, children, transexuals, and so on differ considerably in interpretations of what counts as male versus female. Given significant variations in such rules from one segment of society to another, the assumption of objective, real-world gender differences becomes unsupportable. Other investigators have inquired into the manner in which people construct such entities as "mind" (Coulter, 1979), envy and other moralities (Sabini & Silver, 1982), personal death (Sudnow, 1967), legal codes (Bittner, 1967), and so on (cf. Psathas, 1979).[31]

The second major impact of hermeneutic thought on contemporary social science has occurred within the metatheoretical domain (Taylor, 1964). Although there has been comparatively little ethnomethodological inquiry into the means by which social scientists themselves generate "what there is" through their rules of meaning, this possibility has hardly escaped scrutiny by those concerned with the potential of the social sciences (cf. Berger & Luckmann, 1966; Fay, 1976, Radnitsky, 1970; Wilson, 1970). Both Giddens (1976) and Bauman (1978) have furnished extensive accounts of the hermeneutic critique of empirical sociology, and outlined the bases for an interpretive form of science. As Giddens (1976) argues, sociology should not be concerned with a "pre-given universe of objects," but with social patterns in a continuous state of autonomous reconstitution. For Bauman (1978), sociology should attempt to scrutinize critically the common consensus reached

---

[31] Special note must also be taken of inquiry within the domain of descriptive psychology (Davis, 1981). Such work attempts to penetrate the various rules or conventions governing the process of understanding persons, and in doing so shares much with the hermeneutic tradition. Perhaps the only important difference now separating descriptive from hermeneutic inquiry is in the different attitudes toward the relationship between the analytic units and "what is the case." Descriptive psychologists often tend to view the "structures of understanding" described by their analyses as maps of possibilities in the real world.

in society, and enable people to generate larger frameworks of meaning within which they may better understand each other.

The arguments for "generative theory" (see Chapter 3) extend this analysis. To the extent that commonsense agreements delimit the range of possible actions, the scientist may serve as an agent for undermining such consensus. In the theoretical challenge to common sense, the scientist generates new alternatives for action. Less troublesome roles for the social psychologist have been outlined by Gauld and Shotter (1977) and Brickman (1980). In the former case, the scientist is to serve as an important arbiter for clarity where commonsense perspectives create social conflict. In the latter, the social scientist attempts to translate earlier understandings of human behavior into contemporary language. In each of these cases, the chief concern of the scientist shifts from the observation and recording of behavior to the realm of creative interpretation.

Dialectics

Within early Greek philosophy, as in later formulations, "dialectic" denoted a form of reasoning examining the relation of an idea to its opposite. As it is held, the process of relating these opposing or contradictory ideas ultimately leads to transformations in thought. The history of dialectical thinking is punctuated by Hegel's designation of these opposites (the thesis and antithesis) and their resolution (synthesis). According to Hegel, each synthesis provides a thesis for continuing the process of change, and the direction of change is toward a fully enlightened state, ironically termed the "objective mind." Although overshadowed by the growing enchantment of scientific naturalism and positivism during the late nineteenth and early twentieth centuries, dialectical thinking was integral to the philosophies of Marx, Dewey, Mead, and Freud, among others. Recently, psychologists have begun to unearth the long history of psychological ideas that have drawn sustenance from dialectic thinking (Buss, 1979b; Lawler, 1975; Rychlak, 1968, 1977).

As in the case of the hermeneutic–interpretive movement, dialectic thinking has been employed not only in the analysis of social science metatheory (cf. Parker, 1981), but as well in research on a wide range of substantive problems. Broadly conceived, a dialectic orientation may be used both as a method of understanding, and as a device for describing patterns of action across time (Buss, 1979b; Hook, 1957; Kosok, 1976; Rychlak, 1968). In the case of metatheory, the work of Riegel (1973, 1976, 1979) and Rychlak (1968, 1975) has been perhaps most influential in its effects within psychology. Among the most prominent characteristics of dialectic metatheory is its emphasis on contradiction. Standing in opposition to the Aristotelian logic of identities, dialectic metatheory is concerned with the interdependence of being and negation, with an entity and its opposite. Thus, rather than viewing the scientist's task as that of describing social activity *as it is*, the dialectically oriented investigator might ask whether any existing entity (1) may not in actuality be its own opposite, (2) may not be oppressing its opposite, (3) may not depend for its existence on its opposite, or (4) may be opposed by its opposite in a cross-time process that may yield transformation. In any case, the dialectic investigator is not content to accept that which seems "given" in human affairs. The concern with being, negation, and transformation also sets the stage for a second important emphasis in dialectic metatheory. From the dialectic standpoint, patterns of social action are essentially tenuous, and the tension of oppositions is viewed as essential in fostering historical change. Thus, rather than engaging in the traditional empiricist search for patterns of cause and effect that repeat themselves across time, the dialectician will be far more concerned with patterns of change and possible directions implied by these patterns.

To illustrate, the dialectician would not be content to view sex roles (including androgyny) as the simple product of socialization. Any given sex role might first be viewed in terms of those forces with which it conflicts, and in terms of possible transitions occurring within the society. In the life of an individual, a given sex role may be viewed as but a stage in an ongoing process of transformation, with the possible end point a total rejection of sex-role stereotyping. A dialectician might also take a critical view of much existing sex role theory and research, with particular attention given to (1) the way in which existing theory of sex roles accommodates itself to the contemporary historical circumstances, (2) the traditional use of bipolar conceptions of sex roles, and (3) the underlying ideological commitments represented in the scientist's thinking about sex roles (Hefner, Rebecca, & Oleshansky, 1975; Rebecca, Hefner, & Oleshansky, 1976).

Two additional emphases of dialectic metatheory are also worthy of note. First, there is general acknowledgment of the scientist as a fully participating member of the society. The separation of the role of scientist from that of citizen, typically derived from empiricist metatheory, is held to be illusory. The scientist affects society through his or her scientific activities and the knowledge produced by the science is influenced by contemporary social circumstances. Further, it is argued, knowledge at the scientific level may evolve from "praxis," or the concerted action of the scientist in society. The value of existing knowledge may indeed be evaluated within praxis. The generation of knowledge and concerted action within society are thus seen to be closely linked (Cvetkovich, 1977; Janousek, 1972; Kytle, 1977; Rappoport, 1975; White, 1977). As a second emphasis, the dialectician generally takes a positive view of disruption and conflict. The traditional scientist within the liberal tradition tends to carry out research with an avowed aim of reducing conflict—whether at the personal or social level. Personal crises and social disruptions are frequently viewed as undesirable and worthy of elimination from the psychological or social system. In contrast, the dialectical perspective holds that both for the individual and the society conflicts may be constructive. The discord created by contradictory forces may be a valuable source of further development (Riegel, 1979).

As dialectical psychology often emphasizes multiple dimensions of change (biological, social, personal) and plural methods of study (linguistic, longitudinal, historical), it does not easily fall into any single subdiscipline within contemporary study. However, dialectical analysis and research has gained the increasing interest of those concerned with social interaction. Much of this work has been specifically concerned with issues relating development and social activity. Thus, dialecticians have examined mother–child interactions (Harris, 1975; Riegel, 1973, 1976), socially oriented revisions to Piagetian theory (Buck-Morss, 1975; Freedle, 1975; Lawler, 1975), the sociohistorical context of ego development (Hogan, 1974; Meacham, 1975a; Van den Daele, 1975a, 1975b), the relation of learning and memory processes to broad cultural circumstances (Kvale, 1977; Meacham, 1975b, 1977; Reese, 1977), and changes in family structure across time (Gadlin, 1978). Closely allied with several traditional social psychological issues is dialectical research on the development of privacy (Altman, 1977), family relations (L. K. Brown, 1975; Sameroff, 1975; Ziller, 1977), interpersonal attraction (Adams, 1977), the self-concept (Chandler, 1975), social intervention research (Weeks, 1977), environmental settings (Altman & Gauvain, 1981), decision making (Mitroff & Betz, 1972), and language processes (Israel, 1979b). In all cases the dialectic perspective has been used as an analytic tool, a means of organizing diverse observations, or a means of describing patterns of cross-time change.

The Critical Perspective

The debunking and criticism of conventional thought has always been an important component of intellectual life. However, this orientation has acquired a central role within one identifiable school. The "critical theory" of the Frankfurt school assimilated Marx's critique of the ideological underpinnings of capitalistic economic thought and his conception of history as a process moving toward a state of emancipation. Members of the Frankfurt school, including Adorno, Habermas, Horkheimer, and Marcuse, adopted as primary tasks (1) the explication of ideological biases through critical analysis and (2) the design of alternative perspectives for shaping future society. As a secondary aim, the critical theorist often shares with the dialectic theorist an interest in praxis. In attempting to delineate the forces that influence knowledge structures, and to understand the dynamics of historical change, several members of the school shifted the focus of their critiques from political economy to psychology, from Marx to Freud. Yet, the essential tasks remained unaltered: Critical theory entails inquiry into the conditions affecting the character of knowledge and the development of alternatives for purposes of social action.

Since the inception of the Frankfurt school in the 1920s, critical theory has been both hybridized and absorbed into various intellectual pursuits, and can no longer be associated with any single economic, political, or psychological orientation (see Connerton, 1976; Freiberg, 1979; Holzkamp, 1976; Jay, 1973; Ray, 1979). At present, critical appraisals consistent with the Frankfurt writings are being made by psychologists who have had very little (sometimes, no) contact with the corpus of German writing. Thus, psychological analysis traced to these earlier conceptions more properly falls within the rubric of "critical perspective." Within this perspective the dual conception of criticism is retained: to examine critically the valuational underpinnings and normative dictates underlying existing theories, and to develop alternative conceptualizations. A general preference is expressed for theories that do not mirror commonsense conceptions but transform them. As

Moscovici (1972) has put it, the aim of science is "not only to systematize existing knowledge but to postulate entirely new concepts. It is now fully recognized that the exact sciences create new aspects of nature; social sciences must create new aspects of society" (p. 65). And it is hoped, through criticism and the generation of new alternatives, people may be emancipated from their present interpretations of reality and may realize more fulfilling life patterns (Bauman, 1976; Israel, 1972; Moscovici, 1972; Rommetveit, 1972, 1976).

Within current social psychology, many critical analyses have focused on ways in which psychological knowledge is shaped by the broader social context (Buss, 1979a). It is widely recognized that psychological research is influenced by the organizational features of the scientific community: granting procedures (McGrath & Altman, 1966), publication policies (Cartwright, 1973), disciplinary boundaries (Campbell, 1969), and elite systems of power and prestige (Lubek, 1976; Morawski, 1979a; Strickland, Aboud, & Gergen, 1976). However, a critical perspective extends beyond elucidation of the constraints imposed by the internal structure of a scientific community. It attempts to identify economic, political, ideological, and metatheoretical investments that may fashion what otherwise appears to be neutral or objective knowledge. To do so, it is necessary to examine theories in their historical context. It is also necessary to assess theories for their potential to yield understanding that can emancipate rather than bind people to existing forms of social reality.

It is in this vein that Archibald (1978) has, for example, examined assumptions in classical social psychological theories as they are related to their political, economic, and cultural origins. Sampson (1977) has critiqued concepts of androgyny, moral development, and mental health for the ideology of "self-contained individualism" hidden within their premises. As he points out, the ideology has its origins in the early history of American society, but today it is neither a necessary nor even a preferable basis for social theory. Other analysts have isolated valuational bases of ostensibly neutral theories of human values and moral development (Hogan, 1978; Smith, 1978), prejudice (Harrison, 1974), person perception and nonverbal communication (Hogan, 1978), aggression (Lubek, 1979), dissonance theory (Israel, 1979), social conflict (Apfelbaum & Lubek, 1976; Plon, 1974), social equality (Sampson, 1975), locus of control (Furby, 1979), the interactionist paradigm in social psychology (Gadlin & Rubin, 1979), ethnomethodology (Young, 1971), as well as the character of research methods (Brenner, 1978; Rowan, 1974). In other analyses, it has been shown how positivist–empiricist metatheory dictates theoretical conceptions in social psychology (see Chapter 3) and produces an image of human functioning that is unnecessarily damaging to the culture more generally (Argyris, 1975; Zũñiga, 1975).

A second important line of work in the critical perspective has concentrated on historical accounts of the discipline. As discovered in the case of sociology (Gouldner, 1970; Schwendinger & Schwendinger, 1974), contemporary histories of psychology generally serve to justify an empiricist metatheory (Baumgardner, 1976, 1977; Morawski, 1979a; O'Donnell, 1979; Samelson, 1974; Yaroshevskii, 1973). Allport's (1954) classic treatment of the history of social psychology is thus viewed as presentist; it organizes historical evidence in a way that justifies the existing paradigms of inquiry. Empiricism itself has been shown to be an outgrowth of a particular moral and political climate (A. F. Blum, 1970; Leary, 1978; Shields, 1975; Steininger, 1979). Empiricist beliefs about proper scientific conduct cannot themselves be grounded in observation. Belief in them may thus be traced to the sociohistorical climate in the same way one might link the growth of religious movements to particular historical circumstances.

Historical research further points to various cultural factors affecting the success of a theory and the growth of the discipline. Critical reassessment of social psychology's heritage has unearthed important theoretical ideas previously ignored because of their divergence from mainstream ideological investments (Buck-Morss, 1977; Buss, 1979b; Lubek, 1979). For instance, the history of aggression research suggests that such inquiry has been particularly successful because it adopts the assumption of individual blame, and the view that aggression is a deviation from the kind of normative social standards that favor strong, centralized control (Lubek, 1979). Trends in the study of groups have been shown to be related to the general political climate (Steiner, 1974), and to the cultural backgrounds of the researchers (Gorman, 1979). Critical inquiry has also shown how social conditions such as unemployment (Finison, 1976, 1978), legislation, and the ethnic composition of the profession (Samelson, 1978, 1979) may have influenced patterns of professional interest and association.

Much work within the critical perspective also argues for alternative conceptions of human behavior and of science. For example, Sampson (1977) counters the dominant thesis of self-contained individualism with that of communal "interdependence." Theories of interdependence would locate the responsibility for social actions in the larger community rather than with the individual. This emphasis on interdependence as the desired end to be served by social theory is shared by many others (cf. Argyris, 1975; Gadlin & Ingle, 1975; Rommetveit, 1976). Along similar lines, others have argued for a perspective that treats humans as active, responsible, and changing agents (Gross, 1974; Harré, 1979; Shotter, 1974, 1978). It is this perspective many hope will underlie a new conception of science. As others argue, the new science must inherently be one that attacks the myth of the given (cf. Connerton, 1976; Wexler, 1982).

The Ethogenic Alternative

With the 1972 publication of the volume, *The Explanation of Social Behavior*, British philosopher Rom Harré and American social psychologist Paul Secord outlined a rationale for an alternative form of social psychology termed "ethogenic." The volume, along with numerous others congenial to its fundamentals (cf. Armistead, 1974; Brenner, 1980; Collett, 1977; Ginsburg, 1979; Harré, 1979; Marsh & Brenner, 1978; Shotter, 1975), has had a profound effect on British social psychology, and has begun to generate sympathetic support within a steadily increasing number of American institutions. Ethogenics may be viewed essentially as a composite of ordinary language philosophy and structural anthropology. As a result of its former alliance, ethogenecists are highly critical of the behavioral model in psychology, with its emphasis on deterministic principles of human conduct. From the ethogenic perspective, human action is seen as relying on an agent's ability to evaluate his or her performance according to rules and plans. Deterministic, mental mechanisms are eschewed, as action is seen as performed by people for specific purposes in particular situations. People also monitor and reflexively consider their actions and may thus decide to alter their behavior—to disobey a rule or abandon a given plan.[32]

Along with structural anthropology, the ethogenicist centers concern on the structured actions of people in everyday life. Laboratory research is thus impugned as the laboratory can only distort common patterns of action in unknown ways. More important, individual acts are viewed by the ethogenecist as embedded in larger structures from which they derive their meaning. From this perspective, individuals do not respond to punctate, temporally isolated stimuli, with all other factors held constant. Rather, they are typically engaged in complex sequences of action in which any individual act takes on significance only as it is related to other acts in the sequence (see Chapter 3). It is the scientist's task, in this case, to develop intelligible statements about the underlying structure of events. To this end, investigators have set out to describe the structure of seemingly disorderly acts of hooligans at football matches (Marsh, Rosser, & Harre, 1978), rituals for incorporating strangers into social groups (Harre & DeWaele, 1976), the way intonation patterns are used as markers for the identification of meaning units in communication (Kreckel, 1980), rules of social address (Kroger, in press), the structure of unwanted but repetitive patterns (Pearce & Cronen, 1980), and the common rules for ending encounters (Albert & Kessler, 1978). Such work also bears a close affinity with that of sociolinguistics, ethnomethodology, and rule-role research in sociology. Studies of turn taking and closing sequences in ordinary conversation (Schegloff & Sacks, 1973), rules governing pedestrian behavior (cf. Wolff, 1973), and the manner in which people control their environment by using various rules or roles (cf. Gross & Stone, 1965; Zurcher, 1973) are all quite compatible with the ethogenic orientation.

Metatheoretical Bases for a Unified Alternative

Many of the arguments, concepts, and methods adopted within the above domains are evidenced in the traditional, hypothesis testing sectors of the science. However, in such cases the arguments, concepts, and methods usually serve an ancillary function; their full implications are left unexplored. In each of the domains here reviewed, a self-conscious attempt has been made to break with certain fundamental tenets of the empiricist tradition. The question we must now ask is whether one may discern broad metatheoretical agreement across these domains. If such agree-

---

[32] It is also important to note the close affinity between ethogenic research and "action" theory within Western Europe (cf. Cranach & Harré, 1981; Laucken, 1974; Luckmann, 1981).

ments can be located, could they serve as a metatheoretical base for a
alternative to the traditional account of scientific activity? Is it possible
alliance among these disparate domains could foster a major evolution in
acter of behavioral study? As a general surmise, there appear to be five major assumptions that would evoke substantial agreement within the domains thus far
described. Each of these assumptions stands in strong contrast to pivotal suppositions within the traditional perspective; each is supported by preceding arguments
in the present volume.

Knowledge as Socially Constituted

From the traditional standpoint, the investigator ideally operates as a passive recording device, charting the contours of nature and developing theories to map the
world as observed. However, within each of the domains discussed above, the investigator is viewed as one who creates through his or her theoretical lens what
facts there are to be studied. From this standpoint, facts emerge as the result of
a theoretical perspective. As it is reasoned, knowledge systems are fundamentally
linguistic systems—signals that are used by people in relationships. In this respect,
knowledge would appear vitally dependent on the vicissitudes of social negotiation.
Its constraints would not essentially be experiential but social. Statements employing such terms as aggression, attitudes, economic class, reciprocity, and the like may
or may not be supported by observation, depending on how one chooses to relate
such terms to observation. Typically such relationships depend on the usage of the
terms within social interchange. Because language usage depends on coordinated
actions among people, or "joint action" in Shotter's (1980) terms, behavioral
knowledge is fundamentally a social product.

This view is most fully articulated within the hermeneutic–interpretive and critical domains. In the former case, we found that in the interpretations of others'
behavior, one necessarily projects meaning and intention into their actions. It is to
the projected meaning of such actions and not to behavior itself that one reacts.
Within the critical domain, stress was placed on inherent, valuational underpinnings
of behavioral theory, and the manner in which theory shapes social life as its meanings are absorbed by the society. Theory is not thus data driven, but fashioned by
social circumstances.

Within both the ethogenic and dialectic domains, one may discern some controversy over the assumption of social ontology. At times, ethogenic investigators
speak as if the structure of conduct were available for public observation and the
proper ethogenic investigation simply records the patterns of rule-governed behavior within society. This position would be consistent with traditional empiricism.
At the same time, their analysis suggests that scientists, too, follow investigatory
rules, and that the particular rules they follow will lead to certain forms of interpretation, while suppressing others. Thus, the rules of scientific comportment at any
given time will fashion the kind of knowledge that will result. Dialectic theorists,
and particularly those moved by the concept of dialectic materialism, will often
speak of human behavior as governed by economic structure. In doing so they take

for granted certain social facts that may exist independent of the observer, and thus join the empiricist tradition. However, other dialectic theorists have more fully adopted symbolic interactionist concepts in analyzing the social and ideological basis for various forms of behavioral knowledge (cf. Berger & Luckmann, 1966; Buss, 1979b). In effect, while not complete, agreement with the assumption of a socially constructed world of action may be found within each of the dissident camps.

It is important to note at this point that, while sensitive to the many persuasive arguments for the "social construction of reality," the emerging view does not simultaneously commit the scientist to the endogenic extreme: reality as subjective. That is, one may accept the empiricist assumption of a real world but simultaneously separate the construction of knowledge systems, or the way one communicates about the world, from the experience itself. One may experience without communication and communicate without benefit of experience. From the present standpoint, knowledge about social life is not to be viewed as a "reflection" of what there is, but as a "transformation" of experience into a linguistic ontology. To reiterate, the constraints on knowledge as a language are thus not furnished by reality but by social process.

The latter line of argument applies no less strongly to statements about psychological states or processes (cf. Coulter, 1979). That is, one may argue that what we take to be psychological knowledge is not fundamentally dependent upon self-experience but is a system of language governed by continuously evolving rules. In the case of talk about psychological states, however, we may anticipate a particularly elastic set of rules with a high degree of terminological negotiation. This is because the process of pointing, or saying *"That's* what I mean by X," cannot be easily accompanied by shared experience. In saying, "he possesses a *concept* of writing," for example, one cannot conveniently point to what we take to be an object, as a way of furnishing an experiential anchor for the term "concept." One can usually do so when saying, *"That* is a book" (see Chapter 2). In effect, knowledge of the "mind" is a social construction.

As suggested by this discussion, the social psychologist could come to play a pivotal role in the intellectual community. To the extent that the generation of knowledge is a social process and the social psychologist is committed to an understanding of such processes, then social psychological inquiry does not parallel that of the physicist, chemist, historian, or economist; rather, the social psychologist becomes indispensable in elucidating the grounds upon which physical, chemical, historical, or economic knowledge is based. In this sense it is social rather than philosophic inquiry that may elucidate our understanding of the nature of knowledge and its acquisition. In no way is the discipline prepared for such an undertaking at the present time. However, the seeds for such an enterprise are sown both within the discipline and adjoining domains.[33]

---

[33] A rich array of sources do exist for such an enterprise. See, for example, Campbell (1979), Barnes (1974), Rommetveit (1974), Fleck (1979), Mitroff (1974), and Latour and Woolgar (1979).

The Voluntary Basis of Social Action

Within the traditional perspective, human behavior is believed to reflect principles of the natural order. Thus, social psychologists attempt to establish invariant principles of social behavior that might emulate principles of color perception in experimental psychology, or impulse transmission in physiological psychology. In contrast, theorists in the above domains tend to view social action as fundamentally unprogrammed, and thus capable of a virtual infinity of variations. Social order at any given point is viewed as the product of broad social agreement. Patterns of action termed aggressive, altruistic, intelligent, emotional, and so on are seen as rule, norm, or convention governed (cf. Pepitone, 1976). In effect, such activities are more adequately explained by a series of voluntary decisions, rather than a body of immutable laws. This view of behavior as voluntary is most fully elaborated within the ethogenic domain. A major product of scientific inquiry should, from the ethogenic standpoint, be an account of the prevailing rules within society, rules that may be broken by choice. This view is also quite congenial to the hermeneutic-interpretive standpoint. Here, the major concern is with culturally bounded rules of meaning. Indeed, within this domain, ontological structure is a product of rules in use. Although not explicit in the critical domain, the supposition of rule-based action is fundamental to the critical program. It is assumed by the critical theorist that such analyses have the capacity to alter common understanding, and through enhanced understanding, the individual is liberated from the constraints of previous assumptions. If patterns of behavior were fixed by laws of nature, the emancipatory program would have little hope of success. Within the dialectic school, conflict of opinion may again be discerned. For some traditionalists, dialectic processes proceed with natural force toward inevitable ends. It is this form of dialectic theory that Popper (1957) has critically addressed. However, for others, dialectic thinking is essentially an advanced heuristic that may be employed at any time for purposes of changing self or social surrounds (cf. Basseches, 1980). From this standpoint, dialectic theory is wholly congenial with the assumption of rule-governed action. Again, strong elements of agreement may be discerned among the four domains.

The Historical Embeddedness of Social Knowledge

As we have seen, traditional science is generally committed to the view that scientific knowledge is cumulative and progressive. Through continuing research one may hope to discard empirically invalid theories, and sustain or improve those receiving empirical support. The problematic character of these assumptions has been explored in previous chapters. However, we also find opposition to the traditional view inherent in each of the above domains. As argued within the hermeneutic-interpretive movement, all actions are subject to multiple interpretations, and those interpretations favored during any given epoch may be replaced in the next. Historically situated conventions thus govern what is taken to be true or valid. This view is amplified by those dialectic theorists who view systems of understanding, including science, as undergoing transformation over time according to dialectic processes. Whether dialectic transformation in systems of understanding increasingly approximates "the truth" becomes moot. Work in the critical tradition is closely associated with dialectics in this respect. The critical theorist is one who attempts to elucidate the historical conditions sustaining currently objectified forms of knowledge. Thus, it is hoped that people may be freed to seek new and more emancipated life forms. Yet, as many argue, each newly acquired form carries with it inherent investments that must be opened to critique. The critical program, then, is inherently oriented toward continuous change. Finally, the ethogenics program is based on the assumption of changing patterns of action. To the extent that action is predicated on rules, people are free to seek transformations in conventional conduct.

Theory as Agency

As we have seen, the logical empiricist tradition has typically considered theoretical description and explanation as mapping devices. From this standpoint, social theory serves society by furnishing reliable predictions in the world as given. However, as we have also seen, this characterization of theory appears critically flawed. As indicated, it may be more fruitful to view theories as linguistic signals with a negotiable relationship to experience. If we further accept the argument for a socially constituted order, and grant a functional link between the linguistic practices of the culture and its other patterns of conduct, then alterations in linguistic practices have implications for the social order. In this way social psychological theory acquires an agential role in social life. It can serve as a linguistic tool to be employed by the theorist or others to strengthen, sustain, or obliterate various forms of human activity. When such terms as equity, reciprocity, conformity, reactance, and so on enter the scientific vocabulary, they also enter the ontological system in its linguistic aspect. When such terms are used to "describe" various actions, one's dispositions toward such actions may be vitally altered (see Chapter 1).[34]

This line of argument has been pivotal for scholars working within the critical framework. Their numerous demonstrations of ideological bias underlying theories held to be value neutral, and of bias undergirding the historical accounts sustaining present-day inquiry, all imply that theory is agential in character. Interpretive theorists have further demonstrated that social description does not essentially reflect the empirical world, but shapes the observer's conceptual construction of this world. Thus, theoretical description cannot in principle be data driven. Its source must lie elsewhere than in the world of experience itself. Both critical and interpretive theorists generally agree as well that theoretical accounts may enter

---

[34] As Pearce and Cronen (1980) put it, "The development of a theory is an autonomous act, inextricably linked to the previous assumptions, biases and social climate that the theorist brings to the situation and also fully a cause of those assumptions, biases and social climate. Viewing the theorist as an autonomous actor suggests the irrelevance of truth or falsity in evaluating a theory" (p. 110).

into the common conceptual agreements of the culture, and in this way have the capacity to alter society. Thus, whether desired or not, theory influences social action—even if the reactions to such theory are boredom, misunderstanding, or scorn. Finally, as argued by the same ordinary language philosophers who played such an instrumental role in the development of ethogenics, descriptions of human action inevitably rely on assumptions of intentionality. Thus, in the attempt to describe social life, one inevitably allocates intention. In assigning intention to action, one makes a silent pronouncement on matters of moral responsibility. To describe an experimental subject's actions as "aggression," for example, is automatically to establish an intentional basis for the action. In calling it aggression the theorist is impugning the character of the subject. Such imputations appear virtually inescapable as long as one employs common descriptive terms within the culture.

Valuational Foundations of Knowledge

As we see, there is broad agreement across the groups here discussed that the traditional fact–value dichotomy is woefully misleading. Values, ideologies, or visions of an improved society may legitimately enter the arena of "knowledge making." Critical theorists demonstrate the ideological bases of commonly accepted theories in an attempt to "emancipate" people from their implications. Both ethogenic and ethnomethodological investigators have used their inquiries to criticize common practices in the society and thereby to open the way to preferred alternatives. Dialectic theory is often employed as a means of understanding those institutional structures given normative support by the universalistic theories favored by the logical empiricist tradition. In effect, within the emerging metatheory, the life of the passions is reintegrated with the life of reason.

This line of argument places the scientist in a position at once enviable and precarious. To the extent that society furnishes the means by which the scientist gains special proficiency in communication, it also grants him or her enhanced power to alter or sustain patterns of human conduct. The public thus entrusts to the scientist skills that may affect its well-being. Further, when the psychologist is looked to for authoritative descriptions and explanations of human activity, he or she is being granted license to employ that skill. In this way the theorist may acquire what could in some cases become enormous powers of influence in society. Often the chief lever of social change may lie in the theoretical interpretation of existing ills and their solutions. At the same time, this position confronts scientists with a range of formidable problems—in fact, those that many exogenic thinkers had misleadingly argued were irrelevant to behavioral inquiry. These are problems of value: What forms of human conduct are to be favored? Which are to be discouraged? If theoretical language inevitably carries with it implications for action, then the scientist can no longer take refuge in the Shangri-la of "pure description." The sociobehavioral scientist is thus invited, if not compelled, to return to the moral concerns so central to August Comte's view of the science. Moral debate must come to play an increasingly important role in the new science.

Research as Vivification of Theory

Consistent with a belief in cumulative science, traditional research generally attempts to test hypotheses relating behavior to its antecedents. Through such tests, it is believed, one may emerge with theories containing a high degree of correspondence with existing fact. Yet, from the perspective emerging within the dissident domains, this general process of "testing hypotheses" is rendered suspect. First, if the scientist essentially creates a phenomenon through a particular interpretive stance, then virtually any intelligible hypothesis can be "verified" or "falsified." If one wishes to test the view that crowding leads to aggression, for example, one is led to select a context in which one can generate interpretive agreement that people are "crowded" and that they subsequently "aggress." Neither crowding nor aggression exists in a behavioral world; rather, they are essentially states of conception, and may thus be discerned wherever one has the conceptual capacity to "see" them. One may view oneself as crowded by the presence of a single person, or socially unencumbered in a sea of thousands. Further, from the standpoint of historical relativity, we find that the investigator is faced with an immense panoply of behavioral exemplars under continuous change. Thus, to "test" an hypothesis, the investigator essentially engages in the process of searching out specific exemplars that will best serve interpretive interests. Using this procedure, support or threat may be generated for virtually any sensible hypothesis.[35]

Such criticisms of traditional hypothesis testing do not entail an abandonment of "empirical" work. Rather, they suggest that alternative functions be assigned to this form of activity. One of the principle functions of research implicit in the domains under study is that of theoretical vivification. That is, one may usefully employ research accounts of the traditional variety as forms of illustration. In adding imagery to the abstract theoretical terms the research also invites others to employ the terms of the theory in interpreting their experience. Thus, when the ethogenecist purports to examine the structural features of a particular interaction, he or she is essentially proposing that the structural lens will elucidate the situation; research accounts are then employed for persuasive illustration. Within the interpretive framework, the investigator attempts to document the rules of meaning within a specific context; the documentation in this case serves not as a validating device, but as rhetorical support. Although critical theorists have been little concerned with carrying out systematic empirical studies, the critical program is quite consistent with the above reasoning. The critical theorist would be forced to agree that the critical documentation of others' value biases is no less open to value biases than the work that is criticized. It must be supposed that some disagreement would be found among dialectic theorists concerning the function of empirical research, a disagreement that would again reflect differing views toward materialism

---

[35] The present analysis is in agreement with McGuire's (1980) "constructivist" orientation to theory with respect to his argument that all hypotheses may be supported. However, it disagrees with McGuire's contention that the proper aim of research is thus to determine the range of circumstances under which each hypothesis is valid.

and determinism. However, in general, we find that across the various dissident domains, observational reports play a vital role, although a role other than that traditionally assigned.

Toward a Sociorationalism

Assaying these metatheoretical developments, we see that the decay of the exogenic position has been accompanied by the revitalization of endogenic thought. When science is viewed as a human construction rather than a pawn to nature, one's die is cast in favor of the endogenic tradition. When knowledge is derived from value-interested conceptual standpoints rather than accurate mappings of the facts of nature, a significant shift has occurred from an exogenic to an endogenic world view. Yet, as we see, this contemporary shift does not represent a full embracing of the endogenic perspective. To argue the endogenic view in its extreme is equally as vulnerable as the logical empiricist commitment on which psychology has foundered during the past century. To argue that reality is solely a product of one's internal or conceptual constructions is to be reduced to an otiose solipsism. In adopting this position, one loses the capacity to account either for this knowledge (On what grounds can it be claimed that one is creating the experiential world?), or the ability to communicate about it to others (On what grounds can one explain the existence of others with whom to communicate?).[36]

Rather than a pure, endogenic rationalism, we have in the present confluence what may be termed the emergence of a *sociorationalist* metatheory. That is, in contrast to the empiricist position, we find a metatheory that places the locus of knowledge not in the minds of single individuals, but in the collectivity. It is not the internal processes of the individual that generate what is taken for knowledge, but a social process of communication. It is within the process of social interchange that rationality is generated.[37] Truth is the product of the collectivity of truth makers. Thus, from the sociorationalist perspective knowledge is no longer the exclusive property of a cloistered profession deploying an arsenal of sophisticated and rarefied methods. Nor is knowledge a gift of God, a product of the gene structure, or a product of skilled intuition. Within the emergent paradigm knowledge is a communal creation. *Interpersonal* colloquy is necessary to determine "the nature of things." The emphasis on the negotiation of accounts in ethogenetics, social rules of facticity in ethnomethodology, conventional criteria for determining meaning in the hermeneutic–interpretive tradition, and the historical context of knowl-

---

[36] Also see Hollis' (1977) attempt to reconcile the endogenic and exogenic perspectives (for him, embodied in the autonomous and plastic models of man). He views such an attempt as necessitated by the decline of positivism and the failure of other alternatives to take its place.

[37] For further elaboration of the social basis of rationality see Phillips (1977) and Karatheodoris (1979). See also Cronen and Pearce's (1980) analysis of the coordinated management of meaning.

edge generation in the domains of dialectics and critical theory are all illustrative.[38]

It is difficult to determine the future of the amalgamated views here termed sociorationalist. Like the interlocking tenets of logical empiricism, behaviorism, and experimentalism, the various assumptions of sociorationalism do approach a coherent unity. A commitment to any of them increases susceptibility to the remainder. Advances in any of these domains thus enhances the strength of the meta-theory and weakens the grip of empiricism. Should sociobehavioral study continue to shift in this direction, it would find enthusiastic support within other academic disciplines. Vital movements within philosophy (cf. Gadamer, 1975; Ricoeur, 1970; Taylor, 1971), sociology (Bauman, 1978; Berger & Luckmann, 1966; Giddens, 1976; McHugh, 1970), anthropology (Douglas, 1970; Geertz, 1973; Shweder, 1980), political science (Almond & Genco, 1977; Hirschman, 1970), communications theory (Pearce & Cronen, 1980), and literary analysis (Burke, 1966; Fish, 1979) would all be congenial to the flourishing of such a view. Yet much resistance remains within the traditionalist camps. There is great comfort to be derived from following the well-trodden paths; hypothesis testing is an activity open to all; there are numerous outlets for its expression, and abundant promises of professional advancement. As many fear, when one sits smugly beside warm fires, the murmurs of cold winds only increase one's comfort. Others believe that professional gate-keepers will stifle the interests of the beginning professional in "new paradigm" inquiry. Such inquiry may seem merely an irritant to be eradicated.

Much will depend on whether those within the sociorationalist framework can develop powerful and compelling theoretical ideas. The orientation in itself is no safeguard against mediocre thought. Many have asked for new methods of study. If there were new activities to replace the old, it is argued, they would be willing to try them. However, this demand is only partially warranted. As we have seen, traditional research methods are not necessarily counterproductive. It is the ends to which they are put that are at stake. The sociorationalist invites the investigator to abandon the misleading practice of "testing" hypotheses and to consider ways of using methods in the service of intellectual expression, and intellectual expression in the service of his or her vision of the good. Much will also depend on whether traditionalists can discern the possibility inherent within the sociorationalist perspective for full personal expression within the confines of the profession.

Complicated conceptual issues also remain unsolved for the sociorationalist. For one, the concept of socially constructed reality must be further elaborated. The spector of subjectivism and relativism will prove too fearsome for many professionals. Even among the dissident camps there are many who do not wish to give up the ontological validity of all theoretical accounts. Some are struggling with new

---

[38] As Garfinkel (1967) and others in the ethnomethodological camp point out, linguistic reality is a social achievement. It requires cooperative participation. At any moment a participant begins to raise questions concerning the precise meaning of another's words, or treats common expressions as if they were not truly intelligible, he or she may not only throw the speaker into a state of unrelieved frustration, but may threaten the relationship itself.

concepts of objectivity that can avoid the pitfalls of both empiricist and rationalist accounts (cf. Ossorio, 1978; Sabini & Silver, 1982). However, much remains to be done in this domain. A satisfactory account of natural science progress must also be rendered by the sociorationalists. The function of psychological explanation must be evaluated; the status of rules, roles, and plans as guides for action must be closely assessed; and the extent to which values can guide theory construction without endangering the discipline must be examined.

However, in light of the new vistas for theoretical inquiry, there is good reason to believe that, with the solidification of the new paradigm, the sciences will witness a level of unparalleled intellectual stimulation. With a fundamental alteration in the grounding rationale, we may anticipate a revolution in theoretical activity, new forms of investigation, fresh proposals concerning what it is "to practice" science, innovative forms of advanced training, and a rejuvenated sense of professional significance.

To conclude, during the past century the sociobehavioral sciences have participated in one of humankind's greatest intellectual adventures. They have, in J. L. Austin's (1962a) terms, joined in the "pursuit of the incorrigible," or certain knowledge, a pursuit that has challenged thinkers from Heraclitus to the present. Early in this century, it appeared that the means had been discovered for gaining certainty in the behavioral sciences. Yet subsequent examination has found such means sadly wanting. The search for certainty is a child's romance, and like most, one holds fast to even the most fragile shard attesting to continued life. The question that must now be confronted is how to pass successfully into the maturity of a second century. A new romance is required to extinguish the old, and it appears that the overtures are at hand.

References

Abelson, R. *Persons. A study in philosophical psychology.* New York: St. Martin's Press, 1977.

Abelson, R. P., Aronson, E., McGuire, W. J., Newcomb, T. M., Rosenberg, M. J., & Tannenbaum, P. H. (Eds.). *Theories of cognitive consistency: A sourcebook.* Chicago: Rand McNally, 1968.

Abramson, L. Y., Seligman, M. E. P., & Teasdale, J. D. Learned helplessness in humans: Critique and reformulation. *Journal of Abnormal Psychology,* 1978, *87,* 49-74.

Adams, G. R. Physical attractiveness research: Toward a developmental social psychology of beauty. *Human Development,* 1977, *20,* 217-239.

Adams, J. S. Inequity in social exchange. In L. Berkowitz (Ed.), *Advances in experimental social psychology* (Vol. 2). New York: Academic Press, 1965.

Adams, J. S., & Jacobson, P. R. Effects of wage inequities on work quality. *Journal of Abnormal and Social Psychology,* 1964, *69,* 19-25.

Adorno, T. W., Frenkel-Brunswik, E., Levinson, D. J., & Sanford, R. N. *The authoritarian personality.* New York: Harper & Row, 1950.

Ajzen, I., & Fishbein, M. Attitudes and normative beliefs as factors influencing behavioral intentions. *Journal of Personality and Social Psychology,* 1972, *21,* 1-9.

Albert, S., & Kessler, S. Ending social encounters. *Journal of Experimental Social Psychology,* 1978, *14,* 541-553.

Alexander, C. N., & Sagatun, I. An attributional analysis of experimental norms. *Sociometry,* 1973, *36,* 127-142.

Allport, D. A. The state of cognitive psychology. *Quarterly Journal of Experimental Psychology,* 1975, *27,* 141-152.

Allport, F. H. *Social Psychology.* Boston, Mass.: Houghton-Mifflin, 1924.

Allport, G. W. The historical background of modern social psychology. In G. Lindzey (Ed.), *Handbook of social psychology* (Vol I). Reading, Mass.: Addison-Wesley, 1954. (2nd ed. 1968.)

Almond, G. A., & Genco, S. J. Clouds, clocks and the study of politics. *World Politics*, 1977, *29*, 489-522.

Altman, I. Privacy regulation: Culturally universal or culturally specific. *Journal of Social Issues*, 1977, *33*, 66-84.

Altman, I., & Gauvain, M. A cross-cultural and dialectic analysis of homes. In L. Liben, N. Newcombe, & A. Patterson (Eds.), *Spatial representation and behavior across the life span: Theory and application.* New York: Academic Press, 1981.

Anscombe, G. E. M. *Intention.* Oxford: Blackwell, 1976. (Originally published 1957.)

Apel, K. O. *Analytic philosophy of language and the "Geisteswissenschaften."* Dordrecht, Holland: Reidel, 1967.

Apfelbaum, E. *Some overlooked early European social psychologies.* Paper presented at the meeting of the American Psychological Association, New York, N.Y., Aug. 1979.

Apfelbaum, E., & Lubek, I. Resolution vs. revolution? The theory of conflicts in question. In L. Strickland, F. Aboud, & K. Gergen (Eds.), *Social psychology in transition.* New York: Plenum Press, 1976.

Archibald, W. P. *Social psychology as political economy.* New York: McGraw-Hill, 1978.

Argyris, C. Dangers in applying results from experimental social psychology. *American Psychologist*, 1975, *30*, 469-485.

Argyris, C. *Inner contradictions of rigorous research.* New York: Academic Press, 1980.

Armistead, N. (Ed.). *Reconstructing social psychology.* Baltimore, Md.: Penguin, 1974.

Armstrong, D. M. *Nominalism and realism* (Vol. I & II). London: Cambridge University Press, 1978.

Aronson, E., & Mills, J. The effect of severity of initiation on liking for a group. *Journal of Abnormal and Social Psychology*, 1959, *59*, 177-181.

Asch, S. Forming impressions of personality. *Journal of Abnormal and Social Psychology*, 1946, *41*, 258-290.

Asch, S. *Social psychology.* Englewood Cliffs, N.J.: Prentice-Hall, 1952.

Asch, S. E. Studies of independence and conformity: A minority of one against a unanimous majority. *Psychological Monographs*, 1956, *70*, Whole No. 416.

Atkinson, R. *Orthodox consensus and radical alternatives: A study in sociological theory.* New York: Basic Books, 1972.

Atkinson, R. C. Teaching children to read using a computer. *American Psychologist*, 1974, *29*, 169-178.

Austin, J. L. *Sense and sensibilia.* London: Oxford University Press, 1962a.

Austin, J. L. *How to do things with words.* Cambridge, Mass.: Harvard University Press, 1962b.

Averill, J. A. A constructivist view of emotion. In R. Plutchik & H. Kellerman (Eds.), *Emotion: Theory, research and experience.* New York: Academic Press, 1980.

Ayer, A. J. *The foundations of empirical knowledge.* New York: Macmillan, 1940.

Ayer, A. J. Man as a subject for science. In P. Laslett & W. R. Runciman (Eds.), *Philosophy, politics and society*. Third series. Oxford: Blackwell, 1967.

Bakan, D. *On method*. San Francisco, Calif.: Jossey-Bass, 1969.

Baltes, P. B., & Brim, O. G., Jr. (Eds.). *Life-span development and behavior* (Vol. 3). New York: Academic Press, 1980.

Baltes, P. B., & Cornelius, S. W. The status of dialectics in developmental psychology: Theoretical orientation versus scientific method. In N. Datan & H. Reese (Eds.), *Life-span developmental psychology: Dialectical perspectives on experimental research*. New York: Academic Press, 1977.

Baltes, P., & Labouvie, G. Adult development of intellectual performance: Description, explanation, and modification. In C. Eisdorfer & M. P. Lawton (Eds.), *The psychology of adult development and aging*. Washington, D.C.: American Psychological Association, 1973.

Baltes, P. B., & Reinert, G. Cohort effects in cognitive development of children as revealed by cross-sectional sequences. *Developmental Psychology*, 1969, *1*, 169-177.

Baltes, P. B., & Schaie, K. W. On life-span developmental research paradigms, retrospects and prospects. In P. B. Baltes & K. W. Schaie (Eds.), *Life-span developmental psychology: Personality and socialization*. New York: Academic Press, 1973.

Bandura, A. *Aggression: A social learning analysis*. Englewood Cliffs, N.J.: Prentice-Hall, 1973.

Bandura, A., & MacDonald, F. J. The influence of social reinforcement and the behavior of models in shaping children's moral judgments. *Journal of Abnormal and Social Psychology*, 1963, *67*, 274-281.

Barnes, B. *Scientific knowledge and sociological theory*. London: Routledge & Kegan Paul, 1974.

Bartley, W. W. *The retreat to commitment*. New York: Knopf, 1962.

Basseches, M. Dialectical schemata: A framework for the empirical study of the development of dialectical thinking. *Human Development*, 1980, *23*, 400-421.

Bauman, Z. *Towards a critical sociology*. London: Routledge & Kegan Paul, 1976.

Bauman, Z. *Hermeneutics and social science*. New York: Columbia University Press, 1978.

Baumgardner, S. R. Critical history and social psychology's crises. *Personality and Social Psychology Bulletin*, 1976, *2*, 460-465.

Baumgardner, S. R. Critical studies in the history of social psychology. *Personality and Social Psychology Bulletin*, 1977, *3*, 681-687.

Becker, G. S. *The economic approach to human behavior*. Chicago, Ill.: University of Chicago Press, 1976.

Becker, H. S. *Outsiders: Studies in the sociology of deviance*. New York: Free Press, 1963.

Befu, H. Gift giving and social reciprocity in Japan. *France-Asia*, 1966, *188*, 161-177.

Bell, R. Q., & Hertz, T. W. Toward more comparability and generalizability of developmental research. *Child Development*, 1976, *47*, 6-13.

Bem, D. J. An experimental analysis of self persuasion. *Journal of Experimental Social Psychology*, 1965, *1*, 199-218.

Bem, D. J. Self-perception theory. In L. Berkowitz (Ed.), *Advances in experimental social psychology* (Vol. 6). New York: Academic Press, 1972.

Ben-David, J., & Collins, R. Social factors in the origins of a new science: The case of psychology. *American Sociological Review*, 1966, *31*, 451-465.

Benedict, R. *The chrysanthemum and the sword.* Boston, Mass.: Houghton-Mifflin, 1946.

Berger, P., & Luckmann, T. *The social construction of reality.* Garden City, N.Y., Doubleday, 1966.

Berlyne, D. E. *Conflict, arousal and curiosity.* New York: McGraw-Hill, 1960.

Bernholz, P. *Flexible exchange rates and exchange rate theory in historical perspective.* Unpublished manuscript. University of Basel, Switzerland, 1981.

Berscheid, E., & Walster, E. H. A little bit about love. In T. Huston (Ed.), *Foundations of interpersonal attraction.* New York: Academic Press, 1974.

Berscheid, E., & Walster, E. H. *Interpersonal attraction (2nd ed.).* Reading, Mass.: Addison-Wesley, 1978.

Bernstein, A. M., Stephan, W. G., & Davis, M. H. Explaining attribution for achievement: A path analytic approach. *Journal of Personality and Social Psychology*, 1979, *37*, 1810-1821.

Bernstein, R. *The restructuring of social and political theory.* Philadelphia: University of Pennsylvania Press, 1978.

Bexton, W. H., Heron, W., & Scott, T. H. Effects of decreased variation in the sensory environment. *Canadian Journal of Psychology*, 1954, *8*, 70-76.

Bhagat, R. S. *Evaluating the current intellectual performance of organizational behavior: A philosophy of science critique.* Unpublished paper, 1979, University of Texas. School of Management and Administration, Dallas, Texas.

Bhaskar, R. *A realist theory of science.* New York: Humanities Press, 1975.

Bickman, L., & Henchey, T. (Eds.). *Beyond the laboratory: Field research in social psychology.* New York: McGraw-Hill, 1972.

Bills, A. G. Changing views of psychology as a science. *Psychological Review*, 1938, *45*, 377-394.

Birren, J. E. *Relations of development and aging.* Springfield, Ill.: Charles C. Thomas, 1964.

Birren, J. E., & Woodruff, D. S. Human development over the life span through education. In P. B. Baltes & K. W. Schaie (Eds.), *Life-span developmental psychology: Personality and socialization.* New York: Academic Press, 1973.

Bittner, E. The police on skid row. *American Sociological Review*, 1967, *32*, 699-715.

Bloor, D. *Knowledge and social imagery.* London: Routledge & Kegan Paul, 1976.

Blum, A. F. Theorizing. In J. D. Douglas (Ed.), *Understanding everyday life.* Chicago, Ill.: Aldine Press, 1970.

Blum, G. S. *Psychoanalytic theories of personality.* New York: McGraw-Hill, 1964.

Blumenthal, A. L. Wilhelm Wundt and early American psychology: A clash of two cultures. *Annals of the New York Academy of Sciences*, 1977, *291*, 13-20.

Blumenthal, A. L. The founding father we never knew. *Contemporary Psychology*, 1979, *24*, 547-550.

Blumer, H. *Symbolic interactionism: Perspective and method.* Englewood Cliffs, N.J.: Prentice-Hall, 1969.

Boring, E. G. *A history of experimental psychology.* New York: Century, 1929.

Borstelmann, L. J. *Periodization in the history of American childhood.* Paper presented at the Meeting of Cheiron, Washington, D.C., May 1976.

Botwinick, J. Learning in children and aged adults. In L. R. Goulet & P. B. Baltes (Eds.), *Life-span development psychology: Research and theory.* New York: Academic Press, 1970.

Boulding, K. Dare we take the social sciences seriously? *American Psychologist*, 1965, *22*, 879-887.

Bradley, G. W. Self-serving biases in the attribution process: A re-examination of the fact or fiction question. *Journal of Personality and Social Psychology*, 1978, *36*, 56-71.

Braithwaite, R. B. *Scientific explanation.* London: Cambridge University Press, 1953.

Bramel, D. A dissonance theory approach to defensive projection. *Journal of Abnormal and Social Psychology*, 1962, *64*, 121-129.

Bramel, D. Selection of a target for defensive projection. *Journal of Abnormal and Social Psychology*, 1963, *66*, 318-324.

Bramel, D., & Friend, R. Hawthorne, the myth of the docile worker, and class bias in psychology. *American Psychologist*, 1981, *36*, 867-878.

Brandt, L. W. Behaviorism—The psychological buttress of late capitalism. In A. R. Buss (Ed.), *Psychology in social context.* New York: Irvington, 1979.

Brehm, J. W. *A theory of psychological reactance.* New York: Academic Press, 1966.

Brehm, J. W., & Cohen, A. R. *Explorations in cognitive dissonance.* New York: Wiley, 1962.

Brehm, J. W., & Wicklund, R. *Perspectives on cognitive dissonance.* Hillsdale, N. J.: Erlbaum, 1976.

Brenner, M. Interviewing: The social phenomenology of a research instrument. In M. Brenner, P. Marsh, & M. Brenner (Eds.), *The social context of method.* London: Groom Helm, 1978.

Brenner, M. (Ed.). *The structure of action.* Oxford: Blackwell, 1980.

Brickman, P. A social psychology of human concerns. In R. Gilmour & S. Duck (Eds.), *The development of social psychology.* New York: Academic Press, 1980.

Brim, O. G., & Kagan, J. Constancy and change: A view of the issues. In O. G. Brim & J. Kagan (Eds.), *Constancy and change in human development.* Cambridge, Mass.: Harvard University Press, 1980.

Brislin, R. W. Translation and content analysis of oral and written materials. In H. C. Triandis & J. W. Berry (Eds.), *Handbook of cross-cultural psychology* (Vol. 2). Boston, Mass.: Allyn & Bacon, 1980.

Broadbent, D. E. The minimization of models. In A. J. Chapman & D. M. Jones (Eds.), *Models of man.* Leicester: British Psychological Society, 1980.

Brodbeck, M. Meaning and action. In M. Brodbeck (Ed.), *Readings in the philosophy of the social sciences.* New York: Macmillan, 1968.

Bronfenbrenner, U. Socialization and social class through time and space. In E. E. Maccoby, T. M. Newcomb, & E. L. Hartley (Eds.), *Readings in social psychology* (3rd ed.) New York: Holt, Rinehart & Winston, 1958.

Bronfenbrenner, U. Toward an experimental ecology of human development. *American Psychologist,* 1977, *32,* 513-531.

Brown, E. D., & Sechrest, L. Experiments in cross-cultural research. In H. C. Triandis & J. W. Berry (Eds.), *Handbook of cross-cultural psychology* (Vol. 2). Boston, Mass.: Allyn & Bacon, 1980.

Brown, L. K. Familial dialectics in a clinical context. *Human Development,* 1975, *18,* 223-238.

Brown, R. *Explanation in social science.* Chicago, Ill.: Aldine Press, 1963.

Brown, R. *Social psychology.* New York: Free Press, 1965.

Browning, D. *Philosophers of process.* New York: Random House, 1965.

Bruner, J. S. Psychology and the image of man. Herbert Spencer Lecture delivered at the University of Oxford, 1976, and reprinted in the *Times Literary Supplement,* Dec. 17th, 1976.

Bruner, J. S., & Allport, G. W. Fifty years of change in American psychology. *Psychological Bulletin,* 1940, *37,* 757-776.

Buck, R. C. Do reflexive predictions pose special problems for the social scientist? *Philosophy of Science,* 1963, *30,* 153-162.

Buck-Morss, S. Socio-economic bias in Piaget's theory and its implications for the cultural controversy. *Human Development,* 1975, *18,* 35-49.

Buck-Morss, S. The Adorno legacy. *Personality and Social Psychology Bulletin,* 1977, *3,* 707-713.

Burke, K. *Language as symbolic action: Essays on life, literature and method.* Berkeley: University of California Press, 1966.

Burtt, E. A. The value presuppositions of science. *Bulletin of the Atomic Scientist,* 1957, *13,* 99-106.

Buss, A. R. Generational analysis: Description, explanation and theory. *Journal of Social Issues,* 1974, *30,* 55-71.

Buss, A. R. (Ed.). *Psychology in social context.* New York: Irvington, 1979.   (a)

Buss, A. R. *A dialectical psychology.* New York: Halsted Press, 1979.   (b)

Buss, A. R. The emerging field of the sociology of psychological knowledge. In A. Buss (Ed.), *Psychology in social context.* New York: Irvington, 1979.   (c)

Buss, A. R., & Royce, J. R. Note on the temporality of trait constructs. *Journal for the Theory of Social Behavior,* 1976, *6,* 171-176.

Byrne, D. *The attraction paradigm.* New York: Academic Press, 1971.

Byrne, D., & Kelly, K. *An introduction to personality.* Englewood Cliffs, N. J.: Prentice-Hall, 1981.

Campbell, D. T. A phenomenology of the other one: Corrigible, hypothetical and critical. In T. Mischel (Ed.), *Human action: Conceptual and empirical issues.* New York: Academic Press, 1969.

Campbell, D. T. Ostensive instances and entitivity in language learning. In W. Gray & N. D. Rizzo (Eds.), *Unity through diversity: A Festschrift for Ludwig Von Bertalanffy*. New York: Gordon & Breach, 1973.

Campbell, D. T. Qualitative knowing in action research. In M. Brenner, P. Marsh, & M. Brenner (Eds.), *The social context of method*. New York: St. Martin's Press, 1978.

Campbell, D. T. A tribal model of the social system vehicle carrying scientific knowledge. *Knowledge: Creation, diffusion, utilization*, 1979, *1*, 181-201.

Caplan, N., & Nelson, S. D. On being useful: The nature and consequences of psychological research on social problems. *American Psychologist*, 1973, *28*, 199-211.

Carnap, R. *An introduction to the philosophy of science*, M. Gardner (Ed.). New York: Basic Books, 1966.

Cartwright, D. Risk taking by individuals and groups: An assessment of research employing choice dilemmas. *Journal of Personality and Social Psychology*, 1971, *20*, 361-378.

Cartwright, D. Determinants of scientific progress: The case of research on the risky shift. *American Psychologist*, 1973, *28*, 222-231.

Cartwright, D. Theory and practice. *Journal of Social Issues*, 1978, *34*, 168-180.

Cartwright, D. Contemporary social psychology in historical perspective. *Social Psychology*, 1979, *42*, 82-93.

Chandler, M. J. Relativism and the problem of epistemological loneliness. *Human Development*, 1975, *18*, 171-180.

Chapanis, N. P., & Chapanis, A. Cognitive dissonance. *Psychological Bulletin*, 1964, *61*, 1-22.

Chein, I. *The science of behavior and the image of man*. New York: Basic Books, 1972.

Cherulnik, P. D. Gergen's reappraisal of experimentation in social psychology: A critique. *Journal of Mind and Behavior*, 1981, *2*, 65-70.

Ching, C. C. Psychology in the People's Republic of China. *American Psychologist*, 1980, *12*, 1084-1089.

Chomsky, N. A review of B. F. Skinner's *Verbal behavior*. *Language*, 1959, *35*, 26-58.

Chomsky, N. Current issues in linguistic theory. In J. A. Fodor & J. J. Katz (Eds.), *The structure of language*. Englewood Cliffs, N. J.: Prentice-Hall, 1964.

Chomsky, N. *Language and mind*. New York: Harcourt, Brace & World, 1968.

Christie, R., & Geis, F. *Studies in Machiavellianism*. New York: Academic Press, 1970.

Cicourel, A. V. *The social organization of juvenile justice*. New York: Wiley, 1968.

Cohen, A. R. Some implications of self-esteem for social influence. In C. I. Hovland & I. L. Janis (Eds.), *Personality and persuasibility*. New Haven, Conn.: Yale University Press, 1959.

Cohen, T. Metaphor and the cultivation of intimacy. *Critical Inquiry*, 1978, *5*, 3-12.

Collett, P. (Ed.). *Social rules and social behavior*. Oxford: Blackwell, 1977.

Collingwood, R. G. *The idea of history.* Oxford: Clarendon Press, 1946.

Connerton, P. (Ed.). *Critical sociology: Selected readings.* Baltimore, Md.: Penguin, 1976.

Cooley, C. H. *Human nature and the social order.* New York: Scribners, 1902.

Cooper, D. E. *Knowledge of language.* New York: Humanities Press, 1978.

Coulter, J. *The social construction of the mind.* New York: Macmillan, 1979.

Cowan, P. A., Langer, J., Heavenrich, J., & Nathanson, M. Social learning and Piaget's cognitive theory of moral development. *Journal of Personality and Social Psychology,* 1969, *11,* 261–274.

Cranach, M. von & Harré, R. (Eds.). *The analysis of action: Recent theoretical and empirical advances.* Cambridge: Cambridge University Press, 1981.

Cronbach, L. J. Beyond the two disciplines of scientific psychology. *American Psychologist,* 1975, *30,* 116–127.

Crowne, D. P., & Marlowe, D. *The approval motive.* New York: Wiley, 1964.

Cumming, E., & Henry, W. *Growing old.* New York: Basic Books, 1961.

Cvetkovich, G. Dialectical perspectives on empirical research. *Personality and Social Psychology Bulletin,* 1977, *3,* 688–698.

Dachler, H. P., & Wilpert, B. Conceptual dimensions and boundaries of participation in organizations: A critical evaluation. *Administrative Science Quarterly,* 1978, *23,* 1–39.

Danziger, K. The history of introspection reconsidered. *Journal of the History of the Behavioral Sciences,* 1980, *16,* 241–262.

Dasen, P. R. Cross-cultural Piagetian research: A summary. *Journal of Cross-Cultural Psychology,* 1972, *3,* 23–40.

Datan, N. After the apple: Post-Newtonian metatheory for jaded psychologists. In N. Datan & H. Reese (Eds.), *Life-span developmental psychology: Dialectical perspectives on experimental research.* New York: Academic Press, 1977.

Davidson, D. Action, reasons and causes. *Journal of Philosophy,* 1963, *60,* 685–700.

Davis, J. *Group performance.* Reading, Mass.: Addison-Wesley, 1969.

Davis, K. E. *Advances in descriptive psychology* (Vol. 1). Greenwich, Conn.: JAI Press.

Deese, J. *Psychology as science and art.* New York: Harcourt, Brace, Jovanovich, 1972.

Demos, J., & Demos, V. Adolescence in historical perspective. *Journal of Marriage and the Family,* 1969, *31,* 632–638.

Dennett, D. C. *Brainstorms.* Montgomery, Vt.: Bradford Books, 1978.

deSantillana, G., & Zilsel, E. The development of rationalism and empiricism. *International Encyclopedia of Unified Science,* Vol. II, No. 8. Chicago, Ill.: University of Chicago Press, 1941.

Dethier, V. G., & Stellar, E. *Animal behavior* (3rd ed.). Englewood Cliffs, N. J.: Prentice-Hall, 1970.

Deutsch, M. Field theory in social psychology. In G. Lindzey (Ed.), *Handbook of social psychology.* Reading, Mass.: Addison-Wesley, 1958.

Deutsch, M. Introduction. In M. Deutsch & H. Hornstein (Eds.), *Applying social psychology*. New York: Wiley, 1975.

Dewey, J. *The influence of Darwin on philosophy and other essays in contemporary thought*. New York: Columbia University Press, 1910.

Dewey, J. *Experience and nature*. New York: Dover, 1958. (Originally published in 1929)

Dewey, J. *Philosophy and civilization*. New York: Minton, Balch, 1931.

DiRenzo, G. J. Toward explanation in the behavioral sciences. In G. J. DiRenzo (Ed.), *Concepts, theory and explanation in the behavioral sciences*. New York: Random House, 1966.

Dixon, T. R., & Horton, D. L. (Eds.). *Verbal behavior and general behavior theory*. Englewood Cliffs, N. J.: Prentice-Hall, 1968.

Dohrenwend, B. S., & Dohrenwend, B. P. (Eds.). *Stressful life events: Their nature and effects*. New York: Wiley, 1974.

Dollard, J., Doob, L. W., Miller, N. E., Mowrer, O. H., & Sears, R. R. *Frustration and aggression*. New Haven, Conn.: Yale University Press, 1939.

Dollard, J., & Miller, N. E. *Personality and psychotherapy*. New York: McGraw-Hill, 1950.

Douglas, J. D. (Ed.). *Understanding everyday life*. Chicago, Ill.: Aldine Press, 1970.

Duck, S. Taking the past to heart: One of the futures of social psychology? In R. Gilmour & S. Duck (Eds.), *The development of social psychology*. London: Academic Press, 1980.

Duhem, P. *The aim and structure of physical theory* (P. Wiener, transl.). Princeton, N. J.: Princeton University Press, 1954. (Originally published in 1906.)

Dumont, M. Social science and the survival of cities. *Psychiatry and Social Science Review*, 1969, *3*, 161-169.

Durkheim, E. *The elementary forms of religious life*. London: George Allen & Unwin, 1954. (Originally published 1895.)

Duval, S., & Wicklund, R. A. *A theory of objective self-awareness*. New York: Academic Press, 1972.

Dyal, J. A., Corning, R., & Willows, J. *Readings in psychology: In search of alternatives*. New York: McGraw-Hill, 1975.

Eagly, A. H. Sex differences in influenceability. *Psychological Bulletin*, 1978, *85*, 86-116.

Elder, G. H., Jr. *Children of the great depression*. Chicago, Ill.: University of Chicago Press, 1974.

Elder, G. H., Jr. Social structure and personality: A life course perspective. In P. Baltes & O. Brim (Eds.), *Life-span development and behavior* (Vol. 2). New York: Academic Press, 1979.

Ellis, H. *The dance of life*. Boston, Mass.: Riverside Press, 1923.

Elms, A. C. The crisis in confidence in social psychology. *American Psychologist*, 1975, *30*, 967-976.

Emmerich, W. Socialization and sex-role development. In P. Baltes & K. W. Schaie

(Eds.), *Life-span developmental psychology: Personality and socialization*. New York: Academic Press, 1973.

Erikson, E. *Childhood and society* (2nd ed.). New York: Norton, 1963.

Erikson, E. Identity and identity diffusion. In C. Gordon & K. J. Gergen (Eds.), *The self in social interaction*. New York: Wiley, 1968.

Erikson, E. *Identity and the life cycle*. New York: Norton, 1980. (Originally published 1968.)

Farrell, B. A. The progress of psychology. *British Journal of Psychology*, 1975, *66*, 253-255.

Fay, B. *Social theory and political practice*. London: Holmes & Meir, 1976.

Feigl, H. Principles and problems of theory construction in psychology. In W. Dennis (Ed.), *Current trends in psychological theory*. Pittsburgh, Pa.: University of Pittsburgh Press, 1951.

Feigl, H. *Reduction of psychology to neurophysiology*. Paper presented at the meeting of the American Association for the Advancement of Science, Denver, 1961.

Festinger, L. A theory of social comparison processes. *Human Relations*, 1954, *7*, 117-140.

Festinger, L. *A theory of cognitive dissonance*. Evanston, Ill.: Row, Peterson, 1957.

Festinger, L. Looking backward. In L. Festinger (Ed.), *Retrospections on social psychology*. London and New York: Oxford University Press, 1980.

Feyerabend, P. K. *Against method*. New York: Humanities Press, 1976.

Finison, L. J. Unemployment politics and the history of organized psychology. *American Psychologist*, 1976, *31*, 747-755.

Finison, L. J. Unemployment politics and the history of organized psychology, II, The Psychologists League, the WPA, and the National Health Program. *American Psychologist*, 1978, *33*, 471-477.

Finkleman, D. Science and psychology. *American Journal of Psychology*, 1978, *91*, 179-199.

Fish, S. Normal circumstances, literal language, direct speech acts, the ordinary, the everyday, the obvious, what goes without saying, and other special cases. In P. Rabinow & W. Sullivan (Eds.), *Interpretive social science: A reader*. Berkeley: University of California Press, 1979.

Fishbein, M., & Ajzen, I. *Belief, attitude, intention and behavior*. Reading, Mass.: Addison-Wesley, 1975.

Fishman, S. A. *Language and rationalism: Two integrative essays*. Rowley, Mass.: Newbury House, 1972.

Fiske, D. W. *Strategies for personality research*. San Francisco, Calif.: Jossey-Bass, 1978.

Fleck, L. *Genesis and development of a scientific fact*. Chicago, Ill.: University of Chicago Press, 1979. (Originally published, Benno Schwabe, Basel, 1935.)

Foa, U. G., & Foa, E. B. *Societal structures of the mind*. Springfield, Ill.: Charles C. Thomas, 1974.

Fodor, J. A. *Psychological explanation.* New York: Random House, 1968.

Fodor, J. A. *The language of thought.* New York: Crowell-Collier, 1975.

Ford, C. S., & Beach, F. A. *Patterns of sexual behavior.* New York: Harper & Row, 1951.

Forsyth, D. R. Crucial experiments and social psychological inquiry. *Personality and Social Psychology Bulletin,* 1976, *2,* 454–459.

Foucault, M. *The archaeology of knowledge.* London: Tavistock, 1972.

Fowler, H. *Curiosity and exploratory behavior.* New York: Macmillan, 1965.

Fox, R. The cultural animal. In J. F. Eisenberg & W. S. Dillon (Eds.), *Man and beast: Comparative social behavior.* Washington, D.C.: Smithsonian Institute Press, 1971.

Freedle, R. Dialogue and inquiring systems: The development of a social logic. *Human Development,* 1975, *18,* 97–118.

Freedle, R. Psychology, Thomian topologies, deviant logics, and human development. In N. Datan & H. Reese (Eds.), *Life-span developmental psychology: Dialectical perspectives on experimental research.* New York: Academic Press, 1977.

Freedman, J. L. *Social psychology.* Paper presented at the meeting of the Psychology Section, New York Academy of Sciences, New York, N. Y., 1975–1976.

Freedman, J. L., Carlsmith, J. M., & Sears, D. O. *Social psychology.* Englewood Cliffs, N. J.: Prentice-Hall, 1970. (Later editions, 1974, 1978.)

Freedman, P. E., Cohen, M., & Hennessy, J. Learning theory: Two trials and tribulations. *American Psychologist,* 1974, *29,* 204–206.

Freiberg, J. S. *Critical sociology: European perspectives.* New York: Irvington, 1979.

Fried, S. B., Gumper, D. C., & Allen, J. C. Ten years of social psychology: Is there a growing commitment to field research? *American Psychologist,* 1973, *28,* 155–156.

Fromm, E. *Escape from freedom.* New York: Rinehart, 1941.

Frye, N. *The critical path.* Bloomington: Indiana University Press, 1971.

Furby, L. Individualistic bias in studies of locus of control. In A. Buss (Ed.), *Psychology in social context.* New York: Irvington, 1979.

Gadamer, H. G. *Truth and method.* G. Barden & J. Cumming (Eds.). New York: Seabury, 1975. (Originally published as *Wahrheit und Methode.* Tübingen: J. C. B. Mohr (Paul Siebeck), 1960.)

Gadamer, H. G. *Philosophical hermeneutics* (D. E. Linge, transl.). Berkeley: University of California Press, 1976.

Gadlin, H. Child discipline and the pursuit of self: An historical interpretation. *Advances in child development and behavior* (Vol. 12). New York: Academic Press, 1978.

Gadlin, H., & Ingle, G. Through a one-way mirror: The limits of experimental self-reflection. *American Psychologist,* 1975, *30,* 1003–1010.

Gadlin, H., & Rubin, S. H. Interactionism. In A. R. Buss (Ed.), *Psychology in social context.* New York, Irvington Press, 1979.

Gandhi, M. *All men are brothers.* New York: Columbia University Press, 1958.

Garfinkel, H. *Studies in ethnomethodology.* Englewood Cliffs, N. J.: Prentice-Hall, 1967.

Gauld, A., & Shotter, J. *Human action and its psychological investigation.* London: Routledge & Kegan Paul, 1977.

Geertz, C. *Interpretation of cultures.* New York: Basic Books, 1973.

Gergen, K. J. The effects of interaction goals and personalistic feedback on presentation of self. *Journal of Personality and Social Psychology,* 1965, *1,* 413-425.

Gergen, K. J. Personal consistency and the presentation of self. In C. Gordon & K. J. Gergen (Eds.), *The self in social interaction.* Reading, Mass.: Addison-Wesley, 1968.

Gergen, K. J. Social psychology as history. *Journal of Personality 'and Social Psychology,* 1973, *26,* 309-320.

Gergen, K. J. Social psychology, science and history. *Personality and Social Psychology Bulletin,* 1976, *2,* 373-383.

Gergen, K. J. Stability, change and chance in understanding human development. In N. Datan & H. Reese (Eds.), *Life-span developmental psychology: Dialectical perspectives on experimental research.* New York: Academic Press, 1977.

Gergen, K. J. Experimentation in social psychology: A reappraisal. *European Journal of Social Psychology,* 1978, *8,* 507-527.

Gergen, K. J. Toward generative theory. *Journal of Personality and Social Psychology,* 1978, *36,* 1344-1360.

Gergen, K. J. The positivist image in social psychological theory. In A. R. Buss (Ed.), *Psychology in social context.* New York: Irvington, 1979.

Gergen, K. J. Toward intellectual audacity in social psychology. In R. Gilmore & S. Duck (Eds.), *The development of social psychology.* London: Academic Press, 1980. (a)

Gergen, K. J. The emerging crisis in life-span developmental theory. In P. Baltes & O. Brim (Eds.), *Life-span development and behavior* (Vol. III). New York: Academic Press, 1980. (b)

Gergen, K. J., & Basseches, M. The potentiation of psychological knowledge. In R. F. Kidd & M. Saks (Eds.), *Advances in applied social psychology.* New York: Academic Press, 1980.

Gergen, K. J., & Benack, S. Metatheoretical influences on conceptions of human development. In M. Lewin (Ed.), *Woman, man and child as seen by psychology: A critical history.* New York: Columbia University Press, in press.

Gergen, K. J., & Gergen, M. M. International assistance from a psychological perspective. In *Yearbook of World Affairs, 1971* (Vol. 25). London: Institute of World Affairs, 1972.

Gergen, K. J., & Gergen, M. M. Form and function in the explanation of human conduct. In P. Secord (Ed.), *Paradigms in the social science.* Beverly Hills, Calif.: Sage, 1982.

Gergen, K. J., & Gergen, M. M. The social construction of helping relationships. In J. D. Fisher, A. Nadler, & B. DePaulo (Eds.), *New directions in helping, Vol. 1: Recipient reactions to aid.* New York: Academic Press, in press.

Gergen, K. J., Gergen, M. M., & Barton, W. Deviance in the dark. *Psychology Today*, 1973, *7*, 129-130.

Gergen, K. J., & J. Morawski. An alternative metatheory for social psychology. In L. Wheeler (Ed.), *Review of personality and social psychology*. Beverly Hills, Calif.: Sage, 1980.

Gergen, K. J., & Taylor, M. G. *Role playing and modifying the self-concept*. Paper presented at the meeting of the Eastern Psychological Association, New York, March 1966.

Gergen, K. J., & Taylor, M. G. Social expectancy and self-presentation in a status hierarchy. *Journal of Experimental Social Psychology*, 1969, *5*, 79-92.

Gergen, K. J., & Wishnov, B. Others' self-evaluations and interaction anticipation as determinants of self presentation. *Journal of Personality and Social Psychology*, 1965, *2*, 348-358.

Gewirth, A. Can man change laws of social science? *Philosophy of Science*, 1954, *21*, 229-241.

Ghiselli, E. E. Some perspectives for industrial psychology. *American Psychologist*, 1974, *29*, 80-87.

Gibson, J. J. *The perception of the visual world*. Boston, Mass.: Houghton-Mifflin, 1950.

Gibson, J. J. *The senses considered as perceptual system*. Boston, Mass.: Houghton-Mifflin, 1966.

Giddens, A. *New rules of sociological method*. New York: Basic Books, 1976.

Gilmour, R., & Duck, S. *The development of social psychology*. New York: Academic Press, 1980.

Ginsburg, G. P. (Ed.). *Emerging strategies in social psychological research*. New York: Wiley, 1979.

Glass, D. C. *Behavior patterns, stress and coronary disease*. Hillsdale, N. J.: Erlbaum, 1977.

Glass, D. C., & Singer, J. E. *Urban stress*. New York: Academic Press, 1972.

Glenn, S. S., Grant, L., Whaley, D. L., & Malott, R. W. *Introduction to the science of psychology*. Kalamazoo, Mich.: Behaviordelia, 1976.

Godow, R. A., Jr. Social psychology as both science and history. *Personality and Social Psychology Bulletin*, 1976, *2*, 421-427.

Goffman, E. *The presentation of self in everyday life*. Garden City, N. Y.: Doubleday, 1959.

Goffman, E. *Asylums*. New York: Doubleday Anchor, 1961.

Goffman, E. *Stigma: Notes on the management of spoiled identity*. Englewood Cliffs, N. J.: Prentice-Hall, 1963.

Goldschmidt, W. *Comparative functionalism*. Berkeley: University of California Press, 1966.

Goodman, N. *Ways of worldmaking*. Indianapolis, Ind.: Hackett, 1978.

Gordon, M. E., Kleiman, L. S., & Hanie, C. A. Industrial-organizational psychology, Open thy ears O house of Israel. *American Psychologist*, 1978, *33*, 893-905.

Gordon, T. Notes on white and black psychology. *The Journal of Social Issues*, 1973, *29*, 87-96.

Gouldner, A. *The coming crises of western sociology*. New York: Basic Books, 1970.

Graumann, C. F. Die Scheu des Psychologen vor der Interaktion. Ein Schisma und seine Geshichte. *Zeitschrift für Sozialpsychologie*, 1979, *10*, 284–304.

Greenberg, J. H. Some universals of grammar with particular reference to the order of meaningful elements. In J. H. Greenberg (Ed.), *Universals of language* (2nd ed.). Cambridge, Mass.: MIT Press, 1966.

Greenwald, A. G. On the inconclusiveness of "crucial" cognitive tests of dissonance versus self-perception theories. *Journal of Experimental Social Psychology*, 1975, *11*, 490–499.

Greenwald, A. G. Transhistorical lawfulness of behavior: A comment on two papers. *Personality and Social Psychology Bulletin*, 1976, *2*, 391.

Grice, P. Meaning. *Philosophical Review*, 1957, *78*, 377–388.

Griffitt, W. *Density, "crowding" and attraction. What are the relationships?* Paper presented at the meeting of the American Psychological Association, New Orleans, 1974.

Gross, G. Unnatural selection. In N. Armistead (Ed.), *Reconstructing social psychology*. Baltimore, Md.: Penguin, 1974.

Gross, E., & Stone, G. P. Embarrassment and the analysis of role requirements. *American Journal of Sociology*, 1965, *70*, 1–15.

Grünberg, E., & Modigliani, F. The predictability of social events. *Journal of Political Economy*, 1954, *62*, 465–478.

Gutmann, D. Parenthood: A key to the comparative study of the life cycle. In N. Datan & L. Ginsberg (Eds.), *Life-span developmental psychology: Normative life crisis*. New York: Academic Press, 1975.

Habermas, J. *Knowledge and human interest*. Boston, Mass.: Beacon Press, 1971.

Haines, H., & Vaughan, G. M. Was 1898 a "great date" in the history of social psychology? *Journal of the History of the Behavioral Sciences*, 1979, *15*, 323–332.

Hale, M. *Psychology and social order: An intellectual biography of Hugo Münsterberg*. Unpublished doctoral dissertation, University of Maryland, 1977.

Hamlyn, D. W. Behaviour. *Philosophy*, 1953, *28*, No. 105.

Hampden-Turner, C. *Radical man: The process of psycho-social development*. Cambridge, Mass.: Schenkman, 1970.

Hampshire, S. *Thought and action*. London: Chatto & Windus, 1959.

Hanson, N. R. *Patterns of discovery*. London: Cambridge University Press, 1958.

Harding, J., Proshansky, H., Kutner, B., & Chein, I. Prejudice and ethnic relations. In G. Lindzey & E. Aronson (Eds.), *Handbook of Social Psychology* (Vol. 5). Reading, Mass.: Addison-Wesley, 1969.

Harlow, H. F., & Harlow, M. K. The affectional systems. In A. M. Schrier, H. F. Harlow, & F. Stollnitz (Eds.), *Behavior of nonhuman primates*. New York: Academic Press, 1965.

Harré, R. Some remarks on "rule" as a scientific concept. In T. Mischel (Ed.), *Understanding other persons*. Oxford: Blackwell, 1974.

Harré, R. *Social being*. Oxford: Blackwell, 1979.

Harré, R. Making social psychology scientific. In R. Gilmour & S. Duck (Eds.), *The development of social psychology.* New York: Academic Press, 1980.

Harré, R., & DeWaele, J. P. The ritual for incorporation of a stranger. In R. Harré (Ed.), *Life sentences.* New York: Wiley, 1976.

Harré, R., & Secord, P. F. *The explanation of social behaviour.* Oxford: Blackwell, 1972.

Harris, A. E. Social dialectics and language: Mother and child construct the discourse. *Human Development,* 1975, *18,* 80-96.

Harris, B., & Harvey, J. H. Self-attributed choice as a function of the consequence of a decision. *Journal of Personality and Social Psychology,* 1975, *31,* 1013-1019.

Harris, R. J. Two factors contributing to the perception of the theoretical intractability of social psychology. *Personality and Social Psychology Bulletin,* 1976, *2,* 411-417.

Harrison, G. A bias in the social psychology of prejudice. In N. Armistead (Ed.), *Reconstructing social psychology.* Baltimore, Md.: Penguin, 1974.

Hastie, R., Ostrom, T., Ebbesen, E. B., Wyer, R. S., Hamilton, D., & Carlston, D. E. (Eds.), *Person memory: The cognitive basis of social perception.* Hillsdale, N. J.: Erlbaum, 1980.

Hastorf, A. H. The "reinforcement" of individual actions in a group situation. In K. Gergen & D. Marlowe (Eds.), *Personality and social behavior.* Reading, Mass.: Addison-Wesley, 1970.

Hebb, D. O. *The organization of behavior.* New York: Wiley, 1949.

Hefner, R., Rebecca, M., & Oleshansky, B. Development of sex role transcendence. *Human Development,* 1975, *18,* 143-158.

Heider, F. Attitudes and cognitive organization. *Journal of Psychology,* 1946, *21,* 107-112.

Heider, F. *The psychology of interpersonal relations.* New York: Wiley, 1958.

Helmreich, R. Applied social psychology: The unfulfilled promise. *Personality and Social Psychology Bulletin,* 1975, *1,* 548-560.

Hendrick, C. Social psychology as history and as traditional science: An appraisal. *Personality and Social Psychology Bulletin,* 1976, *2,* 392-403.

Hendrick, C. (Ed.). *Perspectives on social psychology.* Hillsdale, N. J.: Erlbaum, 1977.

Henshel, R. L. The purposes of laboratory experimentation and the virtues of deliberate artificiality. *Journal of Experimental Social Psychology,* 1980, *16,* 466-478.

Henshel, R. L., & Kennedy, L. W. Self-altering prophecies: Consequences for the feasibility of social prediction. *General Systems,* 1973, *18,* 119-126.

Heritage, J. C., & Watson, D. R. Formulations as conversational objects. In G. Psathas (Ed.), *Everyday language.* New York: Irvington, 1979.

Hermann, T. *Psychologie als problem.* Stuttgard: Klett-Cotta, 1979.

Higbee, K. L., & Wells, M. G. Some research trends in social psychology during the 1960's. *American Psychologist,* 1972, *27,* 963-966.

Hirsch, E. D., Jr. *Validity in interpretation.* New Haven, Conn.: Yale University Press, 1967.

Hirsch, E. D., Jr. *The aims of interpretation.* Chicago, Ill.: University of Chicago Press, 1976.

Hirschman, A. *Exit, voice and loyalty: Responses to decline in firms, organization and states.* Cambridge, Mass.: Harvard University Press, 1970.

Hitler, A. *Mein Kampf.* (Ralph Manheim, trans.) Boston, Mass.: Houghton-Mifflin, 1943.

Hogan, R. T. Dialectic aspects of moral development. *Human Development,* 1974, *17,* 107–117.

Hogan, R. T. Theoretical egocentrism and the problem of compliance. *American Psychologist,* 1975, *30,* 533–540.

Hogan, R. T. & Emler, N. P. The biases in contemporary social psychology. *Social Research,* 1978, *45,* 478–534.

Hollis, M. *Models of man.* London: Cambridge University Press, 1977.

Holt, E. B. The whimsical condition of social psychology, and of mankind. In H. M. Kallen & S. Hook (Eds.), *American philosophy today and tomorrow.* New York: Furman, 1935.

Holzkamp, K. *Kritische Psychologie.* Hamburg: Fischer Taschenbuch Verlag, 1976.

Hook, S. *Dialectical materialism and scientific method.* Manchester, England: Special supplement to the Bulletin of the Committee on Science and Freedom, 1957.

Hooper, F. Cognitive assessment across the life span: Methodological implications of the organismic approach. In J. Nesselroade & H. Reese (Eds.), *Life-span developmental psychology: Methodological issues.* New York: Academic Press, 1973.

Horkheimer, M. *Critical theory.* New York: Seabury Press, 1972.

Houston, J. P., Bee, H., Hatfield, E., & Rimm, S. *Essentials of psychology.* New York: Academic Press, 1981.

Hovland, C. I., Janis, I. L., & Kelley, H. H. *Communication and persuasion.* New Haven, Conn.: Yale University Press, 1953.

Hudson, L. *The cult of the fact.* New York: Harper Torchbooks, 1972.

Hultsch, D. F., & Hickey, T. External validity in the study of human development: Methodological and theoretical issues. *Human Development,* 1978, *21,* 76–91.

Huston-Stein, A., & Baltes, P. Theory and method in life-span developmental psychology: Implications for child development. In H. W. Reese & L. P. Lipsitt (Eds.), *Advances in child development and behavior.* New York: Academic Press, 1976.

Ingleby, D. The psychology of child psychology. In M. P. M. Richards (Ed.), *The integration of the child into the social world.* London: Cambridge University Press, 1974.

Insko, C. A. *Theories of attitude change.* New York: Appleton-Century-Crofts, 1967.

Ions, E. *Against behavioralism: A critique of behavioral science.* Totowa, N. J.: Rowman & Littlefield, 1977.

Israel, J. Stipulation and construction in the social sciences. In J. Israel & H. Tajfel (Eds.), *The context of social psychology: A critical assessment.* London: Academic Press, 1972.

Israel, J. From level of aspiration to dissonance (or, what the middle class worries about). In A. Buss (Ed.), *Psychology in social context*. New York: Irvington, 1979. (a)

Israel, J. *The language of dialectics and the dialectics of language*. Atlantic-Highlands, N. J.: Humanities Press, 1979. (b)

Israel, J., & Tajfel, H. (Eds.). *The context of social psychology: A critical assessment*. New York: Academic Press, 1972.

Ittelson, W. H. (Ed.). *Environment and cognition*. New York: Crowell-Collier, 1961.

Ittelson, W. H. Environment perception and contemporary perceptual theory. In W. H. Ittelson (Ed.), *Environment and cognition* (2nd ed.). New York: Seminar Press, 1973.

Jaeger, M. E. *Antecedents and consequences of cognitive consistency: Implications for the Fishbein model*. Unpublished doctoral thesis, Temple University, 1981.

James, W. *The varieties of religious experience; a study in human nature*. New York: Modern Library, 1936. (Original copyright New York: Longmans, Green & Co., 1902).

Janis, I. L. Effects of fear arousal on attitude change: Recent developments in theory and experimental research. In L. Berkowitz (Ed.), *Advances in experimental social psychology* (Vol. 3). New York: Academic Press, 1967.

Janis, I. L. *Victims of groupthink: A psychological study of foreign policy decisions and fiascoes*. New York: Free Press, 1972.

Janis, I. L., & Gilmour, J. B. The influence of incentive conditions on the success of role playing in modifying attitudes. *Journal of Personality and Social Psychology*, 1965, *1*, 17-27.

Janis, I. L., Hovland, C. I., Field, P. B., Linton, H., Graham, E., Cohen, A. R., Rife, D., Abelson, R. P., Lesser, G. S., & King, B. T. (Eds.), *Personality and persuasibility*. New Haven, Conn.: Yale University Press, 1959.

Janousek, J. On the Marxian concept of praxis. In J. Israel & H. Tajfel (Eds.), *The context of social psychology: A critical assessment*. New York: Academic Press, 1972.

Jay, M. *The dialectical imagination*. London: Heinemann, 1973.

Jones, E. E., & Davis, K. E. From acts to dispositions. In L. Berkowitz (Ed.), *Advances in social psychology* (Vol. 2). New York: Academic Press, 1965.

Jones, E. E., & Gerard, H. B. *Foundations of social psychology*. New York: Wiley, 1967.

Jones, E. E., & McGillis, D. Correspondent inferences and the attribution cube: A comparative reappraisal. In J. H. Harvey, W. J. Ickes, & R. F. Kidd (Eds.), *New directions in attribution research* (Vol. 1). Hillsdale, N. J.: Erlbaum, 1976.

Jones, E. E., & Nisbett, R. *The actor and the observer: Divergent perceptions of the causes of behavior*. Morristown, N. J.: General Learning Press, 1971.

Jourard, S. M., & Kormann, L. Getting to know the experimenter and its effect on psychological test performance. *Journal of Humanistic Psychology*, 1968, *8*, 155-160.

Joynson, R. B. Models of man: 1879-1979. In A. J. Chapman & D. M. Jones (Eds.), *Models of man*. Leicester: British Psychological Society, 1980.

Kagan, J. Perspectives on continuity. In O. G. Brim & J. Kagan (Eds.), *Constancy and change in human development.* Cambridge, Mass.: Harvard University Press, 1980.

Kagan, J., & Moss, H. A. *Birth to maturity.* New York: Wiley, 1962.

Kamin, L. J. *The science and politics of I.Q.* New York: Halsted Press, 1974.

Kant, I. Critical examination of practical reason, 1788. In *Critique of practical reason and other works* (T. K. Abbott, trans.). New York: Longmans, 1909.

Kaplan, A. *The conduct of inquiry: Methodology for behavioral science.* San Francisco, Calif.: Chandler, 1964.

Karatheodoris, S. Logos: An analysis of the social achievement of rationality. In A. Blum & P. McHugh (Eds.), *Friends, enemies, and strangers.* New York: Ablex, 1979.

Kelley, H. H. Attribution theory in social psychology. In D. Levine (Ed.), *Nebraska symposium on motivation, 1967* (Vol. 15). Lincoln: University of Nebraska Press, 1967, pp. 192-238.

Kelley, H. H. *Causal schemata and the attribution process.* Morristown, N. J.: General Learning Press, 1972.

Kelly, G. *The psychology of personal constructs.* New York: Norton, 1955.

Kelman, H. C. *A time to speak: On human values and social research.* San Francisco, Calif.: Jossey-Bass, 1968.

Kelman, H. C. The rights of the subject in social research: An analysis in terms of relative power and legitimacy. *American Psychologist, 1972, 27,* 989-1016.

Kelman, H. C., & Pettigrew, T. F. How to understand prejudice. *Commentary, 1959, 28,* 436-441.

Kemeny, J. G. *A philosopher looks at science.* Princeton, N. J.: Van Nostrand-Reinhold, 1959.

Kemp, M. C. Economic forecasting when the subject of the forecast is influenced by the forecast. *American Economic Review, 1962, 52,* 492-496.

Kendler, H. *Psychology: A science in conflict.* New York: Oxford University Press, 1981.

Kessler, S. J., & McKenna, W. *Gender: An ethnomethodological approach.* New York: Wiley, 1978.

Kirsch, I. The impetus to scientific psychology: A recurrent pattern. *Journal of the History of the Behavioral Sciences, 1976, 12,* 120-129.

Knight, R. C. *Good faith, social science and the activity of inquiry.* Unpublished doctoral dissertation, University of Massachusetts, Department of Psychology, 1978.

Koch, S. Epilogue. In S. Koch (Ed.), *Psychology: A study of a science* (Vol. III). New York: McGraw-Hill, 1959.

Koch, S. Reflections on the state of psychology. *Social Research, 1971, 38,* 669-709.

Koch, S. The nature and limits of psychological knowledge. *American Psychologist, 1981, 36,* 257-269.

Kohlberg, L. Stage and sequences: The cognitive-developmental approach to socialization. In D. A. Goslin (Ed.), *Handbook of socialization theory and research.* Chicago, Ill.: Rand McNally, 1969.

Kohlberg, L. From is to ought: How to commit the naturalistic fallacy and get away with it in the study of moral development. In T. Mischel (Ed.), *Cognitive development and epistemology.* New York: Academic Press, 1971.

Köhler, W. *The mentality of apes.* London: Routledge & Kegan Paul, 1925.

Kosok, M. The systematization of dialectical logic for the study of development and change. *Human Development,* 1976, *19,* 325-350.

Krech, D., Crutchfield, R. S., & Ballachey, E. L. *Individual in society.* New York: McGraw-Hill, 1962.

Kreckel, M. A framework for the analysis of natural discourse. In M. Brenner (Ed.), *The structure of action.* Oxford: Blackwell, 1980.

Kroger, R. O. Explorations in ethogeny: With special reference to the rules of address. *American Psychologist,* in press.

Kuhn, T. S. *The structure of scientific revolution.* Chicago, Ill.: University of Chicago Press, 2nd Revised edition, 1970. (Originally published in 1962.)

Kurtines, W., & Grief, E. The development of moral thought: Review and evaluation of Kohlberg's approach. *Psychological Bulletin,* 1974, *81,* 453-470.

Kvale, S. Dialectics and research on remembering. In N. Datan & H. Reese (Eds.), *Life-span developmental psychology: Dialectical perspectives on experimental research.* New York: Academic Press, 1977.

Kytle, J. Ideology and planned change: A critique of two popular change strategies. *Personality and Social Psychology Bulletin,* 1977, *3,* 697-706.

Labouvie, E. W. The dialectical nature of measurement activities in the behavioral sciences. *Human Development,* 1975, *18,* 205-222.

Lacey, H. *Fact and value.* Unpublished manuscript. Swarthmore College, 1977.

Lacey, H. M. Psychological conflict and human nature: The case of behaviourism and cognition. *Journal for the Theory of Social Behaviour,* 1980, *10,* 131-155.

Lacey, H., & Rachlin, H. Behaviour, cognition and theories of choice. *Behaviorism,* 1978, *6,* 177-202.

Lakatos, I. Falsification and the methodology of scientific research. In I. Lakatos & A. Musgrave (Eds.), *Criticism and the growth of knowledge.* London: Cambridge University Press, 1970.

Lake, D. G., Miles, M. B., & Earle, R. B., Jr. (Eds.). *Measuring human behavior.* New York: Teachers College, Columbia University, 1973.

Langer, E. J., & Roth, J. Heads I win, tails it's chance: The illusion of control as a function of the sequence of outcomes in a purely chance task. *Journal of Personality and Social Psychology,* 1975, *32,* 951-955.

Latour, B., & Woolgar, S. *Laboratory life, the social construction of scientific facts.* Beverly Hills, Calif.: Sage, 1979.

Laucken, U. *Naive Verhaltens Theorie.* Stuttgart: Klett, 1974.

Laudan, L. *Progress and its problems.* Berkeley: University of California Press, 1977.

Lawler, J. Dialectic philosophy and developmental psychology: Hegel and Piaget on contradiction. *Human Development,* 1975, *18,* 1-17.

Leahey, T. H. The myth of operationism. *Journal of Mind and Behavior,* 1980, *1,* 127-144.

Leary, D. The philosophical development of the conception of psychology in Germany. *Journal of the History of the Behavioral Sciences,* 1978, *14,* 113-121.

Lecky, P. *Self-consistency, a theory of personality.* New York: Island Press, 1945.

Leichtman, M. Gestalt theory and the revolt against positivism. In A. R. Buss (Ed.), *Psychology in social context.* New York: Irvington, 1979.

Lemaine, G. Social differentiation and social conformity. *European Journal of Social Psychology,* 1974, *4,* 17-52.

Lerner, M. J. The desire for justice and reactions to victims. In J. R. Macaulay & L. Berkowitz (Eds.), *Altruism and helping behavior.* New York: Academic Press, 1970.

Leventhal, H. Findings and theory in the study of fear communications. In L. Berkowitz (Ed.), *Advances in experimental social psychology* (Vol. 5). New York: Academic Press, 1970.

Levinger, G. Toward the analysis of close relationships. *Journal of Experimental Social Psychology,* 1980, *16,* 510-544.

Lewin, K. *A dynamic theory of personality.* New York: McGraw-Hill, 1935.

Lewin, K. *Field theory in social science.* New York: Harper, 1951.

Lewin, M. Kurt Lewin's view of social psychology: The crisis of 1977 and the crisis of 1927. *Personality and Social Psychology Bulletin,* 1977, *3,* 159-172.

Lewin, K., Dembo, T., Festinger, L., & Sears, P. S. Level of aspiration. In J. McV. Hunt (Ed.), *Personality and the behavior disorders.* New York: Ronald Press, 1944.

Lieberman, M. Adaptive processes in late life. In N. Datan & L. Ginsberg (Eds.), *Life-span developmental psychology: Normative life crises.* New York: Academic Press, 1975.

Linton, H., & Graham, E. Personality correlates of persuasibility. In C. I. Hovland & I. L. Janis (Eds.), *Personality and persuasibility.* New Haven, Conn.: Yale University Press, 1959.

Lipetz, M. E., Cohen, I. H., Dworin, J., & Rogers, L. S. Need complementarity, marital stability and marital satisfaction. In K. Gergen & D. Marlowe (Eds.), *Personality and social behavior.* Reading, Mass.: Addison-Wesley, 1970.

Lippitt, R., & Radke, M. New trends in the investigation of prejudice. *Annals of the American Academy of Political and Social Sciences,* 1946, *244,* 167-176.

Loevinger, J. The measuring and measurement of ego development. *American Psychologist,* 1966, *21,* 195-206.

London, I. D. Convergent and divergent amplification and its meaning for social science. *Psychological Reports,* 1977, *41,* 111-123.

London, I. D., & Poltaratsky, N. P. The problem of contemporary analysis in history and psychology. *Behavioral Science,* 1958, *3,* 269-276.

London, I. D., & Thorngate, W. Divergent amplification and social behavior: Some methodological considerations. *Psychological Reports,* 1982, Monograph Supplement I-V48, 203-228.

Lonner, W. J. The search for psychological universals. In H. C. Triandis & W. W. Lambert (Eds.), *Handbook of cross-cultural psychology* (Vol. 1). Boston, Mass.: Allyn & Bacon, 1980.

Looft, W. Socialization and personality throughout the life span: An examination of contemporary psychological approaches. In P. B. Baltes & K. W. Schaie (Eds.), *Life-span developmental psychology: Personality and socialization.* New York: Academic Press, 1973.

Lorenz, K. *On aggression.* New York: Bantam, 1967.

Louch, A. R. *Explanation and human action.* Berkeley: University of California Press, 1969.

Lubek, I. Power structure in social psychology. *Representative Research in Social Psychology,* 1976, *7,* 87-88.

Lubek, I. A brief social psychological analysis of research on aggression in social psychology. In A. R. Buss (Ed.), *Psychology in social context.* New York: Irvington, 1979.

Luckmann, T. Individual action and social knowledge. In M. von Cranach & R. Harré (Eds.), *The analysis of action. Recent theoretical and empirical advances.* Cambridge: Cambridge University Press, 1981.

Luginbuhl, J. E., Crowne, D. H., & Kahan, J. P. Causal attributions for success and failure. *Journal of Personality and Social Psychology,* 1975, *31,* 86-93.

MacCorquodale, K., & Meehl, P. E. On a distinction between hypothetical constructs and intervening variables. *Psychological Review,* 1948, *55,* 95-107.

MacIntyre, A. The idea of a social science. In B. R. Wilson (Ed.), *Rationality.* Oxford: Blackwell, 1970.

MacIntyre, A. Ideology, social science and revolution. *Comparative Politics,* 1973, *5,* 321-341.

MacKenzie, B. Darwinism and positivism as methodological influences on the development of psychology. *Journal of the History of the Behavioral Sciences,* 1976, *12,* 330-337.

MacKenzie, B. D. *Behaviourism and the limits of scientific method.* Atlantic Highlands, N. J.: Humanities Press, 1977.

Mahoney, M. J. *Scientist as subject.* Cambridge, Mass.: Ballinger, 1976.

Malinowski, B. *A scientific theory of culture.* Chapel Hill: University of North Carolina Press, 1944.

Mandelbaum, M. *The problem of historical knowledge.* New York: Harper Torchbooks, 1967.

Manis, M. Social psychology and history: A symposium. *Personality and Social Psychology Bulletin,* 1976, *2,* 371-372.   (a)

Manis, M. Is social psychology really different? *Personality and Social Psychology Bulletin,* 1976, *2,* 427-436.   (b)

Marsh, P., & Brenner, M. *The social context of method.* London: Croom-Helm, 1978.

Marsh, P., Rosser, E., & Harré, R. *The rules of disorder.* London: Routledge & Kegan Paul, 1978.

Martindale, C. *Romantic progression: The psychology of literary history.* New

York: Wiley, 1975.

Marx, L. Reflections on the neo-romantic critique of science. *Daedalus,* 1978, 61–74.

Maslach, C. The social psychologist as an agent of change: An identity in crisis. In M. Deutsch & H. Hornstein (Eds.), *Applying social psychology.* New York: Wiley, 1975.

Mayo, C. *Toward an applicable social psychology.* Presidential address to the New England Psychological Association, Worcester, Mass., Nov. 1977.

McClelland, D. *Power: The inner experience.* New York: Irvington, 1975.

McClintock, C. G. The metatheoretical bases of social psychological theories. In C. McClintock & J. Maki (Eds.), *Social psychological theories.* New York: Holt, Rinehart & Winston, in press.

McClure, J. *Paradigms of attribution and illusion: A critical analysis.* Unpublished Master's thesis, University of Auckland, New Zealand, 1980.

McDougall, W. *Introduction to social psychology.* London: Methuen, 1908.

McGrath, J. E., & Altman, I. *Small group research, a synthesis and critique of the field.* New York: Holt, Rinehart & Winston, 1966.

McGuire, W. J. Some impending reorientations in social psychology: Some thoughts provoked by Kenneth Ring. *Journal of Experimental Social Psychology,* 1967, *3,* 124–139.

McGuire, W. J. The nature of attitudes and attitude change. In G. Lindzey & E. Aronson (Eds.), *The handbook of social psychology* (Vol. 3). Reading, Mass.: Addison-Wesley, 1968.

McGuire, W. J. Theory-oriented research in natural settings: The best of both worlds for social psychology. In M. Sherif & C. W. Sherif (Eds.), *Interdisciplinary relationships in the social sciences.* Chicago, Ill.: Aldine Press, 1969.

McGuire, W. J. The yin and yang of progress in social psychology: Seven Koans. *Journal of Personality and Social Psychology,* 1973, *26,* 446–456.

McGuire, W. J. The development of theory in social psychology. In R. Gilmour & S. Duck (Eds.), *The development of social psychology.* New York: Academic Press, 1980.

McHugh, P. On the failure of positivism. In J. D. Douglas (Ed.), *Understanding everyday life.* Chicago, Ill.: Aldine Press, 1970.

McKeachie, W. J. The decline and fall of the laws of learning. *Educational Researcher,* 1974, *3,* 7–11.

Meacham, J. A. A dialectic approach to moral development and self-esteem. *Human Development,* 1975, *18,* 159–170. (a)

Meacham, J. A. Patterns of memory abilities in two cultures. *Developmental Psychology,* 1975, *11,* 50–53. (b)

Meacham, J. A. A transactional model of remembering. In N. Datan & H. Reese (Eds.), *Life-span developmental psychology: Dialectical perspectives on experimental research.* New York: Academic Press, 1977.

Mead, G. H. *Mind, self and society from the standpoint of a social behaviorist.* Chicago, Ill.: University of Chicago Press, 1934.

Medawar, P. B. *Induction and intuition in scientific thought.* London: Methuen, 1960.

Meehl, P. E. Theoretical risks and tabular asterisks: Sir Karl, Sir Ronald, and the slow progress of soft psychology. *Journal of Consulting and Clinical Psychology,* 1978, *42,* 806-834.

Melden, A. I. *Free action.* London: Methuen, 1961.

Menzel, H. Meaning—Who needs it? In M. Brenner, P. Marsh, & M. Brenner (Eds.), *The social context of method.* New York: St. Martin's Press, 1978.

Mertens, W., & Fuchs, G. *Krise der Sozialpsychologie?* Munich: Ehrenwirth, 1978.

Merton, R. K. The bearing of empirical research upon the development of social theory. *American Sociological Review,* 1948, *13,* 505-515.

Merton, R. K. *Social theory and social structure.* New York: Free Press, 1957.

Mettee, D. R., & Wilkins, P. C. When similarity "hurts": Effects of perceived ability and a humorous blunder on interpersonal attraction. *Journal of Personality and Social Psychology,* 1972, *22,* 246-258.

Milgram, S. *Obedience to authority.* New York: Harper & Row, 1974.

Mills, C. W. Situated actions and vocabularies of motive. *American Sociological Review,* 1940, *5,* 904-913.

Mills, J. *Experimental social psychology.* New York: Macmillan, 1969.

Mills, J., & Aronson, E. Opinion change as a function of communicator's attractiveness and desire to influence. *Journal of Personality and Social Psychology,* 1965, *1,* 173-177.

Mischel, T. Psychological explanations and their vicissitudes. In W. J. Arnold (Ed.), *Nebraska Symposium on Motivation, 1975* (Vol. 23). Lincoln: University of Nebraska Press, 1976.

Mishler, E. G. Meaning in context: Is there any other kind? *Harvard Educational Review,* 1979, *49,* 1-19.

Mitroff, I. *The subjective side of science.* Amsterdam: Elsevier, 1974.

Mitroff, J. J., & Betz, F. Dialectic decision theory: A metatheory of decision making. *Management Science,* 1972, *19,* 11-24.

Mixon, D. Instead of deception. *Journal of the Theory of Social Behavior,* 1972, *2,* 145-177.

Montada, L., & Fillipp, S. H. Implications of life-span developmental psychology for childhood education. In H. Reese (Ed.), *Advances in child development and behavior.* New York: Academic Press, 1976.

Morawski, J. G. The structure of social psychological communities: A framework for examining the sociology of social psychology. In L. H. Strickland (Ed.), *Soviet and Western perspectives on social psychology.* Oxford: Pergamon Press, 1979. (a)

Morawski, J. G. *Human interest and psychological utopias.* Unpublished doctoral dissertation, Carleton University, 1979. (b)

Morgan, C. T., King, R. A., & Robinson, N. M. *Introduction to psychology.* New York: McGraw-Hill, 1979.

Morse, S. J., & Gergen, K. J. Social comparison, self-consistency and the presentation of self. *Journal of Personality and Social Psychology,* 1970, *16,* 148-159.

Moscovici, S. Society and theory in social psychology. In J. Israel & H. Tajfel (Eds.), *The context of social psychology: A critical assessment.* New York: Academic Press, 1972.

Mueller, C. *The politics of communication.* New York: Oxford University Press, 1973.

Mueller, C. G. Some origins of psychology as science. *Annual Review of Psychology,* 1979, *30,* 9-29.

Müller, H. J. *Freedom in the western world.* New York: Harper & Row, 1963.

Mummendey, A. Zum nutzen des Aggressionsbegriffes fur die psychologische Aggressionsforschung. In R. Hilke & W. Kempf (Eds.), *Menschliche Aggression, Naturwissenschaftliche Perspektiven der Aggressionsforschung.* Bern-Stuttgart-Wien: Hans Huber, in press.

Murchison, C. *Social psychology.* Worcester, Mass.: Clark University Press, 1929.

Murdock, G. P. The common denominator of cultures. In R. Linton (Ed.), *The science of man in a world crisis.* New York: Columbia University Press, 1945.

Mynatt, C., & Sherman, S. J. Responsibility attribution in groups and individuals: A direct test of the diffusion of responsibility hypothesis. *Journal of Personality and Social Psychology,* 1975, *32,* 1111-1118.

Nagel, E. *The structure of science.* New York: Harcourt, Brace & World, 1961.

Naroll, R., Michik, G. L., & Naroll, F. Holocultural research methods. In H. C. Triandis & J. W. Berry (Eds.), *Handbook of cross-cultural psychology* (Vol. 2). Boston, Mass.: Allyn & Bacon, 1980.

Nederhof, A. J. *De wetenschappelyke vooruitgang van do sociale psychologie.* Unpublished doctoral dissertation, Vakgroep sociale en organisatie psychologie, Ryksuniversiteit Leiden, 1978.

Neisser, U. *Cognition and reality.* San Francisco, Calif.: Freedman, 1976.

Nelson, C. E. Social psychology in crisis—A study of references in the handbook of social psychology. *Personality and Social Psychology Bulletin,* 1972, *2,* 14-21.

Nesselroade, J. R., & Baltes, P. B. Adolescent personality development and historical change: 1970-1972. *Monographs of the Society for Research in Child Development,* 1974, *39* (1), Serial Number 154.

Nesselroade, J. R., Jacobs, A., & Pruchno, R. *Reliability versus stability in the measurement of psychological states: An illustration with anxiety measures.* Unpublished manuscript, Pennsylvania State University, 1981.

Nesselroade, J. R., & Reese, H. (Eds.). *Life-span developmental psychology: Methodological issues.* New York: Academic Press, 1973.

Neugarten, B. L. *Adaptation and the life cycle.* Paper presented at the meeting of the Foundations Fund for Research in Psychiatry, Puerto Rico, June 1968.

Neugarten, B. L. Time, age and the life cycle. *American Journal of Psychiatry,* 1979, *7,* 887-894.

Neugarten, B. L., & Datan, N. Sociological perspectives on the life cycle. In P. B. Baltes & K. W. Schaie (Eds.), *Life-span developmental psychology: Personality and socialization.* New York: Academic Press, 1973.

Newcomb, T. M. *The acquaintance process.* New York: Holt, Rinehart & Winston, 1961.

Newell, A. You can't play 20 questions with nature and win. In W. G. Chase (Ed.), *Visual information processing.* New York: Academic Press, 1973, 283-310.

Newtson, D. Attribution and the unit of perception of ongoing behavior. *Journal of Personality and Social Psychology,* 1973, *28,* 28-38.

Newtson, D., Enquist, G., & Boris, J. The objective basis of behavior units. *JSAS Catalog of Selected Documents in Psychology,* 1976, *6,* 5. (Ms. 1173)

Nietzsche, F. The use and abuse of history. In Oscar Levy (Ed.), *Human, all-too-human* (Vol. 6), *The complete works of Fredrich Nietzsche.* New York: Russell & Russell, 1964. (Originally published 1909-1911.)

Nisbet, R. A. *Social change and history.* New York: Oxford University Press, 1969.

Nisbet, R. A. *Sociology as an art form.* New York: Oxford University Press, 1977.

Nisbett, R. E., & Bellows, N. Verbal reports about causal influences as social judgments: Private access versus public theories. *Journal of Personality and Social Psychology,* 1977, *35,* 613-624.

Nisbett, R. E., & Ross, L. *Human inference: Strategies and shortcoming of social judgment.* Englewood Cliffs, N. J.: Prentice-Hall, 1980.

Nisbett, R. E., & Wilson, T. D. Telling more than we can know: Verbal reports on mental processes. *Psychological Review,* 1977, *84,* 231-259.

Novak, D., & Lerner, M. J. Rejection as a consequence of perceived similarity. *Journal of Personality and Social Psychology,* 1968, *9,* 147-152.

O'Donnell, J. The crisis of experimentalism in the 1920s: E. G. Boring and his uses of history. *American Psychologist,* 1979, *34,* 289-295.

Ollman, B. *Alienation, Marx's conception of man in capitalist society.* London: Cambridge University Press, 1971.

Orne, M. On the social psychology of the psychological experiment: With particular reference to demand characteristics and their implications. *American Psychologist,* 1962, *17,* 776-783.

Oskamp, S. *Attitudes and opinions.* Englewood Cliffs, N. J.: Prentice-Hall, 1977.

Osgood, C. E., Suci, G. J., & Tannenbaum, P. *The measurement of meaning.* Urbana: University of Illinois Press, 1957.

Ossorio, P. G. *What actually happens.* Columbia: University of South Carolina Press, 1978.

Ossorio, P. G., & Davis, K. E. The self, intentionality, and reactions to evaluations of the self. In C. Gordon & K. Gergen (Eds.), *The self in social interaction.* New York: Wiley, 1968.

Overton, W. R., & Reese, H. W. Models of development: Methodological implications. In J. R. Nesselroade & H. W. Reese (Eds.), *Life-span developmental psychology: Methodological issues.* New York: Academic Press, 1973.

Palmer, R. E. *Hermeneutics: Interpretation theory in Schleiermacher, Dilthey, Heidegger and Gadamer.* Evanston, Ill.: Northwestern University Press, 1969.

Palmonari, A. (Ed.). *Problemi attuali della psicologia sociale.* Bologna: Molino, 1976.

Parisi, D., Castelfranchi, C., & Benigni, L. Eight points for a discussion on social psychology. In A. Palmonari (Ed.), *Problemi attuali della psicologia sociale.* Bologna: Molino, 1976.

Pearce, W. B., & Cronen, V. E. *Communication, action and meaning.* New York: Praeger, 1980.

Pearlin, L. Sex roles and depression. In N. Datan & L. Ginsberg (Eds.), *Life-span developmental psychology: Normative life crises.* New York: Academic Press, 1975.

Peele, S. Reductionism in the psychology of the eighties: Can biochemistry eliminate addiction, mental illness and pain? *American Psychologist,* 1981, *36,* 807–818.

Pencil, M. Salt passage research: The state of the art. *Journal of Communication,* 1976, Autumn, 31–36.

Pepitone, A. Toward normative and comparative social psychology. *Journal of Personality and Social Psychology,* 1976, *34,* 641–653.

Pepitone, A. Lessons from the history of social psychology. *American Psychologist,* 1981, *36,* 972–985.

Perrin, S., & Spencer, C. The Asch effect—A child of its time? *Bulletin of the British Psychological Society,* 1980, *32,* 405–406.

Pepper, S. *World hypotheses.* Berkeley: University of California Press, 1972.

Peters, R. S. *The concept of motivation.* London: Routledge & Kegan Paul, 1958.

Petrinovich, L. Probabalistic functionalism. *American Psychologist,* 1979, *34,* 373–390.

Petty, E., & Cacioppo, J. T. *Attitudes and persuasion: Classic and contemporary approaches.* Dubuque, Iowa: W. C. Brown, 1981.

Phares, E. J. *Locus of control in personality.* Morristown, N. J.: General Learning Press, 1976.

Phillips, D. L. *Abandoning method.* San Francisco, Calif.: Jossey-Bass, 1973.

Phillips, D. L. *Wittgenstein and scientific knowledge.* Totowa, N. J.: Rowman & Littlefield, 1977.

Piaget, J. *The origins of intelligence in children.* New York: Norton, 1952.

Piaget, J. *Understanding causality* (D. & M. Miles, trans.). New York: Norton, 1974.

Pierce, C. S. The law of mind. *Monist,* 1982, 1–3. Present citation from D. Browning, *Philosophers of process.* New York: Random House, 1965.

Pitts, J. R. The hippies as contra meritocracy. *Dissent,* 1969, *16,* 326–337.

Plon, M. On the meaning of the notion of conflict and its study in social psychology. *European Journal of Social Psychology,* 1974, *4,* 389–436.

Poincaré, H. *Science and hypothesis.* New York, 1952. (Originally published in London, 1905.)

Popper, K. R. *The poverty of historicism.* London: Routledge & Kegan Paul, 1957.

Popper, K. R. *The logic of scientific discovery.* New York: Harper & Row, 1968. (Originally published as *Logik des Forschung.* Vienna: Springer-Verlag, 1935.)

Powdermaker, H. *Probing our prejudices.* New York: Harper & Row, 1944.

Prentice, N. M. The influence of live and symbolic modelling on promoting moral judgment of adolescents. *Journal of Abnormal Psychology,* 1972, *80,* 157–161.

Psathas, G. (Ed.). *Everyday language: Studies in ethnomethodology.* New York: Irvington, 1979.

Quine, W. V. O. Two dogmas of empiricism. *Philosophical Review,* 1951, *60,* 20-43.

Quine, W. V. O. *From a logical point of view.* Cambridge, Mass.: Harvard University Press, 1953.

Quine, W. V. O. *Word and object.* Cambridge, Mass.: M.I.T. Technology Press, 1960.

Radnitzsky, G. *Contemporary schools of metascience.* Goteborg, Sweden: Scandinavia University Books, 1970.

Randall, J. H. *Making of the modern mind.* New York: Appleton-Century-Crofts, 1956.

Rappoport, L. On praxis and quasirationality. *Human Development,* 1975, *18,* 194-204.

Rappoport, L. *Renaming the world: On psychology and the decline of positive science.* Unpublished manuscript, Kansas State University, 1978.

Ray, L. J. Critical theory and positivism: Popper and the Frankfurt School. *Philosophy of Social Science,* 1979, *9,* 149-173.

Rebecca, M., Hefner, R., & Oleshansky, B. A model of sex-role transcendence. *Journal of Social Issues,* 1976, *32,* 197-206.

Reese, H. W. *Discriminative learning and transfer: Dialectical perspectives on experimental research.* New York: Academic Press, 1977.

Reese, H. W., & Overton, W. F. Models of development and theories of development. In L. R. Goulet & P. B. Baltes (Eds.), *Life-span developmental psychology: Research and theory.* New York: Academic Press, 1970.

Reynolds, V. The origins of a behavioral vocabulary: The case of the Rhesus monkey. *Journal for the Theory of Social Behavior,* 1976, *6,* 105-142.

Rickmann, H. P. *Understanding and the human sciences.* London: Routledge & Kegan Paul, 1967.

Ricoeur, P. *Freud and philosophy: An essay on interpretation.* New Haven, Conn.: Yale University Press, 1970.

Ricoeur, P. *Interpretation theory: Discourse and the surplus of meaning.* Fort Worth: The Texas Christian University Press, 1976.

Riegel, K. F. Time and change in the development of the individual and society. In H. Reese (Ed.), *Advances in child development and behavior.* New York: Academic Press, 1972.

Riegel, K. F. Dialectic operations: The final period of cognitive development. *Human Development,* 1973, *16,* 346-370.

Riegel, K. F. From traits and equilibrium toward developmental dialectics. In W. Arnold (Ed.), *Nebraska symposium on motivation* (Vol. 23). Lincoln: University of Nebraska Press, 1975.

Riegel, K. F. The dialectics of human development. *American Psychologist,* 1976, *31,* 689-700.

Riegel, K. F. *Foundations of dialectical psychology.* New York: Academic Press, 1979.

Riesman, D. *The lonely crowd.* New Haven, Conn.: Yale University Press, 1950.

Riley, M. W. Age strata in social systems. In R. Binstock & E. Shanas (Eds.), *Handbook of aging and the social sciences*. Princeton, N. J.: Van Nostrand-Reinhold, 1976.

Ring, K. Some sober questions about frivolous values. *Journal of Experimental Social Psychology*, 1967, *3*, 113-123.

Robinson, D. N. *An intellectual history of psychology*. New York: Macmillan, 1976.

Rodin, J., & Langer, E. Long-term effects of a control-relevant intervention with the institutionalized aged. *Journal of Personality and Social Psychology*, 1977, *35*, 897-902.

Rodrigues, A. Social psychology—Current problems and future outlook. *Arguivas Brasileiros Psichologica*, 1976, *28*, 3-19.

Rogers, C. R. Some observations on the organization of personality. *American Psychologist*, 1947, *2*, 358-368.

Rommetveit, R. Language games, syntactic structures and hermeneutics. In J. Israel & H. Tajfel (Eds.), *The context of social psychology: A critical assessment*. New York: Academic Press, 1972.

Rommetveit, R. *On message structure*. New York: Wiley, 1974.

Rommetveit, R. On "emancipatory" social psychology. In L. H. Strickland, F. E. Aboud, & K. J. Gergen (Eds.), *Social psychology in transition*. New York: Plenum Press, 1976.

Rosenberg, M. J. When dissonance fails: On eliminating evaluation apprehension from attitude measurement. *Journal of Personality and Social Psychology*, 1965, *1*, 28-42.

Rosenberg, M. J., & Hovland, C. I. (Eds.). *Attitude organization and change*. New Haven, Conn.: Yale University Press, 1960.

Rosenberg, S. V., & Sedlak, A. Structural representations of implicit personality theory. In L. Berkowitz (Ed.), *Advances in experimental social psychology* (Vol. 6). New York: Academic Press, 1972.

Rosenthal, R. *Experimenter effects in behavioral research*. New York: Appleton-Century-Crofts, 1966.

Rosenthal, R., & Rosnow, R. L. *Artifact in behavioral research*. New York: Academic Press, 1969.

Rosnow, R. L. The prophetic vision of Giambattista Vico: Implications for the state of social psychological theory. *Journal of Personality and Social Psychology*, 1978, *36*, 1322-1331.

Rosnow, R. L. *Paradigms in transition*. New York and London: Oxford University Press, 1981.

Ross, L. The intuitive psychologist and his shortcomings: Distortions in the attribution process. In L. Berkowitz (Ed.), *Advances in experimental social psychology* (Vol. 2). New York: Academic Press, 1977.

Rowan, J. Research as intervention. In N. Armistead (Ed.), *Reconstructing social psychology*. Baltimore, Md.: Penguin, 1974.

Rudner, R. The scientist qua scientist makes value judgments. *Philosophy of Science*, 1953, *20*, 1-6.

Runyan, W. M. A stage-state analysis of the life-course. *Journal of Personality and Social Psychology,* 1980, *38,* 951-962.

Russell, B. *Our knowledge of the external world.* New York: Menton Books, 1956.

Rychlak, J. F. *A philosophy of science for personality theory.* Boston, Mass.: Houghton-Mifflin, 1968.

Rychlak, J. F. A humanist looks at psychological science. In W. J. Arnold & J. K. Cole (Eds.), *Nebraska symposium on motivation* (Vol. 22). Lincoln: University of Nebraska Press, 1975.

Rychlak, J. F. *The psychology of rigorous humanism.* New York: Wiley, 1977.

Rychlak, J. F. The false promise of falsification. *The Journal of Mind and Behavior,* 1980, *1,* 183-195. (a)

Rychlak, J. F. Concepts of free will in modern psychological science. *Journal of Mind and Behavior,* 1980, *1,* 9-32. (b)

Rychlak, J. F. The case for a modest revolution in modern psychological science. In R. A. Kasschau & C. N. Cofer (Eds.), *Psychology's second century.* New York: Praeger, 1981.

Ryle, G. *The concept of mind.* London: Hutchinson, 1949.

Sabini, J., & Silver, M. Introspection and causal accounts. *Journal of Personality and Social Psychology,* 1981, *40,* 171-179.

Sabini, J., & Silver, M. *The moralities of everyday life.* London and New York: Oxford University Press, 1982.

Sacks, H. Hotrodder: A revolutionary category. In G. Psathas (Ed.), *Everyday language.* New York: Irvington, 1979.

Samelson, F. Paradigms, labels, and historical analysis. *American Psychologist,* 1973, *23,* 1141-1144.

Samelson, F. History, origin, myth, and ideology: Comte's 'discovery' of social psychology. *Journal of the Theory of Social Behavior,* 1974, *4,* 217-231.

Samelson, F. *Reactions to Watson's behaviorism: The early years.* Paper presented at the annual meeting of the Cheiron Association, 1978.

Samelson, F. Putting psychology on the map: Ideology and intelligence testing. In A. Buss (Ed.), *Psychology in social context.* New York: Irvington, 1979.

Sameroff, A. Transactional models in early social relations. *Human Development,* 1975, *18,* 65-79.

Sampson, E. E. On justice as equality. *Journal of Social Issues,* 1975, *31,* 45-64.

Sampson, E. E. Psychology and the American ideal. *Journal of Personality and Social Psychology,* 1977, *35,* 767-782.

Sampson, E. E. Scientific paradigms and social values: Wanted—A scientific revolution. *Journal of Personality and Social Psychology,* 1978, *36,* 1332-1343.

Sampson, E. E. Cognitive psychology as ideology. *American Psychologist,* 1981, *36,* 730-743.

Sampson, E. E. *Justice and the critique of pure psychology.* New York: Plenum, in press.

Sarason, S. *Psychology misdirected.* New York: Free Press, 1981.

Sarbin, T. R. Contextualism: A world view for modern psychology. In A. W. Landfield (Ed.), *1976 Nebraska Symposium on motivation: Personal construct psychology* (Vol. 24). Lincoln: University of Nebraska Press, 1977.

Schachter, S. The interaction of cognitive and physiological determinants of emotional state. In L. Berkowitz (Ed.), *Advances in experimental social psychology* (Vol. 1). New York: Academic Press, 1964.

Schachter, S., & Singer, J. L. Cognitive, social and physiological determinants of emotional state. *Psychological Review, 1962, 65,* 121-128.

Schank, R. C., & Abelson, R. P. *Scripts, plans, goals and understanding.* New York: Wiley, 1977.

Schegloff, E. A., & Sacks, H. Opening up closings. *Semiotica, 1973, 8,* 289-327.

Scheibe, K. E. The psychologist's advantage and its nullification: Limits of human predictability. *American Psychologist, 1978, 33,* 869-881.

Scheibe, K. E. *Mirrors, masks, lies and secrets.* New York: Praeger, 1979.

Schlegel, A. Situational stress: A Hopi example. In N. Datan & L. Ginsberg (Eds.), *Life-span developmental psychology: Normative life crises.* New York: Academic Press, 1975.

Schlenker, B. R. Social psychology and science. *Journal of Personality and Social Psychology, 1974, 29,* 1-15.

Schlenker, B. R. Social psychology and science: Another look. *Personality and Social Psychology Bulletin, 1976, 2,* 418-420.

Schopler, J., & Layton, B. D. Determinants of the self-attribution of having influenced another person. *Journal of Personality and Social Psychology, 1972, 22,* 326-332.

Schuler, H. *Ethische Probleme psychologischer Forschung.* Toronto: Hogrefe, 1980.

Schutz, A. *Collected papers, Vol. 1.* The Hague: Nijhoff, 1962.

Schutz, A. On multiple realities. *Philosophy and Phenomenological Research,* 1945, *5,* 533-551. (Reprinted in C. Gordon & K. Gergen, Eds.), *The self in social interaction.* New York: Wiley, 1968.)

Schwartz, B. Does helplessness cause depression or do only depressed people become helpless? Comment on Alloy and Abramson. *Journal of Experimental Psychology: General, 1981, 110,* 429-435.

Schwartz, B., Lacey, H., & Schuldenfrei, R. Operant psychology as factory psychology. *Behaviorism, 1978, 6,* 229-254.

Schwendinger, H., & Schwendinger, J. R. *The sociologists of the chair. A radical analysis of the formative years of North American sociology (1883-1922).* New York: Basic Books, 1974.

Scriven, M. A possible distinction between traditional scientific disciplines and the study of human behavior. In H. Feigl & M. Scriven (Eds.), *Minnesota studies in the philosophy of science* (Vol. 1). Minneapolis: University of Minnesota Press, 1956.

Scriven, M. The exact role of value judgments in science. In K. Scheffner & R. Cohen (Eds.), *Proceedings of the 1972 biennial meetings of the Philosophy of Science Association.* Boston, Mass.: Reidel, 1974.

Searle, J. R. *Speech acts.* London: Cambridge University Press, 1970.

Sechrest, L. Personality. In M. R. Rosenzweig & L. W. Porter (Eds.), *Annual Review of Psychology*, 1976, *27*, 1-28.

Secord, P. F. Transhistorical and transcultural theory. *Personality and Social Psychology Bulletin*, 1976, *2*, 418-420.

Secord, P. F. Social psychology in search of a paradigm. *Personality and Social Psychology Bulletin*, 1977, *3*, 41-50.

Seligman, M. E. P. *Helplessness*. San Francisco, Calif.: Freeman, 1975.

Senn, D. J. Attraction as a function of similarity–dissimilarity in task performance. *Journal of Personality and Social Psychology*, 1971, *18*, 120-123.

Shackle, G. L. S. *Epistemics and economics*. Cambridge: Cambridge University Press, 1972.

Shaver, K. G. *An introduction to attribution processes*. Cambridge, Mass.: Winthrop, 1975.

Shaw, M. E., & Costanzo, P. R. *Theories of social psychology*. New York: McGraw-Hill, 1970.

Sherif, C. W., Sherif, M., & Nebergall, R. E. *Attitude and attitude change: The social judgment-involvement approach*. Philadelphia, Pa.: Saunders, 1965.

Sherif, M. Crisis in social psychology: Some remarks towards breaking through the crisis. *Personality and Social Psychology Bulletin*, 1977, *3*, 368-382.

Sherif, M., & Hovland, C. *Social judgment*. New Haven, Conn.: Yale University Press, 1961.

Shields, S. A. Functionalism, Darwinism and the psychology of women: A study in social myth. *American Psychologist*, 1975, *30*, 739-753.

Shimony, A. "Braithwaite on scientific method." *Review of Metaphysics*, 1953-1954, *7*, 644-660.

Shoemaker, S. *Self-knowledge and self-identity*. Ithica, N. Y.: Cornell University Press, 1963.

Shotter, J. What is it to be human? In N. Armistead (Ed.), *Reconstructing social psychology*. Baltimore, Md.: Penguin, 1974.

Shotter, J. *Images of man in psychological research*. London: Methuen, 1975.

Shotter, J. The cultural context of communication studies: Theoretical and methodological issues. In A. Lock (Ed.), *Action, gesture and symbol*. New York: Academic Press, 1978.

Shotter, J. Action, joint action and intentionality. In M. Brenner (Ed.), *The structure of action*. Oxford: Blackwell, 1980.

Shotter, J. Telling and reporting: Prospective and retrospective uses of self-ascriptions. In C. Antaki (Ed.), *The psychology of ordinary explanations*. London: Academic Press, 1981.

Shotter, J. Critical notice: Are Fincham's and Shultz's findings empirical findings? *British Journal of Social Psychology*, in press.

Shweder, R. A. Rethinking culture and personality theory. Part 3, From genesis and typology to hermeneutics and dynamics. *Ethos: Journal of the Society for Psychological Anthropology*, 1980, *8*, 60-94.

Silverman, I. Self-esteem and differential responsiveness to success and failure. *Journal of Abnormal and Social Psychology*, 1964, *69*, 115-119.

Silverman, I. Why social psychology fails. *Canadian Psychological Review*, 1977, *18*, 353-358.

Simon, H. *Models of man*. New York: Wiley, 1957.

Simon, W. The social, the erotic and the sensual: The complexities of sexual scripts. In J. K. Cole & R. Dienstbier (Eds.), *Nebraska Symposium on Motivation, 1973* (Vol. 21). Lincoln: University of Nebraska Press.

Simonton, D. K. Multiple discovery and invention: Zeitgeist, genius or chance? *Journal of Personality and Social Psychology*, 1979, *37*, 1603-1616.

Simpson, G. E., & Yinger, J. M. *Racial and cultural minorities: An analysis of prejudice and discrimination* (3rd ed.). New York: Harper & Row, 1965.

Skinner, B. F. *Walden two*. New York: Knopf, 1948.

Skinner, B. F. *Verbal behavior*. Englewood Cliffs, N. J.: Prentice-Hall, 1957.

Skinner, B. F. *Beyond freedom and dignity*. New York: Random House, 1971.

Smedslund, J. Bandura's theory of self-efficacy; a set of common sense theorems. *Scandinavian Journal of Psychology*, 1978, *19*, 1-14.

Smith, M. B. Editorial. *Journal of Abnormal and Social Psychology*, 1961, *63*, 461-465.

Smith, M. B. *Social psychology and human values*. Chicago, Ill.: Aldine Press, 1969.

Smith, M. B. Is experimental social psychology advancing? *Journal of Experimental Social Psychology*, 1972, *8*, 86-96.

Smith, M. B. *Humanizing social psychology*. San Francisco, Calif.: Jossey-Bass, 1974.

Smith, M. B. Psychology and values. *Journal of Social Issues*, 1978, *34*, 181-199.

Smith, M. B. Attitudes, values and selfhood. In H. E. Howe, Jr., & M. M. Page (Eds.), *Nebraska Symposium on Motivation, 1979* (Vol. 27). Lincoln: University of Nebraska Press, 1980.

Snow, C. P. The moral un-neutrality of science. In P. Obler & H. Estrin (Eds.), *The new scientist: Essays on methods and values of modern science*. Garden City, N. Y.: Doubleday, 1962.

Snyder, C. R., & Fromkin, H. L. *Uniqueness: The human pursuit of difference*. New York: Plenum Press, 1980.

Snyder, M. L., Stephan, W. G., & Rosenfield, D. Egotism and attribution. *Journal of Personality and Social Psychology*, 1976, *33*, 435-441.

Sommer, J. *Dialogische hermeneutik*. Unpublished manuscript. Universität Heidelberg, 1980.

Sprowls, J. W. Recent social psychology. *Psychological Bulletin*, 1930, *27*, 380-393.

Steele, R. S. Psychoanalysis and hermeneutics. *International Review of Psycho-Analysis*, 1979, *6*, 389-411.

Steiner, I. D. Whatever happened to the group in social psychology? *Journal of Experimental Social Psychology*, 1974, *10*, 94-108.

Steininger, M. Objectivity and value judgments in the psychology of E. L. Thorndike and W. McDougall. *Journal of the History of the Behavioral Sciences*, 1979, *15*, 263-281.

Sterns, H. L., & Alexander, R. A. Cohort, age and time of measurement: Biomorphic considerations. In N. Datan & H. Reese (Eds.), *Life-span developmental psychology: Dialectic perspectives on experimental research.* New York: Academic Press, 1977.

Stokols, D. On the distinction between density and crowding: Some implications for future research. *Psychological Review,* 1972, *79,* 275-278.

Strickland, L. H., Aboud, F. E., & Gergen, K. J. (Eds.). *Social psychology in transition.* New York: Plenum Press, 1976.

Stryker, S. Developments in "two social psychologies": Toward an appreciation of mutual relevance. *Sociometry,* 1977, *40,* 145-160.

Sudnow, D. *Passing on: The social organization of dying.* Englewood Cliffs, N. J.: Prentice-Hall, 1967.

Sullivan, E. V. A study of Kohlberg's structural theory of moral development: A critique of liberal social science ideology. *Human Development,* 1977, *20,* 352-376.

Suomi, S. J., & Harlow, H. F. Social rehabilitation of isolate-reared monkeys. *Developmental Psychology,* 1972, *6,* 487-496.

Surkin, M., & Wolfe, A. (Eds.). *An end to political science.* New York: Basic Books, 1970.

Tajfel, H. Experiments in a vacuum. In J. Israel & H. Tajfel (Eds.), *The context of social psychology.* New York: Academic Press, 1972.

Taylor, C. *The explanation of behavior.* London: Routledge & Kegan Paul, 1964.

Taylor, C. Interpretation and the sciences of man. *The Review of Metaphysics,* 1971, *25,* No. 1.

Taylor, L., & Walton, P. Industrial sabotage: Motives and meanings. In S. Cohen (Ed.), *Images of deviance.* Baltimore, Md.: Penguin, 1971.

Taylor, S., & Mettee, D. When similarity breeds contempt. *Journal of Personality and Social Psychology,* 1971, *20,* 175-181.

Tedeschi, J. T., Smith, R. B., & Brown, R. C. A reinterpretation of research on aggression. *Psychological Bulletin,* 1974, *81,* 540-562.

Thomas, C. W. The system-maintenance role of the white psychologist. *Journal of Social Issues,* 1973, *29,* 57-65.

Thomas, D. *Naturalism and social science.* London: Cambridge University Press, 1979.

Thomas, E. J. Role conceptions, organizational size and community context. In B. J. Biddle & E. J. Thomas (Eds.), *Role theory: Concepts and research.* New York: Wiley, 1966.

Thorngate, W. Process invariance: Another red herring. *Personality and Social Psychology Bulletin,* 1975, *1,* 485-488.

Thorngate, W. Possible limits on a science of social behaviour. In L. H. Strickland, F. E. Aboud, & K. J. Gergen (Eds.), *Social psychology in transition.* New York: Plenum Press, 1976.

Toulmin, S. *Foresight and understanding.* New York: Harper & Row, 1961.

Toulmin, S. *Human understanding,* Vol. I. Princeton, N. J.: Princeton University Press, 1972.

Toulmin, S. Toward reintegration: An agenda for psychology's second century. In

R. A. Kasschau & C. N. Cofer (Eds.), *Psychology's second century.* New York: Praeger, 1981.

Triandis, H. C. Cross-cultural social and personality psychology. *Personality and Social Psychology Bulletin,* 1977, *3,* 143-158.

Triandis, H. C. Some universals of social behavior. *Personality and Social Psychology Bulletin,* 1978, *4,* 1-16.

Triandis, H. C., & Brislin, R. (Eds.). *Handbook of cross-cultural psychology: Social Psychology* (Vol. 5). Boston, Mass.: Allyn & Bacon, 1980.

Triandis, H. C., & Lambert, W. W. (Eds.). *Handbook of cross-cultural psychology* (Vol. 1). Boston, Mass.: Allyn & Bacon, 1980.

Turner, S. P. Complex organizations as savage tribes. *Journal for the Theory of Social Behavior,* 1977, *7,* 99-108.

Tyler, L. E. *Individuality.* San Francisco, Calif.: Jossey-Bass, 1978.

Unger, R. M. *Knowledge and politics.* New York: Free Press, 1975.

Urdang, L. (Ed.). *Random House dictionary of the English language.* New York: Random House, 1968.

van den Berg, J. H. *The changing nature of man.* New York: Norton, 1961.

van den Daele, L. D. Ego development and preferential judgment in life-span perspective. In N. Datan & L. H. Ginsberg (Eds.), *Life-span developmental psychology: Normative life crises.* New York: Academic Press, 1975. (a)

van den Daele, L. D. Ego development in dialectic perspective. *Human Development,* 1975, *18,* 129-142. (b)

Ventimiglia, J. C. *Theoretical convergences in the two social psychologies: Some comments on the crisis in the field.* Paper presented at the annual meeting of the American Sociological Association, San Francisco, September 1978.

Verhave, T., & van Hoorn, W. The temporalization of the ego and society during the nineteenth century: A view from the top. *Annals of the New York Academy of Science,* 1977, *291,* 140-221.

Veroff, J., Depner, C., Kulka, R., & Douvan, E. Comparison of American motives: 1957 versus 1976. *Journal of Personality and Social Psychology,* 1980, *39,* 1249-1262.

Vining, R. Methodological issues in quantitative economics: Variations upon a theme. *The American Economic Review,* 1950, *40,* 266-284.

von Wright, G. H. *Explanation and understanding.* Ithica, N. Y.: Cornell University Press, 1971.

Walster, E., Walster, G. W., & Berscheid, E. *Equity, theory and research.* Boston, Mass.: Allyn & Bacon, 1978.

Warr, P. Aided experiments in social psychology. *Bulletin of the British Psychological Society,* 1977, *30,* 2-8.

Watson, J. B. *Behaviorism.* Chicago, Ill.: University of Chicago Press, 1924.

Weary, G. Examination of affect and egotism as mediators of bias in causal attributions. *Journal of Personality and Social Psychology,* 1980, *38,* 348-357.

Webb, E. J., Campbell, D. T., Schwartz, R. D., & Sechrest, L. *Unobtrusive measures: Nonreactive research in the social sciences.* Chicago, Ill.: Rand McNally, 1966.

Weber, M. *The methodology of the social sciences* (E. A. Shils & H. A. Finch, trans.). New York: Free Press, 1949.

Weeks, G. B. Toward a dialectical approach to intervention. *Human Development,* 1977, *20,* 277-292.

Weick, K. E. Systematic observational methods. In G. Lindzey & E. Aronson (Eds.), *Handbook of social psychology* (Vol. 2). Reading, Mass.: Addison-Wesley, 1968.

Weimer, W. B. *Notes on the methodology of scientific research.* Hillsdale, N. J.: Erlbaum, 1979.

Weinstein, G., & Platt, G. *The wish to be free.* Berkeley: University of California Press, 1969.

Weiss, J. R. Transcontextual validity in developmental research. *Child Development,* 1978, *49,* 1-12.

Westcott, R. W. Of guilt and gratitude: Further reflections on human uniqueness. *The Dialogist,* 1970, *2,* 69-85.

Wexler, P. *Critical social psychology.* London: Routledge & Kegan Paul, 1982.

Wheeler, L. (Ed.). *Review of personality and social psychology* (Vol. 1). Beverly Hills, Calif.: Sage, 1980.

White, S. H. Social proof structure: The dialectic method and theory in the work of psychology. In N. Datan & H. W. Reese (Eds.), *Life-span developmental psychology: Dialectical perspectives on experimental research.* New York: Academic Press, 1977.

Whitehead, A. N. *Process and reality.* New York: Free Press, 1969. (Originally published 1929.)

Wicker, A. W. *Getting out of conceptual ruts.* Invited address, Western Psychological Association, Los Angeles, April, 1981.

Wicklund, R. A. *Freedom and reactance.* New York: Wiley, 1974.

Wicklund, R. A., & Brehm, J. W. *Perspectives on cognitive dissonance.* Hillsdale, N. J.: Erlbaum, 1976.

Williams, R. *Traditional mechanism and the emerging humanisms: Review and prolegomenon.* Paper presented at the American Psychological Association, Montreal, September, 1980.

Wilson, T. P. Normative and interpretive paradigms in sociology. In J. D. Douglas (Ed.), *Understanding everyday life.* Chicago, Ill.: Aldine Press, 1970.

Winch, P. *The idea of a social science.* London: Routledge & Kegan Paul, 1958. (Originally published in 1946.)

Wishner, J. Reanalysis of impressions of personality. *Psychological Review,* 1960, *67,* 96-112.

Wittgenstein, L. *Philosophical investigations* (G. Anscombe, trans.). New York: Macmillan, 1963.

Wohlwill, J. F. A conceptual analysis of exploratory behavior. In H. Day (Ed.), *Advances in intrinsic motivation and aesthetics.* New York: Plenum Press, 1981.

Wolff, M. Notes on the behavior of pedestrians. In A. Birenbaum & E. Sagarin (Eds.), *People in places: The sociology of the familiar.* New York: Praeger, 1973.

Wortman, L. B., & Dintzer, L. Is an attributional analysis of the learned helplessness phenomenon viable?: A critique of the Abramson-Seligman-Teasdale reformulation. *Journal of Abnormal Psychology,* 1978, *87,* 75-90.

Wrightsman, L., & Deaux, K. *Social psychology in the 80s.* Monterey, Calif.: Brooks/Cole, 1981.

Yaroshevskii, M. G. Categorical analysis of the evolution of psychology as an independent body of knowledge. *Soviet Psychology,* 1973, *12,* 23-52.

Young, T. R. The politics of sociology: Gouldner, Goffman & Garfinkel. *American Sociologist,* 1971, *6,* 276-281.

Ziller, R. C. Group dialectics: The dynamics of groups over time. *Human Development,* 1977, *20,* 293-308.

Zinn, H. *The politics of history.* Boston, Mass.: Beacon Press, 1970.

Zũniga, R. B. The experimenting society and radical social reform. *American Psychologist,* 1975, *30,* 99-115.

Zurcher, L. A., Jr. The "friendly" poker game: A study of an ephemeral role. In A. Birenbaum & E. Sagarin (Eds.), *People in places: The sociology of the familiar.* New York: Praeger, 1973.

Zwier, A. G. *The crisis in social psychology. A theoretical and empirical study.* Unpublished master's thesis, University of Auckland, 1980.

Author Index

Subject Index